D0783229

Wo

Middle Ages

Women and Power in the Middle Ages

Edited by

Mary Erler
Maryanne Kowaleski

The University of Georgia Press

Athens and London

© 1988 by the University of Georgia Press
Athens, Georgia 30602
Designed by Kathi L. Dailey
Set in Mergenthaler Bembo
Typeset by The Composing Room of Michigan
Printed and bound by Thomson-Shore, Inc.
The paper in this book meets the guidelines for permanence
and durability of the Committee on Production Guidelines for
Book Longevity of the Council on Library Resources.

92 91 90   5 4 3 2

Library of Congress Cataloging in Publication Data

Women and power in the Middle Ages.

Includes bibliographies and index.
1. Women—History—Middle Ages, 500–1500. 2. Power,
(Social sciences) I. Erler, Mary. II. Kowaleski, Maryanne.
HQ1143.W63 1988   305.4'09'02 87-5840
ISBN 0-8203-0957-5 (alk. paper)
ISBN 0-8203-0958-3 (pbk.: alk. paper)

British Library Cataloging in Publication Data available

Title-page illustration: The lady smiling into her flower
represents La Belle Dame Sans Merci, the merciless woman
who refuses the repeated entreaties of her would-be lover. "Ye
noy me sore," she rebukes him; "free am I now and free wil I
endure." The woodcut comes from Richard Pynson's 1526
edition of the poem. Reproduced by permission of the
Houghton Library, Harvard University.

Contents

Contents

Acknowledgments

We are most grateful to Fordham University, whose financial support of this volume has made it possible to include the color plates. In particular we want to acknowledge the leadership of Richard E. Doyle, S. J., late dean of the Graduate School of Arts and Sciences, whose devotion to Fordham and encouragement of scholarship will long be remembered by members of this community.

The volume's initial impetus came from Thelma Fenster, director of Fordham's Center for Medieval Studies, whose idea it was to offer a conference on the topic of medieval women and power. Together we organized "Women and Power: Intrigue, Influence, and Insubordination," the meeting in March 1985 at which many of the following essays were first presented. During his term as director of the Center for Medieval Studies, Joseph O'Callaghan most generously supported this project. We are also indebted to Rosemary DeJulio, the Center's secretary, for her persevering and comradely help.

M.E.

M.K.

Women and Power
in the
Middle Ages

Introduction

Mary Erler and Maryanne Kowaleski

L aw and force are the contexts in which power has always been examined. Through these two agents, lives are changed, wills imposed, and the surface of public life inscribed. Traditionally, power has been equated with public authority; the getting and spending of this legitimated and sanctioned power have in fact provided the main subject of the discipline of history. This limited view of power as public authority carries two corollaries: it assumes that women were largely powerless and thus marginal, and it discourages investigation of women's actions in society as seemingly inconsequential.

Medieval society, with its wars, territorial struggles, and violence, seems particularly hostile to the exercise of female initiative and power. Indeed, the prevailing cultural attitudes of the Middle Ages considered women, as the descendants of Eve, intellectually and emotionally inferior to men and thus incapable of wielding authority effectively. Women could not vote or run for public office, nor could they participate fully in other power structures such as the Church, the military, or the guilds. Denied access to institutions of higher learning and handicapped by legal systems which in many instances made them mere chattels of their husbands or fathers, medieval women had few opportunities to enjoy public power.[1] It is within this medieval period, however—so apparently constricting—that the following essays attempt to reconsider the traditional view of power as public authority.

Building upon recent feminist scholarship, the essays offer a more exact view of women's actions in the Middle Ages and assess medieval women's power more precisely. This feminist scholarship, which broadens the conventional understanding of power to include new forms of power and new areas for its exercise, in part responds to the larger question of gender asymmetry: why are women so widely (if not universally) subordinated to men? One answer to this question has been to redefine its terms: to understand power more largely and thus to draw women within its circle. This answer, however, which denies the totality of women's subordination, can be considered only a partial response to the problem of gender inequality.[2]

So, for instance, history has made some movement away from a limited and traditional view of power as public authority to a wider view of power which encompasses the ability to act effectively, to influence people or decisions, and to achieve goals. Under the influence of social historians, with their wider interests in the community and its operations, the place of women in society has become a legitimate, even a fashionable, topic of scholarly investigation. With the aid of anthropological and sociological models, too, scholars have begun to examine more closely the gender-based allocation of power and the cultural devaluation of women and their activities.

The work of anthropologists has been particularly relevant. The distinction made, for example, by Michelle Rosaldo and Louise Lamphere, based on the work of Talcott Parsons and Max Weber, between authority (the socially sanctioned "right" to make decisions binding on others) and power (informal influence) is one which has been applied to medieval women's lives, in this volume, by Judith Bennett and Martha Howell and others.[3] Bennett argues that English peasant women were not isolated from the public world; they owned land, appeared in court, and worked in the marketplace. Still, their access to public power was limited by both their gender and their position in the household. Common law and customary law alike barred women from exercising the legal and landholding rights accorded men. Married women labored under the most severe legal handicaps because peasant economy and society gave their husbands, as heads of households, the fullest rights. This system could, however, work to the advantage of women when they reached widowhood. As the head of a household, a widow enjoyed extensive rights and participated more actively in the public community. Yet as Bennett also notes, women's access to public power always stopped short of sanctioned authority. Participation in politics and public office (for instance, as tithing representatives or pledges in court) was restricted to men. Indeed, women were excluded from the village office of aletaster even though their regular (public) activities as brewers made them best suited to oversee the industry.

Similarly, Martha Howell, in her essay on the public role of women in the cities of northern Europe, suggests that a demonstrated decline in the number of women enjoying citizenship rights can be considered a consequence of the developing conception of citizenship as an individual's access to public authority. When town communes first formed, citizenship was regarded as a brotherhood (*Genossenschaft*) and was based on the familial household. The family basis of the brotherhood, however, could not survive once the urban community became self-governing, because family rule proved too fractious and because the values of urban "civil society" stressed individualism in these northern cities. When individual rule replaced familial rule, women lost citizenship rights and therefore lost access to public power. Howell goes on to suggest that the so-called "democratic" urban revolutions of the late Middle Ages may actually have speeded up the exclusion of women from the political realm.

Howell also relies on the influential theory, developed most fully by anthropologists, that the functional division of human activity into private (domestic) and public spheres accounts for gender asymmetry. This public/private dichotomy has been used to explain both the cultural devaluation of women's activities and their lack of public power and subordination to men. In this model, the public sphere, the domain of men, encompasses the worlds of politics, legal rights and obligations, and the market and is thus the sphere of "real" power, prestige, and authority. The private or domestic sphere, to which women are confined by virtue of their role as wives and mothers, encompasses the family and immediate household. Besides helping to understand why women had little access to public power, this model has also been used to explain why women took different avenues from men to gain prestige or influence and why the exercise of public authority by women is often viewed as illegitimate. Many of the essays in this volume reflect this theory in the reiterated theme of women's dependence on position in the family for access to authority. This insight, couched by Rosaldo in theoretical terms ("Women's status will be lowered in those societies where there is a firm differentiation between domestic and public spheres of activity")[4] is supported by the historical particulars which these essays provide.

Thus Brigitte Bedos Rezak, in her analysis of French women's seals, shows that unmarried women from the middle ranks of landowners more often sealed acts in their own names, and wives of this group more often sealed along with their husbands, than did aristocratic women. The greater legal independence and relative power of these women, Rezak submits, derived from their vital role within a family economic structure in which women played an active part in household and estate management. The imagery of these seals is also relevant to the topic of power. Since women mostly lacked public authority, they were forced either to adopt male images (the equestrian figure) or to use conventions which emphasized female sexuality (breasts, hair, and thighs). Here in these seals the relationship of sexuality and power seems clear. When less sexually charged images appear, they are ambiguous, however: the fleur-de-lis, for example, either represents kingship or recalls the Marian Tree of

Jesse, and after 1250, the hawk links women with men's perception of more-or-less controllable Nature.

The relevance of family position for women with access to public power is also clear in the classic essay by Jo Ann McNamara and Suzanne Wemple, initially given as a paper at the first Berkshire Conference in 1973, published in 1974, and reprinted here. McNamara and Wemple show how the involvement of women in the private realm of the family and kinship networks could favor women when the line between public and private spheres was indistinct. Their essay focuses on the power that women exercised through the family from the sixth to twelfth centuries when central authority was weak and the family served crucial political as well as social roles. As women's ability to acquire property through marriage or inheritance improved in the early Middle Ages, their economic and political position within the family, and consequently within the wider public sphere, was also enhanced.[5] The conditions of early feudal society, which placed public power in private hands, also endowed some noblewomen with considerable public authority because their normal domestic functions as the wives or widows of powerful lords involved control over vital resources and institutions. When political office and economic wealth could be inherited, women possessed greater opportunities to gain access to political power by virtue of their family ties.

Recently some scholars have expressed reservations about the universal applicability of the public/private model. Rosaldo herself has admitted that it may be responsible for equating women with their biological function and for establishing a too-simple bipolarity or "understanding shaped by oppositional modes of thought."[6] Gender inequity, she insists, is shaped by a multitude of particulars, including class and culture, rather than by either bipolar or universalizing solutions. The focus on female biology, manifested in the idea that family shapes women, leads us "to forget that families themselves are things that men and women actively create and that these vary with particulars of social context. . . . the roles the sexes play contribute to and are in turn shaped by all other inequalities in their social world."[7]

Neither Rosaldo nor other critics of the public/private dichotomy, however, advocate abandoning the model altogether. The construct can be made more flexible and can serve as a useful analytical device for understanding the relationship between women and power. Several sociologists, for example, have questioned the implicit assumption that the domestic sphere is necessarily subordinate or secondary to the public sphere. They argue that men's domination of the public sphere is actually made possible by the advantages they accrue through their rights to female service in the private or domestic realm.[8] "It is the flow of services from women to men (especially, but not exclusively) in the marriage relationship which creates that time, space and energy for men in the public sphere and unites them all. Female servicing constructs a firm base for male social solidarity; it defines the common interests of men otherwise divided by class and power."[9] In the medieval context, for instance, women's management of the feudal household allowed knights to leave home regularly to fight and thereby to accumulate prestige and power through their military efforts.

McNamara and Wemple also make a significant contribution to the debate on women and power because they suggest a chronology for shifts in the status and public power of women and determine some of the factors involved in these shifts. The public power of aristocratic women, they say, decreased significantly after the twelfth century when the growing power of the state and the rise of formal education restricted women from following previous avenues of power. At the same time, changes in inheritance practices, dowry, and dower reduced the economic power women enjoyed within families. McNamara and Wemple have also traced similar changes in the power and influence exerted by women in religious life.[10] The ecclesiastical reforms espoused by the Cluniac and Gregorian movements, for example, curtailed the considerable public power wielded by abbesses in the early Middle Ages. By emphasizing the sexually provocative, unstable nature of women, these movements discouraged the endowment of nunneries and advanced the control of male monastic orders over female ones. One of the reasons the essays by McNamara and Wemple continue to be influential is the complexity of their analyses, which suggest economic, political, and ecclesiastical causes for changes in the power of both secular and religious women in the Middle Ages. Their understanding of women's power as interacting with a myriad of other cultural forces thus constitutes a warning against any too simple adoption of the public/private dichotomy.

The changes in the power of religious women noted by McNamara and Wemple receive detailed attention in the essay by Jane Schulenburg. Examining those women judged saintly by the medieval Church, she traces shifts in female sanctity, in itself a reflection of the religious prestige or power gained by certain women. The golden age of female sanctity occurred in the century between 650 and 750, when almost one-quarter of all saints were women. These women often achieved sainthood through their position in a powerful family which allowed them to exercise influence in conversion, appointments to church offices, and the foundation or endowment of nunneries. Schulenburg notes, as do McNamara and Wemple, that religious women (especially abbesses) of the early medieval period enjoyed particular visibility at synods, in education, and in their control of landed wealth.[11] The situation changed, however, with the Carolingian and later reforms. Except for a brief rise in the number of female saints in the tenth century, the proportion of female to male saints had declined greatly by the twelfth century. This decrease in the public recognition of saintly (and therefore religiously powerful) women was paralleled by changes in the styles of female sanctity. Increasingly, new female saints received recognition for their private rather than public accomplishments, for achievements in the domestic arts or motherhood—a change which corresponds to the declining role they played in secular affairs at about the same time.

Stanley Chojnacki, in his essay on Venetian wives and husbands, also suggests a chronology for shifts in the influence wielded by women, locating this shift, as have others, in the context of the family. He traces these changes through an examination of the language, bequests, and arrangements set out in patrician wills. From 1400 onward the growing importance of marriage in the fortunes of patrician families led to an increase in the amount of dowries, thereby adding to the economic leverage of wives. These developments had an impact on the attitudes of husbands toward their wives, exhibited in the wills' new language of affection. In order to secure women's favor, moreover, men had to depend on personal loyalties rather than on family or lineage connections. In this behavior they followed the lead of women, displaying a more personal, affective, social orientation.

Thus five essays in this volume attempt a difficult task indeed: the development of a chronology of women's power. McNamara and Wemple's, the earliest essay, is also the most ambitious; even so, its focus is limited to the upper stratum of medieval society. The other essays are somewhat more restricted in the time they encompass, but by focusing on particular periods, locations, and social groups they show how women's power could change greatly in response to specific historical circumstances. These essays, in addition, do not all deal with the same kind of power. Chojnacki, for instance, discusses cultural or behavioral influence exerted by women, Schulenburg examines religious prestige in the form of sainthood, and Howell and McNamara and Wemple focus on public power. Even when the authors discuss the same social class in the same time period, their conclusions may conflict if they employ different sources. Thus Rezak, using seals as a reflection of the power of women in feudal society, shows that the use of seals by women in the second half of the thirteenth century doubled; in this period, according to McNamara and Wemple, the power of feudal women had drastically declined.[12] At the moment, therefore, attempts to construct a chronology for the power of women must be considered preliminary. Even the discovery of societies in which women held a degree of public authority, or the discovery of strategies which empowered them, can only be said to be partial. Still less visible are the ways in which men's authority and women's power are interwoven, though several of the volume's essays attempt to deal with this latter question (Bennett, Hanawalt, and Hansen).

At least two essays in the volume suggest the possibility of women's influence on the larger culture. Chojnacki postulates the reversal of gender-associated styles of language, initiated by women's growing economic power. Susan Groag Bell, in an important essay (first published in 1982) demonstrates the substantial power that female book owners exercised over vernacular literatures as readers, literary patrons, and mothers in charge of the education of children. Because of their exclusion from formal education and from clerical status, women's access to standard avenues of learning was impaired, hence their reliance on books as intellectual and spiritual teachers. Bell is particularly interested in cultural change and suggests that the frequent images of the Virgin reading validated this activity for contemporary women. In fact, the influence may have worked in the opposite direction as well: as the numbers of women book owners increased in the fourteenth and fifteenth centuries, so too did the numbers of such Marian images. Bell also stresses the matrilineal role in the passage of both texts and ideas across national boundaries. As mothers chose books from which to teach their daughters and to bequeath to daughters who married and moved elsewhere, women powerfully influenced the transmission of culture.

Chojnacki and Bell both demonstrate the complex relationship between female and male networks of influence. Barbara Hanawalt examines such ties in detail by focusing on one English female aristocrat's connections and comparing these with her husband's in composition and social purposes. Honor Lisle's network, while similar to that of her husband, served male goals as well as its own female ones. Hanawalt shows how Honor Lisle used gifts, favors, hospitality, letters, and patronage to advance her own reputation and the interests of her family by garnering goodwill and building ties of reciprocity. Lady Lisle's networks with other women helped in particular ways: in solving domestic problems, placing female relatives in advantageous situations, keeping up with fashions and gift etiquette, and supplying household and personal items. Lady Lisle also enjoyed a good deal of public power in business and through her influence over political and religious appointments—yet only, of course, through her position as the wife of a wealthy and politically powerful man. Indeed, her influence over her husband, the main source of her power, was ultimately viewed as suspect and excessive by her husband's political enemies. Honor Lisle's life thus illustrates one of the classic problems in the relation of women to power: that even the near approach of women to public authority is usually viewed as illegitimate and is classified in culturally disapproved ways.

As history has enlarged its boundaries in response to the influence of sociology and anthropology, so literature has responded to new critical perspectives, many of which focus directly on language. The subject of women's relation to language—with its implications for loss and gain in power—has preoccupied many writers. Can different types of discourse be ascribed to women and men? Can individual "social and cultural realities of women's situations generate 'feminine' styles of language use"? What are the characteristics of public and private language?[13] Answers relevant for medieval women have been offered by Elizabeth Alvilda Petroff, who points to the survival of oral characteristics in medieval women's devotional writings and suggests this may be due to the nature of visionary experience (a frequent female subject) with its elements both of visual iconography and dialogue. She also notes the early use of the vernacular by women to describe complex interior states.[14]

Perhaps the earliest movement in the critical examination of medieval women in literature can be said to have proceeded under the rubric of Joan Ferrante's pioneering study *Women as Image*.[15] In a well-known essay, Elaine Showalter has identified two sorts of feminist literary criticism. The earlier of these did indeed study the image of women in literature, exploring misconceptions or stereotypes, probing "fissures in male-constructed literary history" or critical theory.[16]

Recently attention has focused on scholarship which might be called more centrally female. It includes the study of women writers, or patrons, or readers as well as such theoretical questions as whether it is possible to characterize a female mode of discourse (poetics) or to isolate female themes or interests in literature. Since this second emphasis stresses the recovery of women's writing, it is possible to see it as moving literature and history closer together. Showalter here speaks of constructing "a female framework for the analysis of woman's literature, [developing] new models based on the study of female experience."[17]

Bell's essay in the present volume describes Showalter's categories in slightly different terms: it speaks of "women as literary subject matter (Showalter's first category) rather than as creators or users of books" (the second category). Bell's use of literature and history together falls, of course, within the latter category. It provides data to support the familiar idea of medieval women as patrons of literature and in so doing gives a realistically complex picture of women both as literary audience and as economic consumers.

Ferrante's essay in this volume likewise operates in both disciplines and, in addition, neatly subsumes both of Showalter's critical categories. Its first half consists of a survey of female characters in romance and epic who employ subversive strategies: trickery, cursing, manipulation, various sorts of undercutting speech (the hidden promise, the false oath, the forged letter, the benevolent fiction, and the malicious lie), and, finally, magic. The essay's second half then focuses on three woman writers, Hrotsvit, Hildegarde of Bingen, and Christine de Pizan, who, like the literary characters, use an indirect strategy—the modesty topos of formulaic authorial self-deprecation—to mark exterior events, through words, in a powerful way. Though this convention is employed by both male and female authors, the particular forms of it used by Hrotsvit, Hildegarde, and Christine provide illuminating variations on a theme— especially Christine's mixture of diminutive and subversive in her self-characterization "little knife." Like the fictional character of Griselda in Elaine Hansen's essay, Ferrante's historical women consciously adopt a conventional posture unthreatening in the extreme as a deliberately chosen means to power. Ferrante's essay is thus a central one for this volume, since, in making explicit one way in which social constructs determine female authorial voice, it strongly suggests the mutual influence of life and art. Together with Hansen's essay it connects passivity and power—in the worlds of both literature (Hansen) and life (Ferrante).

All three literary essays, in fact, offer variants on this single strategy: the paradoxical achievement of power through its renunciation. Ferrante's female authors employ rhetorical methods here and succeed through abandoning the rhetoric of power, but for both Michelle Freeman and Hansen the battle is joined on moral grounds. These latter two essays deal, of course, with retellings of the Patient Griselda legend in Chaucer's *Clerk's Tale* and Marie de France's "Le Fresne." Although both contributors see their heroines' perfect virtue as posing a puzzle and implying a reproach to a world conditioned to the exercise of power-as-force, their readings of this perfect virtue differ. Freeman suggests that we understand Marie to be offering her heroine Le Fresne as a Christ-like figure, the suffering servant, while Hansen, in contrast, refuses to equate power with submissive goodness, viewing the latter as self-destructive. Hansen sees Griselda as consciously subversive, employing the power of silence for her own ends, while Le Fresne's motives in renouncing power are not self-interested. In both the *Clerk's Tale* and "Le Fresne," the strategy is the same—deliberate abdication of power brings the restoration of equilibrium—but the motives of this identical strategy differ: calculation is opposed to abnegation.

Both Freeman and Hansen are interested in the relation of the author to her/his text. Freeman suggests that Marie, the female poet, is able to exalt the nurturing and sheltering work of a group of women through her own authorial work. Both Marie's activity and that of the women in her text, in providing an alternative, first, to male learning and, second, to male lineage, seem to recall Showalter's second critical category, which elevates the rediscovery of female work. Hansen's essay perhaps fits more easily into Showalter's first category: in asking new questions about traditional texts, it attempts to show how the male poet (and the male narrator) simultaneously empowers himself and controls women—paradoxically by speaking from a marginal status not unlike female marginality.

For the most part, however, the essays in this volume focus not on male dominance but on female empowerment. This approach does not deny the powerful advantages or greater prestige enjoyed by men in the Middle Ages. Indeed, most of the essays keep the subordinate position of medieval women firmly in mind. Yet they dwell at greater length on the more positive theme of how and when women wielded power. In so doing, they make us take a different view of the medieval world and the place of women in this world. Their innovative analyses, moreover, have ramifications beyond the theme of women and power, forcing us to rethink such issues as the periodization of history, the centrality of public authority and military might in history writing, and how and why value is attached to literary works.

In focusing on the empowerment of women, the contributors note that medieval women employed a wide variety of strategies to exert influence. Even within the empowering agency of the family, women possessed a number of options; economic contribution (through dowry, wage labor, or household work and production), sexual attraction, affection, wifely persuasion, and motherly guidance all strengthened women's position. Some of these methods, of course, were also viable outside the domestic sphere. In the larger community, as in the family, sexuality and work, for example, endowed some women with a measure of influence, as did such other (in some cases almost exclusively female) sources of power as gossip,[18] deceit, patronage, and hospitality.

Female motives in seeking power, as well as the ends to which this power was put, could of course vary widely. While the family dominates here also—wives and mothers commonly worked to advance the interests of their husbands and offspring—we should not underestimate the frequency with which self-interest lay behind women's pursuit of influence. Nor should we view medieval women as exclusively the victims of societal forces beyond their control. The presence of a strong motivation or intensely desired end was in itself empowering because of the force and direction it gave to women's lives. On the other hand, medieval women may frequently have defined self-interest in terms of their relationship with men. Thus sexuality was exercised to attract a rich and powerful husband, and hospitality and patronage were bestowed in order to further the careers of male family members.

Contemporaries certainly acknowledged both the potential power that women could wield and the variety of female approaches to power. Strategies which supported male authority—hospitality, for instance—received tacit approval. Wifely persuasion, as one scholar has recently shown, was encouraged by monastic authors and scholastic theologians so that wives could influence their husbands' financial support of ecclesiastical institutions or could dissuade them from usurious behavior.[19] Other scholars have noted the Church's appreciation for wives who persuaded pagan husbands to convert to Christianity. On the other hand, female strategies which could undermine male authority—gossip and sexuality, for instance—were feared, labeled subversive, and condemned as socially unacceptable avenues to power.

One of the strongest common threads that draws together the volume's essays is their interest in female networks. The frequency with which the authors are attracted to this topic suggests the presence of a cultural pattern which has repeatedly supported the efforts of marginalized persons and which perhaps indicates the psychological need common to any subordinated group. The extent to which women's networks differ from men's is a complicated question which cannot be answered here. More important, however, such networks can be seen as providing the basis for activity which either interacts with male authority or responds to it. Thus in this volume women's networks are described as interacting with the dominant male world of politics (Hanawalt), influencing the dominant male world of literature (Bell) and social behavior (Chojnacki), or creating a literary artifact of their own (Freeman). In taking this direction, the essays have attempted to move beyond simple bipolarity and into more realistically complex analyses of the power relations between men and women. The volume's other overarching concern is represented by its various attempts to provide chronologies (for longer or shorter periods of time) which chart the rise and fall of women's power and link it to particular historic situations.

While united in theme, the volume's essays draw upon the widest variety of sources: wills (Bell and Chojnacki); property transactions (McNamara and Wemple, Chojnacki); letters (Hanawalt); manuscript illuminations and miniatures (Bell); manorial records (Bennett); saints' lives (Schulenburg); seals (Rezak); civic records (Howell); legal codes (McNamara and Wemple)—and of course literary texts. Diverse as they are, the essays share the organizing belief that the use of gender as an analytical category can illuminate familiar material. Thus in Bennett's hands manorial records yield information about marriage as female exclusion from authority, while in Freeman's treatment of Marie de France's text, both the tale itself and its heroine are transformed into the product of women's communal efforts.

A number of issues germane to the question of women and power are not touched upon in this volume. In history, for instance, the area of formal subversion—witchcraft—still offers an opportunity for much absorbing work.[20] Natalie Davis's ideas about the relationship between the symbolic impact of sexual inversion and the increasing legal and cultural restrictions placed on women in the early modern period remain to be tested for the Middle Ages.[21] Literary and historical scholars still argue over the significance of the twelfth-century rise of courtly love poetry, which praised upper-class women and encouraged men to seek their approval. Yet a recent overview has called courtliness "less a phenomenon of love . . . than an expression of the difficulties inherent in male-female relations."[22] The ramifications for female power of the confluence of courtly love poetry and the growing cult of the Virgin Mary (promoted mostly by male clerics) also need further investigation. Some scholars, for example, observe that these two movements, which appear to empower women and elevate their status, actually coincided with a decrease in the real political power exercised by these women.[23] Similarly paradoxical is the problem of women and the Renaissance. While some scholars have focused on the prevalence of powerful queens and the greater educational options available to women in this period, others have found evidence of an increasing dependence of women on men.[24] At the intersection of theology and history much also remains to be said. God language and female forms of religious power, both immanent and transcendent, have received scholarly attention recently, but the connection between female visionary experience and authority has been little explored. An exception is Caroline Walker Bynum's recent work on "food behavior" as a nexus of power for medieval women. Bynum argues that, through food, women were able to achieve self-definition, to reject family standards, to bypass forms of clerical control, to claim a priestly role, and to criticize contemporary spirituality.[25]

Though the literary texts treated in this volume are traditional ones, long part of the accepted canon, the question of revision of this canon, and the acceptance of nontraditional kinds of women's writing (with the accompanying need to revise literary methods of responding to new kinds of writing) remains vexed.[26] Canonicity poses a more serious problem the closer we come to the modern period and the larger the body of women's writing. For the medieval period, however, it is not impossible for us to hope that we may uncover more women's writing, probably in nontraditional forms such as letters—and that we may have comparable success in uncovering women's history. Two examples, both of which link history and literature, may be relevant: the *Book* of Margery Kempe, a document of compelling interest both spiritually and socially, came to light as recently as the 1930s and provided, in its surprising reappearance, what constitutes the first English autobiography.[27] In the early modern period, an examination of the most recent bibliography on the topic of women writers in Tudor England suggests that scholarship in this large area has been centrally devoted to the recovery and printing of texts; critical work on these early modern women writers is scarce indeed. The bibliography's compiler, in fact, believes that the main unanswered questions here too center on the issues of power: did Tudor women writers influence their female successors, their male contemporaries, or "the course and character of the English literary Renaissance"?[28] Answers to these questions of literary history, like answers to more specifically historical questions, will depend on the provision of two kinds of texts: those of women's writings and those of their lives.

As the simple opposition between the public and the private spheres must be transcended by a more inclusive examination of the realities of male-female power, so a simple opposition between literature and history must likewise yield to perceptions of their interdependence. Instead of seeing history and literature in their familiar compartments, history providing a background for literature's products, the "new historicism," as it has developed in literary studies, sees both literature and history as imaginative constructions, products of a culture, and interpreters of it. Stephen Greenblatt's well-known formulation speaks of the wish to "investigate both the social presence to the world of the literary text and the social presence of the world in the literary text."[29] We read a series of texts—social and written—to gain our understanding of experience. Literature shapes a culture's sense of itself: similarly, history, in being filtered through individual consciousnesses, is created by them and cannot accurately be described as objective. The use of both these constructs offers a more complex version (or vision) of the past.

To say we focus on the issue of women and power is to say that we are concerned with the deepest questions about women's identity and cultural roles. To ask *when* women have been powerful and *how* is to attempt to provide a new understanding of women's lives and work.

Notes

1. For a general discussion of the cultural and legal handicaps facing women in the Middle Ages, Eileen Power's work is still relevant. See "The Position of Women," in *The Legacy of the Middle Ages,* ed. C. G. Crump and E. F. Jacob

(Oxford, 1926), pp. 401–34, reprinted with her other essays in *Medieval Women,* ed. M. M. Postan (Cambridge, 1975). See also Carolly Erickson, "The Vision of Women" in *The Medieval Vision* (New York, 1976), pp. 181–212.

2. Even a more sophisticated understanding of the constituent elements of power, and of the way in which authority and power interact, however, still leaves untouched the question of why societally recognized expressions of power are so slanted in the direction of maleness. The introduction to Sherry B. Ortner and Harriet Whitehead's *Sexual Meanings: The Cultural Construction of Gender and Sexuality* (Cambridge, 1981) provides a provocative discussion of this topic, suggesting that where male prestige activity depends on the sphere of women's activity, or is closely connected with it, the female sphere will be subject to much male scrutiny and anxiety (fears about female disruptiveness or threat). See also Peggy Reeves Sanday, *Female Power and Male Dominance: On the Origins of Sexual Inequality* (Cambridge, 1981). For a recent summary of the debates on the issue of gender inequality, see Margot I. Duley and Mary I. Edwards, *The Cross Cultural Study of Women: A Comprehensive Guide* (New York, 1986), particularly pp. 26–47 and 78–90.

3. Michelle Zimbalist Rosaldo and Louise Lamphere, eds., *Woman, Culture, and Society* (Stanford, 1974), pp. 21, 99–100. Rosaldo notes: "Whether power is exercised through influence or force, it is inherently competitive, whereas authority entails a hierarchical chain of command and control. Although the idea of authority implies positive actions and duties, the exercise of power has no positive sanctions, only rules that specify 'the conditions of illegality of its operation'" (p. 21n).

4. Rosaldo, "A Theoretical Overview," in *Woman, Culture, and Society,* p. 36.

5. These points are elaborated in Suzanne Fonay Wemple, *Women in Frankish Society: Marriage and the Cloister, 500 to 900* (Philadelphia, 1981). See also David Herlihy, "Land, Family, and Women in Continental Europe, 701–1200," *Traditio* 18 (1962):89–120; Janet L. Nelson, "Queens as Jezebels: The Careers of Brunhild and Balthild in Merovingian History," in *Medieval Women,* ed. Derek Baker (Oxford, 1978), pp. 31–78; Pauline Stafford, *Queens, Concubines, and Dowagers: The King's Wife in the Early Middle Ages* (Athens, Ga., 1983); Christine Fell, *Women in Anglo-Saxon England* (London, 1984).

6. M. Z. Rosaldo, "The Use and Abuse of Anthropology: Reflections on Feminism and Cross-Cultural Understanding," *Signs* 5 (1980):389–417 (quotation on p. 6). This essay of Rosaldo's recalls the similar warnings, in a very different intellectual context, of the French theoretician Hélène Cixous, for whom binary oppositions, such as male/female or culture/nature, embody masculine thought, the more powerful destroying the weaker of these oppositions, which is always identified with the feminine; see Hélène Cixous and Catherine Clement, *The Newly Born Woman,* trans. Betsy Wing (Minneapolis, 1986), pp. 63–64; see also Sherry B. Ortner, "Is Female to Male as Nature Is to Culture?" in Rosaldo and Lamphere, *Woman, Culture, and Society,* pp. 67–87. The insights of literary theorist and anthropologist are echoed by a recent essay written by historian Susan Stuard which suggests that the application of classical and scholastic gender bi-

polarities (right/left, limited/unlimited, straight/curved) influenced medieval women's denigration and their progressive exclusion from power ("The Dominion of Gender: Women's Fortunes in the High Middle Ages," in *Becoming Visible: Women in European Society,* ed. Renate Bridenthal, Claudia Koonz, and Susan Mosher Stuard, 2d ed. [Boston, 1987], pp. 139–58).

7. Rosaldo, "Use and Abuse of Anthropology," p. 416. See also the essays in Sherry B. Ortner and Harriet Whitehead, eds., *Sexual Meanings: The Cultural Construction of Gender and Sexuality,* which argues that gender is to be understood not only as a biological given but also as a product of various social and cultural processes.

8. Eva Gamarnikow, David H. J. Morgan, June Purvis, and Daphne Taylorson, eds., *The Public and the Private* (London, 1983), especially Eva Gamarnikow and June Purvis, Introduction, pp. 1–6, and Linda Imray and Audrey Middleton, "Public and Private: Marking the Boundaries," pp. 12–27.

9. Gamarnikow and Purvis, Introduction, p. 4.

10. Jo Ann McNamara and Suzanne F. Wemple, "Sanctity and Power: The Dual Pursuit of Medieval Women," in *Becoming Visible: Women in European History,* ed. Renate Bridenthal and Claudia Koonz (Boston, 1977), pp. 90–118. Also see Wemple, *Women in Frankish Society,* for a further elaboration of this theme.

11. McNamara and Wemple, "Sanctity and Power"; see also Joan Nicholson, "*Feminae Gloriosae:* Women in the Age of Bede," in *Medieval Women,* ed. Derek Baker (Oxford, 1978), pp. 15–30.

12. Other scholars have also discussed changes in the power and influence of feudal women. Their reliance on different sources and focus on different regions accounts in part for the variations in the chronologies they establish for the decline in feudal women's power. See, for example, Marion F. Facinger, "A Study of Medieval Queenship: Capetian France, 987–1237," *Studies in Medieval and Renaissance History* 5 (1968):3–48, and Herlihy, "Land, Family, and Women in Continental Europe, 701–1200."

13. For a discussion of these questions, see Sally McConnell-Ginet, Ruth Borker, Nelly Furman, eds., *Women and Language in Literature and Society* (New York, 1980); the quoted passage appears on p. xiv.

14. Elizabeth Alvilda Petroff, "Introduction: The Visionary Tradition in Women's Writing: Dialogue and Autobiography," *Medieval Women's Visionary Literature* (Oxford, 1986), pp. 30, 49.

15. *Women as Image in Medieval Literature* (New York, 1975).

16. Elaine Showalter, "Toward a Feminist Poetics," in *Women's Writing and Writing about Women,* ed. Mary Jacobus (London, 1979), and "Feminist Criticism in the Wilderness," *Critical Inquiry* 8 (1981):179–205. Both essays are reprinted in *The New Feminist Criticism: Essays on Women, Literature, and Theory,* ed. Elaine Showalter (New York, 1985), pp. 125–43, 243–70. The quoted statement appears on p. 128. A similar analysis is provided by Elizabeth Abel in her introduction to *Writing and Sexual Difference* (Chicago, 1982), pp. 1–7.

17. Showalter, "Toward a Feminist Poetics," p. 131.

18. See, e.g., Susan D. Amussen, "Féminin/masculin: Le genre dans l'Angleterre de l'époque moderne," *Annales* 40:2 (1985):269–87, for a discussion of the relationship between gossip and reputation in local communities.

19. Sharon Farmer, "Persuasive Voices: Clerical Images of Medieval Wives," *Speculum* 61:3 (1986):517–43.

20. The witch craze was largely a phenomenon of the early modern period. The accusation of witchcraft clearly contained a fear of women's imagined magical powers, though examination of the trial records confirms the actual powerlessness of female victims. Interpretations of the witch craze and its relationship to the status of women vary greatly. See, e.g., E. William Monter, ed., *European Witchcraft* (New York, 1969), and his "The Pedestal and the Stake: Courtly Love and Witchcraft," in *Becoming Visible,* pp. 119–23. Also see Christina Larner, *Enemies of God: The Witch-Hunt in Scotland* (Baltimore, 1981), chapter 1, for a recent survey of the scholarly work on witches.

21. Natalie Zemon Davis, "Women on Top," *Society and Culture in Early Modern France* (Stanford, 1977), pp. 124–51.

22. E. Jane Burns and Roberta Krueger, Introduction to "Courtly Ideology and Women's Place in Medieval French Literature," special issue of *Romance Notes* 25 (1985):208.

23. See John Benton, "Clio and Venus: An Historical View of Medieval Love," in *The Meaning of Courtly Love,* ed. F. X. Newman (Albany, 1972), pp. 19–42; Georges Duby, *The Knight, the Lady, and the Priest: The Making of Modern Marriage in Medieval France,* trans. Barbara Bray (Chicago, 1983). Penny Schine Gold, in *The Lady and the Virgin: Image, Attitude, and Experience in Twelfth-Century France* (Chicago, 1985), also notes the ambivalent and conflicting attitudes toward women in this period. Burns and Krueger give a fuller bibliography on this question, p. 302.

24. Joan Kelly, "Did Women Have a Renaissance?" in *Becoming Visible,* pp. 137–64, and reprinted in her *Women, History, and Theory,* introduction by Blanche W. Cook, Clare Coss, Alice K. Harris, Rosalind P. Petchesky, and Amy Swerdlow (Chicago, 1984). David Herlihy's response to Kelly appears in *Medievalia et Humanistica* 13 (1985):1–22. Some of these issues have recently been treated, primarily from a literary viewpoint, in *Rewriting the Renaissance: The Discourses of Sexual Difference in Early Modern Europe,* ed. Margaret W. Ferguson, Maureen Quilligan, and Nancy J. Vickers (Chicago, 1986).

25. See, e.g., Eleanor McLaughlin, "Women, Power, and the Pursuit of Holiness in Medieval Christianity," in *Women of Spirit: Female Leadership in the Jewish and Christian Traditions,* ed. Rosemary Reuther and Eleanor McLaughlin (New York, 1979), pp. 99–130; Eleanor McLaughlin, " 'Christ My Mother': Feminine Naming and Metaphor in Medieval Spirituality," *Nashotah Review* 15 (1975):228–48; Caroline Walker Bynum, *Holy Feast and Holy Fast: The Religious Significance of Food to Medieval Women* (Berkeley, 1987), pp. 189–244.

26. Marilyn L. Williamson, "Towards a Feminist Literary History," *Signs* 10 (1984):136–47.

27. W. Butler-Bowdon, ed., *The Book of Margery Kempe* (London, 1936); San-

ford B. Meech, ed., *The Book of Margery Kempe,* Early English Text Society, o.s., 212 (Oxford, 1940).

28. Elizabeth H. Hageman, "Recent Studies in Women Writers of Tudor England," *English Literary Renaissance* 14 (Autumn 1984):409–25; quoted passage on p. 422.

29. Stephen Greenblatt, *Renaissance Self-Fashioning: From More to Shakespeare* (Chicago, 1980), p. 5. For a good recent overview, see Jean E. Howard, "The New Historicism in Renaissance Studies," *English Literary Renaissance* 16 (1986):13–43.

Public Power and Authority
in the
Medieval English Countryside

Judith M. Bennett

Villagers in medieval England lived in a very public world.[1] Bound together by nucleated settlements, common fields, and shared lordships, medieval villagers cooperated with their neighbors in coordinating work and government, monitoring courtship and marriage, and exchanging land and labor. Community interest and control extended even to the most private of acts—sexual relations and marriage.[2] As a result, the notion of a public sphere for males and a private sphere for females was much less important to medieval peasants than it was to the middle class of the nineteenth century. A dichotomy between private wives and public husbands was certainly embedded in the households of the medieval countryside, but it was an ideal, not a real dichotomy. Women were never thoroughly isolated from the public life of medieval villages because their daily activities brought them into regular contact with neighbors, officers, laborers, traders, and the like.

A clear but relatively fluid sexual division of labor also promoted the public activity of medieval countrywomen. Skilled or heavy work away from the domestic croft was usually undertaken by men, and women took responsibility for a wide variety of smaller tasks centered on the household.[3] Household duties did not, however, isolate peasant women. On the one hand, women regularly assisted men in planting and harvesting. Whenever agricultural work required additional laborers, women left their tasks around the croft and joined their fathers, husbands, and brothers in the fields. On the other hand, women's work around the croft was often more public than private. As dairymaids, poulterers, gardeners, bakers, and brewers, medieval countrywomen not only supplied the needs of their own households but also produced mar-

ketable surpluses. The enforcement records of the assize of bread and ale
leave no doubt, for example, that women were some of the most active of
commercial bakers and brewers in the countryside.[4] Rural women and
men worked with equal vigor to support their households and relied
with equal intensity upon each other's labor. The private idealization of
the economically inactive "angel in the house" that so strongly characterized the Victorian middle class had no place in the rural household
economy of the Middle Ages.

Neither the public nature of life in the medieval countryside nor the
economic importance of women's work, however, assured that public
power and authority were shared equally by the sexes. Power, defined as
"the ability to act effectively on persons or things . . . [in ways] not of
right allocated to individuals," can be best assessed for medieval coun-
trypeople through their landholding, legal, and social activities.[5] All medieval peasants did not hold land, were not treated equivalently by their
courts, and were not socially active to the same extent and degree. Still,
the most effective members of rural communities were legally competent
and socially active landholders. Defined in these terms, power was most
readily acquired by men, but it was not denied to women. In contrast,
authority, defined as "recognized and legitimized power," was strictly
reserved for males. Women never served as rural officers and were also
excluded from the formal associations that bound men together into a
political community. In the villages of medieval England, political action
brought sanctioned power, social prestige, and personal profit, benefits
available only to men.

The experiences of the medieval peasantry are set forth in the records
of courts held by manorial lords. Manorial courts usually required the
attendance of all tenants at meetings every three weeks and oversaw a
wide variety of local matters, including inheritances, land conveyances,
trespasses, assaults, disputes, and petty thefts. These courts were rural as
well as seigneurial institutions. Convened by a lord's authority but managed by peasant officers, manorial courts blended the seigneurial need for
control with the local need for community regulation and mingled the
lord's law with local custom. These local forums differed from modern
courts in familiarity (most peasants probably knew their courts as well as
they knew their churches), use (most contacts in manorial courts involved
cooperation rather than the conflict we associate with modern legal action), and form (business was conducted by laypeople who normally
acted without the aid of lawyers). Where manorial court rolls survive in
long and complete series, they provide unparalleled insights into the public affairs of preindustrial rural communities.[6]

The use of such records to study the access of rural women to public power and authority presents, however, two basic problems. First, private influence cannot be traced in court records, and no other sources survive to counterbalance the public focus of court rolls with information about private ideals, aspirations, and actions. Because both male and female peasants were illiterate, they have left no diaries or memoirs that describe their personal hopes and visions. The peasantry was generally despised by the literate minority, and its portrayal in contemporary literature is, at best, highly suspect. The private attitudes and activities of medieval countryfolk are, as a result, hidden from historical view.[7] Still, given the public nature of life in the medieval countryside, there can be no doubt that public activities were important in medieval villages and that the ability of women to act publicly was one significant component of their lives. Neighborliness was vital to rural living, and those whose public options enabled them to be better neighbors accrued not only power but possibly also authority. Manorial court rolls offer only a partial view of medieval rural society, but it is a view focused on essential activities.[8]

Second, since court rolls are best used in studies of specific localities, their findings can be extended to other areas and times only with the greatest care and caution. This essay uses the 549 courts extant for the manor of Brigstock (in Rockingham Forest, Northamptonshire) between 1287 and 1348 to examine the access of women in that community to public power and authority.[9] Were the experiences of women in Brigstock typical of all English countrywomen? Because no single community can represent fully the extraordinary diversity of economy, settlement, and custom found in the English medieval countryside, none was "typical" of all others. And because the history of rural women is a relatively new field in medieval studies, little comparable research is available. Nevertheless, comparison of the Brigstock data with information drawn from the archives of two other manors—Iver, a pastoral community in Buckinghamshire, and Houghton-cum-Wyton, an open-field, mixed farming manor in Huntingdonshire—suggests that gender relations in Brigstock followed a pattern broadly characteristic of most rural communities before the plague.[10]

In these communities, then, public power was less available to women than to men, and public authority was, essentially, a male preserve. No matter what private pressures and influences countrywomen might have mustered to influence events in their communities, they were less able than men to exert formal and public power. This finding is, perhaps, unsurprising, since women have been observed in many societies—urban as well as rural, modern as well as medieval—to be excluded from the formal exercise of power. What distinguishes the experiences of medieval countrywomen, however, is that their gender only indirectly affected access to many types of public power but definitively determined the extent of their participation in public authority. Although rural women, under certain circumstances, acquired many attributes commonly associated with the public power of men, they never attained public authority. Women held land, pursued legal pleas, and forged complex networks of friendship with fellow villagers, but politics remained a male affair.

ACCESS TO PUBLIC POWER in Brigstock was determined as much by household position as by gender. Because of their sex, all women faced obstacles to landholding, legal competency, and social activity that were unknown to men, but these obstacles reflected a presumption of household dependency more than gender distinctions. In rural communities such as Brigstock, the full range of landholding, legal, and social options was reserved for householders (including most males) and was less available to their dependents (including most females). Those men, however, who were not full householders (adolescent sons, bachelors, and retired fathers) were less publicly powerful than male householders, just as those women who were freed of household dependency (widows and, in some measure, adolescent daughters) more nearly emulated the public activities of men. Public power, in short, was most available to heads of households. Since most households were headed by males, an assumption of publicly powerful males (i.e., householders) and publicly passive females (i.e., wives and daughters) underlay the distribution of power in the countryside. These gender distinctions, however, not only were secondary to household status but also were moderated by the many household positions that fit poorly the presumption of male power and female dependency.

Because of the influence of household position upon access to public power in Brigstock, women's power waxed, waned, and waxed again over the course of the female life cycle. During adolescence, as young people of both sexes gradually detached themselves from parental authority in anticipation of marriage, the public opportunities of young women roughly matched those of young men. Consider the adolescent experiences of Cristina Penifader and her future brother-in-law, Henry Kroyl junior. Cristina Penifader first appeared in the court of Brigstock in 1312 when she began to accumulate property, while she was still unmarried, from her father. In 1312, he gave her future control of a plot and croft that he had purchased; in 1314 he granted her the use of a full virgate of meadow; in 1316, he gave her four butts of land valuable enough to merit the high entry fine of two shillings.[11] When she needed a personal pledge or legal assistor during these years, Cristina Penifader turned sometimes to her father, but she was sufficiently well connected in the community to seek such aid, as she usually did, from other men to whom she was presumably not related. She was also, by virtue of her propertied status, a suitor of the Brigstock court, obliged to attend all its meetings unless properly excused. By the time Cristina Penifader married Richard Power in 1317, she was a competent landholder, an experienced court suitor, and a socially active member of her community.[12] The experiences of Henry Kroyl junior during his unmarried years were quite similar. In the three years that preceded his marriage to Agnes Penifader in 1319, he accumulated property through gifts from his parents (acquiring parcels of land in six separate transactions), relied often, but not exclusively, upon his father for legal assistance, and paid suit to the Brigstock court.[13]

Cristina Penifader and Henry Kroyl junior belonged to the more privileged sector of a heterogeneous rural community, but their experiences indicate the many ways in which young people—of both sexes and from both relatively rich and relatively poor households—enjoyed access to public power in early fourteenth-century Brigstock.[14] Young people often established independent economic reserves by acquiring land or saving wages, and daughters, like sons, could hold, sell, and buy land without restriction.[15] Adolescents of both sexes were also treated by the Brigstock court as legally responsible adults who could be trusted as landholders, were liable as criminals, and were competent as suitors.[16] Social experiences were similarly parallel, as both young women and young men slowly expanded their horizons while still maintaining close ties with their parents.[17] The public powers of adolescent daughters and sons were certainly distinguishable; sons came to court more readily than daughters, their economic privileges (including preference in inheritance and better wages) assured them of greater success in establishing economic autonomy, and their networks of friends and associates were usually larger and more diverse than the networks of their sisters. Still, adolescent daughters and sons in Brigstock enjoyed fundamentally similar access to public power even if sons more quickly and more easily exploited the options available to them.

Marriage sharply divided the public power of the sexes. It dramatically expanded men's access to power derived through landholding, legal competency, and social action, and it just as dramatically limited the access of women to the same activities. When such women as Cristina Penifader married, they lost many opportunities they had known as adolescents. A wife no longer enjoyed economic independence; her lands were merged into the conjugal property and could not be conveyed or sold without her husband's concurrence (a husband's lands were not similarly encumbered).[18] A wife also lost legal competency; she no longer owed court suit (her husband did it for her), and she no longer invariably took personal responsibility for her own actions (her husband could be implicated for her crimes and pleas).[19] And whereas marriage brought men an expansion of social opportunities and decreased reliance upon family, it had the opposite effect upon women; the court associations of wives were distinguished from those of all other adults (whether male or female) by their small size and heavy focus upon kin.[20] The public powers of women and men were most distinct when they lived together as wives and husbands.

Widowhood and old age brought a new equivalency in the public power of the sexes in Brigstock. The extant records preclude the study of male widowhood, but many men clearly began to exercise their public options less vigorously as they aged. Without formally retiring, they dispersed some landed property among their grown children, they less frequently attended court or brought matters to the court's attention, and they associated less intensely and less widely with others in the community. The means of exercising public power were not closed to aging men, but they nevertheless seem to have activated those means much less commonly than they had done when they were younger.[21] For women, however, the later years of life often brought an expansion, rather than a contraction, in both the availability and the exercise of public power. When widows took over the households left by their husbands, they acquired public opportunities that surpassed those of all other women. Widows freely traded and sold their personal properties, and many managed in addition to circumvent the custodial restrictions placed upon the "free bench" lands assigned, from the conjugal property, for their use. More than daughters or wives, widows most emulated the participation of men in the Brigstock land market—independently trading, exchanging, and selling small parcels of property.[22] Widows were also distinguished by their legal actions. They, like daughters, owed suit to the Brigstock court and answered complaints and pursued litigation without the *couverture* of a male. In addition, they, like husbands, could be legally liable for the actions and problems of their dependents.[23] The social experiences of widows betray a similar breadth of social activity and power. Although the court associations of most women were characterized by a strong focus upon kin, the associations of widows more closely matched the male pattern of wide and varied reliance upon neighbors as well as kin.[24]

As an adolescent daughter or widow, then, a woman in early fourteenth-century Brigstock faced many more public opportunities and responsibilities than she encountered as a married woman. Her experiences suggest that the conjugal households of the medieval countryside had a contradictory effect upon the sexual distribution of power. Conjugality, by creating an expectation of powerful male householders and powerless female dependents, certainly played a crucial role in defining gender. Norms of female and male behavior in the medieval countryside drew heavily upon the private subordination of wives to their husbands. Femaleness was defined by the submissiveness of wives who were expected to defer to their husbands in both private and public. A popular saying advised, "Let not the hen crow before the rooster."[25] Maleness was defined by the private authority of husbands who, as householders, controlled most domestic and community matters. The distinction between a private, female sphere and a public, male sphere received its fullest elaboration in the nineteenth century, but a dichotomy of private wives and public husbands was already firmly established in the households of medieval communities such as Brigstock.

The public-private distinction in the medieval countryside, however, applied more to husbands and wives than to men and women. At the same time that conjugality defined gender, it also moderated the severity of gender distinctions by sustaining many domestic circumstances that did not accord with the expectation of male power and female powerlessness. As long as adolescent daughters had to prepare for independent marriage and widows had to take over the households left by their husbands, power wielded by women, no matter how anomalous, had to be tolerated. Despite the public reticence expected of wives, the access of women to public power varied enormously, according to whether "be she mayde or wydwe or elles wyf."[26]

IN CONTRAST to the relatively fluid and wide dispersion of public power in medieval rural communities, public authority, or legitimated power, was more rigidly and more narrowly distributed. Medieval communities like Brigstock were, perhaps, overorganized and overgoverned. Local order was preserved through peace-keeping groups whose members were mutually responsible for each others' behavior. Legal judgments were enforced through a system of sureties or pledges, who guaranteed that persons would meet court-ordered obligations. Governance was maintained through a wide variety of officers who served either manor or village. In Brigstock, reeves and bailiffs supervised manorial operations, affeerors determined the fines assessed against offenders, jurors judged disputes and claims, chief pledges managed the tithings, messors oversaw harvest operations, and aletasters ensured that ale sold in the community was sound, well measured, and properly priced. The authority that could be obtained through political action—as tithing members, as pledges, and as officers—was available only to men.

The basic peace-keeping system of medieval England, the frankpledge or tithing, never included women. These groups, originally containing only ten persons each, were responsible for bringing their members to court to answer for crimes or offenses. If a tithing, headed by a chief pledge, failed to produce an errant member, it was fined. This system of mutual responsibility was carefully maintained through most of the English countryside. In Brigstock, annual views of frankpledge fined those illegally outside tithings, inducted new members, and considered the chief pledges' presentments of offenses against the peace. With very few exceptions, all men in England, both free and unfree, were expected to join tithings at twelve years of age, but women, considered to be legal dependents of their householders, never joined these groups.[27]

Women were also barred from a variety of legal actions that enabled men to solidify friendships and to enlarge political influence. Men frequently assisted one another in court, acting as attorneys who stood in for absent litigants, as essoiners who brought other suitors' excuses for failing to attend court, and especially as pledges who guaranteed that a person would fulfill a stipulated legal obligation. Almost all persons judged liable by the Brigstock court to pay a fine, perform an assigned task, or answer a specific plea had to produce a personal pledge, who promised that the legal obligation would be met. If such persons defaulted, their pledges were liable for a fine or other punishment. The private arrangements that accompanied pledging are unknown, but most people probably pledged not for remuneration in cash or goods but for ties of friendship and mutuality. The political ramifications of pledging are best illustrated by the fact that the people who most actively served as pledges in Brigstock were, as in most medieval villages, among the wealthiest and most influential members of the community.[28] Although men of all social ranks and ages were accepted as pledges by the Brigstock court, women were rarely allowed to act in this capacity; of the thousands of pledges recorded in the rolls of the court, only forty-six were women. Brigstock was unusual in this respect; on most medieval manors, no female pledges were ever accepted by the court.[29] In Brigstock, as elsewhere, women never served their neighbors as either attorneys or essoiners.

The Brigstock court yielded the right of pledging to women only in unusual and restricted circumstances. Most female pledges were widows; of the twenty-four women accepted by the court as pledges, at least fourteen were widows, and the unknown marital status of the others raises the strong possibility that they were also widowed heads of households.[30] Indeed, the major status requirement for acceptance of a female pledge was widowhood; women from the various social strata of Brigstock (as shown by the activities of their husbands or other males presumably related to them) acted in this capacity.[31] Most female pledges also acted within a restricted sphere, pledging only for the petty liabilities of kin. The extremely high rate of familial pledging by female pledges (twenty-six cases of forty-six, or 57 percent) was matched by a tendency for such sureties to guarantee the payment of the small fines levied for minor crimes (thirty-eight cases) or baking infractions (two cases). The few women who served as pledges in other, more momentous legal transactions were personally involved in other aspects of the case.[32] Clearly the occasional pledging privileges extended to women in Brigstock responded to the practical reality that widows, as heads of households, had to accept responsibility for their dependents.

In the end, female pledging was so limited that it lacked the political ramifications that it carried for men. Any man could serve as a pledge—adolescent sons as well as householders, laborers as well as landholders. Furthermore, men used pledging both to aid family members in minor distress and to form political alliances. Standing as a surety not only for petty matters but also for the weightier obligations involved in land transactions, contracts, and inheritances, Henry Kroyl junior built up a complex political network of obligation and reciprocity that involved literally hundreds of his neighbors. He was unusually active, but most of his brothers and brothers-in-law also pledged on a fair number of occasions for their friends and neighbors in the Brigstock court.[33] Of the seven women in their familial generation, only one ever acted as a pledge; Alice Kroyl pledged once, for a child guilty of a minor field infraction.[34] For Henry Kroyl junior, pledging was an important and commonly used political tool. For his female kin, pledging was a rare obligation that offered no political benefit.

The public authority of women was severely restricted by their inability to form political associations with others through tithings, pledgings, or other forms of legal assistance. The exclusion of women from public office, however, constituted the major obstacle to female authority in medieval rural communities. The method of selecting bailiffs, reeves, messors, aletasters, affeerors, and jurors is unknown. Court records simply note that a particular person was chosen (*electi est*) to a particular office, without specifying either electors or selection procedures. The criteria for selection, however, are much clearer; most rural officials were married males who possessed substantial landholdings.[35] Not all men served their communities as officers, but only men did so.[36]

The official career of Henry Kroyl junior of Brigstock again provides a pertinent example. During his adolescent years, Henry Kroyl junior began to build a political network both through his tithing and through assisting others in court as a pledger, essoiner, and attorney. He did not embark upon a distinguished career of official service, however, until after his marriage. Active in the local court since 1316, Henry Kroyl junior first served as an officer in September 1319, just a few months after his marriage to Agnes Penifader. As adolescents, young men participated in the basic political organizations of rural communities such as Brigstock; as married householders, they gained the additional opportunity of controlling political processes through local offices. Those men who were most able to seize this opportunity came from the elite of their communities. Both Henry Kroyl junior and his brother John Kroyl held extensive properties in Brigstock, and both served often as officers. Their brothers, Robert and William, possessed much more modest landholdings and never served as local officers. The normal prerequisites for officeholding included not only male sex but also married status and comparative wealth.

Official service was not an unmitigated benefit. In addition to time lost from other pursuits, officers in Brigstock were liable for fines for dereliction of duty and attacks from disgruntled villagers. As a result, some attempted to avoid official duties, as did William ad Stagnum, who paid two shillings in 1314 to be excused from serving as reeve.[37] Attempts to avoid office were rare, however, because official activity not only signaled privileged status but also enhanced privilege. On the one hand, officers used their authority to personal advantage, taking gifts, arranging lucrative contracts, and using the lord's labor services to work private lands.[38] On the other hand, officers also worked together to control the poorer and more marginal members of their communities. Rural officers decided what pleas would be disallowed, what crimes would be ignored, and what customs would govern land use and devolution. Their decisions on such matters reflected the concerns of a male elite working to control marginal males, poorer households, and women.[39]

The clerks of manorial courts never noted any protests by women about their lack of political opportunity or any formal efforts by men to exclude women from political matters. Instead, the relegation of politics to men was likely accepted as natural by both sexes. Just as medieval people expected wives to be submissive and husbands to be dominant, so they expected women to accept the government of men. Although it is reasonable to suppose that countrywomen exercised some informal say over political processes, such influence cannot belie the basic power held by the men who controlled rural politics.[40] Informal influence is, of course, inherently limited. It usually exists only to compensate for a lack of formal authority and not only lacks authority but also easily erodes. Moreover, public institutions in the medieval countryside were so highly articulated that the ability of women to influence public matters informally was necessarily curtailed. In communities where all adult males belonged to tithings, where community matters were regulated with numerous by-laws enforced by numerous officers, and where triweekly seigneurial courts required the attendance of all tenants, political life was so active and varied that informal influence was correspondingly limited. Indeed, even in the highly unlikely event that some sort of equilibrium existed in rural communities between male political authority and female informal influence, that balance would have been destroyed by the advantages that those men who wielded formal authority exercised in the world beyond the village. The same men who helped govern a community and run its court also acted as brokers with the outside world— dealing with manorial officials, negotiating with royal tax collectors, and testifying at county courts.[41] Because they lacked political authority, medieval women stood in relation to the men of their villages as those men stood to their manorial lords; the medieval world was a hierarchical world with peasant women at the bottom.

THE EXPERIENCES of medieval countrywomen suggest that political authority was the first sector of public action to be denied to women. Rural women were, under certain circumstances, permitted to hold land, pursue legal claims, and form public associations with neighbors and friends, but they were not allowed to participate in matters political. Such patterns indicate that women were, for convenience's sake, allowed to exercise certain forms of power but that such power was under no circumstances allowed to become sanctioned authority.

Women's exclusion from political authority was strictly maintained despite its legal inconsistencies and practical inconveniences. Unmarried or widowed tenants were as obliged as male tenants to attend all sessions of the manorial court and to observe local by-laws, but they were never— despite their acceptance of the legal responsibilities of landholders—eligible for political authority. Because some of these female landholders were as wealthy as the males who served as reeves, aletasters, jurors, and the like, it seems that their sex was the major barrier to political authority. Unmarried and widowed women also often lived outside the control of a male householder who could be trusted to bring them to court for petty crimes and offenses. Such spinsters and widows, however, were never inducted into tithings to ensure that they kept the peace; again, their sex seems to have been the excluding factor. Similarly, the acceptance of some female pledges demonstrates the legal sufficiency of such actions, but custom limited the political impact of female pledging by only infrequently allowing widows to pledge for their dependents. Moreover, the exclusion of women from the office of aletaster—despite the fact that they, as brewers, were the most knowledgeable and skilled candidates—again illustrates the importance of barring women from authoritative positions. When it came to extending political authority to women, legal precedents and practical requirements had no importance; politics was the business of men.

F. W. Maitland's summary of the public functions of women under the common law in the thirteenth century applies just as well to women under the customary law of communities like Brigstock: "In the camp, at the council board, on the bench, in the jury box there is no place for them."[42] Indeed, the extension of public power to women when convenient, and their exclusion from political authority no matter how inconvenient, might apply to medieval Englishwomen generally. All women, regardless of rank or class, were effectively excluded from formal political activity in medieval England. Countrywomen never served as reeves, townswomen never acted as mayors, and gentlewomen never went to Parliament to advise their king. All these women, however, especially when widowed, could aspire to public power, not only as heads of households, but also as controllers of the economic resources left by their husbands. Medieval Englishwomen, in short, were often powerful, but they were never authoritative.

Notes

1. This essay draws upon material discussed at greater length in my book *Women in the Medieval English Countryside: Gender and Household in Brigstock Before the Plague* (New York, 1987). Readers might particularly wish to consult chapters 4 (on adolescence), 5 (on marriage), and 6 (on widowhood) for specific data and analyses that support the generalization presented here.

2. Manorial lords, for example, often levied fines not only for the marriage of their bondswomen (merchets) but also for sexual activity by unmarried women (leyrwytes) and the birth of illegitimate children (childwytes).

3. These distinctions were reflected in contemporary literature. In the late medieval "Ballad of a Tyrannical Husband," for example, the husband spent his days plowing, while the wife watched children, cleaned house, prepared meals, brewed, baked, cared for poultry and dairy animals, made butter and cheese, and worked wool and flax into cloth. See the printed edition of this poem in *Reliquiae Antiquae,* ed. Thomas Wright and James Orchard Halliwell, vol. 2 (London,

1845), pp. 196–99. For discussions of the sexual division of labor in the medieval countryside, see chapter 5 of my book and Barbara Hanawalt, "Peasant Women's Contribution to the Home Economy in Late Medieval England," in *Women and Work in Pre-Industrial Europe,* ed. Barbara Hanawalt (Bloomington, 1986), pp. 3–19; Rodney Hilton, "Women in the Village," in *The English Peasantry in the Later Middle Ages,* ed. Rodney Hilton (Oxford, 1975), pp. 95–110; Christopher Middleton, "The Sexual Division of Labor in Feudal England," *New Left Review* 113–14 (1979):147–68; Michael Roberts, "Sickles and Scythes: Women's Work and Men's Work at Harvest Time," *History Workshop* 7 (1979):3–29.

4. The extent of female commercial brewing varied widely, but rural women were always active in the industry during the Middle Ages. In early fourteenth-century Brigstock, for example, women completely dominated the trade (men accounted for only 1 percent of the ale amercements levied); in Houghton-cum-Wyton during the same decades, men accrued only 11 percent of ale amercements; in Iver 71 percent of assize infractions were cited against males. The importance of commercial brewing in the lives of many countrywomen is illustrated by the fact that more than one-third of the women identified in the court rolls of Brigstock were cited on at least one occasion for selling ale. See my essay "The Village Ale-Wife: Women and Brewing in Fourteenth-Century England," in *Women and Work in Pre-Industrial Europe,* pp. 20–36.

5. Both this definition of power and the following definition of authority come from Peggy Sanday's discussion of M. G. Smith's definitions in "Female Status in the Public Domain," in *Woman, Culture, and Society,* ed. Michelle Zimbalist Rosaldo and Louise Lamphere (Stanford, 1974), p. 190.

6. For a discussion of the uses and limits of court roll evidence, see my article "Spouses, Siblings, and Surnames: Reconstructing Families from Medieval Village Court Rolls," *Journal of British Studies* 23 (1983):26–46.

7. The culture and attitudes of the peasantry were probably deeply influenced by elite traditions. As judged by R. H. Hilton, one of the leading scholars of rural society, "in so far as one has evidence at all, the ruling ideas of medieval peasants seem to have been the ideas of the rulers of society as transmitted to them in innumerable sermons" (*English Peasantry,* p. 16). If this was the case, medieval peasants accepted a cultural tradition whose ideas about women were, at worst, misogynistic and, at best, ambivalent. For two excellent introductions to elite attitudes toward women, see Eileen Power, *Medieval Women,* ed. M. M. Postan (Cambridge, 1975), pp. 9–34, and Carolly Erickson, *The Medieval Vision* (New York, 1976), pp. 181–212.

8. The study of rural women includes an intellectual tradition that purports to describe a balance in rural societies between female informal power and male formal power. The examples proffered to support such arguments are highly controversial and, in the opinion of this author, unconvincing. See especially Susan Carol Rogers, "Female Forms of Power and the Myth of Male Dominance: A Model of Female/Male Interaction in Peasant Society," *American Ethnologist* 2 (1975):727–56, and Martine Segalen, *Love and Power in the Peasant Family,* trans. Sarah Matthews (Chicago, 1983). The most recent application of such theories in a medieval context can be found in Ivan Illich, *Gender* (New York, 1982). See

criticisms of his arguments in *Feminist Issues* 3 (1983), especially the article by Nancy Scheper-Hughes, "Vernacular Sexism: An Anthropological Response to Ivan Illich," pp. 28–37.

9. These rolls are deposited in the Montagu Collection (Boxes X364A, X364B, and X365) at the Northamptonshire Record Office (hereinafter cited as NRO with the court date) and at the Public Record Office (hereinafter cited as PRO).

10. Local studies not only have a long and distinguished place in medieval rural historiography (as exemplified by estate studies and more recently, by studies of particular villages) but also are particularly suited to the sorts of anthropological enquiries that attend any study of gender relations. Detailed comparisons of women's experiences in Brigstock, Iver, and Houghton-cum-Wyton can be found in my book *Women in the Medieval English Countryside*. The manorial records of Iver are deposited with the Buckinghamshire Archaeological Society in Aylesbury and at St. George's Chapel in Windsor Castle. The manorial records of Houghton-cum-Wyton are deposited in the British Library and at the PRO.

11. Virgates and semi-virgates were the standard holdings in Brigstock. Their precise acreage is unknown, but a virgate commonly covered from twenty to thirty acres of land. Butts, plots of irregular size and shape that remained after fields were divided into strips, were usually small parcels of land.

12. For Cristina Penifader's landholdings, see NRO, January 22, 1312, August 8, 1314 (land granted *ad opus*), and October (n.d.) 1316. Statements about the social horizons of Cristina Penifader and other Brigstock inhabitants are based partly upon network analysis, a system of charting and analyzing each individual's contacts in court. For a full explanation of this complex methodology and its findings, see the appendix and appropriate chapters of my book and my article "The Tie That Binds: Peasant Marriages and Families in Late Medieval England," *Journal of Interdisciplinary History* 15 (1984):111–29. Social activities have also been estimated by tracing patterns of pledging, that is, from the identity of persons chosen to be a surety in court. The findings from this analysis, which are relatively straightforward, are summarized in the notes to illustrate the social distinctions described in the text. Cristina Penifader required legal assistance on eleven occasions before her marriage; her father came to her aid in four instances. For her obligation to attend court, see general essoins (or excuses) offered in such courts as NRO, August 24, 1315, and May 26, 1317.

13. For premarital acquisitions of land by Henry Kroyl junior, see NRO, November 18, 1316, April 14, 1317, May 5, 1317, May 26, 1317, February 4, 1319, and May 31, 1319. For a full discussion of his premarital court network, see "The Tie That Binds." Henry Kroyl junior required legal assistance on eleven occasions before his marriage; his father provided the needed aid in eight instances.

14. For the criteria used to identify adolescents in Brigstock, see pp. 73–75 of my book. As in most rural communities in medieval England, a core group of villagers dominated social life in Brigstock, enjoying both economic privilege (holding semi-virgates or more) and political power (controlling local offices). The fathers of both Cristina Penifader and Henry Kroyl junior belonged to this privileged elite. Since no landholding records are extant for preplague Brigstock,

aggregate assessments of social rank in this essay are based upon officeholding (individuals who held offices or were contemporaneously associated with officeholders—usually fathers or husbands—have been deemed upper rank).

15. The landholding activities of adolescents in Brigstock probably best exemplify the patterns characteristic of this life-cycle stage. First, adolescents were exceptionally active in the local land market; one-fourth of those cited in a sample of 779 conveyors or receivers of land were identified as sons or daughters of other villagers. Second, parents often assisted their children in gaining economic independence; seventeen daughters and twenty-seven sons directly received properties from their parents, and many other young people probably received land with parental assistance that cannot be traced (since parents who purchased lands for their children from third parties would not be mentioned in the legal conveyance of the property). Third, socioeconomic status did not clearly affect the access of adolescents to land; of the 128 adolescent recipients of land whose backgrounds could be traced, 66 were upper rank (with fathers who held local offices), and 62 were lower rank (with fathers who never served in official capacities). Fourth, adolescents freely controlled the properties they obtained on the land market; they seldom held properties that were leased, encumbered, or jointly possessed; they received properties using the legal forms that were employed by adults; and they freely transferred land without any hindrance. Fifth, daughters, although as competent to hold land as sons, were less likely to do so. One daughter conveyed or received land for every four sons who did so. It is worth noting that the active participation of young women and young men in the Brigstock land market represents, in a sense, only the tip of the economic iceberg, since many other economic opportunities (commercial work, employment as servants, and wage work) fostered the growth of economic autonomy during adolescence. Evidence from Iver and Houghton-cum-Wyton suggests that the economic activities of adolescents in Brigstock were not unusual. In Iver, eleven of twenty-nine traced adolescents controlled independent economic resources before marriage. In Houghton-cum-Wyton, daughters regularly paid their own marriage fines; the implication is that they had accumulated means before marriage. For an analysis of the connection between marriage fine payments and economic independence, see my article "Medieval Peasant Marriage: An Examination of Marriage License Fines in the *Liber Gersumarum*," in *Pathways to Medieval Peasants*, ed. J. A. Raftis (Toronto, 1981), pp. 193–246.

16. In a sample of two hundred civil pleas brought before the Brigstock court, sons accounted for thirty-nine defendants and plaintiffs (11 percent of all male litigants) and daughters appeared on seventeen occasions (constituting 20 percent of all female litigants). Although adolescents tended to be involved more in pleas of trespass than in pleas of debt or broken contract, they pursued litigation with forms indistinguishable from those used by full adults.

17. Pledging patterns exemplify the social ambivalence of young people in Brigstock. Young women and men were no longer children completely subsumed under the authority of their householders, but neither were they thoroughly independent. As a result, young people turned to family members for

assistance in meeting their court obligations far more often than did full adults, but they did not invariably do so. In the sample of civil pleas in Brigstock, for example, sons used familial pledges 39 percent of the time (versus the male norm of 13 percent), and daughters used familial pledges 33 percent of the time (versus the female norm of 24 percent).

18. In 1315, for example, the Brigstock court voided the land sale of Quena ad Crucem, declaring that "a wife's sale is nothing in the absence of her husband" ("vendicio illa nulla est de uxore aliter in absentia mariti sui"); NRO, March 20, 1315).

19. These legal changes were not based on a notion of marital reciprocity. Wives did not replace their husbands as court suitors, and they also did not join their husbands in pleas unless personally involved in the case. The experiences of Cristina Penifader illustrate how the change from unmarried adolescent to married wife affected the legal status of women. As an unmarried landholder, Cristina Penifader attended all court sessions or obtained an excuse for her absence. Last appearing as a suitor at the court of June 16, 1317, she married Richard Power in the following month, and he assumed all subsequent obligations for court attendance. For her last essoin, see NRO, June 16, 1317. For an essoin by Richard Power (for lands held by his wife), see NRO, December 4, 1319. While unmarried, Cristina Penifader was also capable of independent legal action. In 1316, she requested and received a court inquisition into her rights to a certain property (see NRO, October [n.d.] 1316). After marriage, she was usually accompanied in legal actions by her husband (see, for example, their joint dispute with Martin Penifader in NRO, June 11, 1344). In general, the legal status of wives under the customary laws of communities such as Brigstock closely paralleled the common-law status of wives. See Frederick Pollock and Frederic William Maitland, *The History of English Law Before the Time of Edward I,* 2d ed., rev. S. F. C. Milsom, 2 vols. (Cambridge, 1968), vol. 2, pp. 399–436.

20. The social shifts occasioned by marriage are discussed fully in "The Tie That Binds." One aggregate index of social activity is the extent to which a person relied upon family members for pledges (sureties required by the court for many legal obligations). In the Brigstock sample of crimes, women used familial pledges much more frequently than men (46 percent of all women guilty of crimes versus 20 percent of all men involved in either crimes or land transactions), but wives used familial pledges at an extremely high rate (75 percent of all wives cited for crimes used a familial pledge).

21. Henry Kroyl senior had a life that provides a particularly good example of this phenomenon because the marriage of his son Henry junior in 1319 clearly marked the beginning of his retirement. He had served his community as an officer on twenty-three occasions in the ten years prior to his son's marriage; although he lived for a decade after the marriage, he never again took on official responsibilities. His three land conveyances in the 1309–19 decade similarly contrast with the single transfer of property accomplished in his last ten years, as do the three disputes that went to litigation in the former period, as opposed to only one in the latter. Although Henry Kroyl senior remained an independent land-

holder until his death in 1329, he nevertheless slowly withdrew, as he aged, from the public life of Brigstock. For similar patterns seen in the careers of five other Brigstock men, see table 6.1 in my book.

22. The precise extent of free bench in Brigstock (whether one-third, one-half, or all of the conjugal holding) is unclear, but widows did hold their free bench for life (i.e., no automatic forfeiture accompanied remarriage). Since men were preferred in inheritance, free bench claims offered many women their best opportunities to obtain large properties; of the sixty people listed in the partial rental of Brigstock in 1319, eleven (18 percent) were women, of whom at least six were widows (and the unknown marital status of the remaining five women suggests that they, too, might have been widowed): see NRO, verso of roll for 1319. Although widows were technically only custodians of their free bench lands (enjoying use but not the right of alienation), they asserted full control over such holdings through a variety of techniques; 54 of the 106 widows identified in Brigstock participated in the local land market. Similarly, one-fourth of the widows identified in Iver brought properties to their local land market (the information on widowhood in Houghton-cum-Wyton was too incomplete for analysis). Although some widows in both Brigstock and Iver used the land market to convey properties to children, others transferred lands outside their families.

23. In 1299, e.g., Letia Fox paid a fine "pro Dulce serviente sua et pro eadem": see PRO, SC 2/194/65, court for May 29, 1299. To take an example from Iver, Katrina, the widow of William Pees, paid a fine in 1337 because she had not prevented her son from fishing illegally; see item 128/53 in the Buckinghamshire Archaeological Society holdings, m. 17, court for May 7, 1337.

24. The peculiar features of widow's social activities can best be seen in pledging patterns. In proffering pledges in the criminal cases sampled, for example, widows used familial pledges 18 percent of the time; men had exactly the same rate of familial pledging, but 75 percent of wives' pledges and 54 percent of daughters' pledges were family members. See table 6.7 in my book.

25. Quoted by Shulamith Shahar in *The Fourth Estate: A History of Women in the Middle Ages,* trans. Chaya Galai (London, 1983), p. 89.

26. Geoffrey Chaucer, "The Knight's Tale," l. 313. See F. N. Robinson, *The Complete Works of Geoffrey Chaucer* (Boston, 1933), p. 32.

27. William Alfred Morris, *The Frankpledge System* (New York, 1910). Maitland suggested that women were not included in tithings because "every woman is in the mainpast of some man" (Pollock and Maitland, *English Law,* vol. 1, p. 482).

28. The informal arrangements that accompanied pledging are unknown. Sometimes officers acted as pledges, and pledges were probably sometimes paid for their services, but usually pledging was performed as an unremunerated favor. See Martin Pimsler, "Solidarity in the Medieval Village? The Evidence of Personal Pledging at Elton, Huntingdonshire," *Journal of British Studies* 17 (1977):1–11. Pimsler also noted both "the frequency with which men in positions of responsibility acted as sureties" and the fact that pledges "tended to come from the wealthier segment of the village" (pp. 6–8). See also R. M. Smith, "Kin and

Neighbors in a Thirteenth-Century Suffolk Community," *Journal of Family History* 4 (1979):223–24 in particular.

29. Pimsler (in "Solidarity?" n. 18) reports one instance of female pledging in Elton but suggests that the scribe may have made an error. He also cites evidence from Wakefield to suggest that women on that manor could serve as pledges as their husbands died. In most manorial courts, however, no women served as pledges (the court records of Iver and Houghton-cum-Wyton, for example, include no instances of pledging by women).

30. One woman who acted as a pledge was cited as being married, but the dating of that instance in the plague year of 1348 lends a suspicion to the attribution that cannot be verified because the 1348 courts are the last series extant for Brigstock for several decades. The other nine female pledges were cited simply by forename and surname, and their marital status cannot be reconstructed from other sources. Widows, however, were more likely than either daughters or wives to be cited by court clerks by name alone, with no marital attribution.

31. Of the twenty-two female pledges whose social backgrounds could be traced, twelve were of upper rank (associated with officeholding males) and ten were of lower rank.

32. Emma Pote, Alice Avice, and Strangia Tulke were the original holders of the lands whose acquisition by others prompted their pledging activities. Alice Somonor was a joint party with her son in the court plea that generated her pledge for his future attendance.

33. Henry Kroyl junior assisted others in court (acting primarily as a pledge but also as an essoiner and attorney) on 245 occasions; only 40 of these assists were rendered to known family members. The figures for other male members of his generation of Kroyls and Penifaders are as follows (figure in parentheses indicates assists to family members): John Kroyl, 159 (16); William Kroyl, none; Robert Kroyl, 13 (2); Robert Penifader, 24 (8); Henry Penifader, 46 (15); William Penifader, 29 (14).

34. NRO, September 18, 1348.

35. The marriage qualification in Brigstock was implicit but clear. First, men explicitly identified by court clerks as sons rarely acted as officers. Second, of the four males in Brigstock whose premarital careers could be traced, none served in offices as bachelors, and all assumed official responsibilities during their married years. Edwin DeWindt's careful study of jurors in Holywell-cum-Needingworth led him to conclude that most jurors were tenants at least thirty years old; most must certainly also have been married by that age. See his *Land and People in Holywell-cum-Needingworth* (Toronto, 1972), pp. 216–20. The connection between officeholding and wealth has been fully explored in many studies. See especially Anne DeWindt, "Peasant Power Structures in Fourteenth-Century King's Ripton," *Mediaeval Studies* 29 (1976):236–67.

36. The only exceptions, to this author's knowledge, occurred in Halesowen, where female aletasters were elected on a few occasions in the late fourteenth and early fifteenth centuries. See Hilton, "Women in the Village," pp. 105–106. A few late medieval instances of women serving in the parochial office of church-

warden have also been found. See Annie Abrams, *English Life and Manners in the Late Middle Ages* (London, 1913), p. 37.

37. NRO, January 3, 1314.

38. For a vivid example of private benefit taken from public office, see George Homans, *English Villagers of the Thirteenth Century* (1941; repr., New York, 1970), pp. 301–302.

39. For a fine study of the social control wielded by officeholders, see Barbara A. Hanawalt, "Community Conflict and Social Control: Crime and Justice in the Ramsey Abbey Villages," *Mediaeval Studies* 39 (1977):402–23. One possible ramification for women in Brigstock was the underreporting of male violence against women in the community; see chapter 2 of my book.

40. Probably the most outstanding example of a rural woman who exercised informal power is the exceptional case of Agnes Sadeler, who was cited as one of the leaders of the Romsley rebellion of 1386. Still, her case reflects more the allowance made for women in protests than the everyday informal influence of women. For a discussion of the special license allowed women in times of disruption and chaos, see Natalie Zemon Davis, "Women on Top," in *Society and Culture in Early Modern France* (Stanford, 1975), pp. 124–51.

41. The fundamental limitations on the informal power exercised by rural women are explored in Rayna Reiter's "Men and Women in the South of France: Public and Private Domains," in *Toward an Anthropology of Women,* ed. Rayna R. Reiter (New York, 1975), pp. 252–82.

42. Pollock and Maitland, *English Law,* vol. 1, p. 485.

Citizenship and Gender: Women's Political Status in Northern Medieval Cities

Martha C. Howell

W omen of all classes in late medieval cities of northern Europe
were active and visible participants in the public realm, much more so
than either the women who came after them from the seventeenth
through the nineteenth centuries or their contemporaries in southern European cities.[1] In this public realm women made and sold textiles,
clothing, beer, bread, pottery, and other goods used both locally and
abroad. They ran taverns and inns; they belonged to guilds and confrater-
nities; they brokered deals between visiting merchants and local manu-
facturers; they borrowed and lent money; they took oaths; they led religious movements; they ran charities; they joined popular political
demonstrations; they sued and were sued; they learned and taught reading, writing, and arithmetic; they delivered babies for pay; and they dispensed medicine and medical advice.[2]

Admittedly, women's presence in the public sphere did not preclude
their subordination to men. Men controlled the crafts and guilds to which
women could belong. Men codified the law that permitted women entry
into public affairs and protected their property. Men ran the Church, the
institution of learning and religion. Men were the legal heads of household. Men also monopolized politics. They alone made, judged, and executed law; they alone voted; they alone held public office, elective or
appointive, as mayor, alderman, judge, or bailiff. In northern European
cities, a line separating a world exclusive to men from the world that men
and women shared was drawn around a small but very significant kind of
public activity—the formal, direct exercise of public authority.

Historians both contemporary and modern have commented on the
existence of this line. Writing in the early sixteenth century, for example,

37

Martin Luther explained that women were excluded from the "public world of governmental authority" in just retribution for their part in original sin. A recent German scholar, remarking on the presence of women in Cologne's medieval register of new citizens, wrote that women, although considered citizens in their own right, "naturally were excluded from participation in government." Natalie Davis has noted as well that women in early modern cities, no matter how visible in reformed worship or in intellectual and cultural life, took no part whatever in government.[3]

Thus the financial acumen, mercantile property, and artisanal skills of medieval urban women never earned them the right to help govern their own professions, much less their own cities. Yet these women—rich, middling, or poor—emphatically did not center their lives on domestic affairs or exclusively on intrafamilial matters. Furthermore, as active participants in the public realm, many of them possessed the objective qualifications for governmental positions. Women merchants could often read and write in the vernacular, probably about as well as their husbands (who had also not attended university and possessed no knowledge of Latin),[4] nor did women's failure to serve as soldiers render them incapable of governing. Although the urban citizenry constituted in theory a defensive unit to which all members contributed, it was common practice for rich or old or otherwise disinclined citizens—including women—to hire others to fulfill their own military obligations.[5]

The rule that reserved political space for men alone in these cities seems to have been unalterable. Not even the demands of the market could force change to occur. Instead, the reverse was true. Cologne's silkwomen had exclusive rights to the craft of silkmaking, and some of them were very important producers. Yet their guild, a fully recognized corporate body, was run by men. Leiden's textile finishers included women as mistresses and apprentices until the craft was awarded political status; thereafter, as the enabling ordinances explained, women could not train for the craft.[6] The many women among Leiden's drapers encountered similar barriers. In 1552, when a group of ninety-two drapers created a supervisory body to regulate cloth sales in nearby markets, not a single one of the thirty-three female members served as an officer.[7]

While the existence and power of this exclusionary principle is evident, the reasons for it are obscure. Contemporary records tell us almost nothing. Political documents such as council minutes or memoirs from the age understandably cannot help us ferret out the reason why women did not enjoy a role in urban government. Legislative and executive records neither require nor discuss women's exclusion from politics; they simply

assume it. These records reveal very little about the constitutional principles that informed political structures and practices. The men who founded
and ran these cities usually expressed their political ideas through their
actions and their specific statutes alone, leaving theory and analysis to later
generations of humanists and historians.

If we hope to understand why political space (but apparently not public space) in late medieval cities of the North was reserved for men, we
must, it seems, approach our task indirectly. Because we cannot plot the
range of women's activities in the formal polity, where women had no
standing and no activities, we must look beyond its membership, to the
community from which a city's political actors were drawn, the civic
community. There we will necessarily encounter women, because they
could not have played their roles in commerce and industry, in the sworn
professions, or in municipal charitable institutions if they had been denied all status in the civic realm. Yet we will undoubtedly also find that
women's civic status was in some ways limited, because full status in the
civic realm would have implied open access to the political realm—and
precisely here, of course, women's civic capacities proved inadequate. By
analyzing the patterns of inclusion and exclusion, acceptance and rejec-
tion, and independence and dependence that describe women's civic status, we may discover the principles that underlay women's absence from
positions of public authority. In so doing, we will explore links between
the history of gender in this age and the constitutional and political
history of late medieval cities.

A person's civic status in late medieval cities of course comprised many
attributes—legal personhood, personal freedom, property and inheritance rights, contractual capacities, and voting privileges—but an analysis of civic status can be approximated through an analysis of citizenship.
People who possessed the privileges, rights, and duties of citizenship in
these cities (termed *Bürger, Poorters,* or *bourgeoises* in the vernacular) were
legal, social, and economic beings new to European civilization and,
some scholars have insisted, new to urban civilization in general.[8] The
essential quality of citizenship was embodied in the "freedoms" or "liber-
ties" citizens held which exempted them from personal, legal, or direct
financial claims by feudal lords and which gave them claims to separate
legal and taxing systems and to unique social services.[9] Citizens also enjoyed nearly exclusive rights within the economic sphere controlled by
their urban government and were, of course, accorded military protection by their cities. In return, citizens owed loyalty, financial and military
support, and obedience to urban law as well as aid and succor to fellow
citizens. Citizenship was thus the route to full participation in urban pub-

lic life. Without it, a person was denied access to certain economic and social resources and inevitably lacked any legitimate claims to formal political authority.

While historians have devoted a great deal of attention to the constitutional and political history of cities in the late medieval North, they have had surprisingly little to say about the actual composition of the citizenry. Scholars have not explained how the variations in the composition of the citizenry correlate with the economic, social, political, and even religious differences discussed in the literature of late medieval urban history. They have had even less to say about women's status in the citizenry beyond occasionally noting that most women, like most men, acquired citizenship by birth and that, unlike most men, women also acquired it by marriage. Because female citizens did not fully enjoy the rights and privileges of citizens, one scholar has characterized them as "passive citizens" who "as collateral and protected partners [*mittelbare Schutzgenossen*] . . . shared the peace, the law and the court of the city and were, in turn, bound to obedience, service and tax obligations."[10]

Yet as the following pages will show, women's passivity was not complete or entirely constant. In some places or at some times, women had freer and more complete access to citizenship than they did at other times and places. Surely these variations, like the variations in the definitions of citizenship itself, reflected deeper differences in the constitutions of these cities as the constitutions changed over time and as they differed from one another in accord with larger shifts in urban society.

A full study of the meaning of citizenship for women (or for men) in late medieval cities of the North is far beyond the scope of this exploratory essay.[11] Although the following pages do not attempt this task, they do presume to illustrate both the possibility and the value of such a study. The essay employs extant rolls registering new citizens from five late medieval cities (Bruges, Leiden, Lille, Cologne, and Frankfurt am Main), along with legislative and constitutional documents that help explain the significance of the rolls. With them, we can roughly describe the variations in women's status as citizens in these urban centers. The essay then attempts to catalog and identify the reasons for these variations. I conclude that demographic and economic forces alone are inadequate explanations for the variations. Using political and constitutional theory drawn from the work of others, I show how the differences might reflect alternative conceptions about the meaning of citizenship. These alternatives may indicate divergent ideas about the nature of the urban community's constituent units: one which allowed women independent status in the citizenry and another which did not. In conclusion I consider the significance of these findings, both for the history of women and for the constitutional history of late medieval and early modern Europe.

THE ESSENTIAL FEATURES of women's status as citizens in these cities on one level appear unambiguous. Women married to or parented by a citizen were explicitly included in the urban citizenry in that they were subject to the city's law and were afforded its protection. Legitimate children born to female citizens were presumed citizens. Women also easily changed their citizenship by marriage. A woman from one city who married a man from another was normally considered to have transferred her citizenship with her residence.[12]

Foreign men who married female citizens, however, received no such automatically favorable treatment, and here some of the ambiguities in women's status as citizens become apparent. In late medieval Lille, female citizens could neither grant foreign-born husbands citizenship nor afford them easier terms of access.[13] In nearby Bruges and in more distant Leiden, in sharp contrast, men who married citizens freely and almost automatically acquired citizenship.[14] Frankfurt am Main adopted an intermediate position. Men who married citizens there were given favorable terms in acquiring citizenship but were not exempted from all requirements, as they were in Bruges and Leiden.[15]

Foreign-born women seeking citizenship along with their husbands met an equally wide variety of possibilities. In a few cities, immigrant wives registered independently along with their husbands in the new citizenship rolls, and in some places these women had to provide separate evidence of their legitimate births. In other cities, women swore an oath with their husbands or as widows repeated the oath their husbands had originally taken for them both.[16]

Adult immigrant women who were single or widowed were subject to an even greater range of practice. In the course of any individual city's history, the relative numbers of women who joined the urban citizenry on their own varied remarkably. The variations between cities were even more marked. In Lille, from 1291, when records begin, until 1459 when the municipal government passed legislation permitting bastards of citizens to register as if foreigners, *no* immigrant women were registered as new citizens. Even then, the numbers were very low (six from 1459 to 1499).[17] In Bruges, however, women averaged about 10 percent of new citizens registered between 1331 and 1460, and in several years women accounted for 20 percent or more of the new citizens (1379, 1388, 1418, 1432, 1441, 1442, 1443, 1454, and 1455).[18] Moving northeast to Leiden, we find women making up about 6 percent of pre-1400 enrollments and about 10 percent of those from 1400 to 1532.[19] In Cologne, the situation was closer to that in Lille; only about 4 percent of new registrants *before* 1396 were female, and afterward, until the mid-fifteenth century, the number fell to less than 1 percent. The pattern in Frankfurt am Main was different still: averaging more than 7 percent in the 1350s, 1360s, and 1370s and reaching 14–20 percent in several of those years, the percentage fell abruptly thereafter to 3.5 percent in the 1380s and 1.3 percent in the first decades of the fifteenth century and then hovered around 2 percent well beyond the middle of that century.[20]

Demographics and economics undoubtedly account for some of these variations. Women as well as men moved to cities in search of wealth and a higher standard of living or more simply in search of jobs and security; immigration rates rose when the prospects for any of these incentives were good and when the need for them was great. Economic booms such as that enjoyed by Leiden in the fifteenth century presumably attracted many newcomers. The labor shortages after the Black Death might well have had similar results. In contrast, the depression that Frankfurt am Main is thought to have suffered in the fifteenth century should have been associated with a falloff in immigration.

Yet there is little reason to attribute much of the variation in women's registration rates in the new citizenship lists of these cities to such factors. The primary reason for skepticism is that immigration rates, no matter how sensitive to demographic and economic factors, were not equivalent to the rates at which new citizens were enrolled. At least we must tentatively draw this conclusion. No cities kept actual immigration records, and we can only estimate numbers of immigrants using statistical reasoning based on the population levels believed to have existed in each of these cities and the influx probably necessary to sustain them. Deaths outnumbered births by significant amounts in cities of this period (the annual shortfall was somewhere between five and ten per thousand) because reproduction rates for much of the married population were low, because a large percentage of the population was celibate, and because life in cities was relatively unhealthy. Even in normal times urban populations could be maintained only by regular immigration. On average, we can roughly estimate, a city needed to register three to five new households per year to preserve each one thousand of population.[21]

Statistics computed using these measures suggest that all but one of the five cities were very far from registering *all* their immigrants as new citizens. Lille would have had to register as many as 150 new householders a year to maintain its purported pre–Black Death population of thirty thousand (in fact, Lille registered about thirty per year) and about seventy-five to maintain its purported population of fifteen thousand after the Black Death (the actual numbers remained at about thirty). Cologne, with a population of perhaps thirty thousand to forty thousand, would have needed as many as two hundred households per year but in fact actually registered only about twenty per year. Leiden, with its population of only about twelve to fifteen thousand, required fewer immigrants and more closely approached the seventy-five needed householders with average annual registrations of forty-five to fifty. Frankfurt, an even smaller city until the end of the fifteenth century, took in only one-third to one-half of the numbers it hypothetically needed. Bruges, like Leiden, frequently came very close to registering most of its new residents as citizens. In the second quarter of the fourteenth century, Bruges regularly registered about two hundred householders a year (a figure which may have increased its population). During years of the Black Death, registrants in Bruges fell dramatically, but the numbers recovered thereafter to about fifty to one hundred per year and remained at that level until the end of the century, when they often fell below fifty.[22]

Another reason for skepticism about the role of demographic and economic factors in determining registration rates, at least for women, is that economic or demographic changes appear almost entirely unrelated to the variations in women's registration rates. As far as we can measure them, employment prospects for women in these cities were not markedly different. Leiden and Lille were dominated by the wool textile industry, which offered women plentiful opportunities for work (at least for low-skilled work), but the other three cities were scarcely less hospitable to women. Bruges and Frankfurt both had important woolen cloth industries, and Cologne boasted a large textile industry comprising wool, linen, silk, and cotton manufacture. The commercial sectors of Cologne's and Bruges's economies, and to a lesser extent that of Frankfurt's, included many positions in retailing and in the service industries which would have attracted additional women. In all of these cities, domestic service was a viable alternative to work in the market economy.[23]

The economic sectors likely to have employed women in each of these cities experienced periods of expansion and decline, but these changes also appear to be unassociated with variations in the rates of female registration. The demise of Leiden's textile industry in the sixteenth century led to no perceptible falloff in female registration. The fifteenth-century expansion of Cologne's silk industry (which employed women almost exclusively) was not associated with an increase in female registrations; in fact, the reverse was true.

In the two cities for which sex ratios can be compared, fifteenth-century Frankfurt and fifteenth-century Leiden, demographic factors seem to have been entirely unrelated to registration rates. Women outnumbered men in both cities by about the same amount, a situation which might be expected to have led to equally low registration rates for women in both cities. Instead, women formed a much higher percentage of Leiden's registrants and in both cities rates were higher than we might expect.

To be sure, total registration rates for *both* men and women sometimes changed with perceptible economic changes in cities, as in fourteenth-century Bruges, where registrations declined with the Black Death and with the economic dislocations associated with the revolutions of the century. The cases of direct temporal correspondence of this kind are, however, remarkably few.

Whatever the relationship between immigration rates and registration rates, common sense alone suggests that the two rates would not have been equally affected by economic and demographic factors and that constitutional or political factors would have played a much greater role in determining the latter rate. For example, when a group of artisans and nonpatrician merchants in Lille temporarily wrested power from the patriciate in 1302–1305, new citizen registrations jumped from an average of 34 for each of the preceding three years to 138 only to fall to their prerevolt level after restoration of patrician rule. Total registrations in Cologne jumped 50 percent after the political revolution of 1396 and remained at the new level for decades thereafter. The fourteenth-century falloff in Bruges's registrations certainly had to do with the political uncertainty and occasional tumult of the period as well as with the associated economic and demographic troubles.

Registration patterns were also associated with the stance a city adopted toward new citizens. Bruges and Leiden adopted hospitable policies. These two cities were, of the five, the most insistent that all tradespeople belong to the citizenry, hence Bruges and Leiden saw the highest proportionate registration rates. In Leiden, citizenship was open to all, both in law and in fact. No residence requirements were imposed on applicants for citizenship. No registration fees were asked until at least 1469 (and then the fees were very low). No oath was required until 1545. Anyone could acquire citizenship simply by marriage, and even the bastards of citizens were considered citizens. Citizenship was not only encouraged for everyone, it was required of most: anyone producing drapery (medieval Leiden's wool cloth made for export), taking on a mastership in a *nering* or *ambacht* (including independent artisans in textile manufacture and trade, bakers, shoemakers, smiths, carpenters, tinsmiths, and wheelwrights), and journeymen in the dyeing trade were specifically named at various times.[24] In Bruges, citizenship was almost as freely available. An early ruling of 1304 granted citizenship to everyone who had lived a year and a day in Bruges and who had paid taxes. Others bought citizenship or married into the citizenry (the latter route was open to both men and women). As in Leiden, all craft (ambacht or *métier*) members were required to register as citizens, and no oath was required of new citizens. The fees charged those who purchased citizenship were surprisingly high, but they applied, let us recall, only to those who had not maintained residence for a year and a day and so exempted everyone except individuals practicing a trade for which guild status was required (citizenship was required for guild membership).[25]

Frankfurt made citizenship somewhat more difficult to acquire but also demanded registration of artisans and merchants, thus inscribing relatively high numbers of new citizens. Frankfurt's citizenry was, city officials boasted, open to all newcomers, and particularly in the fifteenth century, the government regularly issued laws requiring all residents to register as citizens; those who did not do so were to leave the city or to obtain special permission to remain as "residents" (*Beisassen*).[26] Bastards were treated as citizens in Frankfurt, and foreign-born bastards were permitted to join as well. From 1366 onward, guild membership explicitly depended upon citizenship, but there is scattered evidence that the laws were not always strictly enforced until the fifteenth century. New citizens were required to take an oath of loyalty to the city and the emperor (Frankfurt was an imperial city), to produce evidence of financial responsibility, and to pay a fee (the latter two requirements were reduced or eliminated for men who married citizens). The fee was lower than that in Bruges (but significantly was extended to *all* except those who married into the citizenry).[27] Frankfurt's new citizens were, however, also required to post a property bond earning half a mark annually, a requirement replaced after 1373 by higher registration fees (ten pounds heller), which, however, only the well-to-do actually paid. On balance, it seems, Frankfurt's citizenry was more carefully and more restrictively defined than either Bruges's or Leiden's; the more burdensome entrance requirements were offset only partly by Frankfurt's apparent determination to register most residents as citizens (at least, as we shall see, the male citizens).

Lille defined its citizenry even more restrictively and, in opening the crafts to noncitizens, permitted ordinary people to immigrate and work without registering. Thus Lille normally inscribed few new citizens. Until the mid-fifteenth century, even native-born bastards could not obtain citizenship rights. Fourteenth-century Lille also required that new citizens be resident for three years before applying for citizenship, but this requirement was relaxed when Lille was recruiting rich merchants as citizens because these people often had to reside away from Lille for months, even years, at a time. After 1372, when Lille was trying to rebuild a population decimated by the plague, the city reinstated the residence requirement and demanded as well that new citizens be married.

Early in the fourteenth century, Lille had also required, as Frankfurt had done, that new citizens post a bond with the city (it was to represent property worth half a mark per year), but after 1372, this requirement was seldom imposed. Marriage to a bourgeoise did not grant a man citizenship or ease his access to it. The price of citizenship was set at sixty shillings artésienne (equivalent to five shillings gros) early in the fourteenth century and did not change as the value of the gros declined in subsequent decades; consequently the price of citizenship declined in real terms over the centuries, a change entirely consistent with the evident tendency to encourage new citizenship registrations in the late fourteenth century and throughout the fifteenth.

Taken together, the measures imposed in Lille indicate that the citizenry was originally regarded as the personal right of propertied individuals. This conception, however, had to be amended as the city lost population and economic strength after the Black Death and as a result of the economic dislocations caused by war and political upheaval in the late fourteenth and fifteenth centuries in this part of northern Europe.[28]

Similarly, policies in Cologne explain registration rates in this city. Before 1396, citizenship was neither required nor encouraged of new residents.[29] Men who married citizens gained no special privileges, and until 1396 only the wine merchants (members of the *Weinbruderschaft*), wholesalers of imported cloth (*Gewandschneider*), and masters of three organized trades (the bronzesmiths, the butchers, and the hatmakers) were required to register. Membership fees, usually set at six to twelve bulden, were perhaps the highest in Germany.[30] After 1396 citizenship was required of all residents, as was membership in one of twenty-two political-military guilds called *Gaffeln*. Although citizenship was theoretically extended to all, it cannot have been easily obtainable, for the fee remained at six gulden and was raised to twelve gulden in 1421. Predictably, registration rates climbed after 1396 but nevertheless remained at a small fraction of probable immigration rates.

The differences in the proportion of *female* registrants among the new citizens in each of these cities also seem to reflect municipal policy closely. Bruges and Leiden registered a great many independent women because in these cities citizenship was easily acquired and was obligatory for almost all workers. Similarly, Frankfurt registered a great many women (until the late fourteenth century) because its citizenry was also broadly defined to include all people with an economic stake in the community. Cologne rarely registered women, however, because citizenship was effectively restricted to very few and was required of few. In Lille this link seems especially clear. Women did not register as citizens in Lille because they never had to do so and were never encouraged to do so. Market and trade rights did not depend on citizenship, and Lille defined its citizenry as the commune to which all residents might belong only during the years 1302–1305.

Yet while policy differences go a long way in explaining variations in women's registrations, certain variations remain unexplained. After the late fourteenth century, just when official policy seemed to favor women, the proportion of women on Frankfurt's lists fell by two-thirds. In Cologne after 1396, just when citizenship, at least in theory, was expanded to include *all* residents and newcomers and when the overall number of registrants rose almost 50 percent, registrations by women collapsed.

Not policy itself, but changes in the political meaning of citizenship seem to have been correlated with these declines. In both cases, female registration fell off exactly when citizenship was redefined so as to make it directly or indirectly equivalent to access to rule. In Frankfurt, the guilds had gained access to government by 1370 and held a minority of council seats; by that time as well most trades in Frankfurt were organized, and all required citizenship of their members. The changes in the political meaning of guild membership led inexorably to the possibility that female guild members could have voted for and, theoretically at least, could have been eligible for government office. The possibility was a real one, for women had traditionally been full members of many of Frankfurt's organized trades.[31] Instead of taking on new roles now associated with guild membership, however, women shed their existing roles in guilds. After the 1370s, fewer and fewer women sought, or possibly were actively encouraged to seek, registration as citizens. At the same time, fewer sought or were granted guild membership.

The decline in registration was surely related to the decline in guild membership. After the late fourteenth century, women whose trades required membership in Frankfurt's newly corporative guilds had either to change their work or to go elsewhere because they could not assume the political power now associated with the citizenship that their guild membership required. Many potential immigrants apparently chose to go elsewhere, but many others may have chosen to practice unorganized trades which did not imply a claim to public authority. Such women would have turned up in the citizenship lists after the 1370s—and there remained some female registrants after 1370—but their citizenship, not being linked to a corporative organization, would not have implied political participation.

In Cologne, where a similar decline in women registrants is evident after 1396, a comparable process may have been at work. Most women

who immigrated to Cologne after the revolution probably avoided registration, and the few who do appear on the lists were presumably practitioners of trades which did not grant direct access to rule.[32]

Not only were women excluded from positions granting formal political authority in late medieval northern cities, they were deprived of independent access to citizenship and were rendered truly passive citizens
once citizenship implied access to such positions. Their disappearance
from the new citizenship lists occurred because citizen rights had acquired political meaning, because they implied more than market or
trade rights, more than rights to enjoy urban property law, more than the
protection afforded by urban criminal and civil law or by its military
power. Although this study of women and citizenship has merely confirmed what we already know about women's impotence in political affairs, it may also offer a means of explaining that impotence.

Historians concerned with entirely different issues regarding the medieval urban community have provided the tools of analysis. The civic
community typical of Germanic society had deep roots in a distinct asso-
ciational principle, *Genossenschaftsrecht,* or the right to brotherhood.
Brotherhoods were associations of friendship, even love, and of mutual
support created by free individuals whose unanimous decision to constitute themselves as a corporative body gave the body legitimacy. The
oaths that often founded them were, unlike the oaths that sealed feudal
bonds, those of equals. According to Otto von Gierke, who is responsible for the legal theory underlying the scholarship that develops this theory, medieval Germanic political society rested on these notions of brotherhood and was unlike other political societies (classical and feudal)
which were created by their rulers and hence defined by *Herrschaft,* or
lordship.[33]

Later scholars have argued that the moral community of the brotherhood, most often institutionalized in guilds, was not a product of Germanic culture alone but had roots in Christian teachings and was even
legitimated by medieval jurists influenced by Roman civil law. The
"guild" ethos of the brotherhood did not, however, alone inform public
life in late medieval cities. In a 1984 study entitled *Guilds and Civil Society,*
Antony Black has explained that notions underlying what he calls "civil
society" were equally important fundaments of the urban community.
According to Black, civil society rested on principles that in some ways
conflicted with those of solidarity, friendship, equality, and mutual aid
which informed guild societies. These "civil" principles included not
only an emphasis on personal independence and security, government by
law, and equality of individuals before the law but also an acknowledgment of social, economic, and political inequality, respect for contract

and property, and freedom to buy and sell. Although Black locates rudiments of these principles in Christian doctrine and Roman law (indeed, some of them had roots in feudal values as well), he emphasizes that the notions of civil society emerging in late medieval Europe were unique products of socioeconomic conditions peculiar to cities.[34]

Black's analysis helps us to see that the formation of an urban community, usually called the *commune,* or *Gemeinde* in the North, combined several constitutional features. It marked the replacement of lordship by brotherhood, but it also involved an assertion of civil values. Because brotherhood and civil values were in some ways incompatible, both guild and civil ideals could exist in creative tension only if one principle tended to dominate. In general, according to Black, "urban political sentiment was inspired by a conviction that the town was a community in the Germanic genre, analogous to the guild: a group formed by the will of the members and thereby legally valid. That conviction appears also to have lain at the root of attempts, from the thirteenth century, to democratize the commune; craft-guild supremacy (*governo largo*) constituted, as was often claimed, a return to the first principles of the commune. There was no other precedent for decision-making by the people as a whole. This Germanic model runs as a *leitmotiv* through subsequent democratic tradition in Europe: here Gierke's central insight is valid. This is not to say that Germanic political culture was superior or even distinctive; only that it happens to lie at the root of this particular tradition.

"The ideals of civil society—which derived principally from Roman and Christian sources—were more likely to lead to indirect democracy, with the emphasis on accountability, so as to ensure that the conditions of fair exchange are not tampered with. Here popular participation meant consultation, understood as a procedural value based upon justice. This would lead away from a guild outlook towards a republican state."[35]

Brotherhood, lordship, and civil society are, of course, abstract concepts created by theorists, and historians employing them must not mistake them for real entities that can explain change. The categories can nevertheless help us understand the relation between the constitutional and political history of the northern city, on the one hand, and the political status of women within it, on the other. As scholars such as Black have suggested, cities that gained autonomy from feudal lords were undermining the notion of lordship which lay at the base of traditional medieval political society. Most cities gained independence from these lords under the leadership of a small group of wealthy, powerful men whose objectives were, admittedly, simply to assume the privileges of lordship for themselves. The sworn associations these men formed in some cities, however, often incorporated principles of brotherhood. Black notes that these men would also have had reasons to institutionalize the values of civil society, for they were usually merchants and businessmen with interests in free trade, rule by law, and legal equality. Whatever their constitutional principles, however, they rarely opened their ranks to ordinary residents. Even where the entire urban community was included in the citizenry, as in thirteenth-century Frankfurt, political power was no more evenly distributed than was wealth or social status. Rule in these cities remained the exclusive right of rich and well-connected men, who passed it among themselves via marriage and inheritance just as they passed land rights and trade monopolies. In the name of brotherhood but in the service of civil values as well, these men monopolized rule.

Not until after 1250 and then only in some places did a more broadly defined citizenry claim the full political rights long held by the elite. The artisans and smaller merchants who acquired new political powers seldom did so easily, and their struggles (in the southern Low Countries during the fourteenth century and somewhat later in the middle and upper Rhine) constitute important and well-known chapters in the political and institutional history of the medieval city.[36] The timing of these struggles as well as their success depended upon complex interrelations among political, social, and economic conditions particular to the individual cities, so it is dangerous to generalize about their histories.[37] Nevertheless, it is safe to observe, with Black, that these struggles frequently originated in and were carried out in the name of the principles of brotherhood on which the Gemeinde, the urban community, rested. When successful, these struggles led to constitutional reform which formally made the civic community a self-governing brotherhood. Hence, citizenship was extended to all householders, if it had not already been, and was, furthermore, defined to include rights to rule.[38]

The scholarship that underpins this historical narrative also provides a clue to the possible relationship between these constitutional changes and women's civic status. The brotherhood, several scholars have emphasized, was in conception and usual practice an association of households or families.[39] When the citizenry was considered a brotherhood, as it frequently was, even in cities where an elite monopolized rule, the citizenry was itself regarded as an association of families. A document from Frankfurt expresses the concept clearly, characterizing a legal resident as a man and "those who lived with him."[40] One modern scholar has aptly described this conception of citizenship as a "brotherhood of men who lived in the city, headed a household and by virtue of an oath had equal rights and duties. The members' wives and children were not only subject to the protection of the city as were servants and guests but had direct participation in citizenship: they could also be named citizens and their participation became full when they headed a household. . . . It is evident that it was not individualism but the conception of the 'entire' household and especially the contiguous family through marriage and birth [that made up the citizenry]."[41]

It is not difficult to understand why the family would have been counted as the constituent unit in a citizenry conceived as a brotherhood and why women would have shared in that right. The household served as the unit of taxation, the provider of arms for defense, and, of course, the manager and usually the locus of subsistence and market production. Women comanaged these households, and married women in these cities shared property and income with their husbands. Wives were by custom and by testament their husbands' heirs, and daughters inherited movables and immovables from both parents. As comanagers and co-owners of the household and its property, and sometimes as managers and heirs in their own right, women were inevitably full members of citizenries with households as their constituent units. The equation "women = citizen" was, hence, simply an extension of the equation "family unit = citizen."

Strong as the notions of brotherhood and of families as the constituent units apparently were in Frankfurt, however, and as strong as they were in other cities, the notions were not hegemonic. At moments in the city's history, the citizenry was viewed differently. In 1387, for example, all citizens of Frankfurt, new and old, were called to take an oath so that, in the language of the ordinance, "all citizens and residents of Frankfurt might stand together as equals under one oath." While the notion of a communal oath clearly invokes the ideals of brotherhood, the commune being assembled did not consist of households or families. Instead, the oath givers were *all* males over twelve years old—sons and fathers or brothers and cousins who shared a household, some of them as the subordinates of others, were nevertheless considered the citizenry for purposes of this oath.[42]

In Frankfurt we witness a shift from the family to the individual as the constituent civic unit, a shift that involved relinquishing the notion that the brotherhood was an association of families. While the ideals of the brotherhood survived in the oath itself and in the language of the ordinance, this citizenry was no longer the traditional brotherhood of families.

The evidence from Frankfurt, read alongside the body of theory concerning urban constitutions of the age, suggests a rough hypothesis that could help explain women's political and civic status in northern cities. Theory has taught us that two distinct constitutional principles informed the urban community. We can now see that one, resting on civil values, posited that the individual was the basis of the community, but the other,

an expression of guild values, took the family as its constituent unit.
Women actively belonged only to those citizenries in which the latter
principle prevailed. According to this reasoning, I would argue that the
citizenries of Bruges and Leiden were regarded as brotherhoods, that the
brotherhood in fifteenth-century Cologne and Frankfurt was being modified and transformed, and that in Lille guild values had never had primacy. To sustain this argument I must explain why the familial basis of
the urban community could prosper in Leiden and Bruges but was abandoned both in Frankfurt and in postrevolutionary Cologne, where the
ideals of brotherhood itself were nevertheless regularly invoked, serving
to justify artisanal and guild participation in government. Why could the
communal brotherhood as an association of families not easily survive in
settings like Cologne and Frankfurt?

The answer may be that, in these cities, the brotherhood was posited as
the civic ruling body. In Bruges and Leiden, in contrast, the commune or
Gemeinde, while constituting in some sense a brotherhood of families,
did not rule. Communal brotherhoods that ruled in cities like Frankfurt
and Cologne lost their familial base, according to this reasoning, because
families could undermine both the claims cities made to freedom from
feudal overlordship and their struggles to achieve civic unity. Most cities,
it is true, had established their original autonomy from traditional over-
lords through alliances between families of rich residents who then
fought among themselves for hegemony, but we must not forget that in
the end families did not establish themselves as the constituent unit of
rule in northern cities. By 1300, even where oligarchies selected from
rich families still monopolized power (as they did in many places) families themselves did *not* have the political role in late medieval cities of the
North that they enjoyed elsewhere. Membership in a rich and powerful
family was only a young man's essential prerequisite for office; it did not
assure him a place in the government of these cities. A different situation
prevailed elsewhere: in the courts of territorial sovereigns where dynasties ruled (there even retarded or dissolute sons usually retained dynastic
rights to rule) or in southern cities where family clans supplanted urban
institutions (there political authority was transferred from patriarch to
patriarch within the clan).[43]

The shift from familial to individual rule may have begun as cities first
established their independence from feudal rule. Their ties to feudal society explicitly involved kinship. If the early residents of medieval cities
were to assert their freedom from these ties and establish territorial sovereignty, they had to evolve some notion of political rights that exempted
them from the political ties of kin. According to the argument advanced
in this essay, the new ties often entailed a contract between free men

presumed equal before the law—men who shared, in Black's terminology, the values of civil society. Although they retained and invoked
the moral values of the brotherhood, as did the ordinary people who
were later to press for full membership in the civic community, they
could not fully employ the ideals of family if they were to protect their
independence and preserve their unity.

Although the family continued to serve as the constituent unit of public life where the citizenry was simply a union of similar units sharing
such communal resources as market rights, as it was in Bruges and
Leiden, families lost that role in many cities because they undermined the
unity of the commune. Families, after all, speak not for communal interests but for their own. When families rule, private interests become
legitimate public interests and private resources—wealth, heirs, skills, and
so forth which lodge in families, not in individuals—the *legitimate* basis
of public power. In this situation, the commune as a brotherhood of
equals could not have prospered—as it did not in places with family or
clan rule. Possibly for this reason as well families did not establish themselves as the constituent political units in the North. Instead, political
authority passed to individual representatives of commercial or industrial
interests who may well have ruled through corporations that preserved
the concept of brotherhood but jettisoned its familial base.

The research necessary to support this hypothesis has yet to be done,
but even a cursory look at published sources yields evidence in its favor.
From sixteenth-century Lüneberg, for example, we have a record that
illustrates how brotherhoods lost their familial character when they took
on governmental authority. In 1552 the guild of Lüneberg's master tailors
passed laws regarding its *Morgensprache,* the guild's equivalent of council
meetings and its mode of participation in civic government. Not only
could women not attend the meetings, but male masters were sworn to
keep the proceedings of the meeting secret from other family members
belonging to the guild and *specifically* from their wives. While women
still belonged to the guilds, they could take absolutely no part in the
official business these guilds conducted as constituent units of government; only male masters had that right.[44]

THE IDEAS that I have advanced suggest that women were excluded
from positions of public authority in late medieval cities because they
were strictly bound to the family. Because families did not monopolize
rule in these cities, women had no access to rule. The operative prejudice
was not against women rulers as such—although there was abundant
prejudice of this kind in late medieval and early modern Europe—but
against freeing women from the patriarchal authority lodged in families.

Understanding this fact, we can now better understand why Margaret of
Burgundy could have governed the Low Countries and perhaps why
Cathrina Sforza ruled Milan precisely at the time when not a single one of
the successful craftswomen and merchants of Cologne or Frankfurt or
Bruges even sat on their town councils. The former belonged to a political system in which property and political power were linked through
family ties; the latter women lived in a world where those knots had been
cut.

Late medieval cities had thus produced a new and uniquely gendered
definition of political space, one that reserved political authority for individual men (rather than for families) in the interests of civic peace, unity,
and independence. Three consequences of this constitutional innovation,
if it occurred as I have suggested, should be underlined.

First, the many so-called democratic revolutions that occurred in late
medieval cities of the North, although giving men wider access to government, won women no political advantages. In fact, women may well
have lost access to the civic realm precisely to the extent that the revolts
succeeded.

Second, the exclusion of women from government meant that they
took no part in decisions intimately affecting their roles and status. Municipal governments had responsibility for public health and welfare and
set policies for, and even directly managed, industry and commerce. Especially after the Reformation, municipal governments also regularly set
up and ran schools,

Third, not only did the government make policy affecting women
without input from women, but the public world was increasingly being
defined as the province of individuals, not families, as stronger links between governments and public institutions were forged. Guilds, when
they ruled, closed women out. Charity, when taken over by the government, became a male monopoly. The list goes on. The sternly patriarchal
society that was to characterize the seventeenth and eighteenth centuries
in northern Europe was taking shape. In it ordinary women were increasingly relegated to a familial sphere newly distinct from the public
realm. There they were bereft of the civic status they had once borne as
members of families whose place in public associations of equals had
given them public functions.

Notes

1. By "public realm" I mean the realm in which issues not of direct concern to
and not under the control of the domestic unit were located. The public realm, in

contrast to the private, or domestic, realm, can be further defined as the sphere in which community concerns predominated—the locus, e.g., of the production of goods and services to be shared outside the domestic unit or the source of laws, mores, and morals applicable throughout the community. For a fuller discussion of the terms "public" and "private," see M. Z. Rosaldo, "The Use and Abuse of Anthropology: Reflections on Feminism and Cross Cultural Understanding," *Signs* 5:3 (1980):389–417.

2. The best work on urban women's activities in the public realm has concerned Germanic women. For summaries, see Edith Ennen, *Frauen im Mittelalter* (Munich, 1984), and Martha C. Howell, *Women, Production, and Patriarchy in Late Medieval Cities* (Chicago, 1986).

3. The late medieval and early modern period did, however, witness a number of female rulers who acquired political authority as members of ruling dynasties (such as Elizabeth Tudor, Margaret of Burgundy, and Catherine de Medici). Luther's comment can be found in *Lectures on Genesis,* vol. 1, Martin Luther, *Works,* ed. Jaroslav Pelikan (St. Louis, 1958), p. 202. The remark about Cologne's women appears in Hugo Stehkämper et al., eds., *Kölner Neubürger, 1356–1798,* Mitteilungen aus dem Stadtarchiv von Köln 61 (Cologne, 1975). Also see Natalie Zemon Davis, "City Women and Religious Change," in *Society and Culture in Early Modern France* (Stanford, 1975).

4. Many municipalities sponsored elementary schools for girls or for boys and girls together. See Ennen, *Frauen,* for references.

5. Frankfurt am Main, for example, required widows heading households to provide gear sufficient to outfit a soldier.

6. *Bronnen tot de Geschiedenis van de Leidsche Textielnijverheid,* ed. N. W. Posthumus, 6 vols., Rijksgeschiedskundige Publicatiën, nos. 8, 14, 18, 22, 39, 49 (The Hague, 1910–22), vol. 2, document no. 810.

7. Ibid., document no. 1118.

8. The unique features of urban citizenship, particularly in the North, were explored by Max Weber in *Wirtschaft und Gesellschaft;* the sections relating to urban society have been excerpted and separately published in English as *The City* (New York, 1958). Weber's ideas have been followed up especially thoroughly by German scholars. For relevant discussions and guides to the literature, see Otto Brunner, "Zum Begriff Bürgertums," in *Untersuchungen zur gesellschaftlichen Struktur der mittelalterlichen Städte in Europa: Vorträge und Forschungen 10,* ed. Thomas von Mayer (Constance and Stuttgart, 1966), who commented that "the citizenry [*das Bürgertum*], as the term is generally understood today, appeared first in the West at the end of the eleventh century, and 'citizenry' in this special sense appears in no other periods or places." Additional studies of interest include W. Schultheiss, "Das Bürgerrecht der Königs- und Reichsstadt Nürnberg," *Festschrift für Hermann Heimpel,* vol. 2 (Göttingen, 1972), pp. 159ff.; Gerard Dilcher, "Zum Bürgerbegriff im späteren Mittelalter: Versuch einer Typologie am Beispiel von Frankfurt am Main," in *Über Bürger, Stadt, und städtische Literatur im Spätmittelalter,* ed. Joseph Fleckenstein and Karl Stackmann (Göttingen, 1980), pp. 59–105.

9. Dilcher, "Zum Bürgerbegriff," observes that it is somewhat anachronistic

to regard citizenship as a "collection of rights and duties." For contemporaries, citizenship was not something one did or possessed; rather it described who one was.

10. G. K. Schmelzeisen, *Die Rechtsstellung der Frau in der deutschen Stadt-wirtschaft* (Stuttgart, 1935), p. 13.

11. Such an investigation would demand extensive comparative studies of citizenship itself in a variety of cities, as expressed through their legal, political, and constitutional documents, through their membership rolls, and through the occasional contemporary observer or theoretician. It would then require an analysis of women's places in these citizenries, as their places differed from men's and changed over time. Finally, it would entail an examination of how citizenship grew out of the political, economic, and social history of urban Europe.

12. Julius Kirshner, in a comment on an earlier version of this essay that I delivered at the annual meeting of the American Historical Association in December 1986, has reminded me that women may not have transferred citizenship so thoroughly or so easily, because women with inheritances from their natal families would have been required to make some arrangements with their natal city about transfer of their assets to their new homes. Kirshner's evidence, which shows that women sometimes kept dual citizenship, comes mostly from Italian cities (which seem very rarely to have extended citizenship rights to women on their own), but the issue needs to be investigated for northern cities.

13. Pierre Desportes, "Réceptions et inscriptions à la bourgeoisie de Lille aux XIVème et XVème siècles," *Revue du Nord* 62 (1980):541–69.

14. Annie Verspille, "Het Leidsche Poorterschap," *Leids Jaarboekje* (1944); R. A. Parmentier, *Indices op de Brugsche Poorterboeken (1418–1794)* (Bruges, 1938).

15. Dilcher, "Zum Bürgerbegriff."

16. In Frankfurt, widowed women who had been naturalized with their husbands had to repeat the oath; see Dilcher, "Zum Bürgerbegriff."

17. Desportes, "Réceptions et inscriptions."

18. Parmentier, *Indices.*

19. Gemeente archiefdienst, Leiden, *Poortersboeken.*

20. Both Cologne's and Frankfurt's registers have been published: Stehkämper et al., *Kölner Neubürger, 1356–1798;* Dietrich Andernacht and Otto Stamm, eds., *Die Bürgerbücher der Reichsstadt Frankfurt, 1311–1400* (Frankfurt, 1955); Dietrich Andernacht and Erna Berger, eds., *Die Bürgerbücher der Reichsstadt Frankfurt, 1401–1470* (Frankfurt, 1978).

21. Because a disproportionate number of new immigrants to cities were young and single, the average immigrant household probably contained no more than two individuals, including children. For the demographic statistics on which the hypothetical measure of immigration is based, see E. A. Wrigley, *Population and History* (New York, 1969); Carlo Cipolla, *Before the Industrial Revolution,* 2d ed. (New York, 1980); Jan de Vries, *European Urbanization, 1500–1800* (Cambridge, Mass., 1985); R. Mols, *Introduction à la démographie historique des villes d'Europe du XIVème au XVIIIème siècle,* 3 vols. (Louvain, 1954–56); Philippe Dollinger, "Les recherches de démographie historique sur les villes allemandes du Moyen Age," in *La démographie médiévale: Sources et méthodes; Actes du congrès de*

l'Association des historiens médiévistes de l'enseignement supérieur public (Nice, 1970) (Paris, 1972).

22. In the early fifteenth century, a period when Bruges's population is thought to have been maintained at 25,000 to 30,000, the numbers fell well below the hypothetical maintenance rate. Lille's registration figures are presented in Desportes, "Réceptions et inscriptions." Those for Cologne and Frankfurt are published (see n. 20 above). The figures for Bruges have been published as well; see Parmentier, *Indices*. Leiden's are unpublished; see n. 19 above. For the population figures, see Alain Derville, "Le nombre d'habitants des villes de l'Artois et de la Flandre Wallonne (1300–1450)," *Revue du Nord* 65 (April–June 1983), pp. 277–99, for Lille; W. Prevenier, "La démographie des villes du comté de la Flandre aux XIVe et XVe siècles," *Revue du Nord* 65 (April–June 1983), for Bruges; Karl Bücher, *Die Bevölkerung von Frankfurt am Main im 14. und 15. Jahrhundert* (Tübingen, 1886), for Frankfurt; N. W. Posthumus, *De Geschiedenis van de Leidsche Lakenindustrie,* 3 vols. (The Hague, 1908–39), for Leiden; Franz Irsigler, *Die wirtschaftliche Stellung der Stadt Köln im 14. und 15. Jahrhundert* (Wiesbaden, 1979), for Cologne.

23. The economies of each of these cities have been studied in some detail. For guides to the literature on Leiden, Cologne, and Frankfurt, see Howell, *Women, Production, and Patriarchy in Late Medieval Cities;* for guides to the literature on Lille, see R. S. DuPlessis and M. C. Howell, "Reconsidering the Early Modern Urban Economy: The Case of Leiden and Lille," *Past and Present* 94 (February 1982):49–84; for the literature on Bruges, see the extensive bibliography in Jean-Pierre Sosson, *Les travaux publics de la ville de Bruges, XIVe–XVe siècles: Les matériaux, les hommes,* Collection histoire Pro Civitate, série in octavo, no. 48 (Brussels, 1977).

24. A. Verspille, "Het Leidsche Poorterschap," and H. G. Hamaker, ed., *De Middeneeuwsche keurboeken van de stad Leiden* (Leiden, 1873).

25. L. Gilliodts van Severen, *Coutumes de la ville de Bruges,* 2 vols. (Brussels, 1874–75), vol. 1, pp. 298–99. See the introduction to Parmentier, *Indices,* for a full explanation of the laws regarding new citizens and the *Coutumes* for the actual legislation mentioned in this paragraph. The rates began at forty deniers parisis in 1282 but had increased to three pounds parisis in 1349 and in 1352 were raised to six pounds parisis for Flemish born and twelve pounds parisis for those born outside the country. The distinction between Flemish and non-Flemish was maintained until 1441, when in an effort to encourage immigration and registration of skilled workers, the rate was lowered to five shillings gros (the equivalent of three pounds parisis) for both native Flemings and foreigners. In 1454, however, the distinction was reimposed, and the rate was set at twelve shillings gros for Flemings and double that amount for foreigners. The penalties charged foreigners were obviously part of an effort to preserve jobs for Flemings, but only commerce, apparently both petty and large scale, and the unskilled trades were regularly reserved for them: in 1419 it was legislated that non-Flemings could join the citizenry only if they practiced a skilled trade and acquired the freedom of the ambacht. The government's perception that the city needed skilled trades, reflected in this legislation, did not abate in the next decades. By the 1440s the government had eased immigration further for foreigners who mastered

skilled crafts, but the government encountered opposition from the organized crafts in Bruges which were simultaneously issuing legislation designed to exclude newcomers. As late as 1496, the problem remained: the municipal government, now with the support of the territorial sovereign, had to repeat legislation of 1441 requiring the crafts to accept foreigners as newcomers and extending citizenship to non-Flemings at the rates paid by Flemings.

26. Dilcher, "Zum Bürgerbegriff," provides most of the data summarized in this paragraph; see also Armin Wolf, *Die Gesetze der Stadt Frankfurt am Main im Mittelalter* (Frankfurt, 1969).

27. From 1352 onward, the rate for Flemings in Bruges varied between ten shillings gros and twelve shillings gros (with an exceptional period in the midfifteenth century); newcomers to Frankfurt usually paid three pounds heller or three pounds four shillings heller, the former the equivalent of about five shillings gros.

28. For a fuller explication of this thesis, see Desportes, "Réceptions et inscriptions." After the plague the city gradually eased entry requirements for common people but paradoxically never revised its conception that the citizenry was to be made up of the propertied elite rather than craftsmen and ordinary people. Never was citizenship required for craft or simple market rights, and never did common people participate officially in civic affairs.

29. Hugo Stehkämper, *Kölner Neubürger*, provides the data on Cologne's requirements for new citizens.

30. At six gulden, where the fee remained for about a half century after 1371, they were about three times Frankfurt's usual three pounds heller and six times the ten shillings gros charged those Flemish newcomers to Bruges who did not satisfy the residence requirement.

31. See Howell, *Women, Production, and Patriarchy*, for a sketch of women's roles in Frankfurt's trades. Also see Dilcher, "Zum Bürgerbegriff."

32. See Howell, *Women, Production, and Patriarchy*.

33. See Otto von Gierke, *Das deutsche Genossenschaftsrecht*, 4 vols. (1868–1913; repr., Darmstadt, 1954); the concepts of Genossenschaft and Herrschaft have been expanded upon by more recent historians; see Edith Ennen, *Die europäische Stadt des Mittelalters*, 3d ed. (Göttingen, 1979); Georg von Below, *Der Ursprung der deutschen Stadtverfassung* (Dusseldorf, 1892); W. Ebel, *Der Bürgereid als Geltungsgrund und Gestaltungsprinzip des deutschen mittelalterlichen Stadtrechts* (Weimar, 1958); Emile Lousse, *La société d'Ancien Régime: Organisation et représentation corporatives* (Louvain, 1943); Walter Schlesinger, *Beiträge zur deutschen Verfassungsgeschichte des Mittelalters*, 2 vols. (Göttingen, 1963); G. K. Schmelzeisen, *Die Rechtsstellung der Frau*; Société Jean Bodin, *La Ville*, 3 vols. (Brussels, 1954, 1955, 1957).

34. Antony Black, *Guilds and Civil Society in European Political Thought from the Twelfth Century to the Present* (London, 1984).

35. Ibid., pp. 61–62.

36. The best guide to the literature on the constitutional importance of the struggles is Ennen, *Die europäische Stadt des Mittelalters*.

37. Despite the abundance of studies on the history of medieval guilds, there

has been little examination of the variations in the sociopolitical status of such organizations and their place in the complex and changing sociopolitical structures of late medieval cities. For a good discussion of the literature (and its weaknesses), see Jean-Pierre Sosson, "Die Körporschaften in den Niederlanden und Nordfrankreich: Neue Forschungsspecktiven," in *Gilde und Korporation in den nordeuropäischen Städten des späten Mittelalters,* ed. Klaus Friedland (Cologne, 1984). Much of the most important literature treating these and related questions is fairly old. It includes Gunnar Mickwitz, *Die Kartellfunktionen der Zünfte und ihre Bedeutung bei der Entstehung des Zunftwesens* (Helsingfors, 1936); Georg von Below, "Stadtgemeinde, Landgemeinde, und Gilde," *Vierteljahrschrift für Sozial- und Wirtschaftsgeschichte* 7 (1909); idem, *Das ältere deutsche Städtewesen und Bürgertum,* 2d ed. (Bielefeld and Leipzig, 1905); G. des Marez, *L'organisation du travail à Bruxelles au XVe siècle* (Brussels, 1903–1904); idem, *Les origines du droit d'association dans les villes de l'Artois et de la Flandre française jusqu'au XVe siècle,* 2 vols. (Lille, 1941–42); F. Favresse, *L'avènement du régime démocratique à Bruxelles pendant le Moyen Age, 1306–1423* (Brussels, 1932); the work of Hans van Werveke, especially his "Ambachten en erfelijkheid," in *Mededelingen van de Koninklijke Vlaamse Academie, Klasse der Letteren,* IV–1 (Brussels, 1942), pp. 5–26; C. Wyffels, *De oorsprong der ambachten in Vlaanderen en Brabant* (Brussels, 1951).

38. Historians once confidently described these struggles as drives to realize democratic principles. Armed with better evidence about the actual socioeconomic status and the political objectives of the new urban leaders, few scholars today are willing to characterize the revolutions as protodemocratic, but they nevertheless accept that the fourteenth and fifteenth centuries saw a genuine expansion of civic and political status for a number of the urban citizenries in this region. Henri Pirenne's *Early Democracies in the Low Countries* (1910; repr., New York, 1963) is the best known work to argue this case. See also G. Espinas, *Les origines de l'association,* 2 vols. (Lille, 1941–42); Hans Lentze, "Die Kaiser und die Zunftverfassung in den Reichsstädten bis zum Tode Karls IV," *Untersuchungen zur deutschen Staats- und Rechtsgeschichte* 145 (1933); Karl Otto Mueller, *Die oberschwäbische Reichsstädte: Ihre Entstehung und ältere Verfassung* (Stuttgart, 1912); idem, "Das Bürgerrecht in den oberschwäbischen Reischstädten," *Würt. Vierteljahrschrift für Landgeschichte,* n.s., 25 and 26 (1916–17); Franz Petri, *Die Anfänge des mittelalterlichen Städtewesens in den Niederlanden und dem angrenzenden Frankreich* (Reichenau, 1955–56); W. Prevenier, "La bourgeoisie en Flandre au XIIIe siècle," *Revue de l'Université de Bruxelles* 4 (1978): 407–28; Sosson, *Les travaux publics de la ville de Bruges;* R. van Uytven, "Sociaal-econ. evoluties in de Nederlanden voor de Revoluties (14–16de eeuw)," *Bijdragen en Mededelingen van de Geschiedenis van de Nederlanden* 87 (1972); idem, "Plutokratie in de oude democratieën der Nederlanden," *Handelingen der Koninklijke Nederlandse Maatschappij voor Taal- en Letterkunde en Geschiedenis* 16 (1962), pp. 373–409; Wyffels, *De oorsprong der ambachten in Vlaanderen en Brabant;* P. Eitel, *Die oberschwäbische Reichsstädte im Zeitalter der Zunftherrschaft* (Stuttgart, 1970). Also see Dilcher, "Zum Bürgerbegriff," who comments, pp. 81–83, regarding the relationship of Frankfurt's patrician rulers to the Gemeinde; Dilcher sees them as agents.

39. Brotherhoods from all cities in the region regularly described their mem-

berships as consisting of "brothers and sisters" (in context, husbands and wives) and extended social and religious services to all family members. For most of the late medieval period, guilds also included family members in their privileges.

40. Dilcher, "Zum Bürgerbegriff."

41. Ibid.

42. This group was *not*, as we might assume, the city's traditional defensive unit. Heads of household were specifically defined as constituting this group, and women who headed households as citizens were expected to contribute arms to the defense. Moreover, teenage boys did not serve in the militia.

43. A comparative history of urban sociopolitical structures in northern and southern Europe has not yet been written (hardly, indeed, does such a history exist for different areas of the North), but scholars of Italian cities have recently produced important literature which could serve as the basis for such an investigation. Jacques Heers, *Family Clans in the Middle Ages,* trans. B. Herbert (New York, 1977), has claimed that the patrician families of northern cities were similar to southern Italian clans. Most northern historians would disagree, even for the period before 1300, and there is little doubt that, after 1300, "clan" government such as that in Genoa simply did not exist in the North. In addition to Heers's study, see the work of David Herlihy, collected in *Cities and Society in Medieval Italy* (London, 1980), for references to the Italian literature. For the North, W. Prevenier's "La Bourgeoisie en Flandre"; Hellmuth Rössler, *Deutsches Patriziat, 1430–1740* (Limburg/Lahn, 1968); and Wolfgang Herborn, *Die politische Führungsschicht der Stadt Köln im Spätmittelalter* (Cologne, 1977) provide good guides to the literature.

44. Cited in Schmelzeisen, *Die Rechtsstellung der Frau,* pp. 34–35, where he comments: "Das Bemerkenswerte aber sehe ich darin, dass durch das Verlangen solcher Eide und Durch Erlass solcher Schweigegebote der Kreis der Vollgenossen eine betonte Abschliessung gegen den Kreis der übrigen Genossen vornahm, dass diese Abschliessung sich weiterhin des das Vertrauen gegenüber allen anderen ausschliessenden Mittels des Geheimnisses bediente und gerade bei der strammen Begrenzung der durch das Geheimnis Verbundenen ziemlich rücksichtslos sogar vor dem vertraulichen Kreise der Familie nicht Halt machte. Das passte in den Zug einer Zeit, die im Gegensatz zu früher das häusliche vom öffentlichen Leben, das Private vom Amtlichen zu scheiden wusste."

Women, Seals, and Power in Medieval France, 1150–1350

Brigitte Bedos Rezak

T he medieval seal is a *signum*, a sign which embodied personal responsibility and in so doing gave the individual an opportunity to express both self-perception and group consciousness.

Two aspects of seals determine their worth as evidence: first, the primary function of a seal as a personal mark of identity required precise and accurate display of the owner's name and status in order to validate documents. Second, the pattern of seal usage and progressive dissemination through society was a process sensitive to politics and power. Since sealing implied legal capacity linked to rights of property ownership and disposition, seals constituted a crucial element in, and remain a tangible index of, the expression and extent of women's secular power.

The understanding of seals as a source requires analysis and integration of variables such as seal practice, iconographic devices, choice of titles, and their temporal and geographic evolutions. In this way we may come to appreciate the social status of a given group of sealers, mental attitudes within and toward the group, and the degree of power exercised by and within the group.

The present essay will attempt such a treatment for the seals of French women from the mid-twelfth to the mid-fourteenth century. It is based on the study of 817 seals of Ile-de-France, Normandy, Flanders, Poitou, and Provence-Dauphine, regions selected for their geographic and historic diversity (figure 1).[1] I hope to demonstrate how seals shed light on three aspects of feminine power. Prerogatives within society will be evaluated through sealing practice; position within the family structure will be considered by reference to titles and heraldic emblems; finally, the conceptual focus of women within the collective social mentality will be assessed through the iconography of their seals.

From the fourth to the eleventh centuries, the practice of sealing for

61

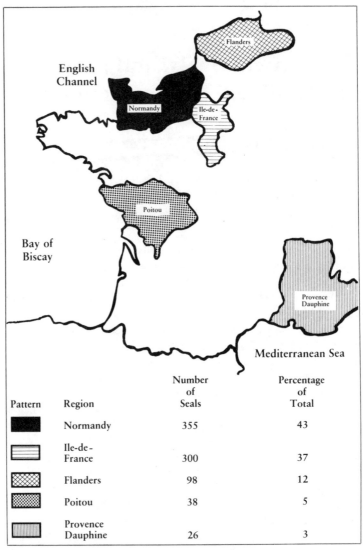

Pattern	Region	Number of Seals	Percentage of Total
	Normandy	355	43
	Ile-de-France	300	37
	Flanders	98	12
	Poitou	38	5
	Provence Dauphine	26	3

1. Distribution of Women's Seals, 1150–1350

documentary validation remained an exclusive kingly prerogative. With the weakening of central authority, ascendant secular and ecclesiastical potentates, dukes, counts, and bishops assumed by mid–eleventh century the privilege of sealing along with other royal rights.[2] Until 1180, this aristocratic group, like the kings before them, viewed the act of sealing as the privilege of superior authority. After 1180, sealing lost this connotation of high status and evolved into the normal way of juridically committing oneself. By 1200, seal usage in this latter, ordinary sense rapidly extended to every stratum of the medieval society, from king to nonnoble landowner.

In France, sealing remained an exclusively male practice up to the twelfth century, in contrast to Germany, where the Empress Kunegund is the first known German female sealer in 1002.[3] In England, Mathilda,[4] the queen of Henry I, used her seal from about 1100. The first French female seal can also be found at the royal level. In 1115, Bertrada of Montfort, the widow of King Philip I, sealed a charter in favor of the abbey of Marmontiers.[5] Remarkably, on this seal, Bertrada is identified as "Queen of the Franks by God's Grace," a title perhaps appropriate for a dowager queen but decidedly less so for one whose marriage to the king had been illegal and was never legitimated by Rome. The apparently unprecedented assumption of sealing by Bertrada may well represent a conscious attempt on her part to assert her royal status by emulating the king's practice in support of her questionable queenly title. During King Philip's lifetime, Bertrada's name as queen was frequently associated with that of the king in the texts of royal diplomas, but she never sealed any document. In fact, Orderic Vital describes how she borrowed the king's seal when she wrote in her own name to the king of England.[6] Only in her widowhood, when her personal influence at court had diminished, did she first undertake to seal. Again in contrast to her foreign predecessors, and despite her use of a royal title, Bertrada used a seal that was *not* that of a reigning queen and was intended for her private documents rather than for official ones. Nevertheless Bertrada's initiative, which reveals both her personal ambitions and the correlation between seal usage and status, led directly to further developments. Bertrada's first husband, Fulk V, Count of Anjou, was the first of his lineage to seal his documents, and this distinction, linked specifically to Bertrada's presence in Anjou, clearly indicates her influence.[7] Furthermore, we may note as perhaps more than mere coincidence that the first nonroyal woman to seal, Sybille of Anjou, Countess of Flanders,[8] was in fact Bertrada's granddaughter. Bertrada's initiative was also not lost on her successor, Adelaide, the queen of Louis VI, whose exceptionally active role in government is well documented by a total of ninety acts which mention her

2. Queen Isabel de Hainaut, wife of
Philip Augustus, king of France. Ca.
1180. Douët d'Arcq, *Sceaux*, n. 153.

participation over a twenty-two-year period. That not one of these acts
refers to her seal, and that there is no mention of her seal before her
widowhood, suggest that Adelaide also started to seal as a dowager, when
she had a need to administer her dower independently and privately.[9]
With the next queen, Eleanor of Aquitaine, there appears for the first
time in France the seal of a reigning consort.[10] This new step, however,
must be appreciated in terms of its precise circumstances. Eleanor was the
first French queen to ascend the throne possessing a personal estate,
the duchy of Aquitaine, and indeed she sealed only in matters relating to
the duchy. The queen's seal thus retained the nonroyal character of its
predecessors. French reigning queens after Eleanor all had seals (figure
2), yet their employment was absolutely limited to private and domestic
matters.[11] They were never affixed to royal charters and were never endowed with the symbolic value of the king's seal, which represented the
authority of the State.[12] So the pattern of queenly seal usage from its very
inception attests to the qualitative difference between the power of queens
and that of kings.

The discussion has so far focused on queenly seals because, until 1150,
they constitute the only female examples in France. Soon after, however,
a greater variety of women's seals is found. Women's sealing (table 1)
reached its peak during the years 1251–1300, as did the general practice of
sealing which became widespread during the thirteenth century and then

Table 1. Women's Seals, 1150–1350, by Social Category

	Percentage of Women's Seals			
	Aristocratic families	Castellan families	Knightly families	Nonnoble landowning families
Before 1200	80	20	—	—
1201–1250	15	30	25	30
1251–1300	8	19	36	37
1301–1350	25	30	19	26

Note: A total of 607 women's seals was analyzed of which 210 displayed counterseals. Totals for the periods were 48 before 1200, 138 for 1201–1250, 366 for 1251–1300, and 55 for 1301–1350.

contracted during the fourteenth century with the development of signatures and the appearance of the notarial system in the North.[13]

The proportions of women's seals gathered for this study are (figure 1): Normandy (43 percent), Ile-de-France (37 percent), Flanders (12 percent), Poitou (5 percent), Provence-Dauphine (3 percent). Women's seals, like seals in general, are concentrated north of the Loire, where diplomatic sealing developed in the absence of an official agency, a public notariat, specially instituted for the validation of documents. By contrast, a notarial system inherited from Roman usage survived in the South. In consequence, sealing in the South remained unusual throughout the Middle Ages and was primarily the practice of a few potentates who imitated the northern custom by way of asserting their juridical independence. The few women found to seal in Poitou and Provence-Dauphine accordingly all belong to the aristocracy and the castellan group. Given the consequent paucity of sigillographic data, the status of southern women,[14] and for that matter of men, is difficult to examine by means of seals. Thus as a result of the bias of our present sources, the following analysis and conclusions will mostly bear on northern women.[15] Even the more substantial northern data base must, of course, be seen in relation to the proportion of men to women sealers and to the social distribution of the latter.

Prior to 1200 (table 1), the aristocrats (i.e., women belonging to ducal or comital families) were virtually the only nonroyal sealers. This group maintained its steady use of seals to the end of the period, about 1350. The castellans (i.e., women belonging to lordly castellan families) in-

creased their seal usage throughout the thirteenth century. Most remarkable, however, is the huge proportion of female sealers of knightly lineage and even of nonnoble landowning families.[16] The latter are found
exclusively in Normandy and are the reason that this province shows the
largest total number of women sealers. It is worth noting that the female
seals of aristocratic and castellan groups together represent no more than
5 percent of all the seals, male and female, in these categories. Female
sealers represent 13 percent of all knightly seals, and the females com-
prise fully 25 percent of extant seals of nonnoble landowners. In contrast,
from the mid-thirteenth century onward, only thirteen bourgeois female
sealers have been found, all located in Normandy, although several hundred male bourgeois seals are known.[17]

Turning to the practice of women sealers,[18] and hence to their legal
power, it was normal for widows and married women to seal alone those
acts which were given in their own names. From 1200 to 1350, however,
the overwhelming majority of married women's seals are found jointly
appended with those of their husbands, fathers, or sons. Widows of any
social stratum almost invariably sealed their documents alone. A novelty,
after 1250, is the appearance of seals used independently by unmarried
girls, exclusively of knightly and nonnoble landowning families.

Women's seals carried as much power of authentication as male ones,
but such power applied only to documents issued in their own names. In
contrast, it was not uncommon for male lords to endow the deed of a
lesser person with greater security by affixing their seals, though they, the
lords themselves, were not party to the transaction. The seals of women,
like the seals of queens mentioned earlier, therefore appear to have been
confined to a strictly personal usage and not to have possessed the public
dimension of the male's.

From the data cited, it is apparent that, in general, male seals are far
more numerous than female seals at all social levels. We should not, however, suppose that there was a substantial majority of men over women in
medieval society. Quite apart from male-only settings, many documents
issued in the names of both spouses were validated only by the seal of the
husband. The question thus arises as to why women ever undertook to
seal.

Among the highest female nobility the very earliest seals, those used
before 1200, functioned as the sole means of validating transactions of
various types, even those, in contrast to the situation for queens, that
were unrelated to women's own personal property. We may therefore
assume that aristocratic and noblewomen started to seal on the basis of
their general importance within the seigneury.[19] Later, however, during
the thirteenth century, these same categories of married noblewomen lost

the independent use of their seals and thereafter sealed only together with their husbands, fathers, or sons. Furthermore, such women thereafter sealed only acts that involved their own property: personal estates, dowers, or dowries.[20] Concurrently, unmarried girls of this higher nobility did not seal. Last, female seals of this group are proportionally very few compared with men's. So it seems that, by the thirteenth century, aristocratic and castellan women experienced a regression of their seal usage, evidence that they increasingly depended upon their male kindred. In short, within the higher nobility, the patrilineal structure of the family and the masculinity of feudal and military obligations, both of which give emphasis to male primacy, tended progressively to reduce women's juridical power and independence.[21]

Women of knightly and nonnoble landowning families present a somewhat different sealing pattern. They did not seal at all before the first quarter of the thirteenth century and, initially, never sealed alone. Yet three points make them seem more independent legally than higher-ranking women: first, unmarried women sealed acts issued in their own names; second, married women sealed a great variety of deeds conjointly with their husbands and not merely those involving disposition of their own rights or properties; third, the proportion of female to male seals is much higher than within the aristocratic and castellan categories. That women of knightly families acted thus independently,[22] as expressed in seal usage, may derive from the practical conditions of their family situations. For though knightly families were formally articulated with reference to the noble concept of lineage, they functioned within the mundane circumstances of a rural household and small estate. In such a household, equality of husband and wife was stressed, and the participation of women in family management was quite important. This statement, of course, was even more true for the Norman nonnoble family. Normandy has been characterized as a region "of strict equality," since the holdings of the lesser nobility and of commoners were equally divided among all children, male and female, at the deaths of the parents.[23] The intensity of seal usage by Norman nonnoble women reflects this equal economic and legal capacity.[24]

In the last analysis, for all women, sealing is a consequence of position and capability within the family unit. The family remains the chief determinant for acquisition or loss of legal and economic power. Therefore sealing may serve as an index to the position of women within their kindreds. This conclusion is further strengthened by the analysis of patterns of names, terms of kinship, and the coats of arms used by women on their seals.

Seals are not the only sources which preserve women's names and titles; these also appear in charters, in literary sources, and on tombstones. Seals were intended for repetitive use under a wide variety of circumstances, however, as representatives of individuals who often had multiple titles and social roles. These conditions of usage, and the small module of seals, compelled economy in seal legends, which thus include only the most essential elements of a sealer's identity. Throughout the period under consideration, most married women of the aristocratic and castellan group designated themselves on seals by their own name followed by the title of their husbands (figures 3–7).[25] In only a very few instances did they insert the word *uxoris* ("wife of").[26] An aristocrat or a castellan who was heiress in her own right usually inscribed her own name, followed by her patronymics, ignoring her husband's title entirely,[27] listing it after that of her father, or mentioning it only on the counterseal, a smaller impression on the reverse of the principal wax impression. After 1300, aristocrats' and castellans' seal legends systematically display the form of name and patronymic followed by the title of the husband (figure 8).[28] In those cases in which the wife came from a very distinguished lineage, this origin was further stressed by the insertion of the term *filiae*, "daughter of," between her name and patronymics.[29] Widowed but unremarried women of the higher nobility often retained a seal bearing the name of their late husbands as well.[30] In the rare instance when a widow remained her father's heir, a new seal might be engraved with only her name and patronymic.[31] Last, I have found only two seals on which widowhood is specifically mentioned.[32]

Women of knightly families, when married, adopted the title of their husbands, quite frequently preceded by the term *uxoris*.[33] Although in the higher nobility the use of patronymics by wives was the privilege of heiresses or dynasts, this usage was common among women of the knightly group (figure 9). Clearly the general family structure stressed economic rather than genealogical concerns and gave equal importance to a wife, whose prior identity did not need to be suppressed or fused with that of her husband. Retention of patronymics may further emphasize the importance of horizontal family solidarity among knights, a pattern which had been displaced, among the higher nobility, by the patrilineal structure.[34]

Again, as with the pattern of sealing, Norman nonnoble women's seal legends are closely related to those described for knightly women. In some cases they simply adopted their husband's name, but in just as many they retained their father's. A still more frequent usage is the husband's name plus the term *uxoris*. The form most typical of nonnoble women's seal legends, however, appearing in quantity from 1250 to 1300, is the simple formulation "Seal of Richeut, his wife" (figure 10).[35] Such

3. Mathilda de Portugal, wife of Philip d'Alsace, count of Flanders. Ca. 1197. Full-length standing figure of a woman holding a fleur-de-lis. Demay, *Flandre,* n. 142.

4. Counterseal of Mathilda de Portugal, wife of Philip d'Alsace, count of Flanders. Ca. 1197. The shield displays the arms of Portugal. Demay, *Flanders,* n. 142 bis.

5. Agathe, wife of Conon, lord of Pierrefonds. 1171. The standing figure of an attractive woman, with long, flowing hair and with her hand on her hips. Douët d'Arcq, *Sceaux,* n. 3214.

6. Adele, wife of Raoul, count of Soissons. 1186. A woman riding a horse and bearing a hawk. Demay, *Flandres,* n. 303.

7. Constance of France, wife of Raymond V, count of Toulouse. Ca. 1194. A woman enthroned and holding in her left hand an orb topped with a fleur-de-lis. Douët d'Arcq, *Sceaux*, n. 741.

8. Isabelle de Rosny, wife of Pierre de Chambli. 1294. Full-length depiction of a woman bearing a hawk and standing between the coat of her husband (the shield on the left bearing three shells) and that of her father (the shield on the right bearing two bars). Douët d'Arcq, *Sceaux*, n. 1693.

9. Agnes de Fleleu, wife of Pierre de Flavacourt. 1281. A woman kneeling in front of the Virgin Mary with Child. Douët d'Arcq, *Sceaux*, n. 2177.

10. Richeut, wife of Geoffroi Beeale. 1258. This seal belongs to a Norman nonnoble landowning woman, and the inscription reads "S' RICEUT SA FAME" ("seal of Richeut his wife"). Demay, *Normandie*, n. 680.

seals stress the marital relationship and simply avoid the issue of a wife's prior identity. They prevent the wife from making any use of her seal independently of her husband's, of course, but we have already seen that, after 1200 at all social levels, only unmarried or widowed women sealed independently. Thus such seals may stress the dependence of wives less than their positive status. Nonnoble seals also offer many examples of legends which use the term *vidua,* widow, a word only rarely found in seals of the nobility.[36]

Thus, as with the pattern of seal usage, seal terminology also shows a major cleavage between the higher nobility and the gentry and nonnoble landowners. In legend selection distinctions are mainly articulated with reference to terms of kinship. Filiation may be stressed among aristocracy and nobility, but only if this ancestry demonstrates wealth or importance. Among gentry and nonnobles what is stressed is conjugality. Furthermore—in contrast to the higher nobility, where assumption of the husband's name normally implies merging of the woman's identity with that of her husband's lineage—for gentry and the nonnoble, conjugality involves a partnership, where a wife is labeled as such but remains differentiated as a person from her husband.[37] Her position is thus given weight within the family unit.

Noblewomen had yet a further means of expressing their position within the lineage: their coats of arms. Heraldry (figures 4, 8),[38] used within the male aristocracy from 1120 onward, was at once the direct product of, and a support for, the organization of noble kinships as linear institutions. The coat of arms, together with patronymics and land, was integral to the male-oriented noble heritage, which it symbolized. In this context, the use of women's bearings was problematic, though women did ultimately acquire heraldic capacity as coats of arms evolved from individual into familial signs. Until 1250, only women of the aristocracy and high nobility displayed arms on their seals. After 1250, women of the knightly class did so as well. Women's seals showing arms are much rarer than other types and of course are but a tiny fraction of the mass of male heraldic seals. Initially, and down to 1250, female coats of arms appear, not on the principal side of the seal, but on the reverse counterseal (figure 4). There seems to have been some confusion over which coat to adopt. The situation for aristocratic and castellan names had been clear: for the married woman, that of the husband; for the heiress, that of the father. Such options are not paralleled by arms selection, however; arms of a father might be used with a husband's name (figures 3, 4);[39] an heiress who had kept her patronymic might display her husband's coat.[40] After 1250, more orderly patterns emerge: thereafter, heiresses of the higher nobility systematically display their father's arms, heraldic devices leave the coun-

terseal for the obverse, and a general tendency develops thoughout the
aristocracy, nobility, and gentry to display coats of both father and husband (figure 8).[41] This heraldic resolution, widely achieved after 1300
within the aristocrats and the castellans, parallels the adoption of both
patronymic and husband's name by that date. This evidence may indicate
that aristocratic and castellan women had now been given more independent recognition within their husband's family units. In fact, women of
knightly descent, who had enjoyed such recognition from the early thirteenth century onward, adopted from the very inception of their bearing
of arms a formulaic display of both husband's and father's coats.

Armorial bearings also reveal something which appears nowhere else
on seals, namely a display of matrilineal descent. (Parenthetically it may
be noted that no woman's seal legend used a matronymic. I have found
only one instance of a son titling himself, "son of X, his mother" upon
his seal. This was the heir of the county of Flanders, through his mother
Marguerite, herself the heiress of the county.)[42] In a very few cases, aristocratic women displayed the coat of their mothers' families.[43] Also,
members of three families from the Ile-de-France (the Clermont, the
Nesle, and the Bouteiller of Senlis) adopted arms that belonged to a
mother's or grandmother's family rather than retaining their paternal
coat.[44] In these instances, as might be expected, maternal lines were of a
higher social status than the paternal. While these few examples prove
that the transmission of arms was not strictly patrilineal, their paucity
emphasizes the general rule of male preeminence within the lineage. Indeed, the rarity of female heraldic seals, the confusion shown in the selection of a coat, the ultimate fusion of father's and husband's arms, all
clearly express the situation of noblewomen, who, by not fitting into the
linear model, did not "exist," at least at the level of signs.

The use and epigraphy of seals defines for knightly and nonnoble
women a more recognized position within their families which parallels
their rather sizable participation within the general juridico-economic
world. This case is the opposite for aristocratic and castellan women,
who after 1200 seem to have had economic power centered only in their
hereditary lands while otherwise being subordinated to a concept of marriage which emphasized their role only within the biogenetic aspects of
lineage.[45]

Despite this restriction, aristocratic and castellan women's seals have
much to reveal about the position of women in the world of sensibilities.
They bear substantial naturalistic depiction of women in contemporary
costume (figures 3, 5–8). By contrast, female seals of the gentry and
nonnoble landowners are generally confined to plant or geometric motives (figure 10), though in some instances nonnoble women's seals dis-

play a distaff (figure 11).[46] Such a limited iconography, manifest also in male nonnoble seals, testifies to the simplicity of rural life and perhaps indicates a narrowness of opportunity, or of financial means, which prevented these modest sealers from employing the services of a good artist. It also reflects a self-perception centered less on the individual than on her environment. To gain a visual impression of women, we shall focus on female seals from the higher nobility, on which all owners were physically depicted.

Money and recourse to good engravers may explain the better quality of depiction but cannot account for the adoption of a full-figure representation. Aristocratic female seals may convey little personal power, but they certainly display the most elaborate iconography. Women of the higher nobility were functionally deprived but were placed upon a sigillographic pedestal (figures 3, 5–8).

The iconography of the secular woman, during the twelfth and part of the thirteenth century, has been characterized as that of "an absence." Art for this period, mainly church art, deals with female representation primarily within the contexts of biblical, Marian, or hagiographic themes. Feminine forms are also all too often used as images that illustrate sin in its many manifestations.[47] When women started to seal, the prevailing masculine seal iconography was role oriented.[48] The king is depicted enthroned with regalia; the lord is an equestrian in arms; the bishop holds his pastoral crozier and lifts up his hand in blessing. Both feudal and ecclesiastical potentates are in fact depicted in the performance of their essential contributions to the tripartite structure of medieval society. Women were not considered at all in this governing social scheme, however, and hence had no functional designation at this general cultural level;[49] they were of course the spouses of those who fought and worked. An examination of their seal iconography, however, does supply information about the place which they occupied, not through the intellectual assessment of clerics and writers, but with reference to their own psychic and emotional environment.

Some few women projected through their seals a self-image borrowed directly from traditional male forms in order to conceptualize their relation to power. In 1220, the countess of Provence and Forcalquier sealed as an equestrian in arms, as did her neighbor, Galberge of Serres.[50] Both of these women were lords in their own right; they had inherited their patrimonies and were thus asserting their willingness to fulfill the feudal obligations inherent in their landholdings. Constance, a southern lady by her marriage to the count of Toulouse but in fact the daughter of the French King Louis VI, is depicted enthroned on her seal to show her affiliation with a royal lineage (figure 7).[51] The selection of this form for a

11. Petronille de Thibivilliers. 1266. The seal displays a distaff and a spindle. Demay, *Picardie*, n. 625.

12. Notre Dame of Rouen, chapter. Twelfth century. The enthroned Virgin Mary. Douët d'Arcq, *Sceaux*, n. 7300.

13. Notre Dame of Chartres, chapter. 1207. The enthroned Virgin Mary with Child. Douët d'Arcq, *Sceaux*, n. 7150.

woman's seal was unprecedented, but subsequent masculine heirs to the county of Toulouse all carefully retained this image, the type of majesty in which a clear superiority inhered.[52] The peculiarity, within France, of Constance's seal is most dramatic when it is compared with queenly seals (figure 2). Whereas, from the eleventh century onward, the king was *always* depicted in majesty, the queen was *never* enthroned. Rather she was standing, the position generally adopted for sealing purposes by noblewomen. In fact, queens could be differentiated from noblewomen only by their crowns and occasionally their scepters (figure 2).[53] In all of seal iconography, only one female figure is depicted as a sovereign, and that is the Virgin who, in about 1150, appeared on ecclesiastical seals,[54] crowned and enthroned, in consequence of the Marian cult (figure 12).

The details of women's effigies on seals include realistic features. Attractive parts of the feminine body are set off to advantage; breasts, thighs, even floating hair (figures 5 and 7), which was considered an instrument of seduction and as such was condemned by the Church, are not infrequently shown on early seals. In most cases, however, the hair is neatly braided (figure 6) or dissimulated within a headdress (figures 3 and 8). Indeed many aspects of feminine costume and the evolution of fashions are accurately documented on these seals.[55] Yet ultimately, female seals carry the abstracted image of woman rather than portraying individual persons. These seals are stereotypes, semiotic conventions of a collective mentality. Remarkably, the express mention of motherhood is excluded; here again, as with queenship, motherly status has, on seals, been appropriated for, and thereafter exclusively reserved to, the Virgin Mary (figure 13).[56] She, alone of all women, may hold a child. This uniqueness as queen and mother subtly underlines how Mary's celebration as a perfect woman resulted in the concomitant denigration of women.[57]

On their seals, noblewomen are endowed with only two attributes. One is the fleur-de-lis (figures 2, 3, and 5),[58] which appears on the earliest seals and is widely used until about 1250, when it retreats in favor of the second attribute, a hawk (figures 6 and 8). The fleur-de-lis had a long-standing tradition as an emblem of kingship and in this capacity had appeared both in Carolingian imperial iconography and on early Capetian seals.[59] During the first half of the twelfth century, the fleur-de-lis became doubly associated with the Virgin (figure 12). First, the flower is carried by Mary as a queen. Second, in the Tree-of-Jesse iconography, the flower stems from Jesse, stretching ultimately to a redemptive Christ through the intermediacy of his mother, who thus gains a clear position within the lineage.[60] The flower motif is thereby equated with female procreation and associated with ancestry. The Tree-of-Jesse theme appearance has been linked to the contemporaneous articulation of the noble family as lineage.[61] Through the bearing of the fleur-de-lis, the medieval woman is connected, metaphorically, with dynastic motherhood and fertility. Parenthetically, I should mention that, simultaneously with the emergence of the flower in the Jesse Tree, there appeared another iconographic theme that expresses fertility through the depiction of a woman with flowers. On calendars of this period and thereafter, the month of April, the month of Venus, of the beginning of spring, of the resumption of life, is illustrated with a female flower bearer.[62] So for a secular woman, the bearing of the fleur-de-lis has a complex meaning. It acknowledges her importance in the biogenetics of lineage but does so by reference to a symbol that evokes the current religious ideal of femininity, the Virgin. Adoption of this ideal type in some sense helped to deny the ordinary woman the plenitude of her own female nature. On the other hand, however, the respect in which Mary was held prompted some sealers to associate themselves fully with her recognized womanly glory. They dedicated their seal iconography to the Virgin while depicting themselves kneeling at her feet (figure 9).[63]

In contrast to this religious and somewhat mutilating symbol, the hawk and other apparatus of the hunt—dogs, horses (figure 6), and horns[64]—clearly emphasize secularity: in a way, Mary is replaced by Eve. Hawking was symbolic of wealth and aristocracy and was an exercise widely enjoyed and practiced by noblemen and noblewomen.[65] This theme, however, is rarely found on men's seals, while it is a principal topos on women's seals. One important reason for the discrepancy is that hawks and hawking were invested, through literature and miniatures, with a semiotic content specifically relating to women. The theme of woman as falconer runs parallel to the motif of amorous conversation. Woman was also described as comparable to a bird of prey on account of her beauty and the careful treatment she required.[66] To these positive and poetic associations, John of Salisbury brought a strong contravention: "Women were better at hawking than men because the worst people were always the most predatory."[67] As with the fleur-de-lis, the sigillographic use of the hawk conveys an ambivalent perception of women. After 1250, the hawk largely supplanted the fleur-de-lis. Indeed, by the thirteenth century, general Marian iconography had shifted its focus from symbolism to realism. No longer the queenly intermediary of the Tree of Jesse, Mary becomes an earthly suffering mother.[68] By this period, too, her genealogical dimension could be expressed by the heraldic devices which, after 1250, are more frequently found on women's seals. The hawking type thus replaces the Virgin as a womanly image at a time of cultural rigidity, of repression, and of doubt. Contemporary literature no longer presents the twelfth-century vision of a woman as a force for good but offers rather a pessimistic assessment of the female as a threat to male psychological balance.[69] At the same time, there appear marginal illuminations showing women engaged in naive but significant challenges to the traditional subordinating attitudes of the Church and male society.[70] Against this background, association of the theme of the chase with women, as exemplified by hawking, takes on additional eloquent significance. The definition of the chase had greatly preoccupied medieval society. It belonged to the configuration of aristocratic power while also providing the locus wherein men could experience the unresolved conflict between the opposing forces of culture and nature.[71] The identification of women with nature is, among other evidences, rooted in the language, the word *mater* (mother) deriving from *materia* (matter).[72] Woman was the biological force, as opposed to the social, which men considered themselves as personifying.

Perhaps what is expressed on late thirteenth-century women's seals through the female metaphor of the chase is the crisis within the medieval experience of power. Women, in their reality, are at the center of such conflict, standing as they do for both nature and otherness. Not ultimately reducible, women stir that male anxiety which stems from the perception of incomplete mastery over the surrounding world. In such images, women symbolize the limits of social power.

Notes

The data used in this paper were gathered for a work in progress entitled *Seals and Social Structure: New Evidence for the Transformation of the French Nobility*. Research for this project has been made possible by a fellowship for independent study from the National Endowment for the Humanities (1984).

1. The corpus of 817 seals considered in this paper consists of all female examples for the period 1150–1350 to be found in the following works: L. Blancard, *Iconographie des sceaux et bulles conservés dans la partie antérieure à 1790 des Archives départementales des Bouches du Rhône* (Marseille-Paris, 1860), hereinafter cited as Blancard, *Sceaux et bulles;* G. Demay, *Inventaire des sceaux de l'Artois et de la Picardie*, 2 vols. (Paris, 1877), hereinafter cited as Demay, *Artois*, or Demay, *Picardie;* G. Demay, *Inventaire des sceaux de la Flandre*, 2 vols. (Paris, 1873), hereinafter cited as Demay, *Flandre;* G. Demay, *Inventaire des sceaux de la Normandie* (Paris, 1884), hereinafter cited as Demay, *Normandie;* M. Deurbergue, *Les sceaux de dames jusqu'en 1350 spécialement en Ile-de-France* (Ph.D. diss., Ecole Nationale des Chartes, Paris, 1966), Paris, Archives Nationales, AB XXVIII/93; hereinafter cited as Deurbergue, *Ile-de-France;* L. Douët d'Arcq, *Collection de sceaux*, 3 vols. (Paris, 1863–68), hereinafter cited as Douët d'Arcq, *Sceaux;* F. Eygun, *Sigillographie du Poitou jusqu'en 1515* (Poitiers, 1938), hereinafter cited as Eygun, *Poitou;* and J.

Roman, *Description des sceaux des familles seigneuriales du Dauphiné* (Grenoble, 1913), hereinafter cited as Roman, *Dauphiné*.

2. B. Bedos, "Signes et insignes du pouvoir royal et seigneurial au Moyen Age: Le témoignage des sceaux," in *Actes du 105e Congrès national des Sociétés savantes* (Paris, 1984), pp. 47–48.

3. E. Kittel, *Siegel* (Braunschweig, 1970), p. 274, and fig. 178, p. 275.

4. T. H. Heslop, "Seals," *English Romanesque Art, 1066–1200* (London, 1984), p. 305 and fig. 336.

5. Her seal, now lost, was recorded and drawn by Gaignières (seventeenth century): Paris, Bibliothèque Nationale, MS. Latin 5441/4, fol. 113; also in MS. Latin 12879, fol. 24 (Dom Martène, *Histoire de Marmoutier*). The document appears on p. 75, n. 1. Comments upon, and a drawing of, Bertrada's seal can be found in A. Maquet and A. Dion, "Sceaux et armoiries des comtes de Montfort-L'Amaury," *Mémoires et Documents de la Société archéologique de Rambouillet* 5 (1879–80), p. 64.

6. Ordericus Vitalis, *Ecclesiastica Historia,* ed. A. Le Prevost, 5 vols. (Paris, 1838–52), vol. 4, p. 195, l. 11, c. 9. On Bertrada, see M. Facinger, "A Study of Medieval Queenship: Capetian France, 987–1237," *Studies in Medieval and Renaissance History* 5 (1968), pp. 6–7, 28. On her contested marriage, see G. Duby, *Medieval Marriage* (Baltimore, 1978), pp. 29–41, especially pp. 37–38.

7. O. Guillot, *Le comte d'Anjou et son entourage au XIe siècle,* 2 vols. (Paris, 1972), vol. 2, p. 12, n. 2.

8. Douët d'Arcq, *Sceaux,* n. 618.

9. On Adelaide's exceptional participation in the government, see Facinger, "Medieval Queenship," pp. 7, 28–30. Her seal, now lost, is attested in Dom J. Mabillon, *De re diplomatica,* 3d ed. (Naples, 1789), p. 622, n. 182: *Adelaidis reginae diploma de villa Sancti Germani prope Compendium—Anno 1153.*

10. Eleanor's seal as queen of France is no longer extant; it is attested in a document dating from 1146–1147, A. Teulet, *Layettes du Trésor des Chartes,* vol. 1, 755–1223 (Paris, 1863), p. 61, n. 92. Still extant are her seals as duchess of Aquitaine (1152), Eygun, *Poitou,* n. 3, and as queen of England, ibid., nn. 4, 5, and Douët d'Arcq, *Sceaux, n.* 10006.

11. See a description of French queens' seals in Douët d'Arcq, *Sceaux,* nn. 151–85. The political and juridical nature of the queen's seal is discussed in Facinger, "Medieval Queenship," pp. 30–31, and in F. Barry, *La reine de France* (Paris, 1964), pp. 165–68.

12. Even during regencies in which the queen assumed authority, in the absence of the king and of his official Great Seal, her personal seal was not affixed on official acts. Rather a specific deputy seal, a "seal in the absence of the great," was created for the purpose. See G. Tessier, *Diplomatique royale française* (Paris, 1962), pp. 198–200; F. Olivier-Martin, *Etudes sur les régences* (Paris, 1931), p. 43.

13. On seal diffusion throughout society, see B. Bedos Rezak, "Les sceaux au temps de Philippe Auguste," *Actes du Colloque international du Centre National de la Recherche Scientifique: La France de Philippe Auguste: Le temps des mutations* (Paris, 1982), pp. 721–36; M. Pastoureau, *Les sceaux* (Brepols-Turnhout, 1981), pp. 25–29.

14. For other means of evaluating the influence of southern medieval women, see D. Herlihy, "Land, Family, and Women in Continental Europe, 701–1200," *Traditio* 18 (1962):89–113, an essay reprinted in *Women in Medieval Society*, ed. Susan Mosher Stuard (Philadelphia, 1976), pp. 13–45. A reassessment of his method and conclusions can be found in P. Toubert, *Les structures du Latium medi-éval*, 2 vols. (Rome, 1973), vol. 1, pp. 734, 766.

15. See a general appreciation of medieval women's condition, in R. Fossier, "La femme dans les sociétés occidentales," *Cahiers de civilisation médiévale* 20 (1977):93–104.

16. Women sealers may be segregated into two principal categories: noble and nonnoble. The first category, nobility, comprises three social subgroups: those of the aristocracy (highest nobility), of the castellans (high nobility), and of the knights (lesser nobility). The nonnoble category includes landowning families, defined primarily on the basis of rural holdings and activities, and the bourgeois, an urban population whose activities consisted of trade, administration, and craftsmanship.

17. One female bourgeois sealer is found in Flanders; see Demay, *Flandre*, n. 4623. For Norman bourgeois female sealers, see Demay, *Normandie*, nn. 1666, 1672, 1674, 1681, 1690, 1696, 1699, 1709, 1713; Douët d'Arcq, *Sceaux*, nn. 4119, 4120.

18. The present study based on a quantitative analysis of female seal usage may be compared with similar analyses of medieval charters relating to women. For a review of such works, see P. Schine Gold, *The Lady and the Virgin* (Chicago, 1985), pp. 116–44, and the author's own analysis and conclusions from a regional analysis of Anjou, in ibid., pp. 118–33, and tables on pp. 135, 137, 139. An overview of female sealing practice, more limited than women's involvement with charters, allows a sharp focus upon the degree of power women exercised in the control of property. None of the analyses reviewed and performed by Gold deals with the sealing of documents in any depth. Superficial references include: Gold, *The Lady and the Virgin*, p. 143, which refers to the fact that "a woman was sometimes excluded from the signing of a charter, even though she was an important participant in the action," and R. Hajdu, "The Position of Noblewomen in the *pays des coutumes*, 1100–1300," *Journal of Family History* 5 (1980):125, where the author presents husband and wife as two equals within the charter, "both participating in the various stages required for the legal transmission of property," while alluding to the fact that this did not automatically result in the affixation of the wife's seal.

19. On responsibilities of women within the seigneurie during this period, see Jo Ann McNamara and Suzanne Wemple's essay "The Power of Women Through the Family in Medieval Europe, 500–1100" in this book; eaedem, "Sanctity and Power: The Dual Pursuit of Medieval Women," *Becoming Visible: Women in European History*, ed. R. Bridenthal and C. Koonz (Boston, 1977), pp. 107–108.

20. Hajdu, "The Position of Noblewomen," p. 127, observed in Normandy a similar narrowing of the scope of the wife's activity; by the mid-thirteenth century, she appears only in charters that deal with land to which she had claims.

21. On the general influence of the patrilineal system on women's condition,

see K.-F. Werner, "Liens de parenté et noms de personne," *Famille et Parenté dans l'Occident médiéval* (Rome, 1977), pp. 14–18, 23–34, especially p. 27; see also below, n. 34. McNamara and Wemple's "The Power of Women Through the Family" and "Sanctity and Power" (pp. 110–13) ascribe the loss of power experienced by women from the thirteenth century onward to the bureaucratization and centralization of government resulting in the exclusion of women from public life.

22. Hajdu, "The Position of Noblewomen," table 1, p. 126, and p. 140, reached similar conclusions. Hajdu noted that Norman women of the knightly group participated in a higher proportion of acts than the aristocrats and castellans and deduced that "knights appear as a transitional stage between more eminent noble and *roturiers.*" These later women are known to have enjoyed more extensive rights than the nobility.

23. R. Howard Bloch, *Etymologies and Genealogies* (Chicago, 1983), p. 164.

24. The extensive economic and legal capacity of nonnoble women has been documented by McNamara and Wemple, "Sanctity and Power," pp. 114, 116, and by Hajdu, see above, nn. 18 and 22.

25. In 1173, e.g., Gertrude, daughter of Thierry d'Alsace, count of Flanders, is styled in her seal legend "sigillum Gertrudis Cameracensis castellane." She was married to Hugh d'Oisy, castellan of Cambrai; Demay, *Flandre*, n. 5507. On the fact that, upon marriage, an aristocratic woman severed ties with her family and became a member of another kindred, see G. Duby, "The Structure of Kinship and Nobility," in *The Chivalrous Society* (Berkeley, 1977), p. 140, and idem, *Medieval Marriage* (Baltimore, 1978), pp. 5–6.

26. In 1216, for instance, Aenor, wife of Robert, count of Dreux and Braine, seals "sigillum Aenor uxoris Roberti de Brenne"; Douët d'Arcq, *Sceaux*, n. 2048.

27. In 1185, for instance, Elisabeth, heiress of Renaud de Courtenay, seals "sigillum Elisabeth de Curtiniaco," though she is married to Peter of France, son of King Louis VI; Deurbergue, *Ile-de-France*, n. 47.

28. In 1313, e.g., S. Isabel de Guerolthezer, dame de Paci et de Nantueil; Douët d'Arcq, *Sceaux*, n. 3142.

29. In 1183, e.g., Adèle, daughter of Robert, count of Dreux, seals "sigillum Aelidis filie comitis Roberti," though she is married to Raoul, count of Soissons; Demay, *Picardie*, n. 36. See, however, her second seal (figure 6), Demay, *Flandre*, n. 303, in which she uses only her husband's title.

30. See examples in Eygun, *Poitou*, n. 209, 423.

31. See example in Douët d'Arcq, *Sceaux*, n. 1559.

32. Demay, *Flandre*, n. 221; Douët d'Arcq, *Sceaux*, n. 2169. See below, n. 36.

33. See examples in Douët d'Arcq, *Sceaux*, n. 2503, 3040; Demay, *Picardie*, nn. 138, 273, 463; Deurbergue, *Ile-de-France*, nn. 154, 191.

34. See above, nn. 21, 22, 24. In patrilineal structure, wives were integrated into the family and served as means of social, political, and economic exchange. Defined in relation to men, these women underwent a type of envelopment that absorbed their personal identity. In the case of lesser women, marriage involved a more equal partnership, hence their recognition on seals as individuals.

35. Demay, *Normandie*, n. 680 (1258, figure 10): "S' Riceut sa fame"; see more examples in ibid., nn. 683, 649, 680, 719, 754, etc.

36. In 1271, e.g., "sigillum Agnetis relicte Johannis Le Barbe"; Demay, *Normandie*, n. 652. The absence of the word *vidua* on noble seals may seem to contradict the fact that women of the higher nobility enjoyed a broader legal capacity precisely in widowhood; see Gold, *The Lady and the Virgin*, p. 130. The lack of reference to widowhood parallels the lack of any reference to marital status on noble seals. Among the numerous examples of nonnoble seals, both *vidua* and *uxoris* are common. Perhaps there was no need for a widowed noblewoman to signal a change in marital status on her seal when such status had virtually never been explicitly mentioned. On the other hand, among nonnobles, where the term *uxor* had been used on seals, *vidua* would be indicated where the legal situation of the sealer required.

37. See above nn. 21, 22, 24, 34.

38. On the beginnings of heraldry and its spread to women, see M. Pastoureau, *Les armoiries* (Turnhout, 1976), pp. 24–30. Howard Bloch, *Etymologies*, pp. 75–78.

39. In 1197, Mathilda, e.g., designated on her counterseal as "countess of Flanders," displays thereon her paternal coat; Demay, *Flandres*, n. 142 (figures 3, 4).

40. In 1198, e.g., Marie, designated on her counterseal as "daughter of the count of Champagne," displays thereon her husband's coat; Demay, *Artois*, n. 53.

41. See examples in Douët d'Arcq, *Sceaux*, nn. 2937, 1672, 1832, etc.

42. Douët d'Arcq, *Sceaux*, n. 625: "sigillum Johannis de Avesnis, filii Margarete comitisse Flandrie et Hanonie."

43. Jeanne de Châtillon, countess of Alençon, e.g., in 1271; Douët d'Arcq, *Sceaux*, n. 887.

44. B. Bedos Rezak, "L'apparition des armoiries sur les sceaux en Ile-de-France et en Picardie (v. 1130–1230)," *Actes du IIe colloque international d'héraldique: Les origines des armoiries* (Paris, 1983), pp. 31–32.

45. See above, nn. 19, 21, 22, 23, 24, 25, 34, and 37 and associated text.

46. For a display of the distaff, see Demay, *Picardie*, n. 625 (figure 11) and Demay, *Normandie*, n. 762, 792, 855, 873, 999; for vegetal motifs, see ibid., n. 798, 808, 896, 901, 975.

47. C. Frugoni, "L'iconographie de la femme au cours des Xe–XIIe siècles," *Cahiers de civilisation médiévale* 20 (1977):177–78; H. Kraus, "Eve and Mary: Conflicting Images of Medieval Women," *Feminism and Art History: Questioning the Litany*, ed. N. Broude and M. D. Garrard (New York, 1982), pp. 79–99.

48. Bedos, "Signes et insignes du pouvoir," pp. 47–62.

49. M. Corti, "Models and Antimodels in Medieval Culture," *New Literary History* 102 (1979):340, 343–44.

50. Seal of the Countess of Provence, in Blancard, *Sceaux et bulles*, p. 11, n. 12, and plate 5, n. 2; seal of Galberge (1256), ibid., p. 53, n. 13, and plate 27, n. 3.

51. Douët d'Arcq, *Sceaux*, n. 741 (figure 7).

52. Ibid., nn. 742–48.

53. See n. 11.

54. See examples in Douët d'Arcq, *Sceaux*, nn. 7252, 7253, 8441, 7300 (figure 12), 7321; Demay, *Flandre*, n. 6811.

55. G. Demay, *Le costume au Moyen Age d'après les sceaux* (1880; repr. Paris, 1978), pp. 91–108.

56. See examples in Douët d'Arcq, *Sceaux*, nn. 9391, 7119, 7150 (figure 13).

57. Gold, *The Lady and the Virgin*, pp. 70–71, 73, 74 and n. 86; M. Warner, *Alone of All Her Sex* (New York, 1983), pp. xxi, 77.

58. See examples in Demay, *Flandre*, nn. 142 (figure 3), 5503, 5485, 914, 1644; Douët d'Arcq, *Sceaux*, nn. 1907, 861, 903, 3578, 153 (figure 2), 3214 (figure 5).

59. Bedos, "Signes et insignes du pouvoir," pp. 48–51. On the multifarious symbolic implications of the fleur-de-lis, see R. A. Koch, "The Origin of the Fleur-de-lis and the *Lilium candidum* in Art," *Approaches to Nature in the Middle Ages,* ed. L. D. Robert (Binghamton, 1982), pp. 109–30.

60. A. Watson, *The Early Iconography of the Tree of Jesse* (London, 1934), pp. 3, 89–90, 142.

61. Howard Bloch, *Etymologies,* pp. 87–90.

62. J. Fowler, "On Medieval Representations of the Months and Seasons," *Archaelogia* 44 (1873):210, n. 39; J. C. Webster, *The Labors of the Months* (Princeton, 1938), pp. 102–103, 176; Heslop, "Seals," p. 306, n. 337.

63. See examples in Douët d'Arcq, *Sceaux*, nn. 2177 (figure 9), 2828.

64. See examples in Douët d'Arcq, *Sceaux*, n. 3770, 723, 2010, 3211; Demay, *Picardie,* nn. 249, 11, 308, 36, and Demay, *Flandre,* n. 303 (figure 6).

65. A. Lehmann, *Le rôle de la femme dans l'histoire de France au Moyen Age* (Paris, 1952), pp. 222–23.

66. O. Cadart-Ricard, "Le thème de l'oiseau dans les comparaisons et les dictons chez onze troubadours de Guillaume IX à Cerveri de Girone," *Cahiers de civilisation médiévale* 21(1978):215–17; P. Verdier, "Woman in Marginalia of Gothic Manuscripts and Related Works," in *The Role of Woman in the Middle Ages,* ed. R. T. Morewedge (Albany, 1975), p. 140; J.-O. Benoist, "La chasse au vol: Techniques de chasse et valeur symbolique de la volerie," *La chasse au Moyen Age* (Nice, 1980), p. 124.

67. Quoted in B. Rowland, *Birds with Human Souls* (Knoxville, 1978), p. 58.

68. J. Ferrante, *Woman as Image in Medieval Literature* (New York, 1975), pp. 12–13. Gold, *The Lady and the Virgin*, pp. 62–67, demonstrates how, by the mid-thirteenth century, images of the Virgin tend to shift from celebrations of queenly dignity and power (Romanesque period) to displays of feminine humility and modesty and of earthly motherhood.

69. Ferrante, *Woman as Image,* esp. synthesis, pp. 99–100.

70. Verdier, "Woman in Marginalia," esp. p. 123; L. Randall, *Images in the Margins of Gothic Manuscripts* (Berkeley, 1966), figs. 706, 708–710, in which mounted women attack a monk or knight with a distaff or lance.

71. P. Harris-Stäblein, "La sémiologie de la chasse dans la poésie de Bertrand de Born," *La chasse au Moyen Age,* pp. 447–49.

72. Ferrante, *Woman as Image,* p. 6; J. Courtès, *Lévi-Strauss et les contraintes de la pensée mythique* (Tours, 1973), pp. 49–50.

The Power of Women Through the Family in Medieval Europe, 500–1100

Jo Ann McNamara and Suzanne Wemple

The concept of public power was more highly developed under the Roman Empire than in any other society before modern times. The role of women in the civic life of the Empire was uncompromisingly clear: "Women are to be excluded from all civil and public offices; and therefore they cannot be judges or act as magistrates, nor can they undertake pleas nor intervene on behalf of others, nor act as procurators."[1] But the same state actively promoted the augmentation of the private rights of Roman women. Under the Republic, the family had held extensive power on every level and women lived in complete subjection to the *patria potestas* (paternal power), being classed as *alieni juris* (minors). Should their fathers die, they were placed under the control of a guardian. Should they marry, they were transferred at the end of a year to the control of their husbands.[2] But as the bureaucracy of the Empire extended its authority systematically over virtually every aspect of life, the power of the family and of the father was correspondingly weakened and the private rights of wives and children came to be protected by the laws of the state.[3] A woman's right to property was protected. The dowry she brought with her into marriage had to be returned intact if her husband repudiated her. The growing custom of marriage *sine manu* enabled a woman to remain under the power of her own family rather than being transferred to her husband's on the simple condition that she live for three days of every year in her father's house. She then had the right to own jointly with her father property over which her husband had no control.[4] After her father's death, the obligatory guardian or tutor was still given power over her, but his authority steadily weakened, and he became a figurehead.[5] By the beginning of the third century, Ulpian said that a woman had to have a tutor to act for her at law, to make contracts, to emancipate slaves, or to undertake civil business. But he added that a woman who had borne three children was no longer subject to this regulation.[6] Thus, the Roman woman, entirely powerless within the public structure, could exercise very considerable power in private life as a result of the wealth and property that she might accumulate by herself or through her family.

In the same period, the Germanic woman appears to have occupied an exceptionally important place in the rudimentary public life of the barbarian tribes. Tacitus, to whom we also owe the saga of the warrior queen, Boudicca, informed the Romans that girls of noble families would provide the best surety from the Germans if held as hostages. He continued: "They believe that there resides in women an element of holiness and prophecy, and so they do not scorn to ask their advice or lightly disregard their replies."[7] At a somewhat later period, Ammianus Marcellinus wrote of the barbarians: "A whole band of foreigners will be unable to cope with one of them in a fight if he calls in his wife, stronger than he by far and with flashing eyes; least of all when she swells her neck and gnashes her teeth and, poising her huge white arms, proceeds to rain punches mingled with kicks."[8]

Yet this awe-inspiring creature enjoyed very few private rights outside the authority of her family. She was barred from the inheritance of any property, and she came to her husband as the object of sale or capture. Whether these practices illustrate the great value that the Germans placed upon their women—Tacitus, for example, praised them for paying for their wives rather than taking a dowry from them[9]—or demonstrates the contempt in which they were held as individuals, it is clear that their economic position was weak indeed, since the bride price went to the woman's family, not to her.

By the fifth and sixth centuries, when the Germanic tribes were setting up kingdoms in the western parts of the decaying Roman empire, the economic position of the women had improved somewhat. Germanic kings, assisted by the growing strength of the *comitatus* (personal followers of the ruler), were gradually weakening the power of the kindred. As the smaller family group began to replace the tribe as the basic social unit, the incapacity of women to inherit property began to disappear along with the old customs of marriage by sale and capture. This process was probably hastened by the influence of the opposing precepts of Roman law and Christianity.

With her position within the family thus enhanced, a woman of that age could expect to share actively in the social role of her family. The Germans drew no distinction between private and public power, or between public and private rights. As a result, women whose families were economically powerful, or who held extensive property in their own names, occupied the public sphere as well as the private. In this investigation of the economic and political power of women, we shall rely heavily on the Germanic codes to chart the changes that occurred in the early Middle Ages. Since most of the aristocratic families who exercised power at that time were Germanic, Roman law will figure only insofar as its influence penetrated those codes.

The Germanic tribes did not impose their own laws uniformly upon the areas they occupied. Instead of territoriality of law, they followed the principle of personality of law, which meant in practical terms that individuals were allowed to live under the law of their ancestors.[10] In areas close to the Mediterranean, where there was a population of Roman descent, Roman law continued to be observed in a simplified codification mixed with Germanic customs. In the Frankish kingdom the population was heterogeneous. But as more and more areas that had never been Romanized were added to the kingdom, Germanic customs came to predominate. In turn, to be sure, these codes were somewhat influenced by Roman precepts as they became the foundation of the feudal customs that were to prevail in the medieval West from the late ninth century on.

Studies of early medieval property and family law, a field that owes much to German scholarship, provide us with valuable information on the extensive area of bride price, marriage settlements, widows' rights, and inheritance. The importance of women's legal position was recognized by the Jean Bodin Society, which devoted two conferences in 1956 and 1957 to women throughout the world from ancient times to the present.[11] Sometimes, however, the laws create problems for scholars. The carefully devised conditions for marriage and its economic arrangements that we find in the codes date from a period when the Germanic tribes were already partially Romanized and Christianized. In actual deeds of settlement and wills and in the accounts of events recorded in chronicles, a more chaotic reality is apparent. Customs barely noticed in the codes died out only gradually. Practices actively condemned by the church continued unabated for some centuries.

Although no trace of the old marriage by capture appears even in the earliest codes, the blood-stained pages of Gregory of Tours, a historian of the late sixth century, are all too full of marriages made on the battlefield.[12] Again and again, the conquering king espouses the widow or daughter of his defeated rival, apparently as part of the loot. But Gregory's care in distinguishing between wives and concubines leaves us in no doubt that these were marriages indeed.

While the codes entirely ignore the possibility of marriage by capture, they do show remnants of the practice of purchasing a bride from her kindred. The German historians of the Nazi period argued in vain that their ancestors never undertook such barbarous arrangements:[13] the careful work of Noel Senn has isolated the traces of the old purchase price (*pretium uxoris, puellae,* or *nuptialis*) in the codes and traced the slow process by which the sale of the bride was converted to sale of the family's rights over her, to a token payment balanced by a growing custom of giving money to the bride herself.[14]

The woman continued to be an object of value for which her suitor was expected to pay a price, but the price itself moved through a series of steps into the hands of the woman rather than those of her family. In the early Germanic kingdoms, a suitor haggled no longer over the price the family would get for the girl herself but over the price to be paid for her *mundium,* the power the father or guardian held over her, which passed to the husband at the time of the marriage.[15] This sum gradually became a symbolic payment, and the bride received as her own an increasingly large portion of the bride gift (*wittemon, meta,* or *dos*) contributed by the bridegroom. For example, Salic law required that the groom pay the bride's father or guardian only the token sum of a gold solidus and one denarius.[16] But if the groom had not already turned a bridegift over to the bride, with written guarantees, she was to receive, on her husband's death, twenty-five or sixty-two and a half solidi, depending on her status, under Salic law and fifty solidi under Ripuarian law.[17] The Burgundian code, issued in the early sixth century, shows a transitional stage, with the bride receiving only a third of the bridegift and the rest going to her father or nearest relative.[18] A woman was allowed to keep the entire bridegift only if she married for a third time.[19] The Visigothic,[20] Bavarian,[21] and Alemannic[22] codes awarded the whole bridegift to the bride. In the earliest version of the Lombard code, issued by Rothari (636–652), the father retained the bridegift, but in the later version, revised by Liutprand (712–744), the bridegift was turned over to the bride and the relatives were given only a token indemnity.[23] The Saxons, who remained farthest outside the Roman sphere of influence, with their customs being codified only under Charlemagne (768–814), continued to award a substantial sum, three hundred solidi, to the bride's father.[24] It was, however, conceded that the wife could keep the bridegift she was given in movable goods.[25] In England, the practice of giving the parents or the guardian a payment was abolished by Cnut (1016–1035), who ruled: "No woman or maiden shall ever be forced to marry a man whom she dislikes, nor shall she ever be given for money unless the suitor wishes to give something of his own free will."[26]

Although the codes usually expressed the amount of the bridegift in money, the formulas and deeds show that, most frequently, real property was turned over to the wife as her bridegift.[27] For example, according to a marriage settlement drawn up in the reign of Cnut, a certain Godwin, when he wooed Brihtric's daughter, "gave her a pound of gold to induce her to accept his suit and he granted her the estate at Street and whatever belongs to it, and 150 acres at Burmash and also 30 oxen and 20 cows and 10 horses and 10 slaves."[28] Deeds frequently gave her unrestricted ownership of this property, although some codes and donations stipulated that she had only the usufruct of her bridegift, which, upon death, would be passed to her children or revert back to her husband's heirs if she should have no children.[29]

In addition to her bridegift, a woman received a *morgengabe,* or morning gift, after the consummation of her marriage. That settlement usually consisted of real property, and customs varied as to whether she held the usufruct or had outright possession of the gift.[30] Through the bridegift and the morning gift, women were able to acquire impressive personal domains and concomitant economic and political power. Probably for that reason, in periods of fairly effective royal power—at the beginning and again at the end of the period we are discussing—efforts were made to restrict their extent. The Lombard code tried to limit the amount of the property that passed into the hands of women by stipulating that the morning gift would not exceed a quarter of the husband's patrimony. Nobles were forbidden to give more than 300 solidi of gold, though an exception was made for judges who could give up to 400 solidi.[31]

When the Merovingian prince, Chilperic I (561–584), married Galswintha in 556–557, he gave her the cities of Limoges, Bordeaux, Cahors, Bearn, and Bigorre as a morning gift. After the murder of Galswintha, that property did not revert to her husband but went to her sister, Brunhilda, wife of Sigibert, Chilperic's brother.[32]

Although, according to Germanic customs, a father was not obliged to give a dowry to his daughter, we know that many doting parents did provide their daughters with generous dowries, perhaps imitating the Roman practice. Riguntha, the daughter of Chilperic and Fredegunda, his third wife, was sent off to her Visigothic fiance with so astounding a quantity of goods that the Frankish nobles objected, fearing that the royal fisc had been stripped to outfit her. This was in fact the case, but the girl's mother claimed that she had provided for the girl out of the property she had amassed as a result of her husband's generosity.[33] Such resources should have meant that a Merovingian queen could well afford to support her own retainers and that a man in her service could not be harmed with impunity, since she had the power to take reprisals. However, it required a strong hand and constant vigilance to retain wealth in those times. Riguntha's fortune never reached Spain. The girl was robbed repeatedly along the road by members of her diminishing entourage, the last of whom finally abandoned her in Toulouse with nothing left. All the formidable rage of her mother was ineffectual in recouping the losses.

This tale acquires additional interest in light of the fact that Fredegunda had nothing of her own when she married Chilperic. All her wealth and power came to her through her marriage. Nor was she unusual among the wives of the Merovingian kings. Among the several wives of Chilperic's brother, Charibert, were two sisters whom he discovered in the service of yet another wife. One of these, "who wore the robe of a nun," attempted to discourage his advances by taking him to see her father, a weaver, at his work. This did nothing to kill his appetite, and the amorous king, who had already married a shepherd girl, added the sisters to his harem. The shepherd's daughter, incidentally, was in possession of vast treasures at his death, though many of them were stolen from her and she came to a sorrowful end in a convent.[34]

Misalliances on such a scale are astonishing today, and the motivations of those early kings in choosing their marriage partners are obscure. King Sigibert is said to have married the Visigothic princess, Brunhilda, because he "saw that his brothers were taking wives unworthy of them, and to their disgrace, were actually marrying slave women."[35] But when a bishop taunted Chilperic with this fact, claiming that the king's sons "could not inherit the kingdom because their mother had been taken to the king's bed from among the slaves of Magnachar," Gregory states that the bishop spoke, "not knowing that the families of the wives are now disregarded and they are called the sons of a king who have been begotten by a king."[36] The lack of a noble origin does not, in this period, appear to have been a substantial barrier to the unlimited exercise of power by women. The history of the Frankish monarchy in the late sixth century is dominated by the ferocious rivalry between Fredegunda, the former slave, and Brunhilda, the Visigothic princess. Their titanic struggle stemmed originally from Brunhilda's sense of family—she was determined to avenge the murder of her sister Galswintha—but the progress of the contest suggests that the power of women in this period was derived from their own personal force rather than from legal protection or from the position of their family.

Only in the tenth century, when the family had entered its age of glory, does the bloodline become a significant factor in determining the position of women. When Hugh Capet advanced his claim to the throne of France against the Carolingian claimant, Charles of Lorraine, his supporters argued that Charles should be disqualified because he had married beneath his station, the daughter of a mere knight. "How could the powerful duke suffer that a woman, coming from the family of one of his vassals, should become queen and rule over him? How could he walk behind one whose equals and, even whose superiors, bend the knee before him?" On the other side, Hugh's wife was the daughter of the Empress Adelaide by her first marriage, and the powerful hand of her mother was guiding her husband's party.[37]

A woman's opportunities to achieve a position of power through marriage were increasingly enhanced as time went on if she controlled inherited property of her own. In the early period, when royal power was still relatively strong in the Germanic kingdoms, women were generally discriminated against in favor of their brothers. In contrast to Roman law, which provided equal rights of succession to the family's property by daughters and sons, the general principle upheld by the Burgundian, Alemannic, Bavarian, and Ripuarian codes was that daughters could inherit only if there were no sons.[38] Lombard law made similar provision, although it enabled fathers to give a third of their property to their daughters.[39] Only the most Romanized of the Germanic codes, the Visigothic law,[40] allowed equal rights of succession to daughters. As Ganshof has demonstrated, the most restrictive laws were those that prevailed in the least Romanized areas of the Germanic lands.[41] The Thuringian code excluded women altogether from the inheritance of immovable property,[42] and the Saxon code conceded that daughters could succeed only if there were no uncles or brothers on the father's side.[43]

As can be seen from the evolution of the Salic Law, the tendency in the sixth and seventh centuries was to relax the inheritance laws designed to keep property intact for the benefit of sons. The most ancient version of the code, issued in the late fifth century, excluded women completely from the inheritance of Salic land.[44] In the late sixth and seventh centuries, the Salic law was somewhat mitigated to allow women to inherit land which had not come to their parents as part of the patrimony. Chilperic admitted women even to the inheritance of Salic land, provided that they had no brothers. Lands acquired by means other than inheritance were equally divided between sons and daughters.[45] In any case, as we have seen, a forceful woman occupying a favorable position was not generally vulnerable to these legal restrictions. Merovingian women, like their men, took what power they could and held it as long as they were not forcibly dispossessed.

Deeds show that the restrictions on inherited Salic land were frequently disregarded, and indeed even resented, by the fathers. In one deed of the late eighth century, a father complained against the "impious custom" which discriminated between his children and which ran contrary to their equality before God and the love he felt for them.[46] Lombard law, while holding to the principle that daughters could succeed only where there were no sons, allowed fathers to leave one-third of their property to their daughters.[47] In England, Alfred the Great (871–899) recognized the intentions of his grandfather in excluding women from the inheritance of his family's land. In his own testament, however, he defended the equal rights of his own daughters. He respected the earlier custom only in his stipulation that if the male heirs wished to keep the land intact they could purchase the portion of land inherited by the females.[48]

By the mid-eighth century, when the Carolingians succeeded to the Frankish throne and began to dominate the West, the restrictive Germanic customs of marriage by purchase and female incapacity to inherit immovables were thus nearly obliterated. The private rights of women to the control of property had been established, giving them, as daughters, sisters, mothers, and wives, a position of economic equality within the family. As we shall see, this condition held inherent difficulties for the family itself, difficulties Charlemagne himself may have perceived—he apparently solved the potential problems of divided inheritances by preventing the marriage of any of his daughters, turning a blind eye to their more informal sexual alliances. Few families, however, followed his example. Most women continued to marry, bringing property of their own with them to strengthen their claims to power within the household they were entering. For the aristocracy, in an age when private power was almost synonymous with public power, this meant that there would be few restrictions on the power of women in any sphere of activity.

In theory, the married woman in Carolingian times did no more than adopt the role that has always been regarded as proper to women. Carolingian queens were housewives. But the houses they kept were the imperial domain itself. In the *Capitulare de villis,* Charlemagne delegated extensive authority to the queen for the regulation of the domestic concerns of the empire and the direction of the royal servants. The breadth of this power is apparent in the fact that persons bearing the humble domestic titles of chamberlain, butler, and steward, for example, were in reality the ministers of the Carolingian state. The emperor was therefore giving his wife very great power indeed when he ordered: "We wish that anything ordered by us or by the queen to one of our judges, or anything ordered by the ministers, seneschals or cupbearer . . . be carried out to the last word. . . . And if someone, through negligence fails to do this, he must abstain from drink . . . until such time that he gains admission to our presence or that of the queen and asks to be absolved."[49]

Two generations after Charlemagne, describing the administration of the palace, Hincmar of Rheims gave the queen, with the assistance of the chamberlain, charge of the royal treasury, arguing that the king, who had to concern himself with the ordering of the entire kingdom, should not be burdened with such domestic trifles.[50] When, under Charlemagne's successors, domestic revolt and armed rivalry once more disturbed Europe, the housewifely role became even more extensive. Like any wife on the American frontier, a woman was expected to defend her home if her husband was absent. It is therefore worthy of only a passing mention by the chroniclers that the wives, mothers, and sisters of the Carolingian kings and their vassals were frequently engaged in holding cities under siege or directing military operations against troublesome subordinates when their lords were engaged elsewhere.

The importance of the queen's role was recognized by the Carolingians and their successors through their practice of having their queens anointed and crowned, to make them sharers in the rather mystical aspects of the king's power. Along with Pepin, the first Carolingian monarch, whose own claims needed all the reinforcement that could be devised, his wife, Queen Bertha, was formally crowned and continued to exercise considerable political power after his death.[51] Praise of the queen was also incorporated into the *Laudes* (hymns of praise), which comprised part of the royal liturgy.[52] The importance of the queen's position in the early medieval empire was recognized by contemporaries not only in the use of such lofty titles as *consors regis* (royal consort), but by the complaints of some writers against queens who were not regarded as capable of the satisfactory performance of their duties. Agobard of Lyons, for example, in his writings against Judith of Bavaria, the wife of Louis the Pious (814–840), complained that in her the emperor did not have a wife "who can be to him a help in administering the palace and the realm."[53]

As a matter of course, these women were also expected to raise their children and protect their heritage when necessary. Here a complication of the greatest magnitude arose. The protecting mother was all too often found to be simultaneously acting the wicked stepmother. In this age, when primogeniture had yet to be introduced, royal patrimonies, and others, were already sufficiently disturbed by the practice of making provision for all sons. But to this, Carolingian conditions commonly added the problem of providing for children of a second marriage. The sons of the first wife of Louis the Pious were sufficiently quarrelsome to do untold damage to the fabric of the empire. But even the hope of a peaceful succession secured by the division of the empire was destroyed by the determination of his second wife, Judith of Bavaria, to secure a favorable place for her own son, the future Charles the Bald.[54] In England, an even more decisive role in the future of the kingdom was played by Elfreda, the mother of Ethelred the Unready (978–1016), who secured the crown for her son by the murder of his half-brother, Edward the Martyr.[55] Similarly, the great German empire of Otto the Great (936–973) came close to foundering on the rock of his second wife's ambition. Here, too, the elder son was driven to rebellion, though, fortunately for all, he met an early death, making place for Adelaide's child, Otto II.[56]

But the quarrels and ambitions of queens, however interesting, are not the most important aspect of the growing power of women in the ninth and tenth centuries. As the great empire of Charlemagne began to lose its cohesion, power slipped from the hands of the monarchs and was seized by the great nobles of the realm. In the development of this "first feudal age," the family entered its age of glory. The key to power in this period was control of landed property, whether through private ownership or through control of royal property received as a fief. Initially, the fief was designed to equip a man for knightly service and was regarded as indivisible. But in 870, Charles the Bald was obligated to issue the Capitulary of Quierzy, acknowledging the heritability of fiefs and therefore subjecting them to the inheritance laws that governed private property.[57] The subsequent development of franc-parage provided for the possibility of dividing the income from a fief among the heirs, although rights over the fief as such remained with the eldest son. When a family held several fiefs, it was customary to divide them among younger sons and daughters. As the power of the Frankish monarchy continued to disintegrate, families developed the custom of willing fiefs to daughters when there were no sons to inherit them.[58]

In addition to this growing freedom in disposing of royal fiefs, the aristocratic families of the ninth and tenth centuries were expanding their control of allodial—freehold—land by force and purchase and through land clearance. There were no serious restrictions on the family's power to distribute such land as it saw fit. Few families were inclined to exclude their daughters from the capacity to inherit allodial land. When such land came into the hands of a woman, it remained her property and did not pass to her husband or her husband's family unless she willed it to do so. It was common for a wife to leave the management of her property to her husband, although he could not alienate it, as is attested by joint signatures on deeds of this type. Forceful women, however, like Matilda of Tuscany in the eleventh century, insisted on excluding their husbands from the management of their property and taking it into their own control.

The most dramatic instance of the movement of a woman's inheritance is the case of Eleanor of Aquitaine. Though Eleanor lived in the twelfth century, her situation conforms with the practices of the tenth and eleventh centuries. When she married the King of France, her great duchy nearly doubled the extent of that monarchy. But when she divorced him and married the King of England, the duchy went with her. When she quarreled with her second husband, she had no hesitation in returning to

Aquitaine as an independent ruler and designating her second, and favorite, son as her heir rather than her elder son, for whom the crown of England had been destined. The career of Eleanor affected the highest seats of power in the Middle Ages. That similar powers were exercised by women of less magnificence is becoming increasingly clear as modern social histories, particularly in England, France and Belgium, broaden the trails blazed by the great Marc Bloch. Out of this growing volume of work, based on the patient examination of local records, the living outlines of medieval society in such areas as the Maconnaise, Bavaria, and Catalonia emerge. Though much remains to be learned, a recent attempt at a synthesis has been made by Georges Duby,[59] and Doris Stenton has begun to apply the findings to the history of women.[60] From collections of English records we have many examples of women able to dispose freely of their property, and in at least one case, in the late tenth century, to disinherit a son in favor of a more distant female relative.[61]

Through their control of the land, lords of various degrees came to control most of the regalian rights formerly held by the kings. They administered justice, made laws, coined money, raised armies and carried on all the normal responsibilities of government. Like Charlemagne's queen, their female partners shared in such responsibilities. However, when a woman inherited her own estate, she inherited the political power that went with it, and frequently exercised it in her own right. To this, she might add independent exercise of her husband's power when she became a widow. Such activities of women were not accepted without complaint. An assembly of bishops at Nantes in 895 demonstrated that they were one at heart with their Roman ancestors when they proclaimed:

> It is astounding that certain women, against both divine and human law, with bare-faced impudence, act in general pleas and with abandon exhibit a burning passion for public meetings, and they disrupt, rather than assist, the business of the kingdom and the good of the commonweal. It is indecent and reprehensible, even among barbarians, for women to discuss the cases of men. Those who should be discussing their woolen work and weaving with the residents of the women's quarters, should not usurp the authority of senators in public meetings just as if they were residents of the court.[62]

But the indignation of the bishops was quite without effect, for the public power at the behest of the Roman Empire was gone. Within a century, the successors of the censorious bishops had to bear the humiliation of women's inheriting the advocacies even of churches.[63] For a period in the tenth century the power of the papacy itself was under the control of the noble Roman ladies Theodora and her daughter Marozia, who bore the proud title "senatrix."[64]

If the capacity to inherit property gave extensive power to women, the freedom to leave the same property wherever they liked put the seal on that power. When a woman married and had children she had to be counted as a member of at least two families and it was by no means inevitable that she would identify primarily with that of her husband. As a wife or as a widow, she could administer her power to further projects that were conceived mutually with her husband. But she might as easily pursue her own ends or those of her original family.

Ethelfleda, the Lady of the Mercians, was the widow of the king of Mercia and the daughter of Alfred the Great of Wessex (871–899) and sister of Edward the Elder. Even during the lifetime of her ailing husband, she took over the active role of governing Mercia and continued in that capacity for years after his death. After a life of campaigning against invading Danes, Irish, and Norwegians to defend her frontiers, Ethelfleda deliberately excluded from succession to the kingdom of Mercia her daughter (whom she had prevented from marrying with that purpose in mind) and brought it into union with her brother's kingdom of Wessex.[65] As regent for her son, the future Henry IV (1056–1106), Agnes of Poitou earned the epithet "the tears of Germany" because she used her power to further policies objectionable to the German nobility.[66] Perhaps it was his awareness of such possibilities that determined Otto II (973–983) to entrust the regency of Germany, during his absences, neither to his Italian mother nor to his Greek wife, both of whom proved to be capable regents after his death, but to his German sister, Matilda, abbess of Quedlinburg.[67]

Archibald Lewis has provided many examples of the power of women as heads of families in southern France in the ninth to the eleventh century. Indeed Lewis believes that this conglomeration of power in the hands of women was the major cause of the breakdown of the family system in the tenth-century Languedoc.[68] Wherever we look during this period, we find no really effective barriers to the capacity of women to exercise power. They appear as military leaders, judges, castellans, controllers of property.[69] Though barred from the priesthood, they even exercised vast power over the church as a result of their family positions.

Before the church required celibacy of its ministers, the wives of priests took ecclesiastical property into their own hands, as is shown by the complaints registered by Atto, Bishop of Vercelli, in the second quarter of the tenth century.[70] In addition, the power of secular women to donate or withhold property and their power to appoint candidates to church offices through exercise of their magisterial powers was an integral part of their general position. In this way, the Roman lady Marozia came to exercise control over the papacy itself for a period in the early tenth century. The proprietary rights of the family of Theophylactus and their great political influence passed first into the hands of Theodora, his wife. Their daughter, Marozia, became mistress of one pope and mother of another, leader of the famous pornocracy which Liutprand of Cremona attacked so violently. The same lady, at one point, nearly succeeded in uniting all of northern Italy under her power only to be thwarted by the anger of one of her sons, who feared the loss of his entire inheritance.[71]

On the other side, the reformed church of the eleventh century owed an incalculable debt to the powerful Countess of Tuscany, Beatrice, and her daughter, Matilda. It was in Matilda's castle of Canossa that the great drama of Pope Gregory's subjection of the Emperor Henry IV was played out. During that pope's lifetime and for decades after his death, it was the armies of Matilda that defended the liberated church in Italy. And when she died, she willed her great Tuscan inheritance to the church to form the bulwark of the papal state.[72]

These extensive powers exercised by women were, as we have seen, largely derived from the rather irregular powers held by the great families of the age. In the eleventh century, throughout Europe, the process of reconstituting some of the institutions of public power was begun, a process that accelerated throughout the twelfth century. Vogelsang,[73] studying the German Empire, called the tenth century the "golden age" of the *consortium regni*. He demonstrated that by the eleventh century the Empire had largely ceased to be governed on a personal basis and, as a result, the empress's power was severely diminished. The same process became apparent in France and England in the next century. In the church, the imposition of celibacy and the prohibition of lay investiture restricted the power of the family, and therefore of women, in the late eleventh century. The resumption of some control of the fief system by contemporary princes weakened their position in the feudal system. In 1037, Konrad II issued the *Constitutio de feudis,* excluding women from the inheritance of fiefs. Although there was a perceptible decrease in the influence and power of women in Germany after this date, Herlihy argued that the Constitution was applied with indifferent success.[74] Other historians point out that only after 1156, when Barbarossa invested Henry of Babenberg and his wife with the Duchy of Austria and granted that in Austria sons and daughters could succeed equally after that date, were women occasionally admitted to the inheritance of fiefs in other areas of Germany.[75] In France, where the consolidation of royal power was far more gradual and the restoration of royal control of fiefs far more difficult, women were never categorically excluded from their inheritance. If they were lucky enough not to have brothers, they could continue to inherit great wealth and play a correspondingly important role.[76] In England, William the Conqueror, following Norman custom, was content to control the succession of fiefs by controlling the marriage of their heirs, both male and female.[77]

Meanwhile, the families themselves had become alarmed at the effects of their inheritance practices. Duby has described their widespread efforts to halt the erosion of estates through split inheritances and thereby protect the position of the family in this period of renewed royal power.[78] As the idea of primogeniture and the indivisibility of the patrimony was again entrenched, the daughters of the nobility suffered a severe diminution of their rights. A daughter's claim on the inheritance gradually gave way to the dowry provided by her family at the time of her marriage, the *maritagium*. Throughout western Europe, by the twelfth century, we find that the dowry was becoming considered a sufficient settlement for a married woman. In some areas, even that right was restricted or simply not recognized. In Normandy, where women's rights were quite restricted, a woman could receive only up to a third of the total patrimony as dowry, and her parents had the right to exclude her altogether if they wished to do so.[79]

During the late tenth and eleventh centuries, the bridegift, given by the husband, came to be transformed into the dower. The bridegift, as we saw it in its earlier form, whether given as usufruct, which had to be passed on to the children after the wife's death, or as property, which the wife owned outright and could alienate or leave to whomever she wished, was turned over to her on her wedding day and usually represented a specific piece of land.[80] But in the tenth and eleventh centuries, fewer deeds gave the wife outright ownership, and even the usufruct was generally restricted to the use of the husband and wife jointly, not to the wife exclusively. Instead of specifying a given piece of property, some deeds spoke only of a fraction of the income derived from the husband's patrimony. That type of agreement was replaced in the twelfth century by the dower arrangement, which gave a widow the usufruct of a portion, usually one-third, of her husband's patrimony. She was thus provided for in case of her husband's decease but her economic independence during his lifetime, and, to some extent, after his death, had vanished.[81]

With the power of their women thus severely reduced, the aristocratic family was in better condition to face the ensuing period of struggle with the resurgent monarchies—a struggle that continued well into modern times. But by the twelfth century, public power was gradually being recaptured from the great aristocratic families by kings and princes. Institutions outside the household were being created to administer public affairs. The success of the aristocracy as a class in adjusting itself to this broad political change was accomplished largely at the expense of the aristocratic women. As the families were resisting princely encroachment upon their rights by insisting upon the indivisibility of the patrimony, the economic rights of women were restricted. Concurrently, as rulers slowly developed an impersonal machinery for government, queens and empresses, as well as ladies on a somewhat more modest level, were excluded from public life. This meant that the heads of the great families— both men and women—were losing the power they had derived from the private power of the family. But while it was possible for aristocratic men to retain the same power by acting as the administrators of the new institutions, such positions were not open to noble women. Their activities were confined to the role of housekeeper, a role whose boundaries were shrinking. With the return of public power and the corresponding loss of family power, women were moving back to the conditions that had existed under the Roman Empire.

Notes

"The Power of Women Through the Family in Medieval Europe, 500–1100," originally appeared in *Feminist Studies* 1 (1973):126–41 and is reproduced here, in somewhat altered form, from Mary S. Hartman and Lois Banner, eds., *Clio's Consciousness Raised: New Perspectives on the History of Women* (New York: Harper and Row, 1974), © 1974 Harper and Row. It is reprinted by permission of *Feminist Studies*.

1. Digest, 50, 17, 2. *Corpus Iuris Civilis*, ed. Georgius Gebaver (Göttingen, 1776), p. 1137.
2. Robert Villiers, "Le statut de la femme à Rome jusqu'à la fin de la République," Société Jean Bodin, *Recueils* 11 (1959):179.
3. Jean Gaudemet, "Le statut de la femme dans l'empire romaine," Société Jean Bodin, *Recueils* 11 (1959):191.
4. Villiers, "Le statut," p. 187.
5. Gaudemet, "Le statut."
6. Ulpian, Regula IX, *Corpus Iuris Civilis*, ed. Galisset (Paris, 1853), p. 6.
7. Tacitus, *Germania*, trans. H. Mattingly, vol. 8 (Harmondsworth, 1960), p. 107.
8. Ammianus Marcellinus, *History* 15:12, ed. J. C. Rolfe, vol. 1 (Cambridge, Mass., 1935), p. 195.
9. Tacitus, *Germania*, pp. 18, 115.
10. L. Stouff, "Etude sur le principe de la personnalité des lois depuis les invasions barbares jusqu'au XIIᵉ siècle," *Revue bourguignonne de l'Enseignement supérieur* 4: 2 (1894); F. L. Ganshof, "L'étranger dans la monarchie franque," Société Jean Bodin, *Recueils* 10 (1958):19–20.
11. "La femme," Société Jean Bodin, *Recueils* 11–12 (1959–62).
12. Gregory of Tours, *History of the Franks*, ed. E. Brehaut (New York, 1969).
13. Although the feminist movement of the Weimar Republic was eradicated under the National Socialists, supporters of that regime retained an interest in this

aspect of women's studies. One extremist went so far as to say that belief in such a practice was *rassfeindlich,* inimical to the race: Gerda Merschberger, *Die Rechtsstellung der germanischen Frau* (Leipzig, 1937), p. 47.

14. Noel Senn, *Le contrat de vente de la femme en droit matrimonial germanique* (Portentruy, 1946).

15. Louis-Maurice-André Cornuey, "Le régime de la 'dos' aux époques mérovingienne et carolingienne" (Thèse, Univ. d'Alger, 1929).

16. *Formulae Salicae Merkelianae,* ed. K. Zeumer, no. 15. *Monumenta Germanicae Historica* (hereinafter cited as *MGH*), *Legum sectio V: Formulae,* p. 247, "idcirco ego in Dei nomine ille, filius illius, puellam ingenuam nomine illa, filiam illius, per solidum et denarium secundum legem Salicam." See also *Formulae Salicae Bignonianae,* no. 6, p. 230 and *Formulae Salicae Lindenbrogianae,* no. 7, p. 271.

17. *Capitula Legi Salicae addita, Pactus Legis Salicae,* 100, 1–2; *MGH Legum sectio I, Legum nationum germanicarum* IV, I, pp. 256–57 (henceforth cited as *MGH, Leg. nat. germ.*). *Lex Ribuaria,* 41 (37), 2; *MGH Leg. nat. germ.* III, II, p. 95.

18. *Leges Burgundiorum,* 86, 2; *MGH Leg. nat. germ.* II, I, p. 108. See also no. 66, 1–3, pp. 94–95.

19. *Leg. Burg.* 69, 2 *MGH Leg. nat. germ.* II, I, p. 96. As to a woman's right when she married a second time, see 69, 1, p. 95, and F. L. Ganshof, "La femme dans la monarchie franque," Société Jean Bodin, *Recueils* 12 (1962):21, n. 47.

20. *Lex Visigothorum* III, 1, 6; ed. K. Zeumer, *MGH Leg. nat. germ.* I, p. 130.

21. *Lex Baiuvariorum,* 8, 14. *MGH Leg. nat. germ.* V, II, p. 359.

22. *Leges Alemanorum,* 54, 1, *MGH Leg. nat. germ.* V, I, p. 112.

23. Rothari, 215; Liutprand, 103; ed. Franz Beyerle, *Die Gesetze der Langobarde* (Weimar, 1947), pp. 84 and 268.

24. *Leges Saxonum,* 40, ed. von Richthofen, *MGH Leg. nat. germ.* V, pp. 60–70; ed. Claudius von Schwerin, *Leges Saxonum und Lex Thuringorum, MGH, Fontes iuris germanici antiqui in usum scholarum* (Hanover, 1918), pp. 27–28; ed. Karl A. Eckhardt, *Germanenrechte* II: *Die Gesetze des Karolinger-Reiches* III (Weimar, 1934), p. 40.

25. *Leges Saxonum* 47, ed. von Richthofen, pp. 73–74; ed. von Schwerin, pp. 29–30; ed. Eckhardt, p. 26.

26. II Cnut 76, A. J. Robertson, *The Laws of the Kings of England from Edmund to Henry I* (Cambridge, 1925), p. 216.

27. According to Cornuey, *Régime de la dos,* p. 46, dowry in the fifth century was usually in the form of movable goods, but in the sixth, it was more commonly given as real property.

28. A. J. Robertson, ed., *Anglo-Saxon Charters* (Cambridge, 1939), pp. 150–51.

29. Cornuey, *Régime de la dos,* p. 53ff.

30. Ibid., pp. 127–31.

31. *Liuprandi Leges,* p. 89, ed. Beyerle, p. 254.

32. Gregory of Tours, *History of the Franks,* pp. 9, 20.

33. Ibid., pp. 6, 45.

34. Ibid., pp. 4, 26.

35. Ibid., pp. 4, 27.

36. Ibid., pp. 5, 20.

37. Richer, *Histoire de France* 4, ed. R. Latouche (Paris, 1936), pp. 9–11.

38. See Biondo Biondi, *Il diritto romano christiano* III (Milan, 1954), pp. 339–41; *Leges Burg.*, 14, 1–2, MGH, *Leg. nat. germ.* II, I, p. 52; *Leges alam.*, 55 MGH *Leg. nat. germ.*, V, 1, pp. 114–15; *Lex Bai.*, 15, 9–10, MGH *Leg. nat. germ.* V, II, pp. 428–29; *Lex Rib.*, 57–(56), 4, MGH *Leg. nat. germ.* III, 11, p. 105.

39. *Liutprandi Leges*, 1 and 65, ed. Beyerle, *Gesetze der Langobarden*, pp. 170, 230.

40. *Lex Vis.* IV, 3, De successionibus, 1, Antiqua; MGH *Leg. nat. germ.* I, p. 174.

41. Ganshof, "La femme dans la monarchie franque," pp. 33–40.

42. *Lex Thur.*, 26–27, ed. von Schwerin, p. 60; ed. Eckhardt, p. 38.

43. *Lex Saxonum*, 41, 44, 46, ed. von Richthofen, pp. 71–72; ed. von Schwerin, pp. 28–29.

44. *Pactus Legis Salicae*, De alodis 6, ed. K. A. Eckhardt, II, 1: 65 *Titel-Text* (Göttingen, 1955) also in MGH *Leg. nat. germ.* IV, I, p. 222. Text A is most ancient, dating to 507–511, Chlodovech's reign; on this Eckhart, *Pactus Legis Salicae*, vol. 1 (Göttingen, 1954), p. 207.

45. *Capitulare IV ad Legem Salicam*, p. 108; MGH *Leg. nat. germ.* IV, I, p. 262.

46. *Marculfi formularum II*, 12, ed. Zeumer, MGH *Form.*, p. 83: see also *Cartae senonicae* (dated 768–75), 45, ed. Zeumer, ibid., p. 205, and the testament of Burgundofara, dated 632, ed. B. Mayer, "Das Testament der Burgondofara," *Mitteilungen des Instituts für Oesterreichische Geschichtsforschung, Ergänzungsband* 14 (1939):11–12.

47. *Liutprandi Leges* 1 and 65, ed. Beyerle, pp. 170, 230.

48. F. E. Harmer, ed., *Select English Historical Documents* (Cambridge, 1914), no. 9.

49. *Capitulare de villis* 16; MGH *Capitularia regum francorum*, I, p. 84.

50. Hincmar of Rheims, *De ordine palatii*, 22; MGH *Capt. reg. franc.*, II, p. 525.

51. P. Krull, "Die Salbung und Krönung der deutschen Königinnen und Kaiserinnen im Mittelalter" (Diss., Halle, 1911).

52. Ernst Kantorowicz, *Laudes Regiae* (Berkeley, 1947).

53. Agobard of Lyons, ed. Migne *Patrologia latina* (cited as *PL*), 104, p. 310.

54. On Judith of Bavaria, see translations of contemporary chronicles by Allen Cabaniss, *Charlemagne's Cousins* (Syracuse, 1967), and *Son of Charlemagne* (Syracuse, 1965); and by Bernard Scholz, *Carolingian Chronicles* (Ann Arbor, 1972).

55. Frank M. Stenton, *Anglo-Saxon England*, 3d ed. (Oxford, 1971), p. 373, casts doubt upon the evidence for Elfreda's guilt but concedes that she was popularly believed to be guilty. The event gave rise to another tradition recorded in the fourteenth-century life of St. Edith of Wilton: C. Horstmann, ed., *St. Editha* (Heilbronn, 1883). There the shocked nobles are said to have tried to avoid bestowing the crown on Ethelred by offering it to the sister of the murdered king, who was living with her mother in the convent at Wilton.

56. The life of Adelaide was written by Odilo of Cluny, *Epitaphium Adelheidae Imperatricis, PL*, 142, pp. 974–75. The marriage of Adelaide and Otto also offers us another problem regarding the inheritance of land by women. After the death

of Adelaide's first husband, she was regarded as the sole heiress of his lands and titles in Italy, which she carried to her second husband, the German Emperor. Perhaps it was in recognition of this authority that Otto took the unusual step of stamping her image on the reverse of his coins.

57. Capitulary of Quierzy. *MGH Leges* II, pp. 343–44.

58. As Ganshof, "La femme dans la monarchie franque," p. 29, points out, a married woman's incapacity under the Germanic laws presents a problem whose solution the laws themselves do not demonstrate. Only the *Lex Burg.* 100, *MGH Leg. nat. germ.* II, V, p. 113 is explicit on the subject. Deeds are few and do not necessarily show that a married woman's incapacity was a general principle in all the codes.

59. Georges Duby, *Rural Economy and Country Life in the Medieval West* (London, 1968).

60. Doris Stenton, *The English Woman in History* (London and New York, 1957).

61. Robertson, *Anglo-Saxon Charters*, pp. 150ff. Domesday Book lists a woman named Asa in Yorkshire who held her land separate and free from the domination and control of her husband, Beornwulf, even when they were together, so that he could neither give nor sell nor forfeit it. They had separated and she had withdrawn all her land and possessed it as its lady. Quoted from Dorothy Whitelock, *The Beginnings of English Society*, 2d ed. (Penguin, 1971), p. 95.

62. Council of Nantes, 895, canon 19, *Acta Conciliorum*, ed. Harduin (Paris, 1714), VI, pt. 1, p. 461.

63. Duby, *Rural Economy,* 493, reprinted a particularly interesting document in which Cunegonde, advocate of Plauen, left her extensive holdings to a sisterhood of which she was a member.

64. Flodoard, *De Christi triumphis apud Ital.* XII, 7, in *Liber pontificalis*, ed. L. Duchesne, 2 (Paris, 1892).

65. *The Anglo-Saxon Chronicle,* ed. G. N. Garmonsway (London, 1953), pp. 94–97, 100–101, 103. Her contribution to the unification of England is examined in detail by F. T. Wainwright, "Aethelflaed, Lady of the Mercians," in *The Anglo-Saxons,* ed. P. Clemoes (London, 1959).

66. Marie Luise Bulst-Thiele, *Kaiserin Agnes* (Leipzig, 1933).

67. An account of her regency, which shows the abbess performing all the secular duties of ruling the empire is to be found in *Annales Quedlinburgenses; MGH SS* 3, pp. 75–76.

68. Archibald Lewis, *The Development of Southern French and Catalan Society* (Austin, 1956), pp. 170 and 210.

69. Aimee Ermolaef, *Die Sonderstellung der Frau im französischen Lehnrecht* (Bern, 1930), pp. 56ff., gives numerous examples for the tenth and eleventh centuries of women leading military expeditions, going on crusade, dispensing justice, etc.

70. Atto of Vercelli, *Epistolae, PL,* 134, pp. 115–19.

71. Liutprand of Cremona, *Tit-for-tat,* III et passim, ed. F. Wright (London, 1930).

72. Matilda's role in the great reform of the eleventh century was noticed by all

the annalists of the age. Her life was recorded in a lengthy poem by Donizo of Canossa, *Vita Matildis,* ed. L. Simeoni, *Rerum italicarum scriptores,* rev. ed., V, 2 (Bologna, 1930), and also in *MGH SS* 12. Alfred Overmann, *Gräfin Mathilde von Tuscien* (1895; repr., Frankfurt a.M., 1965), has brought together all the texts relating to her history.

73. Thilo Vogelsang, *Die Frau als Herrscherin im hohem Mittelalter: Studien zur "consors regni" Formel* (Göttingen, 1954).

74. David Herlihy, "Land, Family, and Women in Continental Europe, 701–1200," *Traditio* 18 (1962):89–113.

75. Hans Thieme, "Die Rechtstellung der Frau in Deutschland," Société Jean Bodin, *Recueils* 12 (1962):351–76. He noted that following Barbarossa's precedent, *Weiberlehen* became more common, women holding Brabant in 1204 and Lüneburg in 1235.

76. Ermolaef, *Die Sonderstellung der Frau.*

77. The condition of women of the aristocracy in eleventh-century Normandy was examined by Anne Prah-Pérochon, "Rôle officielle de Mathilde, femme de Guillaume le Conquérant, 1053–1083" (Thèse, Aix-Marseille, 1973, under the direction of Georges Duby, Collège de France and Aix-Marseille).

78. Duby, *Rural Economy,* p. 183.

79. In Roman Law, the father of the bride, not her husband, provided the dowry, and in areas influenced by Roman Law this arrangement was never abandoned. As early as the first codification of Lombard Law, it stipulated that if a father or brother married off a girl and gave her a dowry, she should remain satisfied and should ask for no more. F. Niccolai, *La formazione del diritto successario* (Milan, 1940), shows the substitution of a *maritagium* for the daughter's share. This was the prevailing practice in Italy, and Rothari's edict was incorporated into the statutes of the Italian cities. "Exclusio propter dotem" meant that preference was given to male descendants. See also G. Rossi, "Statut juridique" in Société Jean Bodin, *Recueils* 12 (1962):115–133.

80. Roger Bataille, *Le droit des filles dans la succession de leurs parents en Normandie* (Paris: 1927).

81. Even crown lands were alienated in this manner when kings turned them over to their brides with the right of unrestricted ownership. Charles the Simple in 907, e.g., gave his bride extensive property from the royal fisc as her irrevocable property. The change is traced in great detail by Cornuey, *Le régime de la dos.*

Female Sanctity:
Public and Private Roles,
ca. 500–1100

Jane Tibbetts Schulenburg

DE TRIBUS ORDINIS SANCTORUM HIBERNIAE: The first order of Catholic saints was at the time of [St.] Patrick. There were then bishops all famous and virtuous and full of the holy spirit. . . . They did not spurn the administration or company of women . . . nor fear the wind of temptation. . . . [In] the second order . . . few were bishops, but many [were] priests. . . . they fled the companionship and administration of women and even excluded them from their monasteries.

De S. Onchuone, Confessore "Ex variis," *Acta Sanctorum Hiberniae*

One indirect index of attitudes toward women, as well as of their power and visibility in the early medieval church and society, is provided by a collective study of saints' lives. Membership in the celestial city had a terrestrial base: those recruited to sainthood embodied the values and hierarchical order of their earthly society. With changes in the structure, values, and needs of society and the Church, shifts occurred in the opportunities available to women which could provide them with the visibility required for elevation to sainthood. During the early Middle Ages, worldly power, high status, and social and economic prominence were all necessary prerequisites for candidates for sanctity. Based on a collective examination of some 2,274 male and female saints listed in the *Bibliotheca Sanctorum* (supplemented by information from the *Acta Sanctorum*), this essay will focus on shifts in styles of sanctity found in the lives of female saints between 500 and 1100 as well as changes in the ratio of female to male saints who lived in the regions of Britain, France, Germany, the Low Countries, and Italy.[1]

Saints' lives, in their edifying intention, are rich in fantasy and contradiction. Until approximately the past two decades, scholars have generally discredited the historical value of the vitae of saints. With the growing interest in social history and the history of mentalities, however, scholars are beginning to take a serious second look at hagiography.[2]

While saints' lives present many difficulties for the historian, they also provide a solid core of social and personal detail not found in any other documentation. They hold remarkable potential for social and cultural historians and are invaluable for historians of medieval women. Unlike many other early medieval sources which are so frustrating in their silence on women's lives and experiences, the vitae of saints pay great attention to women: they are directly concerned with female roles in the Church and society as well as with attitudes toward women. Also the sheer numbers of vitae, the hundreds of lives of male and female saints, afford us an unsurpassed view of changing patterns of female sanctity across the centuries as well as an opportunity to compare women's roles and status with those of their male contemporaries. A collective study of saints' lives thus provides enough information to form a rather crude but accurate evaluation of the status of women in medieval society and specifically within the religious community.

As Delooz has noted, the perception of sanctity was a function of the community: one was after all only a saint *for* and *by* others.[3] In this early period saints were popularly chosen rather than officially canonized. Their selection was predicated on their saintly reputations recognized by their peers and on the energetic expression of this opinion by an informal and usually local pressure group which formulated a public cult. In contrast to many of the later official candidates for canonization, who were promoted by specific orders, the church hierarchy, or the papacy, these early saints reflect the popular collective religious mentality of the period.[4]

Several years ago in an article entitled "Sexism and the Celestial Gynaeceum," I attempted to provide a general statistical overview of the holy dead from about 500 to 1200.[5] I found that despite claims of spiritual egalitarianism by the Church, it was much more difficult for women to be recognized as saints than it was for men. For this period of some seven hundred years, the average percentage of women recognized as saints was less than 15 percent (see table 1 for the years 500–1099). Certain periods seemed to have been more conducive than others to the making of female saints, however. The years 650–750, for example, emerged as a golden age for female saints (especially in France and Belgium, where nearly one

Jane Tibbetts Schulenburg

Table 1. Women Saints in the Middle Ages from 500 to 1099

Years	Total number of saints	Male saints	Female saints	Percentage of female saints[a]
500–49	236	213	23	9.7
550–99	304	281	23	7.6
600–49	201	180	21	10.4
650–99	365	292	73	20.0
700–49	230	176	54	23.5
750–99	194	157	37	19.1
800–49	128	109	19	14.8
850–99	151	132	19	12.6
900–49	64	49	15	23.4
950–99	105	88	17	16.2
1000–49	132	117	15	11.4
1050–99	164	148	16	9.8
Total	2,274	1,942	332	—

Source: Saints listed in the *Bibliotheca sanctorum*.

Note: Because of the nature of our sources, the figures shown are only approximate.

[a]Average = 14.9.

out of every five saints was a woman, and in Britain, where nearly two out of every five saints were female.) After 751, however, with the establishment of the Carolingian dynasty, the total number of male and female saints fell, as did the relative proportion of female saints. This deterioration is temporarily modified in the tenth century, which witnessed a sharp increase in female sanctity tied to ecclesiastical developments in Saxony and the reforms in England. After the year 1000, the decline was further exacerbated and reached its nadir between 1050 and 1100, when only 9.8 percent of all saints were female. (For France these rough statistics for the eleventh century are even more exaggerated; only approximately 4 percent of the saints were female.) These rough statistics seem to provide an indirect index of a progressive deterioration in the status of women and their active roles in the Church.[6]

A closer look at the typology of female sanctity reveals a significant pattern with regard to female prominence and visibility. For the early Middle Ages, access to sainthood came essentially through positions of power and political prominence: high office and high social and economic status. At this time popular sanctity was essentially predicated on public activities—exterior actions—in preference to the interior, mystical, and special charismatic traits which would be important for the making of saints in the late Middle Ages. Male saints were recruited from among the upper secular clergy (popes, archbishops, and bishops), from the cloister (abbots and monks), and sometimes from the throne (kings and emperors). Women, in contrast, denied access to the secular church hierarchy, were rewarded with recognition of sainthood for their roles as pious queens, abbesses, consecrated virgins/nuns, hermits, and martyrs.

What social and cultural arrangements provided the necessary opportunities for women to achieve positions of power and visibility which could in turn promote candidacy for sanctity? During this early period, in the absence of strong, impersonal governmental institutions, royal or aristocratic families assumed the political, economic, and social authority in various areas of Europe. Thus within the context of the irregular powers of the early medieval family, women could achieve positions of authority and control over wealth. With political and economic power situated within the family, the household became the essential locus of power. In the undifferentiated space of the great hall, the distinction between public and private became redundant. The domestic sphere was also the public sphere: it stood at the very center of power and authority. The household served as the noblewoman's "powerhouse"; it provided nearly limitless opportunities for women whose families were politically and economically powerful.[7]

It is therefore within the context of the household that a substantial number of noblewomen and queens of the Merovingian and Anglo-Saxon period achieved sainthood. The early queens were recognized, for example, for their successful work as "domestic proselytizers."[8] While their missions might in some ways be viewed as "privatized," they were in fact part of a concerted "public" strategy of conversion carried out in close cooperation with contemporary popes and bishops. Their crucial role in the missionary effort was recognized by the church hierarchy. The queens' success in their proselytizing activities also had immense public/political repercussions, for the newly baptized Christian king was followed in his new faith by all of his retainers and the entire realm. Thus, through her successful work in converting her husband Clovis to Christianity, St. Clotilda, queen of the Franks, established a prototype which would be followed by many other royal female saints.[9] Clotilda's granddaughter, Clodoswinde, queen of the Lombards, for example, was praised for her work in trying to convert her husband, Alboin, to Catholicism.[10] Clotilda's great-granddaughter, the Anglo-Saxon queen Bertha, was singled out for her role in converting her husband, King Aethelbert of Kent, to Christianity.[11] Following in this same tradition was Bertha's daughter, Ethelberga, queen of Northumbria, who used her influence in the conversion of her husband, King Edwin.[12] This formula can also be found among other royal medieval female saints from both the east and west of Europe.[13]

The early medieval queen-saint achieved prominence through her role as *consocia,* or partner to the king, as regent, and especially as dowager queen. In these positions queens actively participated in the king's council (*curia regis*), which was small and personal.[14] Through their royal offices, pious queens appointed bishops and abbots; they worked to formulate alliances between the crown and bishoprics or monasteries; they influenced and affected religious policy and organization. With the property of the royal domain they endowed churches, founded monasteries and hospitals, and ransomed slaves.[15] Gregory of Tours, for example, praised St. Clotilda's pious activities: "She endowed churches, monasteries and other holy places with the lands necessary for their upkeep; her giving was so generous and so eager that already in her lifetime she was looked upon not as a Queen but as the handmaiden of God whom she served with such zeal."[16] The queen-saints acquired important relics for the royal collections or for their favorite monastic foundations. They established dynastic burial sites which served as royal mausoleums and made provisions for perpetual prayers for the souls of their families.[17] The efficacy of their own personal prayers for the success of the king and kingdom was also recognized. Several royal saints attempted to use their influence and positions of power to secure peace for their nations. While the dossiers of these early saintly queens underscored their piety and charity, their astute deeds were frequently based on political expediency as well as religious motives.

While some of the most famous saints of this early period were selected from the royal courts, nearly one-half of the female saints were recruited from the cloister. The golden age of female saints, the mid-seventh century through the mid-eighth century in France and Britain, and the increase in tenth-century Britain and Germany, was intimately connected with new opportunities for women in the Church, specifically with the early popularity of female monasticism and the enthusiastic establishment of convents by the nobility. We therefore find a striking correlation between the pattern of new religious communities established for women and the making of female saints (see tables 2 and 3).[18] The nobility's eagerness to establish often lavishly endowed family monasteries

Table 2. New Religious Foundations: France/Belgium

Years	New foundations (total)	Men's houses	Women's houses	
			Number	Percentage
500–49	108	100	8	7.4
550–99	156	137	19	12.2
600–49	102	77	25	24.5
650–99	159	107	52	32.7
700–49	63	55	8	12.7
750–99	91	80	11	12.1
800–49	146	134	12	8.2
850–99	107	99	8	7.5
900–49	136	130	6	4.4
950–99	232	219	13	5.6
1000–49	543	515	28	5.2
1050–99	979	946	33	3.4
Total	2,822	2,599	223	—

Source: Based on the monastic foundations listed in L. H. Cottineau, *Répertoire topo-bibli-ographique des abbayes et prieurés* (Mâcon, 1935–37), 2 vols., and E. de Moreau, *Histoire de l'église en Belgique: Circonscriptions ecclésiastiques, chapitres, abbayes, couvents en Belgique avant 1559* (Brussels, 1948).

[a]Average = 7.9 percent.

seems to have owed much of its momentum to the opportunities provided by the new frontiers of these freshly Christianized lands—the rapid influx of landed wealth, the spoils of war, and the enhancement of power and lordship. In part this initial desire to establish convents seems to have been a response of this self-protective aristocratic caste to its own special needs.[19] The family monastery in this early period was in many ways regarded simply as an extension of the noble household. From the perspective of the founders of these new communities, the often substantial endowment did not constitute a permanent alienation of property; rather it was viewed as perhaps a temporary investment in a complementary sphere of influence. Therefore, as a type of strategy, the founding families often attempted to maintain control over their monasteries and properties

Table 3. New Religious Foundations: Britain

Years	New foundations (total)	Men's houses	Women's houses Number	Women's houses Percentage[a]
500–49	8	8	0	0
550–99	39	39	0	0
600–49	29	20	9	31.0
650–99	94	56	38	40.4
700–49	26	19	7	26.9
750–99	16	15	1	6.3
800–49	12	8	4	33.3
850–99	11	9	2	18.2
900–49	22	19	3	13.6
950–99	26	21	5	19.2
1000–49	16	15	1	6.3
1050–99	57	51	6	10.5
Total	356	280	76	—

Source: Based on the monastic foundations listed in David Knowles and R. Neville Hadcock, *Medieval Religious Houses: England and Wales* (London, 1971), and the Ordnance Survey, *Monastic Britain* (Southampton, 1978).

[a] Average = 21.3 percent.

by safeguarding the election of the abbesses and advocacy of the convent for their heirs.[20]

Thus many of the saints of this early period were recruited from the cloister, specifically, from among founding abbesses. The vitae of these abbess-saints often discuss in a very forthright manner the critical relationship between economics (landed wealth) and sanctity. In addition to praising the saints' great generosity in favor of the Church, the lives frequently provide detailed accounts of the extensive landed estates which the abbess or her parents had employed in the establishment of the family monastery.[21] While many of these early family houses were created for daughters of the aristocracy, who would then assume the position of founding abbess, a good number of religious houses were established by widows acting in their own names. They founded these monasteries on their dower lands as places of retirement and security. Many of these noble widows also became abbesses of their new communities and won recognition of sanctity.

The vitae frequently underscore the autonomy and power found among these early medieval widows,[22] whose use of power was manifested in a number of ways. Many of the holy widows refused remarriage and insisted on taking the veil and entering monastic life. Their autonomy became especially apparent in their rather liberal alienations of family properties in favor of the establishment of new monastic communities and churches. While the saints' lives praised and encouraged these independent acts—that is, the generous donations in favor of the Church—in reality many of the bequests appear to have been accomplished as overt acts of defiance carried out against the express wishes of the widow's family. These actions emphasize the helplessness of the family at this time to prevent widows from making what appeared to some as impulsive or excessively generous donations, at odds with family strategies and at the expense of the interests of the patrimony.

The vitae also tell of the success of the founding abbess-saints in augmenting their new community's original endowment, especially through attracting additional bequests and donations from the local nobility. Some of these landed estates accompanied noblewomen who wished to become members of these new monastic foundations. The initial popularity of the movement, together with the widespread fame of the abbess-saints, served to attract great numbers of noblewomen to these newly established communities. While a good number of these proprietary houses appear to have been fairly small, with communities of only a dozen or so female religious, and survived only a generation or two, other monasteries were extremely large and successful and housed several hundred inmates. According to Baudonivia's vita of St. Radegund, the foundress wanted her new monastery to be able to accommodate the greatest possible number of nuns.[23] At the death of St. Radegund in 587, her monastery of Holy Cross at Poitiers had approximately two hundred nuns, plus clergy and monastic familia. Some three hundred women flocked to live under the rule of the founding abbess-saint Aurea in her monastery in Paris. St. Sexburga's new foundation at Sheppey had some seventy-seven inmates. St. Tetta, eighth-century abbess of Wimborne, was said to have had approximately five hundred nuns under her care.[24] Many other vitae mention the large communities of nuns, and monks, in the case of the double monastery, over which these abbess-saints ruled. Thus in the early enthusiasm of monastic life for women, many of these communities were very large and impressive centers. Filled with women from wealthy and powerful families, they provided a significant power base for the rulers of these communities.

The early medieval abbess-saints also exercised their authority and won immortality through impressive building campaigns. The significant role which they assumed as "builder-saints" is again related to the special needs and opportunities found in these newly Christianized lands. The great numbers of new churches and monastic buildings, as well as the rapidity with which many of these construction projects were completed, are truly amazing. Although today very little remains of these early medieval buildings, archaeological finds, the lives of saints, and chronicles all provide hints as to the size, numbers, and extent of these structures. It was apparently traditional for many of these early monastic complexes to have several churches: one specifically for the nuns (or for the nuns and monks or nuns and parishioners), another which served as a funerary basilica or a mausoleum for the community, and perhaps another for the male component of the monastery, the priests and monks.[25] According to the vita of St. Salaberga, this abbess-saint built a large monastery with six churches for her nuns. For the men attached to the community, she constructed a smaller monastery with its own church.[26] The female communities at Nivelles and Soissons each had four churches. We learn from our sources that, in the seventh century, St. Begga made a pilgrimage to Rome. On her return she built a monastery at Andenne, and in imitation of the seven churches of Rome she built seven chapels.[27]

The abbess "builder-saints," like their contemporary abbots and bishops, appeared as commissioners of ecclesiastical buildings. Many oversaw the actual construction of these buildings. An eleventh-century text, for example, praises St. Sexburga for her building activities. "Then it pleased the saintly queen Seaxburg that she would there [in the island of Sheppey] build a minster for delight and for glory; and she had it built, as men used to tell, so that for thirty years there never stilled the sound of groaning wagon nor complaining slave."[28] The German saint Hadeloga, founder and abbess of Kitzingen, was also remembered for her building activities. According to tradition, she was responsible for having built a stone bridge over the river Main at Kitzingen, one which took thirty-two years to be constructed.[29]

A few of the vitae tell of a more direct involvement by female saints in these building activities. The seventh-century German abbess-saint Landrada worked with her own hands in the construction of her church in honor of the Virgin Mary. We learn that she worked "like a man" in preparing the foundations. After clearing away the briars, she dug up and transported stones. Also she personally erected the altar of her church.[30]

The vitae of the eighth-century German abbess-saints Herlindis and Renildis describe the building activities of these two sisters. Each morning they would get up early to work on the family monastery at Eyck, where they carried sand and immense stones for the building. Their monastery was completed with amazing rapidity.[31]

A number of abbess-saints won recognition for enlarging their churches and monastic buildings and for their important roles in procuring precious relics for their convents. Others were lauded for their work in decorating and enriching their new foundations. The seventh-century abbess-saint Eustadiola, founder of the large monastery of Moyen-Moutiers at Bourges, also occupied herself with the decoration of the church. The vita notes that St. Eustadiola embellished its walls with magnificent embroidered wall hangings and covered the altar with expensive cloth fringed with gold. With their own hands the abbess and her nuns had made these works of art. St. Eustadiola also commissioned crosses, candelabra, chalices, and reliquaries for the adornment of the church.[32]

Several founding abbess-saints were remembered for assisting their new foundations in other ways. We learn, for example, that St. Eanswitha's monastery, built on a cliff at Folkestone, experienced serious problems with its water supply. Thus, according to legend, St. Eanswitha dug a canal with the tip of her crozier (the symbol of abbatial power) and made the water run uphill to her foundation![33] A similar incident is associated with St. Bertha, the founder of a convent near Avernay. This monastery also lacked access to a water supply. Through a vision, however, St. Bertha learned of a nearby garden with a spring. She then purchased this land for one pound of silver and traced with her crozier a small ditch from the spring to her monastery.[34]

The vitae and chronicles of the early Middle Ages then recognized these abbess-saints for their "public" activities—especially their economic roles and practical talents. They also endorsed their administrative skills, prudence, and wisdom.

Abbess Ethelburga was praised for running her convent "in a manner worthy of her brother."[35] The early abbess-saints attended royal councils and synods. The great Synod of Whitby (663–64) was held at the double monastery founded and ruled by St. Hilda. Abbess Ebba, aunt of the king, participated in the deliberations of a Northumbrian council of 680–81. St. Mildred, abbess of Minster-in-Thanet, along with four other abbesses, attended a witenagemot (about 696–716) at Baccanceld, in Kent.[36] In the description of Abbess Aelffled's attendance at the Synod on the Nidd, she is called "the best of advisers, and a constant source of strength to the whole province." At this synod she addressed and advised the archbishop, king, bishops, abbots, and chief nobility of the kingdom "with inspired words."[37] In the vita of St. Cuthbert, St. Aelfled is involved in an important political discussion with St. Cuthbert and is described as appearing with "womanly daring" (*audacia feminea*).[38] While the abbatial dignity enhanced the prestige of the noblewoman, the position also extended her networks beyond the family into the hierarchy of the Church, providing increased access to the corridors of power. Frequently through these important connections abbess-saints were able to secure special monastic privileges and immunities. These diplomas helped to ensure their communities' continued autonomy and safeguarded their landholdings.

In addition to providing abbesses with opportunities to exhibit their administrative skills and to be actively involved in the political activities of the period, the early monasteries were important centers of learning and education. In the newly converted regions of northern Europe, they served as local missionary centers, with their abbesses and nuns assisting in conversion efforts through the establishment of schools.

A number of female saints of this period were distinguished for their impressive learning. St. Gertrude of Nivelles was famous for having memorized nearly the entire collection of divine laws ("ut pene omnem bibliothecam divini legis memoriter recondit") and for her ability to lecture on the obscure mysteries of scriptural allegories.[39] The Venerable Bede describes the school which St. Hilda established at Whitby as one of the first and greatest centers of learning in the North of England. He says of St. Hilda, "so great was her prudence that not only ordinary folk, but kings and princes used to come and ask her advice in their difficulties and *take it*."[40] Aelfled is described as a "wise woman and learned in holy scriptures" ("sapiens femina et in sanctis erudita scripturis").[41] The vita of St. Leoba relates that she "made such progress in her teaching that many of [her pupils] afterwards became superiors of others, so that there was hardly a convent of nuns in that part which had not one of her disciples as abbess." The vita also notes: "And because of her wide knowledge of the scriptures and her prudence in counsel they [i.e., bishops, princes, and nobles] often discussed spiritual matters and ecclesiastical discipline with her."[42] A number of female monastic saints were also celebrated for their medical knowledge and famous healing abilities.[43]

As leaders of their monastic communities and of the surrounding areas, abbess-saints were called upon in times of disaster. The seventh-century abbess-saint Godeberta assumed an important role while a plague raged in Noyon. She recommended that for three days the people of Noyon observe a fast, wearing sackcloth and ashes. They followed her advice, and the plague was dissipated.[44] St. Leoba organized the village of Bischofsheim to extinguish a threatening fire. She was also sought out to calm a devastating storm.[45] A servant of the monastery of Holy Cross, sent to fish in the sea, was saved from a storm by an invocation to St. Radegund.[46] According to their vitae, St. Gertrude of Nivelles, St. Edith of Wilton, and a number of other female saints were also said to have used their supernatural powers to save men who were under their patronage from impending disaster at sea.[47]

Although the special privileges and immunities, as well as the presence of *advocati* (bishops and abbots designated as guardians), provided a certain level of security and protection for the monasteries, the female communities still faced frequent attempts on the part of the local nobility and bishops to usurp their lands. Especially at these times, when the monastery's lands were threatened, the founding abbess-saints displayed their formidable powers and appeared as protector saints. (It should be noted, however, that while most of the saintly activities we have been tracing thus far have concerned "living saints," most of the cases in which patron saints exhibited protective powers over their properties were accomplished posthumously, from the saint's tomb.) It was generally believed that the founding abbess/patron saint, although deceased, resided in her tomb and that from this most sacred vantage point she continued to watch over and protect her foundation and its lands. In times of dire necessity, she could be called upon to use her special *potentia* on behalf of her community of nuns. As can be noted in the vitae, the supernatural power of these female patron saints was perceived and feared by men and women of all classes of medieval society.

One example of the exercise of power by the holy dead over their properties can be found in the case of the popular late seventh-century Belgian saint Aya. She was a very wealthy noblewoman who took the veil at Mons under the abbess-saint Waltrudis. She donated extensive properties to the monastery. According to tradition, however, about eighty years after St. Aya's death, her relatives came to reclaim their "family" lands. Since no title deed could be found, the case went to court. Following the nuns' request, the court was held at the tomb of the saint. At the proceedings the nun who was apparently handling the case spoke in a loud voice, "Great Saint, they wish to take from us Guesmes, Nimy, Maisières, and Braine, which you gave us. Speak in favor of your daughters, and confirm the gifts you made in your life." At this point a voice allegedly broke forth from the depths of the tomb, clearly audible to all present, declaring: "I ratify all these gifts which I made to the church." Thus through her "supernatural" intervention, the saint confirmed the monastery's landholdings. (And appropriately enough, Aya became one of the saints invoked in lawsuits.)[48]

Another case in this tradition can be found in the *Translatio* of St. Edith, patron saint of Wilton. During the reign of Cnut, a certain magnate of the king by the name of Agamundus carried off a piece of land belonging to Saint Edith (i.e., Wilton). The usurper then died suddenly ("impenitens morte") without returning the property which he had seized. As punishment for this act, St. Edith directed her wrath toward the dead man and would not let his soul rest. At his wake, the corpse "awoke" and told those around him of St. Edith's anger and asked that the lands be restored to the saint. This accomplished, he then died in peace, with Edith now his protector.[49] A similar case is described in the *Translatio* of St. Edith where the saint visited her wrath on a certain Brixius who had also usurped some of her monastery's property.[50]

The vita of the tenth-century abbess-saint Wulfhild also relates a fascinating case in which a patron saint exercised her protective *potentia* over her community. St. Wulfhild had been abbess of the monasteries of Barking and Horton for many years. Apparently through the ambition of the priests of Barking Abbey and with the assistance of Queen Alftrude, however, the abbess and her nuns were removed from their monastery and were replaced by a male community. As the abbess and her nuns were leaving their convent and lamenting their expulsion, Wulfhild prophesied that in twenty years, at this very gate, she and the nuns would return and would be rightly restored to their monastery. This prophecy came to pass. For at that time, St. Ethelburga, the first abbess and founder of Barking (d. ca. 678) appeared in a vision to Queen Alftrude who was ill. The saint was in vile attire, ragged and rent, complaining of the injury which had been done to her (that is, to her monastic community) by Alftrude. St. Ethelburga then warned the queen to expect death if she did not restore Wulfhild to the monastery. According to the vita, the queen (obviously shaken by this powerful vision), corrected her ways, restored the holy abbess and all of her sisters to the monastery, and then recovered her health.[51]

This survey then emphasizes the significance of the access to political and economic power as well as education in the pursuit of sanctity. During this early period, the intersection of public and private spheres favored the acquisition of wealth and the exercise of power by women. Also the activities which led to recognition of sanctity for the *mulieres sanctae* were essentially indistinguishable from those of their male contemporaries. As Eleanor McLaughlin has observed: "It was a sanctity powerful, public, practical, even administrative, and it was a power and holiness to which women were called coequally with men."[52] It is of special interest to note that at this time we do not find churchmen questioning the propriety of the roles which these public and powerful female figures had assumed. Instead, they were praised for acting *non mulieriter sed viriliter.*

During the ninth century, however, with the emergence of the Carolingian empire and Church reforms, we can see in some regions of Europe a concerted attempt by the reformers at reorganizing society and the Church. In general, the reformers tried to reassert the Church's authority and power. With the Church now established and organized, the earlier practical need for women's talents seems to have subsided. The Church was in a position to attempt to enforce its restrictive policies which had been ignored or necessarily mitigated during its initial stages of development (especially during the period of the missionary movement in the north of Europe). Thus the Carolingian reformers (followed by the Cluniac and Gregorian reformers), introduced policies which tried to regularize activities—to limit women's public involvement and their leadership activities in the Church and society through the demarcation of a "proper" feminine sphere and a delineation of female nature, abilities, rights, and responsibilities.

The reformers' encouragement of ritual purity and fear of the female sex served as an excuse for the growing segregation of the sexes and sharpened the boundaries between them. The reform councils repeatedly legislated strict enclosure for female religious which necessarily restricted their active involvement in the "public sphere."[53] Strict claustration also contributed to a loss of independence and economic hardship for many women's communities. With a loss of autonomy came a similar loss in public influence and general visibility for the abbess and her monastery. As Suzanne Wemple has argued: "Abbesses of both types of monasteries, for Benedictines and canonesses, lost not only their freedom of movement but also their former influence. Although emperors and kings periodically summoned them, undoubtedly to discuss the disposition of monastic resources, abbesses, unlike abbots, did not participate in reforming assemblies."[54] In general there appears to have been an erosion of the abbess's former public role; the emphasis now fell on her private role within the enclosure. The councils also stipulated the necessary separation of the sexes in monastic schools, which in turn led to a growing disparity between the levels of male and female education and the exclusion of female religious from the mainstream of education.[55] The physical arrangement of the double monastery, with its close association of male and female religious, came under attack by the reformers. Eventually this very special experiment in monastic life, which had been extremely favorable to women's autonomy and power, disappeared. The reform councils also strictly excluded women from sacred space, which again worked to restrict their activities and visibility.[56]

This narrowing of female boundaries contributed to the erosion of women's public status. Rather than rewarding women for their pious exercise of power and their leadership in the Church, the reformers now attempted to restrict women to a privatized, domestic realm.

One of the most blatant examples of this deliberate attempt can be found in the following edict of the reform Council of Nantes (895), which warned: "It is astounding that certain women, against both divine and human laws, with bare-faced impudence, act in general pleas and with abandon exhibit a burning passion for public meetings, and they disrupt rather than assist, the business of the kingdom and the good of the commonweal. It is indecent and reprehensible, even among barbarians, for women to discuss the cases of men. Those who should be discussing their woolen work and weaving with the residents of the women's quarters, should not usurp the authority of senators in public meetings just as if they were residents of the court."[57]

Another interesting and well-known ninth-century case underscores the reformers' concern with monitoring women's public roles and their attempts to silence them. In 847 a German woman named Theoda was condemned by the bishop and council of Mainz for her prophesying. According to the *Annales of Fulda* and the Council of Mainz, Theoda preached that the end of the world was close at hand and claimed to know the exact day on which the dreaded end would arrive. Filled with fear, men and women offered the prophetess gifts and asked her to pray for their souls. According to churchmen, however, "What is more serious, [these people] turned away from church doctrines preached by clerks of holy orders to follow her as though she were a teacher sent from heaven." Theoda was then brought before the bishop, where, after extensive questioning, she admitted that she had said such things. The synod determined that she should be punished by a public flogging. According to the sources: "Whereupon with shame she gave up the ministry of preaching that she had irrationally seized upon and presumed to claim for herself against the custom of the church, and perplexed, she put an end to her soothsaying."[58]

Another notorious instance in which women's public roles and power within the Church were condemned occurred in eleventh-century pre-Gregorian-reform Italy. It concerned Abbot Guarinus of Settimo, a reformer who preached against simony and clerical concubinage. When the abbot presented his business before Bishop Hildebrand of Florence, he received his answer not from the bishop whom he had addressed but from the bishop's wife, Alberga, who sat at court beside him. Disgusted and insulted, the abbot railed against the woman: "Accursed Jezebel, are you so sunk in your sinful condition that you dare to speak before a meeting of *bonorum hominum vel clericorum?*"[59] In this incident, the abbot's rage and offended sense of propriety were directed against Alberga's pretentious intrusion, as a woman and wife of a bishop, into the realm of "good men and clerks"—that duly constituted public male sphere.

This effort to limit women's visibility and privatize their existence can be found in many of the reformers' writings. St. Odo of Cluny warns that "the highest virtue in a woman is not to wish to be seen."[60] Cardinal Humbert, originally a Cluniac monk from the Lorraine and an enthusiastic supporter of the reform program of Pope Gregory VII, emphasizes in his writings against simony the necessary exclusion of women from public roles. In his fear of female power within the Church, he specifically notes that women were "permitted neither to speak in church nor to rule over men."[61] The twelfth-century reformer Idung of Prüfening, writing shortly after the period under consideration in this essay, argues for strict female claustration. He warns that members of the female sex should not appear in public. He also suggests that it was not expedient for women to have their own monastic governance because of their natural fickleness and the outside temptations which womanly weakness was not strong enough to resist.[62]

Thus with the reform ideology a new ideal is presented for women, one which denigrated female participation in the public realm while it glorified the private role or cult of domesticity. As Suzanne Wemple has observed, these shifts began in the ninth century and brought with them a new style of female sanctity.[63] Many of the saints' lives now singled out for praise exceptional domestic skills. They lauded and sacralized the expertise of pious women in household management, domestic arts, and motherhood.

St. Maura of Troyes (d. ca. 861) is a good example of this new type of domestic saint or "holy housekeeper." Selflessly devoted to serving the bishop and Cathedral of Troyes, she spent her time filling the lamps of the church with oil, purchasing ecclesiastical vestments with her own money, or making an alb for the bishop-saint Prudentius after having bleached and spun the flax.[64] The contemplative St. Liutberga (ninth century) was another domestic saint. After spending her formative years as a pious household servant, she retired to live as a recluse. We learn that she was especially "skilled in many feminine labors," including the "art of weaving." In her cell she kept a charcoal burner with a vat in which to dye cloth or yarn. Here she held a weaving workshop, teaching the daughters of the nobility the arts of weaving and dyeing cloth in many colors.[65] While the ninth-century life of the abbess-saints Herlindis and Renildis notes their role in building their monastery and in education, it also glorifies the skills of these women in the domestic arts. The author observes that the sisters were "carefully trained in every area of work such as is done by women's hands, in various designs, in different styles; so that they attained a high standard of excellence in spinning, weaving, designing, and embroidering interlace in gold and flowers in silk."[66] The domesticity of St. Wiborada (d. ca. 925) was also praised in her vita. She devoted much of her life to caring for her brother Hitto, who became a priest of St. Gall. She made his clothing and provided for all of his needs in the ministry. Wiborada also worked for the monastery of St. Gall, where she proved to be especially adept at making covers for the books produced in the scriptorium.[67] The eleventh-century life of King Robert by Helgaud describes the pious activities of the French king's mother, Queen Adelaide. The author states that she gave to St. Martin a chasuble worked in very pure gold with Christ in majesty, cherubim, and seraphim, the Lamb of God, and the four beasts of diverse countries. She also made for the blessed confessor a cope of gold cloth and two of silver. For her special protector, St. Denis, she created in the same way a chasuble which was an admirable work.[68] Perhaps the epitome of this type of domestic saint was the noblewoman-saint Hunna. Hunna's popular local cult and fame rested on her pious activity of washing the clothing of the poor: thus her name, "the holy washerwoman."[69]

While the Church perhaps attempted to exercise social control through the promotion of a new female image (a domesticized/privatized saintly ideal for women), it was not entirely successful in removing women from the public sphere. Certain areas of Europe, such as England, Scotland, and regions of Germany, still presented "new frontiers" with fresh opportunities for women to exercise a great deal of power and influence in society and the Church. In addition, the office of queenship continued to provide visibility for women and access to sainthood. We therefore find at the end of this period a saint such as Queen Margaret of Scotland (d. 1093), who in many ways is reminiscent of the prominent Merovingian and Anglo-Saxon women of the golden age of sanctity. As queen (consocia), St. Margaret played a major public role. Renowned for her learning, she was active in the reform movement and attended councils and set policy. The author of her vita also praised the queen's domestic proficiency (especially her involvement in needlework) and her role as mother.[70]

It should be noted that a number of the vitae of the earlier female saints (who were essentially remembered for their "public roles" as founding abbesses of monasteries, as builder-saints, and as administrators), also mentioned the domestic achievements of these saints. The royal saints Radegund and Balthilda, for example, won praise from their hagiographers for their assumption of some of the humblest of domestic tasks. We have already noted the seventh-century founding abbess-saint Eustadiola, who was remembered for her fine embroidery work, which she used to decorate her church. One of the most important and popular of all Anglo-Saxon saints, Etheldreda, founding abbess of Ely, was known for her great skill in orphrey, or gold embroidery work. She is said to have made a stole and maniple worked in gold and precious stones for St. Cuthbert.[71] Several other early examples of female saints follow in this tradition.

In general, however, the attempts of the reformers to relegate women to the domestic sphere resulted in a limited visibility for women. Despite the promotion of the feminine religious ideal of domesticity, these activities were less likely to capture the popular imagination and to inspire the enthusiastic devotion required for the making of saints. Greater value was still attached to the public sphere. (We do not find, for example, a parallel development of a domestic/custodial male saint emerging at this same time; rather, men saints continued to be recruited from among those in the public spotlight—abbots and bishops.) Thus in attempting to restrict the functions of women, the reformers also restricted their access to sainthood.

Perhaps one of the most extreme examples of this shift can be noted in Joseph-Claude Poulin's study of the ideal of sanctity in Carolingian Aquitaine (750–950). Poulin has noted that in this region (which was also the center of Benedict of Aniane's reform movement) the ecclesiastical authors had not been inspired to promote the ideal of female sanctity, nor had they advanced any pilgrimage centers to the relics of a woman saint. Also, while Poulin noted that at least thirty-eight saints' lives had been written for men during this period, he did not find any contemporary vita that promoted a female saint.[72]

Although Church politics beginning with the Carolingian reforms encouraged gendered spheres and worked to shrink public boundaries for women, these efforts were further bolstered by a complex of other political, economic, and social factors.

With the growth of feudal monarchies in the eleventh and twelfth centuries, governments ceased to be ruled on a personal basis but rather developed into large, impersonal institutions. Public power, which had previously been exercised by great aristocratic families through the household, was recaptured by kings who were assisted in their governance by professional bureaucrats. The loss of public power was especially felt by queens and aristocratic women, for with the removal of the power base from the household, noblewomen essentially lost their formal positions of influence. The intersection of the public with the private spheres had encouraged the female exercise of power: this convergence was now replaced by an increasingly rigid separation of public and domestic spheres of influence.[73]

With the reforms of the Church came increased emphasis on male leadership. In contrast to the early Church with its weak and decentralized authority, a new, strong ecclesiastical organization emerged with a changed religious atmosphere. The Church had become a large, complex, inflexible bureaucracy which now provided little opportunity for women to have access to its hierarchy or to be part of its extensive networks. Furthermore, the reform emphasis on the need for ritual purity and on sex-segregated spheres fostered an exaggerated fear of women that often led to a full-blown misogyny. In this atmosphere of restricted functions and distrust, it became extremely difficult for women to gain access to sainthood.

A number of other ecclesiastical, economic, and social factors contributed to the further displacement of women from formal positions of power and influence. The golden age of female sanctity and the tenth-century rise in female saints coincided with the initial rush of women into monastic life and the enthusiastic establishment of family monasteries. While the initial success of the Church had depended on the aristocracy's close cooperation and its establishment of proprietary monasteries and churches, in their reconstitution of monastic life, however, the reformers now advocated the effective release of monasteries from lay control. In their emphasis on the necessary separation of monastic life from "the world," reformers insisted on doing away with the proprietary house, in which the founders maintained control over the monastery's lands and administration. This change seemed to have a critical impact on family strategies and discouraged the aristocracy from endowing new monastic communities for their daughters, which now meant the "permanent" alienation of a portion of their patrimony. In addition, with the destruction and disorder caused by the invasions, the closing of the new frontiers, and diminishing opportunities for profit from war, pillage, and new lands, the initial interest in the founding of convents waned. A rapid decline in the number of new houses followed, as well as decay in the newly established communities. As Leyser has noted (p. 202), during this period the initial need for female houses appears to have been more than satisfied. Perhaps more important, however, Leyser suggests that princes had apparently become less tolerant of wealthy widows who freely alienated their inheritances.[74] Noblewomen were now frequently forced to remarry and to use their possessions to build up territorial lordships rather than piously disposing of them in establishing a female foundation.[75] Other changes also worked to diminish the economic independence of noblewomen, such as policies of patrilineal lineage, primogeniture, and the indivisibility of patrimony as well as shifts in the institution of the bridegift.[76]

Therefore these various political, social, and economic changes seem to underscore a deterioration in the formal power and economic independence of the aristocratic families of Europe. Since female saints of this early period were especially dependent on the irregular powers of the family for their status and influence in society, these shifts seem to have contributed to the decline in the number of mulieres sanctae.

The patterns of change which we have been tracing concern an elite group of women, "women worthies," who were honored by the Church in their saints' lives and popular cults. While a collective study of the vitae provides many important insights into shifts in female sanctity, the lives furnish only very limited and indirect evidence, for example, about women who actively challenged or defied the growing sex-based restrictions of the Church and society, about informal female influences and networks of power, or about lower-class women. Thus in light of the limitations of our sources and the complexity of female experiences in medieval society, we need to be careful not to attribute a wider validity to these patterns of visibility and status than they merit.

Nevertheless, it appears that in barbarian Europe of the early Middle Ages, women enjoyed a certain potentia and indeed wider opportunities in the "public" realm as confirmed by their selection to the celestial gynaeceum. In this pioneering society, when the very survival of the Church depended on the contribution and cooperation of everyone, restrictions upon the activities of the allegedly inferior sex were ignored or temporarily abated. Women with power and property were actively recruited by churchmen to aid in missionary work, to establish churches, monasteries, and centers of education, and to assume positions of leadership with very real power. They partook of the prerogatives and privileges of the newly Christianized lands and were frequently rewarded for their essential contributions through recognition of sanctity.

Although during the golden age of female sanctity (which is set in the midst of the so-called Dark Ages) the Church and society acknowledged women's worth (as witnessed by the relatively high percentage of female saints for the period), they still failed to recognize their equivalence fully. This failure is highlighted by the asymmetrical patterns which emerge from our survey of the dossiers of female and male saints.

Notes

This essay constitutes a revised and expanded version of a paper presented at the American Historical Association meeting, Chicago, in December 1984. I have given a fuller treatment of this topic in *"Forgetful of Their Sex": Female Sanctity and 'Deviancy,' ca. 500–1100* (forthcoming).

1. The most complete compilation of saints can be found in the *Bibliotheca sanctorum*, Instituto Giovanni XXIII della Pontificia Universita Lateranense (Rome, 1961–71), 12 vols. Also see *Acta Sanctorum*, ed. J. Bollandus et al., rev. ed., 68 vols. (Paris and Rome, 1845–1931) (hereinafter cited as *AASS*).

2. During the past twenty years studies on sanctity have proliferated, though most of the works do not treat early medieval saints or specifically focus on female sanctity. A select list of some major studies would include Pierre Delooz, *Sociologie et canonisations*, Collection scientifique de la Faculté de Droit de l'Université de Liège 30 (Liège/The Hague, 1969); André Vauchez, *La sainteté en Occident aux derniers siècles du Moyen Age d'après les procès de canonisation et les documents hagiographiques* (Rome, 1981) (extensive bibliography); Donald Weinstein and Rudolf M. Bell, *Saints and Society: The Two Worlds of Western Christendom, 1000–1700* (Chicago, 1982); Peter Brown, *The Cult of Saints: Its Rise and Function in Latin Christianity* (Chicago, 1981); Richard Kieckhefer, *Unquiet Souls: Fourteenth-Century Saints and Their Religious Milieu* (Chicago, 1984); Sophia Boesch Gajano, ed., *Agiografia altomedioevale* (Bologna, 1976) (extensive bibliography); Stephen Wilson, ed., *Saints and Their Cults: Studies in Religious Sociology, Folklore, and History* (Cambridge, 1983) (extensive bibliography); Sister Benedicta Ward, *Miracles and the Medieval Mind: Theory, Record, and Event, 1000–1215* (Philadelphia, 1982); Alexander Murray, *Reason and Society in the Middle Ages* (Oxford, 1978); Michael Goodich, *Vita Perfecta: The Ideal of Sainthood in the Thirteenth Century* (Stuttgart, 1982); Joseph-Claude Poulin, *L'Idéal de sainteté dans l'Aquitaine carolingienne d'après les sources hagiographiques (750–950)* (Quebec, 1975); F. Graus, *Volk, Herrscher, und Heiliger im Reich der Merowinger: Studien zur Hagiographie der Merowingerzeit* (Prague, 1965).

3. Delooz, pp. 5–25.

4. On canonization, see E. W. Kemp, *Canonization and Authority in the Western Church* (London, 1948).

5. J. T. Schulenburg, "Sexism and the Celestial Gynaeceum—From 500 to 1200," *Journal of Medieval History* 4 (1978):117–33.

6. For another interpretation of the statistics on female saints, one which incorporates both early and late medieval saints, see David Herlihy, "Did Women Have a Renaissance? A Reconsideration," *Medievalia et Humanistica: Studies in Medieval and Renaissance Culture* n.s., no. 13 (1985):1–22.

7. See especially JoAnn McNamara and Suzanne F. Wemple, "The Power of Women Through the Family in Medieval Europe, 500–1100," in this volume; Jo Ann McNamara and Suzanne F. Wemple, "Sanctity and Power: The Dual Pursuit of Medieval Women," in *Becoming Visible: Women in European History*, ed. R. Bridenthal and C. Koonz (Boston, 1977), pp. 90–118; Susan Mosher Stuard, *Women in Medieval Society* (Philadelphia, 1976), pp. 1–12; Janet L. Nelson, "Queens as Jezebels: The Careers of Brunhild and Balthild in Merovingian History," in *Medieval Women*, ed. Derek Baker (Oxford, 1978), pp. 31–77.

8. Godefroy Kurth, *Sainte Clotilde*, (Paris, 1905), pp. 1–19. Schulenburg, "Women and Proselytization in Germanic Society," paper presented at the Thirteenth Conference on Medieval Studies, Western Michigan University, Kalamazoo, May 1978.

9. Gregory of Tours, *History of the Franks,* trans. Lewis Thorpe (Harmondsworth, 1974), bk. 2, chaps. 29–31, pp. 141–45; Kurth, pp. 50–64.

10. See the letter from Nicetius, Bishop of Trier, to Clodoswinde (ca. 568), in which he praises her religiosity and refers to her grandmother Clotilda and her meritorious work in converting Clovis. He then asks Clodoswinde to persist without ceasing in trying to convert her husband Alboin to Catholicism (*Epistulae Austrasicae,* 8, *Monumenta Germanicae Historica* (hereinafter cited as *MGH*), *Epistolae merowingici et karolini aevi,* vol. 1, pp. 119–22).

11. Bede, *A History of the English Church and People,* trans. L. Sherley-Price (Harmondsworth, 1968), bk. 1, chap. 25, pp. 68–70.

12. Bede, bk. 2, chap. 11, pp. 120–22.

13. Kurth, pp. 14–18.

14. See Marion Facinger, "A Study of Medieval Queenship: Capetian France, 987–1237," *Studies in Medieval and Renaissance History* 5 (1968):3–48.

15. There are many examples of these activities in the vitae of the Merovingian and Anglo-Saxon queens and German empresses. Especially active were Sts. Clotilda, Balthild, Radegund, Ethelberga, and Sexberga. See also Nelson, pp. 60–73.

16. Gregory of Tours, bk. 3, chap. 18, p. 182.

17. Schulenburg, "Female Saints and the Holy Dead: Caretakers and Collectors (500–1100)" (Paper delivered at the Nineteenth International Congress on Medieval Studies, Western Michigan University, May 1984).

18. Schulenburg, "Women and Monasticism: Crises of Invasion and Reform" (Paper delivered at the Fourteenth International Congress on Medieval Studies, Western Michigan University, May 1979).

19. Karl J. Leyser, *Rule and Conflict in an Early Medieval Society: Ottonian Saxony* (London, 1979), pp. 63–73.

20. Ibid.

21. In some cases, when the monastery's ownership of certain properties came into question, the vitae were used as legal charters or land titles as proof of possession.

22. See Leyser, pp. 49–62; Suzanne F. Wemple, *Women in Frankish Society: Marriage and the Cloister, 500 to 900* (Philadelphia, 1981), pp. 47–49; Pauline Stafford, *Queens, Concubines, and Dowagers: The King's Wife in the Early Middle Ages* (London, 1983), pp. 171–82.

23. Baudonivia, *De vita sanctae Radegundis liber II; MGH, Scriptorum rerum merovingicarum,* vol. 2, bk. 2, chap. 5, p. 381, hereinafter cited as *MGH, SRM.*

24. *Gregorii episcopi turonensis liber in gloria confessorum, MGH, SRM,* vol. 1, chap. 104, p. 814; (St. Aurea) *AASS,* Octobris II, 477; David Knowles and R. Neville Hadcock, *Medieval Religious Houses: England and Wales* (London, 1971), p. 261; Agnes B. C. Dunbar, *A Dictionary of Saintly Women,* vol. 2 (London, 1905), p. 241.

25. G. A. de Rohan Chabot, Marquise de Maille, *Les Cryptes de Jouarre* (Paris, 1971), p. 26.

26. *AASS,* Septembris VI, 527.

27. Dunbar, vol. 1, pp. 111–12; "De virtutibus sanctae Geretrudis," *MGH, SRM,* vol. 2, bk. 10, p. 469; Maille, p. 41.

28. Cited by Christine Fell in *Women in Anglo Saxon England* (London, 1984), p. 120.

29. *AASS,* Februarius I, 306.

30. *AASS,* Julii II, 626.

31. *AASS,* Martii III, 385.

32. *AASS,* Iunii II, 132.

33. *AASS,* Augusti I, 686.

34. *AASS,* Maii I, 117.

35. Bede, *History,* bk. 4, chap. 6, p. 218.

36. Charles Joseph Hefele and Dom H. Leclercq, *Histoire des conciles,* 3 vols. (Paris, 1909), vol. 3, pt. 1, p. 539; Arthur West Haddan and William Stubbs, *Councils and Ecclesiastical Documents Relating to Great Britain and Ireland,* vol. 3 (1871; repr., 1964), 238–40.

37. Eddius Stephanus, "Life of St. Wilfrid," in *Lives of the Saints,* trans. J. F. Webb (Harmondsworth, 1965), chap. 60, p. 196.

38. *Two Lives of St. Cuthbert,* trans. Bertram Colgrave (New York, 1969), chap. 24, p. 236.

39. *MGH, SRM,* vol. 2, *vita* A, chap. 3, p. 458.

40. Bede, *History,* bk. 4, chap. 23, p. 247 (emphasis added).

41. Bede, "Life of Saint Cuthbert," in *Two Lives of St. Cuthbert,* chap. 24, p. 234.

42. "Life of Leoba," in *The Anglo-Saxon Missionaries in Germany,* trans. C. H. Talbot (New York, 1954), p. 214.

43. *MGH Scriptorum,* vol. 15, chap. 3, p. 540.

44. *AASS,* Aprilis, II, p. 33.

45. "Life of Leoba," pp. 218, 220.

46. *MGH, SRM,* vol. 2, bk. 1, chap. 31, p. 374.

47. *MGH, SRM,* vol. 2, *vita* A. chap. 5, pp. 458–59; *Translatio of St. Edith* by Monk Goscelin, *Analecta Bollandiana* 56 (1938):12, 278. See also Susan Millinger's interesting study, "Humility and Power: Anglo-Saxon Nuns in Anglo-Norman Hagiography," in *Distant Echoes: Medieval Religious Women,* vol. 1, ed. John A. Nichols and Lillian Thomas Shank (Kalamazoo, 1984), pp. 115–29.

48. Dunbar, vol. 1, p. 97.

49. *Translatio of St. Edith,* chap. 12, pp. 278–79.

50. Ibid., pp. 279–80.

51. *Vita sanctae Vulfildae, Analecta Bollandiana* 32 (1913), chap. 8, pp. 20–22.

52. Eleanor McLaughlin, "Women, Power, and the Pursuit of Holiness in Medieval Christianity," in *Women of Spirit: Female Leadership in the Jewish and Christian Traditions,* ed. Rosemary Ruether and Eleanor McLaughlin (New York, 1979), p. 107.

53. See Schulenburg, "Strict Active Enclosure and Its Effects on the Female Monastic Experience, ca. 500–1100," in *Distant Echoes,* vol. 1, pp. 51–86.

54. Wemple, p. 169.

55. Ibid., p. 188.

56. Schulenburg, "Women and the Church: Proscriptions of Sacred Space, ca.

500–1100" (Paper presented at the Eighteenth International Congress on Medieval Studies, Western Michigan University, May 1983).

57. Council of Nantes, 895, chap. 19, *Acta Conciliorum*, ed. Harduin, vol. 6 (Paris, 1714), part 1, p. 461, cited by McNamara and Wemple, "The Power of Women," p. 93 in this volume.

58. *Annales Fuldenses* (847), *MGH, Scriptorum*, vol. 1, p. 365, Charles Joseph Hefele and Dom H. Leclercq, *Histoire des conciles*, vol. 4 (Paris, 1911), part 1, pp. 135–36. This fascinating case is translated and discussed by Wemple in *Women in Frankish Society*, pp. 144–45.

59. *Vita S. Iohannis Gualberti Anonyma*, *MGH, Scriptorum*, vol. 30, pt. 2, chap. 2, p. 1105. See also R. I. Moore, "Family, Community, and Cult on the Eve of the Gregorian Reform," in *Transactions of the Royal Historical Society*, 5th ser., vol. 30 (London, 1980), p. 68.

60. Odo of Cluny, *Collationum, Bibliotheca Cluniacensis*, ed. Dom Martinus Marrier and Andreas Quercetanus (Brussels, 1915), bk. 2, p. 192.

61. *Liber iii adversus simoniacos, MGH, Libelli de Lite*, vol. 1, bk. 3, chap. 12, p. 212.

62. Idung of Prüfening, "An Argument Concerning Four Questions by Idung of Prüfening," in *Cistercians and Cluniacs: The Case for Citeaux*, Cistercian Father Series 33, trans. J. Leahey and G. Perigo (Kalamazoo, 1977), pp. 175–76.

63. Wemple, p. 171.

64. *AASS*, Septembris VI, p. 276.

65. *MGH, Script.*, vol. 4, chap. 35, p. 164.

66. *AASS*, Martii III, p. 385.

67. *MGH, Script.*, vol. 4, chap. 6, p. 452.

68. Helgaldus, *Vie du roi Robert*, in *Collection des mémoires relatifs à l'histoire de France*, ed. M. Guizot (Paris, 1824), vol. 6, pp. 379–80.

69. Dunbar, vol. 1, p. 397. See also a note on St. Hunna in the *Analecta Bollandiana* 66 (1948), pp. 343–45.

70. Turgot, "Life of Queen Margaret," in *Early Sources of Scottish History, A.D. 500–1286*, trans. Alan O. Anderson, vol. 2 (Edinburgh, 1922), pp. 64–73. Turgot also notes: "Her chamber was never empty of these things (that is, of the things that pertained to the adornment of divine service); it seemed to be a kind of workshop, so to speak, of celestial art. There were always seen copes for the cantors, chasubles, stoles, altar-cloths, and other priestly vestments, and decorations for the church. Some were being prepared by the artist's hand; others, finished, were kept as being worthy of admiration" (p. 65).

71. *AASS*, Junii V, 430. St. Etheldreda made for St. Cuthbert "stolam videlicet et manipulum similis materiae, ex auro et lapidis pretiosis, propriis (ut fertur) manibus, docta auritexturae ingenio fecit."

72. Poulin, pp. 42–43.

73. Wemple, especially pp. 194–97; McNamara and Wemple, "The Power of Women," pp. 95–97 in this volume; Stuard, pp. 9–11.

74. Leyser, p. 71.

75. Ibid.

76. McNamara and Wemple, "The Power of Women," pp. 95–97 in this volume; McNamara and Wemple, "Sanctity and Power," pp. 110–16.

The Power of Love:
Wives and Husbands
in Late Medieval Venice

Stanley Chojnacki

In December 1445 Valerio Zeno and Vittoria Vitturi, a Venetian patrician husband and wife, summoned a notary to draw up their wills.[1] In his will, written December 2, Valerio designated Vittoria as his sole executor and, acknowledging his obligation to return her dowry of twenty-four hundred ducats to her, instructed that she was to inherit all his other goods as well, whether she remarried or not. He made a point of underscoring this intention, anticipating "impediments or opposition" to Vittoria's inheritance from his agnatic kinsmen, who would be reluctant to see his property escape them, especially if Vittoria should remarry (as, in the event, she did, twice).[2] Still, that he favored his wife over kin did not signal alienation from his lineage, for he asked to be buried "in our tomb of Ca' Zeno at SS. Giovanni e Paolo." In her will nineteen days later, Vittoria reciprocated by making Valerio her sole executor and universal heir—except for one other bequest, a four-hundred-ducat dowry contribution to a daughter of Valerio's late brother, Basilio Zeno. This generous bequest surprisingly shows Vittoria more beneficent toward her husband's kin than he himself was and indeed more than she was to her own natal family, which then included one brother with a son just entering adulthood.[3] Yet although like Valerio she favored her spouse over her kinsmen in tangible bequests, also like him she wanted to be buried "in the tomb where my father, *Dominus* Andrea [Vitturi], and my mother are buried."[4]

The wills of Valerio and Vittoria Zeno, fairly typical examples of the genre, expose the rich complexity of social relations among married patricians in late medieval Venice. They show married people's enduring loyalty to family and lineage of origin, expressed here in the symbolically weighty choice of burial sites, but they also show deep trust and generosity between husband and wife. Such strong bonds between spouses had the potential to subvert other, older loyalties, notably those to the natal clan.[5] The Zeno wills, and others like them, however, reveal that married patricians did not always face a sharp either/or choice between natal and marital family. Rather, they inhabited a dense interwoven thicket of social and psychological relationships, through which they navigated in a variety of ways, limited by the constraints of individual circumstance but also following the urgings of individual desires. Family and lineage ties were important, as was calculation of personal interest, but affection also figured in married people's choices in bestowing loyalty and largesse. In the following pages I make an initial foray into the uncharted realm of affection between spouses, with special concern for its place in patricians' overall social orientation.[6] I pay particular attention to husbands' regard for their wives, for there are signs that husbandly affection deepened in the fifteenth century. This development appears to have been influenced by an increase in the status and power of women in patrician society. At the same time, it contributed toward expanding still further women's influence—economic, social, and cultural.

On the whole, the literature on marriage among the late medieval and Renaissance Italian elites has tended to emphasize, properly and profitably, its alliance aspect, viewing marriage as an instrument of family and lineage strategy, a means of promoting the family's status and advancing its interests.[7] Although less concerned with the strictly social dimensions of family history than scholars working on other cities, historians of Venice have also studied patrician marriage and have emphasized the political and economic stakes in families' matrimonial strategies.[8] Such family-centered concerns were manifestly important, but emphasis on alliances can give the impression that marriage had little to do with the personalities or even identities of the spouses, who figure in this picture chiefly as instruments of family interest, especially the teenaged brides (grooms, in contrast, often took part in marriage negotiation).[9] When we stress alliances, too, we take a perspective that shows all parties—contracting families, spouses, even children—operating chiefly, if not solely, from calculated interest.

Although marriage was an important vehicle of patricians' family and individual interest, attention to alliances did not necessarily preclude intense relations between spouses. Indeed, it would be surprising if close bonds did not often develop. As instruments of family strategy, spouses might be drawn to each other by mutual sympathy. For that matter, family strategy encouraged good relations between the two joined links as a guarantee of the alliance's enduring success. Over the course of years and decades of proximity and intimacy, during which the contours of their families were constantly being reshaped and their shared experiences accumulating in scope and complexity, husbands and wives could develop feelings of companionship, loyalty, and affection for one another. A full picture of marriage must consequently consider husband–wife relations over time. The interfamilial dimension is important, but so are the years after the bride and groom were thrown willy-nilly into connubial bliss by the interests of their families, the long postnuptial period when spouses had the opportunity to forge a relationship of their own.

Special attention should be given the experience of wives over the uxorial cycle, the long evolution that saw them change, in many cases, from terror-stricken child brides into mature wives and mothers and finally into widows who often commanded formidable resources. Because each of these phases has its own dense and busy reality, distinct from those of other phases, no one moment in the wifely experience captures its essence. Nor can a "typical" wife be found. Different women went through the uxorial cycle in different ways. Some had many children, some had few or none. Some kept close ties to their natal families; others forged warm affinal associations. Some built relationships of loyal tenderness with their husbands; others suffered through marriages marked by strain and alienation. Some predeceased their husbands; others lived into long widowhoods and, like Vittoria Vitturi Zeno, contracted second and even third marriages.

Sparse documentation makes it difficult to reconstruct married persons' concerns and sentiments in detail, but one type of source offers abundant insights into the attitudes of patricians at moments of social and economic assessment. The source is wills. Wills, or testaments, allow us to observe women, and men as well, confronting the last things, taking careful stock of the contents of their lives, and expressing their ultimate preferences and hopes. Because the concerns of Venetian testators emerge with remarkable clarity from the thick undergrowth of formulas that often mark wills, these documents are a rich mine of information about husbands' and wives' opinions of each other. Accordingly, the principal documentation in this essay is a group of 361 wills drawn up between 1290 and 1520 by patricians with living spouses.[10]

Fourteenth- and fifteenth-century wills reflect changing attitudes during the period. We must be wary of assigning neat dates or precise causes to attitudes and especially of devising too clear-cut a chronology of sentiment. Whether historical conditions trigger new kinds of emotional relationships among people is a hugely delicate and complex question and a controversial one.[11] Nevertheless, evidence is strong that the fifteenth century saw the emergence among Venetian patricians of a higher regard for women and a deepening of husband-wife affection. These tendencies appear tied to certain general developments in patrician marriage during the period.

In his will, Valerio Zeno acknowledged the large dowry of 2,400 ducats that his wife Vittoria had brought to their marriage. He declared that half of it had come in the form of real estate which he treated as his own while he was alive but which should be returned to her at his death.[12] Vittoria's family, the Vitturis, had thus considered her marriage to Valerio worth a substantial investment of movable and immovable Vitturi wealth. As Vittoria's will showed, such marriage portions could take permanent flight from the wife's lineage. Had Valerio outlived his wife, her bequest to him would have given him the real estate her family had put into her dowry. The construction of patrician marriages on big and growing dowries is a phenomenon that Venice shared with other Italian cities during this period.[13] One of the strongest reasons for it in Venice was the growing importance of marriage in patrician family strategy and a consequent willingness to invest heavily in it. This emphasis on marriage increased women's influence in patrician society by increasing their wealth. This is a vast, many-sided question, but the main points can be stated briefly.

Contributing strongly to women's enhanced power in patrician society were major changes in the nature of the patriciate during the decades around 1400. Briefly, members of the class became at this time more dependent on government support for their economic well-being and more jealous of their status and the prestige and privileges it brought them. The two tendencies led to the erection in the early fifteenth century of a barricade of exclusivist legislation around the ruling class.[14] The officially enforced patrician self-consciousness set a higher premium on the choice of marriage partners, specifically on the prestige and influence of brides' and grooms' families. Already in the early fifteenth century, Venetian legislators were raising the status requirements for patrician wives, and the patrician humanist Francesco Barbaro was attaching at least as much importance to a mother's birth as to that of a father in the breeding of worthy patricians.[15] In these circumstances, matchmaking was a serious business indeed.

The currency of matchmaking was dowries, which climbed steadily throughout the period, as families invested ever larger portions of their substance in marriages that brought prestige and cemented valued friendships.[16] So important to family strategy were advantageous marriages that in the fifteenth century girls' dowries sometimes outstripped their brothers' patrimonies—something occasionally noted by will-writing parents, such as the father who excluded his married daughter because she had already received "much more than all her brothers will get."[17]

By the sixteenth century the impact of the dowry on male-female relations had reached such a point that legislators were blaming Venice's declining commercial enterprise on the tendency of husbands to live off
their wives' dowries.[18]

Still, for all the dowry's importance as a tool of family strategy, in the
end it belonged to the daughter whom it accompanied to marriage. It was
in fact her "patrimonium," to be returned to her or transferred to her
chosen heirs at the end of the marriage.[19] For this reason a testating father
would bid his married daughters to "be well content with their dowries
and have no reason for complaint" when they were denied further bequests. Yet although some fathers (and mothers) were concerned about
the deep bite that dowries were taking out of family wealth, others com-
pounded the effect by leaving additional bequests to their already dow-
ered daughters.[20] These contrasting attitudes alert us to the variety of
patrician family situations and the broad range of personal choice open to
individuals. They also signal that fathers benefited their daughters in a
number of ways over and above dowry provision—benefits that added
further to women's disposable wealth. This wealth, rising pari passu with
dowry levels, gave married women formidable new power in their social
relations. For one thing, they were now in a position to help their own
daughters meet the rising dowry standards—in the process contributing
to their further rise.[21] They could extend their largesse to others as well,
however. The result of the swelling of married women's actual and potential benefactions was to exalt their importance and influence within
their social worlds. A wife's or widow's family and kin had compelling
practical reason to keep in her good graces by showing her every affectionate consideration.

These circumstances magnified the influence of married women on
those near them, notably their husbands. The material expression of a
wife's regard could now literally change her husband's life—as no doubt
Valerio Zeno's life would have changed if, instead of bequeathing him her
twenty-four-hundred-ducat dowry, his wife, Vittoria, had exercised her
legal right to have him restore it to her estate, for the benefit of other kin.
Some wives followed Vittoria in selecting their husbands as prime benefi-
ciary.[22] Others made different choices, however, and favored natal kin, so
that they returned the dowry to the family from which it had come in the
first place.[23] It was the capacity to dispose of their wealth as they liked—on
the basis of calculation but also of inclination—as much as the wealth
itself, that gave married women their potent new presence in patrician
society. A constellation of potential beneficiaries, most prominent among
them fathers hoping that their daughters would return at least some of the
dowry wealth to their natal families and husbands desirous of lodging it

permanently in their own family, was anxious to earn the favor of these increasingly rich benefactresses.[24] The parental bequests to already married daughters, mentioned above, were probably stimulated at least in part by the desire to retain the daughters' continued benevolence and the economic generosity in which it might find expression.

The heightened importance of women affected men in a variety of ways. One was in their attitude toward women's fashions in clothing. This complex subject, on which I can touch only glancingly here, involves important aspects not only of women's economic autonomy but also of individual psychology and the relations between private and collective interests as well.[25] Female fashion, like male fashion, grew increasingly splendid in the fifteenth century and elicited ambivalent responses. Public concern centered on costly attire that proponents of sumptuary legislation saw as unproductive waste, an attitude fully displayed in the preambles to the sumptuary laws that increased in the fifteenth century. These express endless agonizing over women's "excessive expenditures on wicked and impractical [inutilem]" apparel that "consumes their husbands and sons" or, again, leads to the "ruin of their husbands and fathers."[26] Many individual men shared this concern, their votes passing the laws, but others took pride in their handsomely decked-out womenfolk, even encouraging their expenditures. In the sixteenth century, we are informed, family and friends saw brides-to-be display their elaborate trousseaux at betrothal parties, and husbands themselves engaged tailors and mercers to clothe their brides in up-to-date splendor.[27]

Yet the wearing of sumptuous clothing may also have been a way for women with wealth but few opportunities for productive economic (let alone political) outlets to make a gesture of self-assertion. In a culture which narrowly limited women's activities in the public sphere, heavy spending on lavish dress could be viewed as doubly assertive, calling visual attention to individual identity and demonstrating the autonomous possession of wealth.[28] That it might be detrimental to men may have been incidental—or for some it may have been a gesture, with available means, protesting institutional or individual male domination. The significance of female fashion in male-dominated societies is a rich subject, with the erotic as well as the sumptuary aspects touching relations between men and women at several different levels. Whether women wore splendid attire to attract or to challenge men (or without regard to men at all), whether men took pride in their wives' appearance or were sexually or economically threatened by its public display, whether expenditures on dress were regarded as wasteful or as investments in status— these questions deserve extended consideration. Although the answers are incomplete at present, the Venetian legislation makes it clear that women were spending money on fashion, that men were thought to be suffering as a result, and that neither government nor private male society was able to curb these expenditures.

Women's wealth and their autonomy in using it—even in ways that were potentially harmful for men—made women formidable figures. This power inspired a complex variety of responses. Here we venture into psychological waters ill charted in the sources and the literature. The first fruits of research, however, strongly suggest that the increase in married women's wealth led the menfolk to take their mates more seriously and to court their favor more assiduously. This development in turn seems to have produced a deeper bond between spouses, with implications for the whole patrician culture and specifically for the articulation of both male and female gender identity.[29]

The new regard that women gained found varied expression. One form was an increased tendency in the fifteenth century for husbands to name their wives as executors (*commissari*) of their wills. The wills of 104 patricians with living wives give a crude overall idea of the trend. Fifty-five were from the fourteenth century; in these, wives were named as executors by thirty-five of the testating husbands, or 64 percent. Of the forty-nine husbands who wrote their wills in the fifteenth century, however, forty-three, or 88 percent, elected their wives—a striking increase. Moreover a few, such as Valerio Zeno, made the wives their only commissari, while others instructed that, in disputes among executors, the wife would hold the deciding vote. None of the Trecento husbands' wills that I have seen gave such authority to wives.[30]

Practically speaking, these appointments made good sense in the fifteenth century. Well-dowered wives would acquire substantial personal wealth upon becoming widows; as noted, many also had other wealth, from legacies not encumbered with dowry restrictions, to enjoy during their marriage. The practical skills or expert help they used managing their own resources might fruitfully be applied to the benefit of their husbands' estates and especially to that of their common offspring. A family-conscious patrician had every reason to deepen his widow's involvement—and possibly that of her wealth and her brothers—in his sons' grooming for adulthood.[31] To be sure, in entrusting his estate to his wife, a husband effectively removed it from the control of his agnatic kin. The short-term alienation, however, could be counterbalanced by the lineage's potential longer-term benefit from his sons' improved chances for a generous inheritance from their mother and also for the support of her natal familiars, especially the sons' maternal uncles. At any rate, a husband entrusting his estate to his wife's care was likely to be pretty sure of her benevolence toward their children and even (as with Valerio Zeno) toward his other kinsmen. Yet apart from these hardheaded reasons, that husbands placed their wealth in the care of their wives, alone or with others, signifies trust and a sense of shared interest, impulses that marital intimacy could easily blend into strong emotional attachment.

Another sign of men's personal regard for women can be found in fathers' attitudes toward their daughters' vocational preferences. We must tread cautiously here. Family interest weighed heavily on fathers, and marriage was one of the chief weapons in the arsenal of family strategy. An attractive, intelligent daughter and adequate dowry resources added up to a combination of family-enhancing assets a father would only reluctantly avoid using. Alternatively, scant dowry capital might make the convent unavoidable for the daughter.[32] It was a rare father who would or could go against the perceived family interest to satisfy a daughter's choice of adult life. And indeed, most testating fathers left instructions about their daughters' futures with no regard for the girls' thoughts on the matter; the governing principle apparently was that as many daughters should marry as family resources permitted.[33] Yet despite the powerful imperative of family economic and social needs and interests, we do find the occasional father giving weight in his will to his daughters' "intentions" or "desires" when providing for them. Such cases appear more frequently in the fifteenth century than in the fourteenth.[34]

The apparent new fatherly concern for daughters' vocational preferences coincides with a rise during the fifteenth century in the age at which testating parents wanted their daughters married. Indeed, the two tendencies appear to be related manifestations of an increased attention to the timing and substance of female adulthood.[35] Fathers according their daughters greater participation in the choice of their vocations would want the choice delayed until the girls gained greater maturity. Alternatively, a general delaying of the female marriage age, and with it the presumption of adult status, would incline fathers to view their married daughters as more mature persons. These signs of an evolving notion of female adulthood have important implications for changes in Venetian ideas about female, and particularly wifely, gender; they require fuller treatment than is possible here. Still, in the context of the present discussion, it is important to note that fathers' new solicitude for their daughters' preferences may have been encouraged by the example of their wives, who when writing their wills appear even more inclined to offer their daughters the choice between the convent and marriage.[36] Indeed, an emerging maternal tendency to allow daughters complete freedom of vocational choice, including even lay spinsterhood, represented a challenge to traditional male conceptions of family honor, seen as threatened by unmarried daughters' exposure to secular temptation.[37] I have seen no

evidence that husbands permitted women to choose a single life, but the
willingness of even a few of them to entertain their daughters' preferences
in a choice between marriage and the convent may indicate that the increased importance that wives were gaining from their wealth was spill-
ing over into influence on their husbands' cultural attitudes as well as on
family strategy.

The more influential presence of women in the patrician family seems
to have stimulated not only men's regard and solicitude but their affection
as well. Affection arises from many things, and it would be simplistic to
attribute it to the wealth or power of the loved one, even more so to
assume that Venetian spouses had not loved one another before the rise in
dowries. Nevertheless, men in fifteenth-century Venice were more eloquent than their grandfathers in expressing their affection for the women
in their lives. Nowhere is the change more apparent than in the language
of wills, in which terms of endearment became steadily more frequent
and more elaborate during the fifteenth century. A preliminary sense of
the trend emerges from sixty-seven husbands' wills written between 1322
and 1511.[38] Of the thirty-three from before 1400, only eight went beyond simple references to *uxor* or *moier* (or sometimes *muier*), and these
eight all used the conventional adjective *dilecta,* as in "uxorem meam
dilectam." In the thirty-four written between 1402 and 1511, however,
twenty-two of the husbands, almost two-thirds, added an affectionate
adjective when they mentioned their wives. The tendency accelerated as
the Quattrocento advanced: twenty of the twenty-six wills written after
1425, more than three-quarters, include a term of affection for the wife.
Moreover—and more important than the numerical evidence from this
tiny sample—although most fifteenth-century husbands still favored *dilecta* when referring to their wives, growing numbers resorted to such
tender terms as "mia molier charissima," "mia chara e dileta chonsorte,"
or "mia dilectissima consorte."[39] (The new application to spouses of the
old kinship term *consorte,* literally, "destiny-sharer," shows the use of terminology once reserved for kinship to describe matrimonial loyalties—
another sign of the growing importance of marriage in family strategy.)[40]

The new articulateness in affection did not belong only to husbands
and wives but extended to other relations as well. We find in the Quattrocento, for example, a daughter called "dilectissima et dulcissima," a son
"mio fio dilectissimo," a "carissimum" brother, and even—tellingly—
"dilectissimos" brothers-in-law.[41] Still, men had applied similar (though
less effusive) terms to natal kinsmen in the previous century, too. The big
change was their new application to wives. The new language of husbandly love is remarkable not just because of its warmth but because of its

flexible variety, its individuality. Testators chose the exact terms they wanted, supplying their own nuances; superlatives, for example, seem to have been chosen expressly to convey an exceptionally close bond. Sometimes husbands used different terms in different passages of a single will, showing that each instance was an act of personal choice.[42] The contrast with the narrow vocabulary and perfunctoriness of such usage in fourteenth-century wills could not be sharper.

The change owes much to increased literacy and verbal confidence, evident in the greater incidence of wills written not by notaries but by the testators themselves, in the vernacular—although Latin wills from the late Quattrocento also contain far more terms of affection than Latin wills of a century earlier. Especially noteworthy (and worthy of more systematic investigation) is the fact that women as well as men drafted their wills by hand more frequently in the fifteenth century than they had earlier. The personal language in these handwritten wills gives even more weight to their expressions of affection as well as showing women's increased control of language as a means of asserting themselves. While this new expressiveness in conveying marital affection suggests development in literacy and linguistic facility, however, it also shows that new feelings were stimulating a new articulateness. The language of affection was so widespread in wills of the later Quattrocento that it appears to have become a convention, raising the question of whether its use is a valid gauge of individual feeling behind the words—although even its adoption as a cultural convention would suggest that affection between spouses was becoming normative. There is also evidence, however, that the affectionate expressions in fifteenth-century wills were not empty formulas.

The wills reveal still more about sentiment in the testators' descriptions of the relationships that they reward or ignore in their bequests. It is telling, for example, to read a man's instruction that his wife and children not come to his funeral "to avoid compounding their pain" at losing him.[43] However much pain his death actually did cause them, such bereavement at least seemed to him likely or at least natural, and his instruction a touching last thoughtful gesture to his loved ones. Another testating husband declared that he wanted his wife to be aware of "the love I have always borne her."[44] Disarmingly candid was Jacopo Morosini, who in 1448 praised "Cristina, *mia molier charissima,* to whom I am altogether too obliged, for her admirable conduct, and also for all the cash—over and above her dowry—that I have received from her family." In gratitude he made her his universal heir.[45] Such expressions of sentiment, rarely found in fourteenth-century wills, crop up regularly in the fifteenth, displaying a greater male concern with the feelings of wives and children and more openness about sentiment in general.

By giving his whole estate to his wife, Jacopo Morosini, like Valerio
Zeno three years earlier and like other fifteenth-century husbands, backed
up his fond words with deeds. By one deed with symbolic weight, husbands associated themselves with their wives in acts of piety and penance—together in the prayers of the priest as they had been in life.[46]
Another, weightier still, was making joint burial arrangements. In 1499,
Donato Arimondo ordered the construction of a tomb, complete with
carved inscription, for himself and his "chara chonsorte," Madona Bianca—despite Bianca's own wish, nine years earlier, to be buried with
her natal relatives from the Dolfin clan. Here we sense an emotional tug-
of-war, Donato doing his best to steal Bianca's ultimate allegiance away
from her natal family and attach it to himself.[47] Not all husbands provided for joint burial with their wives; even the uxorious Valerio Zeno
preferred entombment in the lineage crypt and made no mention of his
wife's posthumous companionship. Those who did, however, reveal a
powerful desire to preserve symbolically their closeness to their wives.

The complexity and implications of husbands' affection are even more
apparent in their bequests to their wives. Again, variety is the rule. Some
husbands bequeathed nothing, some just their wife's dowry—although
that was not really a bequest at all, for a widow's legal right to her dowry
did not depend on any action by her husband. Indeed, her entitlement to
its restitution was so strong that it took precedence over all other claims
on her husband's estate. Nevertheless, a husband's acknowledgment of
the dowry in his will helped his widow by supplying quick and sure
documentation for the *vadimonium,* the legal action by which a widow (or
her successors) established the fact and amount of her dowry, thus taking
the indispensable first step toward the *diiudicatum,* or dowry-recovery
procedure.[48] Men, however, characteristically went beyond the dowry in
providing for their wives, adding a few hundred ducats, a life annuity,
very frequently food and lodging, and sometimes, like Valerio Zeno or
Jacopo Morosini, the entire estate. To be sure, motives of interest were
not absent from these husbandly bequests. Generous bequests to wives,
like their selection as testamentary executors, could stimulate wifely reciprocity, to the benefit of the husband's family and lineage. Moreover,
husbands normally made bequests to their wives conditional on the latters' willingness to renounce remarriage and stay with the children. Will-
writing husbands were considerate of their wives, but they also thought
hard about their children's reduced prospects of inheritance from a remarried mother.[49]

Yet tender feelings are unmistakably evident in husbands' bequests.
Even childless husbands sometimes offered economic inducements for
their widows to forgo remarriage; Donato Arimondo did so, and so did

his uncle, Marino. Marino, who was very generous to his wife as long as she remained a widow, instructed his kinsmen to treat her "as if she were my own self."[50] Disturbed at the prospect that their wives might desert their memories for other husbands, these men made it worth the wives' while to preserve in death the lifelong marital bond, in Marino's case forged forty-five years earlier, in Donato's, thirty-seven.[51] Yet others, including Valerio Zeno, benevolently encouraged, or at least accepted, their wives' remarriage, explicitly granting the wives benefits whether they married again or not.[52] All these gestures show husbands committed to caring for their companions of many years. The variety in their approaches, however—acknowledging the dowry or not, making outright bequests or not, encouraging widowly celibacy or cheerfully contemplating their wives' remarriage—shows men acting individually, tailoring their bequests to the distinctive qualities of their personal marital relationships. This male behavior can be seen as one of the transforming cultural effects of women's changed place in patrician society. Men did not abandon lineage loyalty in their affection for their wives; on the contrary, one form taken by husbandly love was the association of their wives with the lineage, its fortunes, and its symbols. Indeed, for success, marriage strategies, on which families staked large chunks of their resources, hoping for benefits from matrimonial alliances, required at least tolerable relations between spouses. Nevertheless, the testimony of fifteenth-century patrician wills reveals a new element in men's social orientation, rooted in a new respect and affection for their wives, that was now taking an influential place alongside lineage loyalties. It was a more personal response to the peculiarities of individual relationships. To the extent that a man with finite resources exhibited this responsiveness in concrete ways, as in a bequest to his wife, he necessarily reduced his tangible expression of lineage loyalty. This consequence, however, was offset by the hope that, by being loving and generous to their wives, men could encourage wifely love and generosity in return, to the benefit of family and lineage.

Yet calculations of interest, personal and lineage, alone did not determine these men's choices. The new husbandly attitude is also evident in terms of changed emotional relations between the sexes. Indeed, the validation that women's wealth gave to the sentimental ties that connected men to them—validation from the material standpoint of the lineage—enabled men to complement the lineage-based discipline that had traditionally dictated their social behavior with more personal kinds of loyalty. Thanks to the enhanced importance of marriage in patrician society and the increased stature it gave to well-dowered women, husbands could more closely approach the freer, less circumscribed, less lineage-determined orientation of women, in which individual responses to the contingencies of personal relationships, responses such as gratitude, respect, and affection, were allowed wider scope. Men could respond more fully, more reciprocally, to their wives' personal gestures and in their wills appear to have been more inclined to do so. Maddaluzza da Canal made her husband her universal heir, in the event of childlessness, as a reward for his "excellent companionship."[53] Maddaluzza had her dowry and no particular economic ax to grind; she simply wanted to show her pleasure in her husband's company. The same kindly affection probably led Lucrezia Priuli in 1503 to bequeath her husband Sebastiano a dwelling and one thousand ducats in state securities, along with instructions that, as with Valerio Zeno's strictures about his wife Vittoria's legacy, Sebastiano was not to be subjected to "any molestation" in enjoying his legacy from her.[54]

When well-dowered wives voluntarily bestowed their affection in these ways, their husbands were now able and willing to respond in kind. Marco Loredan, for example, in 1441 admonished his kin not to be surprised that he was making his wife his sole executor and universal heir, for he was obliged to her more than to "any [other] creature in the world" for her ministrations, costly to her own health, during his protracted illness—ministrations that he likened more to the labors of a slave than to the attentions of a wife.[55] Less touching but still full of tender gratitude is the statement of another Loredan, Francesco, who after allocating his wife's dowry repayment, regretted that "I lack the capital to give her what she merits for all her benefits to me."[56] These cases and others like them illustrate how, gradually and always within the limits of family and lineage obligations, men, under the influence of their wives, were now enriching their social culture with a new responsiveness in word and deed to the claims of emotion.

The change in women's wealth and influence thus had a larger significance apart from the fact that men were more respectful and solicitous, and more affectionate and generous, toward women. Women, with their economic weight and their traditionally less lineage-encumbered model of social relationships, were also providing a pattern for male culture and a stimulus toward modifying it and making it more flexible. Women's gender identity was changing with the growth in the power and influence of the wifely state, but men's gender identity was being transformed, too, as male society's changing attitudes toward marriage and wives modified husbandhood.[57] In apportioning bequests in response to personal as well as lineage urgings—in choosing interment with a wife rather than a father, in respecting the convent or marriage preferences of a "dulcissima e charissima" daughter, in thoughtfully apportioning bequests to brothers, nephews, sons, daughters, and also the "dilectissima consorte"—in carving out a structure of bequests that reflected the peculiarities of individual social geographies and the diverse loyalties they evoked, men were modifying their social personages under the influence of their formidable, substantial wives and in a manner more congruent with female patterns of social relations.

Three principal results of women's influence are apparent. One was to perpetuate and enlarge women's influence still further, as the men in their families courted them with ever larger bequests, gifts, and dowry settlements. This swelling of female wealth alarmed patrician legislators as a group, but individual patricians continued to find, in the importance of marriage in patrician relations, compelling reason to assemble large dowries for their daughters. Once under way, the transfer of family resources into female hands was carried along by its own momentum. The second result followed. With so much invested in marriages, patrician families sought to gain more from them. In consequence patterns of social relations altered throughout the patriciate. Lineage remained the principal framework of social orientation, but the desire to capitalize on the investment in marriage led to greater emphasis on affinal ties and the support and prestige they could offer. In this dense blending of kinship and marital association, the mediating role of propertied women, objects of both natal and marital kinsmen's interest, had large and growing significance.[58]

Third and most important, women's large and growing share of patrician wealth and the influence it brought could find expression in an approach to social relations less restricted by lineage obligations than that of men. It is ironic that the heavily patriarchal structure of Venetian lineage patterns made women freer of enforceable lineage discipline. A man was bound to his lineage by an array of legal constraints and economic inducements. A woman, at least a married woman, shared in two lineages and thus was bound tightly to neither except by moral ties which themselves pulled in two directions. In this freer female social space, personal loyalties and sentiments and tangible expressions of them took their place alongside the defined patterns of lineage loyalty and the more adjustable but no less strategically rooted expectations of marriage alliances. Women were the chief proponents of this more individualized approach to social relations, but their impact, on patrician society generally and especially on their own husbands, stimulated a response in kind.

Husbands were obliged, by self-interest and lineage interest—and specifically by the centrality in family strategy of favorable marriage alliances—to pay more attention to their well-dowered wives (and daughters). To do so they had to devote greater efforts to gaining and keeping the women's tangible favor. Women's favor, however, owing to their position outside the strict confines of kinship discipline, responded more to personal loyalties than to family or lineage loyalties and thus had to be earned in personal ways, so that men had a powerful inducement to adapt their male culture to the affective culture of women. This tendency, offered here only as a hypothesis, needs further study, as do a host of related questions—such as the coincidence of increased women's wealth and a rising marriage age, the patriciate's remarkable sociability in the sixteenth century, and the frank sensuality of Venetian art and social behavior in that century.[59] Even at this early point, however, there is reason to believe that changes in the relations between the sexes, in the function and nature of marriage, and, fundamentally, in the status and influence of women had a powerful transforming effect on the culture of Renaissance Venice.

Notes

For Signe and Steve Chojnacki on their fiftieth wedding anniversary.

Research for this essay was supported principally by the American Council of Learned Societies and the College of Arts and Letters, Michigan State University; the author expresses his gratitude to both bodies.

1. Archivio di Stato, Venice (hereinafter cited as ASV), Archivio Notarile, Testamenti (hereinafter cited as NT, followed by *busta* number and notary's name) 558, Gambaro, nos. 123, 124.

2. Vittoria's later marriages are noted in Marco Barbaro, "Libro di nozze patrizie," Biblioteca Nazionale Marciana, Venice, MSS italiani, classe VII, 156 (=8492) (hereinafter cited as Barbaro, Nozze), f. 432 right. Valerio's concern that his bequest to Vittoria might be contested is apparent in his wording: "volo, quod non obstantibus, neque impedientibus aliquibus condicionibus neque oppositionibus, que quo iure, modo, et forma opponi et fieri possent contra hanc presentem meam ordinationem et voluntatem, dicta Vittoria semper et in omni statu et termino, *et tam viduando quam non viduando*, et in quocumque alio statu et termino esse posset et declarari, semper habeat et habere debeat totum illud quod sibi dimitto" (emphasis added).

3. Vittoria's mother, Zacca Vitturi, in her will of 1417 mentions both Vittoria and a son, Nicolò (NT 1157, Croci, prot. 1, f. 25v). This Nicolò registered his son, then eighteen, in the Balla d'Oro lottery for admission to the patrician Great Council in 1442; they were both probably still living when Vittoria testated in 1445 (ASV, Avogaria di Comun, Balla d'Oro [=BO], 163, f. 396). On registration for the Great Council and the Balla d'Oro, see Stanley Chojnacki, "Kinship Ties and Young Patricians in Fifteenth-Century Venice," *Renaissance Quarterly* 38 (1985):240–70, and idem, "Political Adulthood in Fifteenth-Century Venice," *American Historical Review* 91 (1986):791–810.

4. In an earlier will, in 1427, Vittoria had followed the same pattern, making Valerio her sole executor and universal heir (except for a five-ducat bequest to a

daughter of her late brother, Piero Vitturi) but requesting burial "in the tomb of my father and kinsmen [propinquorum meorum]." She also committed ten ducats toward the placement of a marble tablet on the tomb (NT 852, Rizoto, no. 349).

5. The tension between loyalty to natal families and marital families, especially for women, is an important theme in the writings of Diane Owen Hughes and Christiane Klapisch-Zuber. See Hughes, "From Brideprice to Dowry in Mediterranean Europe," *Journal of Family History* 3 (1978):262–96, and "Representing the Family: Portraits and Purposes in Early Modern Italy," *Journal of Interdisciplinary History* 17 (1986):7–38, esp. 10–11; and Klapisch-Zuber, "The 'Cruel Mother': Maternity, Widowhood, and Dowry in Florence in the Fourteenth and Fifteenth Centuries," in *Women, Family, and Ritual in Renaissance Italy,* trans. Lydia G. Cochrane (Chicago, 1985), pp. 117–64.

6. Guido Ruggiero has advanced useful speculations on husband-wife affection in Venice in the context of the tension between marital and extramarital sexual urgings. See *The Boundaries of Eros: Sex Crime and Sexuality in Renaissance Venice* (New York, 1985), esp. p. 64.

7. Hughes, e.g., sees growing lineage consciousness leading to the shift from brideprice to dowry; see "Brideprice," pp. 287–88. Klapisch-Zuber and David Herlihy argue that family interest led fathers to hasten very young daughters onto the marriage market in order to procure sons-in-law at a time when eligible men were in short supply. See *Tuscans and Their Families* (Cambridge, Mass., 1985), p. 223. Elsewhere, however, Klapisch-Zuber raises questions about the supply-and-demand approach. "The Griselda Complex: Dowry and Marriage Gifts in the Quattrocento," in *Women, Family, and Ritual,* pp. 213–46, esp. pp. 215–17. She also cites cases of Florentine men so eager for matrimonial alliances that they forced their widowed sisters to remarry even when doing so meant abandoning young children of the first marriage ("Cruel Mother," pp. 117–31). For discussions of psychological and cultural factors, see Richard A. Goldthwaite, "The Florentine Palace as Domestic Architecture," *American Historical Review* 77 (1972):1009–10; and Julius Kirshner, "Pursuing Honor While Avoiding Sin: The Monte delle Doti of Florence," *Quaderni di studi senesi,* no. 41 (Milan, 1978).

8. On marriage in Venice, see, in addition to the observations in Ruggiero, *Boundaries of Eros,* Bianca Betto, "Linee di politica matrimoniale nella nobiltà veneziana fino al XV secolo: Alcune note genealogiche e l'esempio della famiglia Mocenigo," *Archivio storico italiano* 139 (1981):3–64; Stanley Chojnacki, "Dowries and Kinsmen in Early Renaissance Venice," *Journal of Interdisciplinary History* 5 (1975):571–600. Political implications are discussed in Robert Finlay, *Politics in Renaissance Venice* (New Brunswick, N.J., 1980), esp. pp. 82–89; economic calculations in James C. Davis, *A Venetian Family and Its Fortune* (Philadelphia, 1975). Frederic Lane treated marriage from different angles in many writings, including *Andrea Barbarigo, Merchant of Venice, 1418–1449* (Baltimore, 1944), and several essays in *Venice and History* (Baltimore, 1966).

9. On brides' ages, see, briefly, Stanley Chojnacki, "Patrician Women in Early Renaissance Venice," *Studies in the Renaissance* 21 (1974):192. For an example of a prospective groom contracting his marriage: ASV, Avogaria di Comun, Con-

tratti di Nozze, 111/1, no. 5 (Arimondo-Michiel, 1488). Surviving marriage contracts in Venice have yet to be studied systematically.

10. This sample, a tiny fragment of the huge testamentary holdings in the Venetian State Archives, is the current state of an ongoing survey of the wills of sixteen patrician clans which I am making as part of the research for a general study of patrician marriage. The 361 examined for the present discussion, excluding wills written by single and widowed members of the clans, were drawn up by 104 husbands and 257 wives.

11. The thesis, generally based on prescriptive literature, that affection among family members is an innovation of the early modern period, at least in Europe, is controversial. For statements of it, see Lawrence Stone, *The Family, Sex, and Marriage in England, 1500–1800,* abridged ed. (London, 1979), and Jean-Louis Flandrin, *Families in Former Times,* trans. Richard Southern (New York, 1979). For criticisms of it, see Steven Ozment, *When Fathers Ruled: Family Life in Reformation Europe* (Cambridge, Mass., 1983) and David Herlihy, *Medieval Households* (Cambridge, Mass., 1985), esp. pp. 112–30. The evidence studied for the present discussion suggests strongly that, in Venice, husbands and wives experienced, or at least were moved to express, mutual affection well before the religious developments which Stone in particular and also Flandrin regard as contributing to the emergence of "companionate" family life.

12. Valerio noted that twelve hundred ducats' worth of Vittoria's dowry was secured by "possessionibus et proprietatibus meis de sancto Jacobo de Luprio *quas habui ab ea in dotem*" (emphasis added). Although twelve hundred ducats indicated a substantial amount of property, it is unlikely that this dowry included any of the Vitturis' own residences. The total dowry of twenty-four hundred ducats greatly exceeded the limit of sixteen hundred ducats imposed by the Senate on marriage settlements in 1420; the act is partially reproduced in Giulio Bistort, *Il Magistrato alle Pompe della Repubblica di Venezia,* repr. of 1912 ed. (Bologna, 1969), pp. 107ff.; Bistort also discusses other legislation that attempted to hold back the dowry tide. See Stanley Chojnacki, "Marriage Legislation and Patrician Society in Fifteenth-Century Venice," in *Law, Custom, and the Social Fabric in Medieval Europe,* ed. Bernard Bachrach and David Nicholas, forthcoming.

13. Hughes, "Brideprice," pp. 288–90; Herlihy and Klapisch-Zuber, *Tuscans,* pp. 224–25.

14. I am preparing a monograph tentatively entitled "Public Manhood in Renaissance Venice," in which these developments and their significance for the patriciate's evolution will be discussed at length. See, briefly, Chojnacki, "Political Adulthood," pp. 797–99.

15. *Francisci Barbari de re uxoria liber in partes duas,* ed. Attilio Gnesotto (Padua, 1915), p. 41. On Barbaro, see Margaret L. King, "Caldiera and the Barbaros on Marriage and the Family," *Journal of Medieval and Renaissance Studies* 6 (1976), pp. 31–35. In 1422 the Great Council passed a measure denying patrician status to sons of patricians and low-status women; ASV, Maggior Consiglio, Deliberazioni, 22, Ursa, ff. 47v–48. On the prestige value of marriage and wives in male-dominated societies, see the Introduction to Sherry B. Ortner and Harriet White-

head, eds., *Sexual Meanings: The Cultural Construction of Gender and Sexuality*
(Cambridge, 1981), p. 21.

16. The status of prospective husbands as another important factor in the calculus of marriage is discussed in the context of different levels of prestige and
power in the Venetian patriciate in the forthcoming Chojnacki, "Marriage Legislation."

17. "Ha abudo asa piui de quello havera tutti suo fradelli" (ASV, Cancelleria
Inferiore [hereinafter cited as CI, followed by busta number and notary's name]
175, Rizzo, prot., f. 35v [will of Francesco Loredan, January 22, 1459]). Morosina, widow of Marco Querini, noted that her daughters' dowries had been
constituted partly at the expense of their brothers' inheritance: "Le son sta marida
e ben e ha abudo de quell de suo fradelli" (NT 1149, Benedetto, unnumbered
will, March 6, 1461).

18. ASV, Senato, Terra, 28, f. 151.

19. See the discussion and references in Chojnacki, "Dowries," pp. 590–92.
Observation of Florentine practice prompts Klapisch-Zuber to be skeptical of the
dowry's significance as a share of the paternal estate. See "The Griselda Complex:
Dowry and Marriage Gifts in the Quattrocento," esp. p. 216.

20. The father who wanted his daughters to be content was Vito da Canal, in
1448: "Pro eo, quod eis dedi in dotem ipse habent causam remanendi bene contente, et non se condolendi de aliquo" (NT 558, Gambaro, no. 171). Already in
1393, Antonio Morosini instructed his executors to reserve a certain portion of
his bequest to his daughter "pro so legato e non per docta" (NT 640, Bordo,
unnumbered [July 14, 1393]). Heiresses appear to have had immediate access to
legacies not encumbered by dowry regulations; this subject, however, needs more
study.

21. See Chojnacki, "Dowries," pp. 582–90. Examples of mothers who encouraged further dowry inflation by allocating more for their daughters' dowries
than for their sons' legacies: Maria Balbi, 1438, and Chiara Moro, 1490 (NT 558,
Gambaro, no. 54; NT 41, Bonamico, no. 54). In her 1464 will, Petronella Morosini commanded not only her own wealth but that of her mother in the interest
of her daughter Paolina's marriage, by appointing the Procurators of San Marco
to administer Paolina's one-third share of Petronella's estate and also one thousand ducats that Petronella's mother had bequeathed to her, which would now
enrich Paolina's marriage portion. Petronella expressed concern that her husband,
Zilio Morosini, would be dilatory in arranging Paolina's marriage, which Petronella wanted concluded by the girl's fifteenth birthday. Noteworthy is Petronella's
confidence that her contribution to Paolina's marriage portion was great enough
to compel Zilio to bow to the Procurators' arrangements for his daughter's marriage (NT 1239, Tomei, no. 600 [September 2, 1464]).

22. Lucia Priuli in 1489 (NT 66, Busenello, no. 232), e.g., and Elisabetta Vitturi in 1483 (NT 727, Moisis, no. 92).

23. Most women with children made them the principal beneficiaries, but
women also made alternative provisions in the event that the children died before
reaching adulthood. While some favored husbands as secondary legatees, others

gave all to their natal kinsmen. Agnesina Arimondo in 1411, e.g., provided that, if her two children failed to reach their majority (her son at age twenty, her daughter at marriage), her mother and her sister, a nun, were to receive lifetime annuities from Agnesina's estate, which at their deaths would go to her four brothers—and not a ducat for her husband (NT 364, Darvasio, no. 291). More characteristic were the arrangements of Maria Soranzo, who provided for the possibility that her children would not reach adulthood by giving one-quarter of her *residuum* each to her mother, her husband, her three brothers together, and charity (NT 558, Gambaro, no. 54).

24. An example of a husband's efforts: in 1365 Leonardo Morosini bequeathed his wife 200 lire *a grossi* provided she kept half of her dowry in the family ("lasando la mitade de la so enpromessa in la chasa a utilitade de so fioli"); NT 1023, Caresini, no. 13. In the fifteenth century the inducements were proportionately higher; see below, n. 52.

25. For some preliminary observations, see Stanley Chojnacki, "La posizione della donna a Venezia nel Cinquecento," in *Tiziano e Venezia* (Vicenza, 1980), pp. 65–70. On fashion and its significance, see Jacqueline Herald, *Renaissance Dress in Italy* (Atlantic Highlands, N.J., 1982); Anne Hollander, *Seeing Through Clothes* (New York, 1978); and Alison Lurie, *The Language of Clothes* (New York, 1981). For a perspective on the social forces behind sumptuary legislation, see the valuable study of Diane Owen Hughes, "Sumptuary Laws and Social Relations in Renaissance Italy," in *Disputes and Settlements: Law and Human Relations in the West*, ed. John Bossy (Cambridge, 1983), pp. 69–99.

26. Bistort, *Magistrato*, 123, 154.

27. Cesare Vecellio, *De gli habiti antichi e moderni di diuerse parti del mondo* (Venice, 1590), 126v. A rare look into newlyweds' expenses is offered by the account book of Moisè Venier, who in 1438 recorded expenditures of more than 147 ducats on the apparel of his wife, Cateruzza Vitturi, in the first three months of their marriage; ASV, Procuratori di San Marco, Commissarie miste, Busta 3a, Moisè Venier, red leather account book, ff. 1r–3r. An act of the Senate in 1420 had set a limit of five hundred ducats on husbands' expenditures on their wives' apparel during the first five years of marriage; ASV, Senato, Misti, Reg. 55, f. 103v. In Florence, husbands' gifts of clothing to their wives were seen as only temporary concessions; see Klapisch-Zuber, "The Griselda Complex." For an instance of a Venetian father urging restraint upon his daughters in their expenditures (thus testifying to their freedom in the matter), see the 1447 will of Francesco Morosini, in which, after endowing the daughters with dowries of as much as eighteen hundred ducats and making them his residuary heirs, he "prayed and commanded them, in true paternal obedience, not to spend their wealth on vain and empty things but rather *in honorem dei et proximi*." Procuratori di San Marco, Commissarie miste, Busta 158a, Francesco Morosini, parchment, April 5, 1448. For valuable comments on male ambivalence regarding women's dress, see Hughes, "Sumptuary Laws," pp. 95–99.

28. In contrast to this hypothesis, Georg Simmel, in his famous treatise on the subject, saw fashionable dress as a sign of conformity, associated with subordinate status which induces persons to seek security in the group. In arguing his

point, however, Simmel noted that women in Renaissance Italy, unlike their German contemporaries, enjoyed "full play for the exercise of individuality"; therefore, according to his thesis, there should have been no "particularly extravagant Italian female fashions," in contrast to the situation in Germany; see "Fashion," in *Georg Simmel on Individuality and Social Forms: Selected Writings,* ed. Donald N. Levine (Chicago, 1971), pp. 308–309. Simmel's characterization of Italian Renaissance costume runs counter to all authoritative testimony; see, for a sampling, Hughes, "Sumptuary Laws," pp. 88–92. For comments on the forging of female identity within social and cultural boundaries, especially the family, see Natalie Zemon Davis, "Boundaries and the Sense of Self in Sixteenth-Century France," in Thomas C. Heller et al., eds., *Reconstructing Individualism: Autonomy, Individuality, and the Self in Western Thought* (Stanford, 1986), pp. 53–63.

29. On gender identity as contingent, something continuously being shaped by historical circumstances, see Joan W. Scott, "Gender: A Useful Category of Historical Analysis," *American Historical Review* 91 (1986):1053–75.

30. Examples of other men who either made their wives their only executors or instructed that, in any dispute among executors, the wife's side should prevail: Marino Arimondo, 1477, Donato Arimondo, 1499, Marco Pisani, 1504 (CI, Miscellanea Testamenti, Notai Diversi, 27, no. 2578; NT 66, Busenello, nos. 126, 264).

31. Hughes ("Brideprice," p. 284) and Klapisch-Zuber ("Cruel Mother," pp. 124–25) note men's characteristic concern for the sons of their sisters. For the role of maternal uncles in Venice, see Chojnacki, "Kinship Ties."

32. Testating fathers normally left detailed instructions on the investment of their assets until their daughters were of age to be married, preferably—in the words of Andrea Arimondo in 1427, echoing others—"in uno zentilomo de Veniesia" (CI, Miscellanea Testamenti, Notai Diversi, Busta 27, no. 2697). Similarly, Michele Navagero, in the same year, asserted that his daughter Suordamor "se debia maridar in zentil homo" (NT 1157, Croci, Prot. II, f. 14r).

33. Andrea Arimondo, who wanted his daughter to marry a "zentilomo" (see n. 32), authorized his executors to decide whether his estate had enough to marry off any additional daughters or put them into convents: "Non habiando la summa de dener sel fusse piu de una fia lor [i.e., the executors'] liberta de munegar e maridar qual a lor parera." Lorenzo Loredan in 1440 made similar arrangements: "Item, volio che mia fia Biancha e Loredana siano maridade or munegade segondo aparera . . . a deschrizion de mie chomessarii" (NT 558, Gambaro, no. 86). Giovanni Morosini, however, in 1437 noted "con amaritudine" that his estate had so little that he could not afford even a convent dowry, let alone a marriage dowry, for his daughter Marietta (NT 1232, Stefani, no. 314).

34. Examples of fathers' solicitude: Lorenzo Loredan left it "in libertade dele do mie fie" to decide "se quelle volesse servir a dio" or "se veramente quelle volesse esser maridada." Leonardo Priuli provided dowry money for any daughters who "nubere vellent" (NT 1186, Groppi, no. 71, prot., no. 38). Michele Navagero, who wanted his daughter to marry a patrician (above, n. 32), also gave her the option to "munegar." A rare fourteenth-century father giving his daughter the same choice was Marino Morosini, who in his 1380 will made Ag-

nesina heir to half his *residuum* for her marriage or her religious vocation "como la dita Agnesina mia fia alezera" (ASV Procuratori di S. Marco, Commissarie miste, Busta 167, Marino Morosini, parchment, 6 January 1379 [Venetian style = 1380]).

35. I am preparing a detailed discussion of trends in marriage ages and their larger significance. Broadly speaking, the preferred age for brides rose from the preteens or early teens in the fourteenth century to the middle to late teens in the fifteenth. See, briefly, Chojnacki, "Dowries," p. 585. For intriguing information on changing measures of female maturity from the perspective of prosecution of sexual offenses against young women, see Ruggiero, *Boundaries of Eros,* p. 102.

36. This is a general impression given by women's wills and has not yet been systematically investigated. Examples of mothers who gave daughters the option: Cristina Morosini (1423), NT 560, Gritti, no. 346; Sterina Lando (1458), NT 727, Moisis, no. 142. On the other hand, some mothers made their preferences clear and forceful: Orsa da Canal declared in 1440 that, if her daughters were not married by age seventeen, "nichil habere debeant ipse filie femine de dicto meo residuo" (NT 558, Gambaro, no. 84).

37. Francesca Zeno, wife of Piero Morosini, contemplated with apparent tranquillity the lay single state chosen by her daughter Chiara; Chiara would enter into her inheritance as Francesca's residuary legatee either when she married or, if she did not, at age twenty (Museo Civico-Correr, Venice, MSS P.D./C, No. 916/10 [1427]). Isabetta, widow of Barbon Morosini, wanted her bequest to her granddaughter to stand even if the young woman "vuol star in nel mondo sença maridarse, o munegarse" (NT 1156, Croce, No. 517 [1450]). The dangers to daughters' virtue and family honor are explicitly raised in the Senate act of 1420 attempting to limit dowries. For male fears of the dangers presented by unmarried lay women, see Klapisch-Zuber, "Cruel Mother," pp. 122–23; Kirshner, "Pursuing Honor," pp. 9–10 and passim; and Chojnacki, "Marriage Legislation."

38. The discrepancy between this figure and the larger group of husbands' wills discussed above is a result of my having noted the language of husbands' references to their wives only in the recent stages of my research in the wills. The indications from such tiny documentation will need to be verified in examination of a much larger sampling of husbands' wills. Even in this small sample, however, the consistent difference between the wills of fourteenth- and fifteenth-century husbands strongly suggests a tendency in patrician society at large.

39. Quotations from wills of Jacopo Morosini, 1448, Donato Arimondo, 1499, and Alvise Lando, 1481 (NT 558, Gambaro, no. 168; NT 66, Busenello, no. 126; NT 1186, Groppi, no. 72).

40. I found not one use of the term *consorte* in the thirty-eight wills written before 1427, when it was used by Andrea Arimondo (CI, Miscellanea Testamenti, Notai Diversi, Busta 27, no. 2697). For an example from Tuscany of the more traditional, lineage-focused use of the term, see Christiane Klapisch-Zuber, "'Kin, Friends, and Neighbors': The Urban Territory of a Merchant Family in 1400,'" in *Women, Family, and Ritual,* p. 76.

41. NT 41, Bonamico, no. 150 (will of Nicolò Pisani, 1493); NT 1157, Croci, prot. II, f. 29r (will of Daniele Vitturi, 1440).

42. In his 1499 will, e.g., Donato Arimondo referred to his wife, Bianca, variously as "mia chara chonsorte," "mia chara e dileta chonsorte," "mia dileta chonsorte," and just plain "Madona Biancha" (NT 66, Busenello, no. 126).

43. "Et al osequio mio non voio el ne vegni ne mia moier ne fiuoli ne fie per no i dar pena sora pena" (will of Francesco Loredan, 1459, NT 179, Rizzo, prot., f. 35v).

44. "Bene volio che la chognoscha lamor lio senper portato" (will of Donato Arimondo, 1499, NT 66, Busenello, no. 126).

45. "Ala qual sono tropo ubligato, si per lo bon portamento chomo per assa danari, oltre la dote, ho abuto de i suo" (NT 558, Gambaro, no. 168).

46. In a 1431 will, for example, Sebastiano Vitturi endowed a mansionary to pray for his soul and that of his wife, Suordamor (NT 1157, Croci, prot. 1, f. 88v).

47. Donato also wanted to include two natal kinsmen, sons of his late brother, in the tomb, but only his and Bianca's names were to be inscribed on it (NT 66, Busenello, no. 126). Bianca's will of 1490 is NT 41, Bonamico, no. 30.

48. The procedure for recovering dowries is spelled out in Book I, chap. 62, of the Venetian statutes (*Volumen statutorum, legum, ac iurium D. Venetorum* [Venice, 1564], 28v–29v). Legislation on marriage and dowries in the fourteenth-sixteenth centuries periodically altered it; for example, the Senate act of 1420 in Bistort, *Magistrato*, p. 107; another Senate act of 1505, in ASV, Avogaria di Comun, Contratti di Nozze, 140/1, initial unnumbered folios. Elaborate documentation of dowry claims is evident in, e.g., ASV, Giudici del Proprio, Vadimoni, Reg. 4, ff. 29v–30v (claim of heirs of the late Franceschina Barbaro, May 14, 1460). The evolution of dowry rules and practice will be the subject of a separate study.

49. Francesco Barbaro declared that the upbringing of children was a wife's most serious duty (*De re uxoria*, p. 92), but fathers' concern for the maternal care of children was surely interwoven with fear that a mother's remarriage would transfer her loyalty and her wealth to a new family—a transfer, Klapisch notes, that was urged by widows' brothers in Florence ("Cruel Mother"). For examples of Venetian fathers who conditioned their bequests to wives on the latters' remaining, unmarried, with the children, see the wills of Michele Navagero, 1427, and Sebastiano Vitturi, 1431; NT 1157, Croci, prot. 2, f. 14, prot. 1, f. 88v.

50. "Volio la sia tratada come la persona mia." Marino left her four hundred ducats over and above her dowry, the use of his "caxa granda," in which her widowed sister could also live, at Marino's expense, or—if they preferred another nearby house—remodeling expenses (CI, Miscellanea Testamenti, Notai Diversi, 27, no. 2578).

51. Marino's will was written in 1477; he had married in 1432. Donato's will dates from 1499; his wedding was in 1462. See Barbaro, Nozze, ff. 8 left, 9 left.

52. Michele Navagero (1427), testating with young children, bequeathed his wife four hundred ducats if she remained unmarried but two hundred ducats if she remarried (NT 1157, Croci, prot. II, f. 14r). Sebastiano Vitturi (1431) at first left his wife four hundred ducats "tam viduando quam non" but, later in the will, after providing for his adopted son, apparently thought better of it and made the bequest conditional upon her remaining single and caring for the young man

(ibid., prot. I, ff. 88v–90r). Lorenzo Loredan (1441) conditioned a supradowry bequest of two hundred ducats to his wife upon her caring for their children, but if there were no children, then she had it free and clear and would be free to marry (NT 558, Gambaro, no. 86).

53. "Per haver abudo bonissima chompagnia da lui sino al presente e molto meio spiero per lavegnir" (NT 1186, Groppi, no. 82). Maddaluzza had two married sisters, alternative beneficiaries, but they got only one hundred ducats each.

54. Lucrezia was apparently a rich widow, since Sebastiano moved in with her at their marriage in 1497 (NT 66, Busenello, no. 246; Barbaro, Nozze, f. 369 left).

55. "I son ubiga piu cha criatura di sto mondo per lestremi afani la porta chon mi per chason de la mia infirmita e dano dela soa persona che a tuti puo eser manifesto non chomo muier ma chomo sciava" (NT 1157, Croci, prot. 2, f. 29).

56. CI 175, Rizzo, prot., f. 35v.

57. For a discussion of the effect on gender definitions of kinship, marriage, and "prestige structures," see the Introduction to Ortner and Whitehead, *Sexual Meanings,* esp. pp. 21–24.

58. For instances of women linking their natal and marital families, see Chojnacki, "Kinship Ties."

59. A preliminary statement of some ideas on these matters can be found in Chojnacki, "Posizione della donna."

Medieval Women Book Owners: Arbiters of Lay Piety and Ambassadors of Culture

Susan Groag Bell

This boke is myne, Eleanor Worcester
An I yt lose, and yow yt fynd
I pray yow hartely to be so kynd
That you wel take a letil payne
To se my boke is brothe home agayne.

Inscription in a Book of Hours
belonging to the Duchess of Worcester,
ca. 1440

The power of the word is the greatest and most far-reaching power known to society. In slave societies it was too dangerous to teach slaves to read, as their literacy would surely lead to rebellion. Yet upper-class medieval laywomen were empowered by the ownership of precious books and used these books also for the rudimentary education of sons and daughters with which they were charged. As girls outside the cloister were deliberately unschooled in Latin (a command of that language was the ecclesiastic and scholarly symbol of power during the Middle Ages), women's insistence on owning vernacular compositions and translations of Latin texts confirms female interest in both the spiritual and worldly importance of religious and secular literature. The knowledge that women gleaned from their books and the books' widespread international transportation by their owners further demonstrates medieval women's considerable cultural influence.

I believe that the influence of laywomen in promoting cultural change can be assessed by looking at their special relationship to books, and I offer this article as a pioneer attempt to chart this area. Preliminary research suggests that book-owning women substantially influenced the development of lay piety and vernacular literature in the later Middle Ages. Women frequently bought and inherited religious as well as secular books, and spent considerable time reading them. In particular, as readers of vernacular literature, as mothers in charge of childhood education, as literary patrons who commissioned books and translations, and as wives who married across cultural and geographical boundaries, women had a specific and unique influence.

This essay is divided into three parts. The first deals with the facts of medieval laywomen's book ownership, including the acquisition of books through inheritance, commission, and patronage. The second part focuses on women's special relationship to books: (1) because of their inferior status in medieval Christian thought and their exclusion from scholarship and clerical life, women had an even greater need for the mental and spiritual nourishment offered by books than men did; (2) as mothers they were the primary teachers of the next generation and acquired books as teaching texts; and (3) untutored in Latin, they played an important role in the development of vernacular translations. The last section deals with the importance of women's relationship to books in the development of cultural change, including their influence on iconography as well as book content, and their role in the international movement of art and ideas through their ownership of books.

Patterns of Book Ownership

Many still regard the medieval book as a possession of the cloister or of the male of the family. Traditional textbooks and historiography emphasize medieval culture as a phenomenon associated with either monasticism or feudalism. Monks (rarely nuns) are depicted as scribes or as readers of religious books. Troubadours' tales of lovelorn knights sighing over unattainable ladies did not address these ladies' intellectual or spiritual pursuits, beyond a nod at Eleanor of Aquitaine as a patron of poets. Classic medieval historiography focuses on one of two male institutions—the church or chivalric feudalism. Even the authors of the most widely used recent Western civilization textbook, who are aware of the literacy of medieval laywomen, see those women as literary subject matter rather than as creators or users of books.[1] Scholarly articles concerned with book ownership also largely ignore women book owners. In her 1972 article on fifteenth-century books and their owners, Susan Connel observed, "Exceptional not for the contents, but for being found at all,

Table 1. Identified European Laywomen Owning Books, A.D. 800–1500

	Number of Women, by Century							
Number of books	Ninth century	Tenth century	Eleventh century	Twelfth century	Thirteenth century	Fourteenth century	Fifteenth century	All centuries
One book	3	3	6	9	12	41	76	150
2–10 books	1	—	5	6	3	6	29	50
11–50 books	—	—	—	—	—	7	13	20
51–200 books	—	—	—	—	—	1	13[a]	14
Unspecified number of books[b]	6	1	—	1	—	—	—	8
Total	10	4	11	16	15	55	131	242

[a] One of these women, Gabrielle de la Tour, owned 200 manuscripts in 1474. Nine others, indirect evidence indicates, may have owned between 51 and 100 manuscripts and printed books, although this cannot be positively documented.

[b] Each of these women was referred to as "owning books" or being "busy with her books," although no specific books could be traced to them.

are records of books owned by women."[2] Yet from the ninth to the fifteenth century, particularly in the latter portion of this period, there is
solid evidence that individual European laywomen of the upper classes
read and owned books. Table 1 shows the numbers of laywomen identified by name to whom the ownership of at least one book can be traced.
These women were identified in: (1) rare book library catalogs; (2) medieval wills; (3) medieval inventories of household goods or of libraries;
and (4) dedications to patrons. The 242 women identified who lived between A.D. 800 and 1500 in no way constitute a representative sample,
and their origins are geographically diverse—from Scotland in the north
to Sicily in the south and from the Atlantic in the west to Serbia and
Poland in the east. The evidence, however, suggests that the number of
laywomen book owners increased substantially by the fourteenth century
and multiplied dramatically by the fifteenth century. This preliminary
exploration also strongly suggests that there may be rich, untapped evidence of women book owners between the ninth and fifteenth centuries. I
wish to stress the tentativeness of all but the most general conclusions
based on the figures shown in the table and my awareness of the many
avenues that are open for further work on this subject. That these women
and their books originated in diverse European locations, while they
often journeyed across the Continent and the English Channel on marriage, suggests important trends in the diffusion of medieval culture.

Various medieval developments facilitated the individual search for
spiritual guidance through books. For example, M. T. Clanchy sees the
shift "from memory to written record" that occurred over the eleventh
and twelfth centuries as preparation for the growth of a literate mentality—for people ready to spend time and effort with books.[3] Tech-
nology also played an important part. The chimney flue and fireplace,
developed in the early fourteenth century, provided safety and warmth
indoors by allowing smoke to escape. The fireplace, substituting for the
central open fire in large communal areas, also facilitated the development of smaller rooms which, together with the appearance of window
glass, provided privacy for peaceful and comfortable indoor reading (figure 1).[4] Further, by the thirteenth century eyeglasses became available:
lenses to correct presbyopia, allowing the middle-aged to continue close
work, had been introduced in the late thirteenth century, and concave
lenses for myopia made reading a possibility for the nearsighted by the
mid-fifteenth century.[5] Finally, cheaper production of manuscripts in the
course of the fourteenth and fifteenth centuries and improvements in
printing of small books by the end of the fifteenth century undoubtedly
spurred the growth of individual book ownership and literacy.

Until the advent of incunabula (that is, the earliest printed books, pub-

1. "Annunciation" with two books in a Flemish interior, showing chimney fireplace, windows. Flemish, ca. 1425–1428. The *Merode Altarpiece*, Metropolitan Museum of Art, New York.

lished between 1453 and 1500), medieval books consisted of handwritten rolls or bound pages known as manuscripts. Most of these books owned by the laity that have survived were religious in content, covering sermons, selections of psalms (the Psalter), parts of the Old or the New Testament, or a combination of all of these items in a "Book of Hours," which will be considered in detail later in this article.

While the actual cost of medieval books cannot be measured in modern terms, medieval women's accounts show not only that they bought books but that the books they bought were relatively expensive. We know, for example, that in the eleventh century the Countess of Anjou paid two hundred sheep; one bushel each of rye, wheat, and millet; and a quantity of marten pelts for one volume of the sermons of Haimo of Halberstadt.[6] But we do not know the circumstances of this exchange. The countess may well have accepted the book in part payment for the goods, or she may have made a donation to the monastery to which the scribe belonged and then received the book as an expression of thanks. Fourteenth-century accounts present less ambiguous figures. Thus, for example, the accounts of Mahaut, Countess of Artois, show that in 1308 she paid seven livres and ten sous for copies of the *Histoire de Troyes* and *Perceval;* in 1313 she paid eight livres for a copy of the *Consolations of Boethius.*[7] At about the same time, in 1324, the Countess of Clare paid a scribe eight shillings and his board and lodging for the four months it took him to copy the *Lives of the Church Fathers* for her.[8] It appears that the work of the scribe was a minor part of the total cost. Parchment and illuminations (especially those using gold leaf) largely accounted for the high cost of books. Mahaut, Countess of Artois, paid a female scribe, Maroie, twenty-five sous for writing a Book of Hours in 1312[9] and ordered an even less expensive Book of Hours costing six sous for her niece in 1320.[10] By the end of the fourteenth century, it was possible to acquire tracts, broadsides, and small devotional texts for less than one shilling in England.[11]

However, whether a book cost eight livres or six sous in the fourteenth century, it was still out of reach for anyone except the nobility or upper bourgeoisie. It would have taken a female agricultural laborer in southern France in the early fourteenth century about fourteen days to earn enough to buy the cheapest book purchased by the Countess of Artois between 1306 and 1330 and more than a year's daily labor to buy one of the more luxurious books. A male agricultural laborer could have purchased the cheaper book after seven days of labor, since he earned twice as much as his female companions for the same type of work.[12] By the fifteenth century, however, it appears that such a book came within the reach of the lower bourgeoisie, some of whom were documented book owners.

Perhaps the clearest documentary evidence for the acquisition of books by medieval laywomen comes from bequests by fathers or husbands. It seems likely that the legator would be disposed to bequeath those items for which the legatee had expressed a preference in his lifetime. Such a bequest, then, may indicate a woman's preference for a book rather than some other object that might have been willed to her. Examples of the passage of books from fathers to daughters include the ninth-century Gisela, daughter of Louis the Pious, who inherited her husband's library. Her three daughters were also mentioned individually in the will as legatees of their father's books.[13] Three daughters of the Earl of Devon each inherited one book at his death in 1377.[14] Many of the most exquisite volumes of the Duc de Berry's collection were inherited or purchased by women from his estate in 1416. His famous *Très Riches Heures* was inherited by his daughter Bonne, the Countess of Savoy. In about 1504 Margaret of Austria carried it off to the Netherlands as part of the library she salvaged from her short marriage to the Savoyard Philibert le Bel.[15] Jean de Berry's younger daughter Marie, Duchess of Bourbonnais, specifically requested and received forty of the most prized books from his estate in 1417. These included nine religious books (four Bibles in French, one in Latin, a small Psalter, two copies of the *City of God* in French, two treatises on the Trinity, and at least one Book of Hours).[16] The duke's magnificent *Belles Heures,* now in the Cloisters Collection in New York, was purchased by his nephew's widow, Yolande of Aragon, Countess of Anjou and Queen of Sicily, for the vast sum of three hundred livres.[17] Anne of Brittany inherited the enormous library of her former royal husbands, Charles VIII and Louis XII, who had acquired large collections from Italian libraries through plunder and purchase during their Italian campaigns. But Anne had also collected and commissioned books of her own.[18] By the fifteenth century, the disposition of less expensive books written on paper in the vernacular was frequently mentioned in wills.[19]

Wills and testamentary settlements attest to women's inheritance of books from men. However, women's inheritance of books from women is of greater significance in this analysis of medieval women's book ownership. Solid evidence comes from the *Sachsenspiegel* [The Mirror of the Saxons], a collection of Saxon custom laws first compiled by Eike von Repgow in about 1215, which reflected the social mores of the previous three centuries. Book 1 of the *Sachsenspiegel* discussed the household items that were to be inherited by women. The "gerade" (or Roman "paraphernalia") were to be passed from mother to daughter; they included geese, small farm animals, beds, household furniture, linens, clothing, kitchen utensils—and books (figure 2). The text enumerating

2. The "Gerade" in the *Sachsenspiegel* Law. German, ca. 1350. Sächsische
Landbibliothek, Dresden, MS 32.

items to be passed from woman to woman specifically includes all books connected with religious observance: "Alle Bücher die zum Gottesdienste gehöre [sic]."[20] An additional clause in the 1279 version that remained in later editions added that these devotional books were to be inherited by women, because it was women who were accustomed to reading them: "Bücher die Fraue phlege zu lese [sic]."[21]

The *Sachsenspiegel*, translated from its original Latin into German by Eike von Repgow, was frequently copied and recopied throughout the thirteenth and fourteenth centuries. It was also adapted for non-Saxon areas; the laws applied to wide geographic regions to the east of its birthplace near Magdeburg, reaching far into what is now the Soviet Union. The *Sachsenspiegel* clearly attests to women's role in the transmission of culture, especially lay religious culture, and to the different reading habits and religious observances of men and women.

Women's inheritance of books from women was not confined to *Sachsenspiegel* areas. A Dutch Book of Hours, inscribed with the names of six generations of women, indicates a Western European parallel to the *Sachsenspiegel* custom.[22] Examples in wills of women inheriting books from their mothers also exist.[23] However, testamentary evidence of women's bequests of devotional books to their daughters is scarce, which may suggest that such bequests were customary (as in the *Sachsenspiegel*) and required no documentation.

Fourteenth-century records increasingly reveal names of women who not only owned books but also collected numerous manuscripts of the same book and assembled libraries. Mahaut, Countess of Artois, an outstanding example, ordered thirty books of various types between 1300 and 1330.[24] The countess did not collect merely for the sake of owning luxurious and beautiful treasures. Her accounts indicate that she paid a large sum for a desk that enabled her to read in comfort. In the early years she preferred history and romances: the *Chronicles of the Kings of France, Perceval,* and the *History of Troy.* After the death of her only son in 1316, however, she ordered only books of religion and meditative philosophy. Between 1316 and 1328 she commissioned two different copies of the Bible, both in French; a two-volume Bible written on parchment and bound in red leather; two different copies of the *Lives of the Saints;* a roll of illuminated prayers in a silver container; three Books of Hours; the *Lives of the Church Fathers; Miracles of Our Lady;* and a French translation of Boethius's *The Consolations of Philosophy.*[25] Isabeau of Bavaria's accounts show that her thirty-three books included nine Books of Hours and sixteen other books of devotion.[26] She appointed Katherine de Villiers, one of her court ladies, to be in charge of her books. In 1393 Katherine de Villiers paid forty-eight sous to the trunk maker Pierre de Fou for a leather-covered wooden trunk with lock and key so that the books could be safely transported during Queen Isabeau's travels.[27] An inventory of Gabrielle de la Tour, Countess of Montpensier, found at her death in 1474, listed more than two hundred volumes according to their arrangement in cupboards and chests. At least forty of these were religious texts.[28]

As patrons of authors and of publishers, women also became interested in the new printing presses that sprang up in Western Europe late in the fifteenth century. Most women, as well as men, collectors still preferred the luxurious handwritten books, but some also bought or commissioned incunabula. Margaret of York and Isabella d'Este were notable for their connections with major early printers. While Duchess of Burgundy, Margaret of York encouraged William Caxton to translate from the French and later to print *The History of Troyes*—the first English book, printed in 1476. Caxton's preface describes how Margaret personally helped him through his initial difficulties with the translation and how she later rewarded him well.[29] However, Margaret also continued to collect artistic manuscripts of meditative religious philosophy, such as Boethius's *Consolations* (figure 3). Isabella d'Este was one of many Italian women of the nobility and merchant aristocracy who, as children during the early humanist period, were taught to read Latin and Greek. As the Countess of Gonzaga at Mantua, she became an industrious collector of books. She commissioned the printing of many books, including in 1497 a copy of Jerome's *Letters*. Her regular correspondence with Aldus Manutius, the early Venetian printer and publisher, reveals that she was a determined collector who searched for rarities printed on the finest parchment, for special bindings, and for first copies of printing runs.[30] Isabella clearly encouraged high standards in both the textual and technical execution of Aldus's work.

By the end of the fifteenth century, then, women had become more frequent possessors of many types of books which they had acquired through inheritance, through outright purchase from scribes and booksellers, and through commission.

Women and the Written Word

Throughout the Middle Ages, following the teachings of the early Christian fathers, women were exhorted to model themselves on biblical heroines. In order that they should do so, noble women were taught to read at an early age. "Let her take pattern by Mary," wrote Jerome.[31] Although Jerome had called on women to play an important part in Christianity,

3. Scribe presenting *Consolations of Philosophy* to Margaret of York. Flemish,
1476. Boethius, *Consolatione,* Universitätsbibliothek, Jena,
MS El. f. 85, fol. 13v.

both in monastic communities and as mother-educators, the institutional clerical attitude throughout the following thousand years was ambivalent.[32] Women were excluded from established philosophical Christian debate and from the councils of the church. From the fourth to the twelfth century, however, women took a prominent part in monastic life and from the thirteenth century onward in the resurgence of institutional piety.[33] Women flocked to the leadership as well as the rank-and-file membership of female religious communities such as the Dominicans, the Poor Clares, and the Beguines. "Yet, the ecclesiastical attitude to women," writes Brenda Bolton, "was at best negative if not actively hostile."[34] In that same period, not surprisingly, women were also in the forefront of heretical movements.

Because women's public participation in spiritual life was not welcomed by the hierarchical male establishment, a close involvement with religious devotional literature, inoffensive because of its privacy, took on a greater importance for women. Cicely, Duchess of York, repeated and commented upon her morning devotional reading to her supper companions at night.[35] Margaret Beaufort's confessor wrote that she had "diverse books in French wherewith she would occupy herself [in meditation] when she was weary of prayer."[36] Of the 242 laywomen identified who owned books before 1500, 182, or 75 percent, included books of piety among their possessions (145, or 60 percent, owned books of piety written in the vernacular). In cases where only one book could be attributed to a woman, the book was almost invariably a devotional item. These books of piety included Gospels, Psalters, lives of the saints, and, in large part, Books of Hours.

A Book of Hours was composed of prayers to be read at certain hours of the day and included varied collections of biblical material and saints' lives. According to Victor Léroquais and J. M. L. Delaissé, the Book of Hours was the most popular devotional item developed in the twelfth century. Léroquais described the individual commissioning of Books of Hours as an "escape from Church control."[37] Delaissé contended that the development of Books of Hours implied "a greater concern for the layman by offering him devotional exercises with a more personal approach."[38] It seems likely that the laywoman would be even more interested in this escape from church control, which provided for private devotional reading; Books of Hours were traditional gifts for young girls learning to read and were often included in a bride's trousseau. Furthermore, the contents of Books of Hours could be varied to suit the individual.[39] Most Books of Hours consisted merely of standard versions of the written text embellished with a few ornamental letters. The more magnificent, however, were enhanced with colored illustrations. The margins were occasionally filled with frightening or charming vignettes of everyday life or with mythical and imaginary designs.

Catherine of Cleves's Book of Hours, made during the 1430s in the early years of her marriage to the Duke of Gelders, suggests that one item of devotional literature could cover the whole range of human experience. This book, although exceptionally luxurious, is a good example of the diverse material that might be packed into a Book of Hours and of the emphasis it could throw on women's duties and behavior.[40] The Latin text was supplemented by hundreds of lively illustrations of Old and New Testament scenes and of saints' lives. One illustration showed the birth of Eve from Adam's rib, reminding the reader of woman's subordinate status.[41] Another pictured the crucifixion with Catherine, the book's owner, praying at one side of the cross, and the Virgin with milk spurting from her breast standing at the other, reminding Catherine of her expected duty as a merciful and chaste mother.[42] The illustrations reminded the reader of her duty as a charitable and competent economic manager by portraying her distributing alms, supervising the household production of food, supervising workers such as the dairy women, milking cows, and churning butter.[43] Finally, the book pointed to women's responsibility for their children's education, which included finding tutors for young sons; one of the illustrations showed a schoolmaster with his pupils.[44] It is clear that Books of Hours were much more than simple prayerbooks. They could bring spiritual consolation, edification, and perhaps peace of mind; they could also instruct, distract, and amuse. To dismiss medieval women's devotional books merely as books of piety would demonstrate a misunderstanding both of medieval women's need for spiritual nourishment and of the richly varied contents of their books of devotion.

During the fourteenth and fifteenth century, Books of Hours became the most popular devotional reading. While they were by no means exclusively women's books, women of the nobility and of the upper bourgeoisie were unlikely to be without one. The poet Eustache Deschamps, with whom Christine de Pizan corresponded in 1404 on the subject of men's injustice to women, satirized the ladies of the bourgeoisie for flaunting their luxurious Books of Hours. Queen Isabeau of France chose gold and azure for her daughter's Book of Hours in 1398, and Deschamps caught the brilliance of these colors in his satire of bourgeois women:

> A Book of Hours too must be mine
> Where subtle workmanship will shine
> of gold and azure, rich and smart
> Arranged and painted with great art
> Covered with fine brocade of gold,

> and there must be, so as to hold
> the pages closed, two golden clasps.[45]

Deschamps was not interested in books as aesthetic objects.[46] But because organized medieval Christian ritual revolved around the greatest
artistic treasures, perhaps laywomen, excluded from immediate contact
with these treasures during Christian liturgical celebrations, wished their
one item of devotion to be as beautiful as possible.

Book ownership probably had a second purpose as well. Beginning
with Jerome in the fourth century, Christian moralists repeatedly declared that it was women's duty to concern themselves with the literary
and moral upbringing of their children, and particularly of their daughters. Thus, in A.D. 403 Jerome wrote a letter to the mother of a newborn
daughter:

> Have a set of letters made for her of boxwood or of ivory and tell her their
> names. . . . When she begins with uncertain hand to use the pen, either let
> another hand be put over hers or else have the letters marked on the tab-
> let. . . . Let her every day repeat to you a portion of the Scriptures as her
> fixed task. . . . Instead of jewels or silk let her love the manuscripts of the
> Holy Scriptures, and in them let her prefer correctness and accurate arrange-
> ments to gilding and Babylonian parchment with elaborate decorations. Let
> her learn the Psalter first, with these songs let her distract herself, and then
> let her learn lessons of life in the Proverbs of Solomon. . . . Let her then
> pass on to the Gospels and never lay them down.[47]

Between 1247 and 1249 Vincent of Beauvais wrote a treatise entitled
De eruditione filiorum nobilium ("On the Education and Instruction of Noble Children") at the request of Queen Margaret of Provence, wife of
Louis IX of France (Saint Louis). The queen's commission included details and some chapters specifically on the education of girls.[48] Vincent
relied almost entirely on Jerome's letters concerning girls' education, insisting that by busying themselves in reading and writing, girls could
escape harmful thoughts and the pleasures and vanities of the flesh.[49]

Some seventy years after Vincent of Beauvais's treatise, the Italian
Francesco di Barberino wrote his *Reggimento e Costumi di Donna* (Rules
and Customs for Ladies). Like Vincent of Beauvais and Jerome,
Francesco di Barberino took it for granted that the mother would be
concerned with children's primary and moral education. "And if it is
fitting to her station," he wrote, addressing a mother on how to educate
her daughter, "she should learn to read and write so that if it happens that
she inherits lands she will be better able to rule them, and the acquired
wisdom will help her natural wisdom. But here note well, that the person
who teaches her be a woman or a person above suspicion, since too much
intimacy is the occasion for many evils."[50]

The Italian-born author Christine de Pizan, who spent her life in Paris composing thirty books, among them a number of educational works, wrote in 1405 of the duties of women: "When her daughter is of the age of learning to read, and after she knows her 'hours' and her 'office,' one should bring her books of devotion and contemplation and those speaking of morality."[51]

In keeping with these prescriptions, many types of books—such as Psalters, Gospels, and educational treatises—were commissioned and used specifically for the education of children. First and foremost was the Psalter, or book of psalms, which often served as an alphabet book. Blanche of Castille followed the maxim of Jerome in ordering the now-famous Psalter, housed in the Morgan Library, to teach her son, the future Saint Louis, to read.[52] Isabeau of Bavaria's accounts show that she ordered a Book of Hours including psalms for her daughter Jeanne in 1398 and an alphabet Psalter, an "A,b,c,d, des Psaumes," for her daughter Michelle in 1403.[53] The girls were between six and seven years old when they received these books. A rare pictorial example of a medieval alphabet book can be found in a manuscript that belonged to the Countess of Leicester in about 1300, and is now in the Bodleian Library in Oxford.[54] One illustration shows the Virgin as a small girl holding her alphabet Psalter and standing within the shelter of her mother's ermine-lined cloak (figure 4). "Put to my book, I had learned the shapes of the letters, but hardly yet to join them into syllables, when my good mother eager for my instruction arranged to place me under a schoolmaster," wrote the eleventh-century Guibert de Nogent, describing his mother's determination to educate him for the religious life.[55]

In choosing these books of instruction for their children, mothers pursued their individual interests and ideas. In 1395 Christine de Pizan wrote a book of moral instruction, the *Enseignements moraux*, for her son Jean. A copy of this manuscript, now in the British Library, belonged to Queen Isabeau of France, who may have read it to her own son, the Duc de Guienne.[56] Empress Eleanor of Portugal ordered a sumptuous copy of Pius II's *De Liberorum Educatione* for her son Maximilian I of Austria in 1466. Her interest in new artistic trends and ideas caused her to choose an Austrian scribe and an illuminator who followed the latest Italian ideas on art and architecture in their execution of the manuscript.[57]

It is important to consider as well the power and influence that women, as commissioners of educational volumes, were able to exercise in their choice of subject matter. By commissioning books and by instructing children they were able to influence both artistic and ideological developments. The choice between an alphabet Psalter, a Gospel, a Book of Hours, or an educational treatise may indicate steps in the growth of the

4. Saint Anne teaching the Virgin, who is holding an
alphabet book, to read. English, ca. 1300. *Psalter,*
Bodleian Library, Oxford, MS Douce 231, fol. 3.

student reader or the commissioner. The commissioner of a Book of Hours could choose whether to order Hours of the Cross, Hours of Saint Louis, or Hours of the Virgin. A patron could decide where to place the emphasis in the Testaments—whether, for example, to include the story of Solomon's judgment between the two mothers (emphasizing maternal unselfishness) or whether to include the story of Salome and the beheading of John the Baptist (demonstrating female power). A commissioner had to decide which vignettes of the numerous saints to include, and whether or not to concentrate on female saints' lives in a Book of Hours intended for a young girl.

Books of Hours were certainly used as works of primary education. As noted previously, Isabeau of Bavaria gave her daughter, Jeanne of France, a Book of Hours at the age of six.[58] This example of a commissioned Book of Hours ordered by a mother for her daughter, together with the existing evidence about women's involvement with devotional books and their concern for passing on their culture to the next generation, suggests that it may have been a general practice for mothers to commission books as wedding gifts for their daughters. Through individual choice and collaboration with scribes and artists, women may have exerted a powerful influence on the contents of the Books of Hours handed on to their children.

Educating the young and choosing their reading material was but one aspect of medieval women's cultural contribution in their special relationship to books—another was their concern for vernacular translations. Most devotional literature in the early Middle Ages was written in Latin, a language accessible only to a small sector of lay society. Medieval laywomen's knowledge of Latin was even rarer than that of laymen, who were often taught Latin in preparation for a possible career in the church. Since women were expected to read devotional literature, it is not surprising that they played an important role as instigators of vernacular translations from the Latin and of vernacular literature in general. Nor is it surprising that an upsurge of such translations occurred in the twelfth and thirteenth centuries together with the development of Books of Hours.

Throughout the later Middle Ages, girls educated to remain outside the cloister did not learn a great deal of Latin.[59] The twelfth-century Abbess Herrad's *Garden of Delights,* with its captions in German and Latin, was intended to teach Latin to her novices, who had been taught to read German at home.[60] Christine de Pizan, one of the most scholarly laywomen of the late fourteenth century, knew a minimum of Latin. She always read her sources in French or Italian translations and did not even advocate Latin for girls in her educational treatise for women, *The Book of Three Virtues.*[61]

Bishop John Fisher, the confessor of Margaret Beaufort, mother of Henry VII, wrote soon after her death that although she was a woman who was always interested in scholarship, she "ful often complayned that in her youthe she had not gyven her to the understondynge of latyn wherein she had a lytell perceyvynge."[62] Latin "Instructions" written for an English layman of the early fifteenth century commanded him to "expound something in the vernacular which may edify your wife."[63] Knowledge of Latin also declined in English nunneries in the fourteenth and fifteenth centuries; thus girls sent to them for education were unlikely to learn the language. Similar evidence from the Netherlands demonstrates that the nuns in Dutch and Flemish convents read mostly in the vernacular.[64]

Other evidence of medieval women's lack of proficiency in Latin comes from the first rank of fifteenth- and sixteenth-century humanists. Exceptional male humanists, men like Leonardo Bruni, Vittorino de Feltre, Erasmus, Vives, Ascham, and Thomas More, all wanted girls to be as proficient in Latin as boys and advocated teaching Latin to girls as a new departure from the medieval norm.[65] It is clear that the first rank of humanists did not have their way, however. Walter Ong suggested that the grammar schools and institutions that proliferated from the sixteenth century onward used the study of Latin as a kind of male puberty rite that would make boys independent of women.[66] Clearly the professional institutions that required knowledge of Latin were disinclined to allow women the preparation needed to enter the professional occupations in the church, in academia, and in law and medicine.[67] Thus the aim of Renaissance teachers and humanists to revolutionize primary education by taking boys into institutions and by teaching girls Latin at home was frustrated.

Indeed, women had developed a vernacular home culture during the last four medieval centuries. By the mid-twelfth century, highborn women, still following patristic recommendations, had begun to commission biblical and saintly themes in vernacular translations. An early example is Maud, first wife of Henry I of England, who commissioned the *Voyage of Saint Brendan* in Latin and later in a vernacular Anglo-Norman translation "for her ladies and maidens."[68] Also in the twelfth century, Eleanor of Aquitaine's daughter Marie of Champagne commissioned a French translation of Genesis from Evratt.[69] In 1328 Margaret of Provence commissioned John de Vignai to translate Vincent de Beauvais's *Speculum Historiale* ("Mirror of History") almost as soon as her husband had commissioned the Latin composition of this work (figure 5).[70] In 1382 Anne of Bohemia arrived in England to marry King Richard II, bringing with her a New Testament written in Latin, Czech, and German.[71] Soon after her arrival she ordered an English translation of the Gospels, presumably to learn English.[72]

5. King Louis IX commissioning the *Mirror of History* in Latin, while his queen, Margaret of Provence, commissions a French translation of the same work. French, ca. 1333. *Miroir Historial,* Bibliothèque Nationale, Paris, MS Fr. 316, fol. 1.

Of the 186 laywomen who are known to have owned books between 1300 and 1500, 125 (or 67 percent) definitely owned vernacular translations. The actual percentage must have been higher; it is difficult to be more precise because some of the books were described in inventories or wills without indicating their contents: "a little book," "a bible," "Heures," or "a little book bound in green velvet." It is clear, however, that by the mid-fifteenth century translations proliferated and, aided by cheaper production, made reading and book owning a reasonable proposition for a less wealthy segment of society, one not proficient in Latin. This segment included a good proportion of women.[73]

Women, Books, and Cultural Influence

The significance of medieval women's book owning is apparent in two other areas. First, women influenced the shaping of iconography in books, thereby offering new images of womanhood. Second, women acted as international ambassadors of cultural change through their distribution of books over a broad geographic area.[74]

Medieval devotional manuscripts offer innumerable iconographic portraits of reading women. The woman book owner herself may be shown in a variety of poses with her book: kneeling before the Virgin and Child; standing by the side of the Cross; or kneeling at a prie-dieu, like the Duchess de Berry in her husband's famous *Belles Heures*. Or the new owner might be portrayed in the margin of a manuscript received as a wedding gift long after it was first produced, so that the difference in artistic style and fashion of her dress indicate the years gone by since the manuscript was written (figure 6).[75] A most delightful portrait of a woman book owner is that of Mary of Burgundy reading her book while surrounded by her lapdog and her jewels. She sits in the window overlooking a magnificent gothic church, in which another replica of herself adores a majestic Virgin and Child (figure 7).

Portraits of the Virgin Mary herself surrounded by books provide yet another ingenious artistic confirmation of women's close involvement with devotional literature. Uncountable paintings and sculptures of the Annunciation depict Mary as an avid reader. Mary had been portrayed with a book as early as the eleventh century, but by the fourteenth and fifteenth centuries books were common in Annunciation iconography (figure 6).[76] The Master of Vissi Brod in a fourteenth-century Bohemian Annunciation piece represented two books on the Virgin's delicate desk (figure 8). Robert Campin's Virgin in the *Merode Altarpiece* sits in a comfortable Flemish interior against a fireplace, near a table with two books (figure 1). The Virgin in the *Belles Heures* of the Duc de Berry kneels by a lectern that harbors three books (figure 8.9). The altarpiece of Sainte Marie Madeleine in Aix-en-Provence shows the Virgin kneeling beside a circular stand holding five books, and the Virgin in Catherine of Cleves's manuscript is also surrounded by five books.[77]

The scene is, of course, based on the common literature of the era—the Gospels, the "Golden Legend" of Jacobus de Varagine, and the apocryphal gospel of Pseudo-Matthew. Yet in none of these is there any reference to reading or even to prayer at the time of the Annunciation.[78] Mary is described as fetching water from the well or weaving, if any activity is described at all. Clearly, the artists themselves conceived Mary with books, without benefit of written tradition. Nor did they confine themselves to the scene of the Annunciation. The Virgin reads while two midwives prepare for her confinement at Bethlehem (figure 10); she reads while recuperating from childbirth, relegating Joseph to rocking the baby (figure 11), or while sitting in the garden, watching the children at play.[79] She reads on the donkey while Joseph carries the babe during their

6. "Annunciation" with one book. French, ca. 1382. Later owner reading in margin painted into manuscript in 1438. *Très Belles Heures de Notre Dame,* Bibliothèque Nationale, Paris, MS Nouveau Acquisition Latin 3093, fol. 2.

7. Mary of Burgundy reading in window overlooking Gothic church. Flemish,
ca. 1467–1480. *Book of Hours,* Bildarchiv der Oesterreichischen
Nationalbibliothek, Vienna, Cod. 1857, fol. 14v.

Color plate 8 follows page 174.

9. "Annunciation" with three books. French, ca. 1408. In *Belles Heures of Jean de Berry*, Metropolitan Museum of Art, New York, fol. 30.

Color plate 10 faces page 175.

11. The Virgin reads while Joseph rocks the swaddled Babe. Northern French, early fifteenth century. *Book of Hours,* Walters Art Gallery, Baltimore, MS 10.290, fol. 69.

flight into Egypt (figure 12). She is even shown as the woman in Revelations who escapes the seven-headed monster by flying into the wilderness clutching her book and then peacefully settles with her book in sanctuary (figure 13).

Students of iconography suggest that the book in Christian art symbolizes the Word (that is, Christ),[80] that at the time of the Annunciation Mary was reading the Old Testament prophecy in Isaiah, "Behold a virgin shall conceive and bear a son, and shall call his name Emmanuel,"[81] or that Mary was seen as a symbol of wisdom, learned in the law of God, because only such a woman would be worthy to bear His son.[82] These views may explain the symbolism involved, but artists' insistence on portraying the most significant medieval female ideal, the Virgin Mary, as a constant reader was surely based on the reality of their patrons' lives. It suggests that women were not only acquiring books but spending much of their time perusing them. The developing association of the Virgin with books in fact coincides with the rise in numbers of women book owners during the fourteenth and fifteenth centuries. Saint Anne teaching the Virgin to read, a symbol of the mother as her daughter's teacher, is also more frequently depicted in fourteenth- and fifteenth-century Books of Hours (figure 4).[83] Artists using the circumstances of their patrons' involvement with books to change iconography thus produced a new symbolism. This symbolism showing the Virgin as a constant reader in turn added respectability to laywomen occupying themselves with books.

The most general significance of women's book owning emerges in conjunction with medieval marriage customs, which forced women to move from their native land to their husbands' domains. Medieval marriage bestowed upon women a role of cultural ambassador that it did not bestow upon men who remained on their native soil. It would have been pointless in this analysis to consider, for example, only Frenchwomen's books, or Italian or German women's books. Medieval noblewomen, more often than not, changed their cultural milieu with marriage. Their books are evidence of the influential role these women played as international disseminators of literary, artistic, and religious ideas. Arranged marriages, which forced young girls—indeed, child brides—to travel widely to foreign countries, underscore the importance of a familiar book. The accustomed devotional volumes could teach a new language, minimize the strangeness of new experiences, and comfort the homesick. In addition, the radius of a book's exposure was fairly wide. Noble households were extensive and included many members. Books were often borrowed and sometimes were lost, finding their way to new owners.

12. The Virgin reads on the donkey while Joseph carries the Babe on their flight into Egypt. Flemish, ca. 1475. *Book of Hours,* Bibliothèque Royale Albert ler, Brussels, MS IV 315, fol. 105v.

8. "Annunciation" with two books. Bohemian, ca. 1350. Master of Vissi Brod,
National Gallery, Prague.

10. The Virgin reads while midwives prepare for her delivery. East German or
Bohemian, 1406. *Missal*. Bayerische Staatsbibliothek, Munich,
MS clm 14.045, fol. 41v.

13. The woman escaping a seven-headed monster carrying her book to read in sanctuary. "Revelations," Rhenish, ca. 1320. *Apocalypse of St. John the Apostle,* Metropolitan Museum of Art, New York, fol. 21v.

There are numerous examples of women book owners who functioned as cultural ambassadors throughout medieval centuries. In 1051 Judith of Flanders married Tostig, Earl of Northumbria. As a widow she later married the German Welf of Bavaria. She brought at least two large English Gospels, illustrated for her in Winchester, to her German marriage.[84] Their style was adopted in the Bavarian scriptorium at Weingarten Abbey where Judith retired in her old age. One of these Gospels, bound in thick wooden boards, covered with plates of silver, and encrusted with jewels, is now a treasure of the Morgan Library in New York.[85] Another became Judith's wedding gift to her new daughter-in-law, Countess Matilda of Tuscany, in 1086.[86] Thus, the "Winchester style" traveled from England, to Bavaria, and thence to Tuscany. The "Melissenda Psalter," one of the prized possessions of the British Library, was also an eleventh-century wedding gift.[87] Melissenda, heiress of the

king of Jerusalem, married the crusader Fulk the Young, thereby bringing him the kingdom of Jerusalem. The carved ivory binding and Byzantine figures of her Psalter are part of the artistic heritage that returned
with the crusaders from East to West.

By the end of the fourteenth century, women carried manuscripts of
diverse languages and subject matter in their trousseaux. Anne of Bohemia brought Czech and German Gospels to England.[88] Isabelle of
France, sister of book collectors Charles V and Jean de Berry, was married off to the rich Jean Galeazzo Visconti in 1360 in order to raise the
ransom for her captive father. Isabelle carried her French books to Milan.
A generation later she sent her daughter Valentina Visconti back to France
to marry Louis d'Orléans, sending with her a trousseau containing
twelve books, many of Italian origin. All but one of Valentina's books
were prayerbooks and Psalters.[89] In the second half of the fifteenth century, Yolande of France brought three coffers of books when she married
Amadeo of Savoy.[90] By the end of the fifteenth century brides brought
romances, grammars, and educational treatises as well, but devotional
works remained a part of the literary trousseau. Giovanna di Medici took
a Mass book decorated with miniatures and silver clasps when she married Bernardo Rucellai in 1466.[91] Anna Sforza, who married Alphonso
d'Este as the predecessor of Lucrezia Borgia, brought the De Sphaera, a
fashionable humanist treasure of the Sforza library, to Ferrara, but she
also brought a missal.[92] When Hyppolita Sforza married the son of the
king of Naples in 1465, her trousseau contained twelve books. She carried Cicero's treatise on old age, De Senectute, which she had copied herself as an exercise in writing, together with a variety of other Latin
books. The nucleus of her library, however, consisted of the obligatory
books of piety: the lives of saints, in Italian translation; a luxurious copy
of Augustine's City of God; and a New Testament in Greek, demonstrating Hyppolita's fashionable humanist education.[93] As an eager book collector she stopped to buy manuscripts on her wedding journey from
Milan to Naples.[94]

Anne of Bohemia exemplifies the relationship of these ambassadorial
brides not only to their books but also to the cultural pursuits of those
living on her husband's domain. Anne married Richard II of England in
1382—in the age of Chaucer and Wycliffe. She arrived in England not
only with her books but with Bohemian book illustrators. The influence
of Anne's books and illustrators on English art is clearly established.[95]
The Liber Regalis which documents the coronation of Richard and Anne,
and which was used for English coronation ceremonies until the time of
Elizabeth I, exemplifies the artistic influence Anne brought from Bohemia. The book is illustrated in the style of Bohemian art and is quite

different from any previous English work (figure 14; compare figures 8 and 10).

While Bohemian painters revitalized English art in the late fourteenth century, Anne herself influenced English literature. Critical of Chaucer's *Troilus and Criseyde,* in which he emphasized female infidelity, she inspired the poet by her patronage, which resulted in *The Legend of Good Women:* "And when this book is made / Give it the Queen, on my behalf / at Eltham or at Sheene," Chaucer wrote in the prologue.[96]

But it was in religious matters that the Anglo-Bohemian connection had the greatest impact. Anne came from the *Sachsenspiegel* domain. Her mother was the fourth of her father's wives, three of whom had come from areas served by *Sachsenspiegel* law. Anne's father, the Emperor Charles IV, had founded Prague University and encouraged a free circle of preachers and an impressive production of religious literature written in both local vernaculars, Czech (Bohemian) and German. His daughter clearly took this freedom of reading vernacular biblical texts for granted. When she arrived in London the English reformer John Wycliffe pointed to her in his pleas to legitimize the English translation of the Bible.

Wycliffe's aim was considered heretical by church officials. They objected to translations from the Latin, claiming that untrained minds would misinterpret the Bible and damage Christian principles; no doubt they feared that their own authority would be undermined. In a tract of 1383, a year after Anne had arrived in London, Wycliffe wrote:

> It is lawful for the noble queen of England [Anne] the sister of the Emperor, to have the gospel written in three languages, that is in Czech and in German and in Latin; and it would savor of the pride of Lucifer to call her a heretic for such a reason as this! And since the Germans wish in this matter reasonably to defend their own tongue, so ought the English to defend theirs.[97]

Anne's uninhibited ownership of multilingual Gospels in England was remarked on even in her funeral oration at Westminster, in 1394. Archbishop Arundel spoke to hundreds who mourned the popular queen; she had died of a fever after only twelve years of marriage at the age of twenty-eight. He praised Anne for her biblical studies and for requesting that he critically examine the text of her new English translation and commentaries on the Gospels. He commended her as a woman who was "so great a lady, and also an alien, and would so lowlily study in virtuous books."[98] Moreover, the cultural exchange that Anne initiated from Prague to London also encouraged the reverse: the influence of Wycliffe and other English reformers on Hussite Bohemia accelerated.[99]

Writing of the sixteenth-century Reformation, Roland Bainton states: "The Reformation had a profound influence on women and they in turn

14. Coronation of Richard II of England and Anne of Bohemia. English, ca. 1382. *The Liber Regalis,* Westminster Abbey Library, London, MS 38, fol. 20, reproduced by permission of the Dean and Chapter of Westminster.

upon the church. The translation of the Scriptures into the vernaculars and their dissemination through the printing press stimulated literacy and the will to read."[100] I would suggest that we may find it was women who had a profound influence in bringing about the Reformation by their collective involvement in heresies and by their individual involvement with religious literature in the preceding centuries. Scholars agree that one of the key issues in reformist movements throughout the late Middle Ages was the public's greater familiarity with the teaching of the New Testament—a familiarity obviously deepened by the spread of literacy and the invention of printing, but first and foremost by the translation of scriptural texts into the vernacular. Women played an important role in teaching, in translating, and in loosening the hierarchical bonds of church control through their close and private relationship to religious books.

Medieval laywomen's ownership of devotional books, encouraged by legal convention and marriage customs, increased proportionately with the advent of technical aids to literacy, with the growth of dependence on the written word, and with the disintegration of Christian unity in this period. Because women were not able to take part in the ecclesiastical authority structure of spiritual life, they depended more heavily on books, especially vernacular books. In turn, in their choice of books used as teaching aids, mothers could influence the lives of their daughters. In times when a single book was often the only literary possession, such a choice was indeed of paramount importance.[101]

Medieval women's book ownership reveals a linear transmission of Christian culture and the development of a mother-daughter or matrilineal literary tradition that may also have influenced later generations. The evidence of books chosen by mothers and brought across Europe by their daughters reveals a geographically widespread transmission of culture. These young brides (and widows on remarriage) brought their books across regional and national boundaries, often transmitting artistic style, specific content, and ideas. Economic, political, and diplomatic pressures forcing young girls and widows to traverse the Christian world for arranged marriages may have propelled women's books haphazardly from one cultural milieu to another. But the content of these books was surely not arbitrary; rather, it reflects conscious choice on the part of mothers in shaping their daughters' futures. It would repay us to look more closely at the contents of pre-Reformation devotional books, especially the Books of Hours. These books express something of the medieval mother-child relationship—particularly the mother-daughter relationship—and of the values and ideals dispersed throughout Europe by medieval women.

Notes

"Medieval Women Book Owners: Arbiters of Lay Piety and Ambassadors of Culture" was originally published in *Signs: Journal of Women in Culture and Society* 7:4 (1982):742–68, copyright © 1982 The University of Chicago, and is reprinted by permission. The epigraph is quoted from MS Harley, 1251, British Library, London.

1. Edward McNall Burns, Robert Lerner, and Standish Meacham, *Western Civilizations: Their History and Their Culture* (New York, 1980).

2. Susan Connel, "Books and Their Owners in Venice, 1345–1480," *Journal of the Warburg and Courtauld Institute* 35 (1972):163–86, esp. 163.

3. M. T. Clanchy, *From Memory to Written Record* (London, 1979).

4. LeRoy Joseph Dresbeck, "The Chimney and Fireplace: A Study in Technological Development Primarily in England during the Middle Ages" (Ph.D. diss., University of California, Los Angeles, 1971). The concept of reading by the fireplace in comfort is well illustrated by Robert Campin's Annunciation scene in the *Merode Altarpiece* (figure 1); Campin's *Santa Barbara Reading,* at the Prado Museum, Madrid; or the *Woman Reading by the Fireplace While Stirring a Pot,* in Comestor, "Historia Scholastica," MS Reg. 15 D.I., British Library, London.

5. Vincent Illardy, "Eyeglasses and Concave Lenses in Fifteenth Century Florence and Milan: New Documents," *Renaissance Quarterly* 29 (Autumn 1976):341–60. Also E. Rosen, "The Invention of Eyeglasses," *Journal of the History of Medicine and Allied Sciences* 11 (January–April 1956):13–46 and 183–218.

6. See James Westfall Thompson, *The Medieval Library* (Chicago, 1939), p. 640.

7. Jules Marie Richard, "Les Livres de Mahaut, Comtesse d'Artois et de Bourgogne, 1302–1329," *Revue des questions historiques* 40 (1886):135–41.

8. Thompson, p. 645.

9. Richard, p. 237.

10. Ibid., p. 238. This may have been one of the mass-produced Books of Hours described by Dr. Pieter Obbema in a paper read at the University of California, Berkeley, in 1977 (Library, State University of Leiden, the Netherlands).

11. Malcolm B. Parkes, "The Literacy of the Laity," in *The Medieval World,* ed. D. Daiches (London, 1973), p. 564.

12. A male agricultural laborer in southern Frace during the same period earned between ten and fifteen deniers (or pence), double the daily earnings of a woman (Georges Duby, *L'économie rurale et la vie de campagne dans l'occident medieval,* 2 vols. [Paris, 1962], vol. 2, p. 562).

13. Thompson, p. 265.

14. Margaret Deanesly, "Vernacular Books in England in the Fourteenth and Fifteenth Centuries," *Modern Language Review* 15:4(1920):349–58, esp. 351.

15. Jean Longnon, *The Très Riches Heures of Jean Duke of Berry* (New York, 1969), p. 25.

16. Leopold Delisle, *Recherches sur la Librarie de Charles V, Roi de France, 1337–1380,* 2 vols. (Amsterdam, 1967), vol. 2.

17. Ibid., 2:239; and see also Millard Meiss, *The Belles Heures of Jean Duke of Berry* (New York, 1974), p. 267.

18. Ernest Quentin Bauchart, *Les Femmes bibliophiles de France,* 2 vols. (Paris, 1886), vol. 2, 374–82.

19. In 1434 Agnes Paston, e.g., a member of the English wool trading gentry, inherited a religious tract, the "Prick of Conscience," from a burgess of Yarmouth. See Deanesly, p. 353. Occasionally a resigned notation in a will made it clear that, since a woman had borrowed a book and kept it a very long time, she might as well inherit it permanently. The Countess of Westmorland, however, came close to losing her copy of the *Chronicles of Jerusalem* when King Henry V died before returning the borrowed book to her. See Thompson, p. 402.

20. Hans Hirsch, ed., *Der Sachsenspiegel* (Berlin, 1936), pp. 130–31.

21. Ibid., and see, e.g., the oldest dated *Sachsenspiegel* (May 7, 1295): Märta Äsdahl Holmberg, ed., *Der Harffer Sachsenspiegel* (Lund, 1957), p. 118.

22. *Books of Dyson Perrins,* 3 vols. (London, 1960), vol. 3, pp. 98–100, esp. 98 (lot 139; present whereabouts of lot 139 unknown).

23. E.g., Catherine Payenne inherited a *Book of Our Lady* from her mother Maroie. See Thompson, p. 265. Eleanor de Bohun, Duchess of Gloucester, died in 1399 and left a well-illustrated *Golden Legend* in French to her daughter Anne and a "Book of Psalms" and other "Devotions," which she had used constantly, to her daughter Johanna. See *Collection of All the Wills Now Known to Be Extant* (London, 1780), pp. 182–83. Cicely, Duchess of York, left the *Life of Catherine of Siena,* the *Life of Matilda,* and a *Golden Legend* to her granddaughter Brigitta in 1495. See J. G. Nichols and J. Bruce, eds., *Wills from Doctors' Commons* (London, 1863), pp. 1–8.

24. Richard, pp. 235–41.

25. Ibid.

26. Valet de Viriville, "La Bibliothèque d'Isabeau de Bavière," *Bulletin du Bibliophile* 14 (1858):663–87.

27. Ibid., p. 677.

28. A. de Boislisle, *Annuaire-Bulletin de la Société de l'Histoire de France,* vol. 17 (Paris, 1880), pp. 297–306. There were many other women collectors. Mechthild of Rottenburg, Countess of Palantine, who founded the universities of Tübingen and Freiburg, collected some one hundred books in the mid-fifteenth century. See Philipp Strauch, *Pfalzgräfin Mechthild in Ihren Literarischen Beziehungen* (Tübingen, 1883). Jeanne d'Evreux received Jean Pucelle's now-famous Book of Hours at her marriage. Between 1325 and 1370 she ordered twenty devotional books, among them four breviaries and eight missals. See Paulin Paris, "Livres de Jehanne d'Evreux," *Bulletin du Bibliophile* (1838):492–94. Margaret, Duchess of Brittany, whose books were inventoried at her death in 1469, left eleven prayerbooks. See *Bibliothèque de l'Ecole des Chartes,* 5th ser., no. 3 (1862), p. 45. Bona of Savoy left forty books at her death in 1503, most of which were books of piety. See Theodor Gottlieb, *Die Ambrasser Handschriften: Beitrag zur Geschichte der Wiener Hofbibliothek* (Leipzig, 1900), pp. 122–25, which is an inventory of Bona's books. Valentina Visconti, who had arrived in France with twelve books in her trousseau in 1388, left forty-three volumes at her death in 1408. At least twenty-

six of these were books of devotion. See Pierre Champion, *La Librairie de Charles d'Orléans* (Paris, 1910), pp. 70–74. Marie de Clèves, second wife of the poet Charles d'Orléans, left about thirty books at her death in 1487; see Champion, pp. 115–17.

29. N. F. Blake, *William Caxton and His World* (London, 1969).

30. See Julia Cartwright, *Isabella d'Este*, 2 vols. (London, 1911). In 1501 Isabella ordered the first copies of the poems of Petrarch and Virgil to be printed by the Aldine press, and then had them bound for herself in Flanders. In 1505 she wrote to Aldus, requesting books in Latin that he had printed in a small edition and added: "When you print other volumes, do not forget to print some on fine paper for us, and that as quickly as possible." Later that year she complained: "The four volumes which you sent us are pronounced by everyone who has seen them to be twice as dear as they ought to be. We have given them back to your messenger. . . . When you print some more, at a fair price and on finer paper, with more careful corrections, we shall be glad to see them." See Cartwright, vol. 2, pp. 25, 27.

31. Saint Jerome, *Select Letters of Saint Jerome* with an English translation by F. A. Wright (Cambridge, Mass., 1963), pp. 339–57. On women's education and learned women in the Middle Ages, see Patricia H. Labalme, ed., *Beyond Their Sex: Learned Women of the European Past* (New York, 1980); and Suzanne Wemple, *Women in Frankish Society* (Philadelphia, 1981).

32. See Clara Maria Henning, "Canon Law and Sexism," in *Religion and Sexism: Images of Woman in the Jewish and Christian Traditions,* ed. Rosemary Radford Ruether (New York, 1974), pp. 267–91, esp. pp. 275–77.

33. Rosemary Rader, "Early Christian Forms of Communal Spirituality: Women's Communities," in *The Continuing Quest for God: Monastic Spirituality in Tradition and Transition,* ed. William Skudlarek (Collegeville, Minn., 1982); Lina Eckenstein, *Woman under Monasticism* (Cambridge, 1896); Jo Ann McNamara, "Sexual Equality and the Cult of Virginity in Early Christian Thought," *Feminist Studies* 3:3/4 (1976):145–58; and Brenda M. Bolton, "Mulieres Sanctae," in *Women in Medieval Society,* ed. Susan M. Stuard (Philadelphia, 1976).

34. Bolton, p. 143.

35. J. Nichols, ed., *Collection of Ordinances and Regulations for the Government of the Royal Household* (London: Society of Antiquaries, 1790), pp. 37–39. See also C. A. J. Armstrong, "The Piety of Cicely, Duchess of York: A Study in Late Medieval Culture," in *For Hilaire Belloc,* ed. Douglas Woodruff (London, 1942).

36. John E. B. Mayor, ed., "Month's Mind of the Lady Margaret," in *The English Works of John Fisher,* Extra Series no. 27 of the Early English Text Society (London, 1876), p. 295.

37. Victor Léroquais, *Les Livres d'Heures,* 2 vols. (Paris, 1927), vol. 1, introduction.

38. L. M. J. Delaissé, "The Importance of Books of Hours for the History of the Medieval Book," in *Gatherings in Honor of Dorothy E. Miner* (Baltimore, 1974), pp. 203–205.

39. There are innumerable examples of the varied compositions of Books of Hours. Some, including that given to Jeanne d'Evreux on her marriage in 1325,

included the life of Saint Louis and the tale of his crusade to the Holy Land, which presumably was meant to impress upon the recipient the high achievements of the royal family into which she was marrying. See *The Hours of Jeanne d'Evreux* (New York, 1957). Yolande of Aragon bought a Book of Hours from the estate of the Duc de Berry in 1416 that included an unusual story of how Saint Jerome was tricked into wearing a woman's dress by his envious companions. See Meiss, fol. 184v.

40. John Plummer, ed., *The Hours of Catherine of Cleves* (New York, 1975).

41. Ibid., no. 88.

42. Ibid., no. 96.

43. Ibid., nos. 57, 93, 81, and 13.

44. Ibid., no. 56.

45. Translated in E. Panofsky, *Early Netherlandish Painting*, 2 vols. (Cambridge, Mass., 1953), vol. 1, p. 68.

46. Daniel Poirion, *Le Poète et le Prince* (Paris, 1965), p. 219. Deschamps's poetry was never assembled into an aesthetic object, as were the collected poems of his contemporaries.

47. Saint Jerome, pp. 343–65 (quoted passage on pp. 345–47).

48. The treatise was intended for the use of the royal children, Louis and his sister, Isabelle. See A. Steiner, *Vincent of Beauvais "De eruditione filiorum nobilium,"* Medieval Academy of American Publications no. 32 (Cambridge, Mass., 1938); and Astrik L. Gabriel, *The Educational Ideas of Vincent of Beauvais* (Notre Dame, Ind., 1956).

49. Steiner, pp. 172–76; Gabriel, p. 40.

50. Francesco di Barberino, *Reggimento e Costumi di Donna* (Turin, 1957), p. 344 and app., p. 15. Elsewhere in the book Francesco admitted that he sometimes thought girls should not be taught to read.

51. Christine de Pizan, *Le Trésor de la Cité des Dames* (Paris, Janot, 1536), fol. xxxiv. This book is sometimes known as *Le Livre des Trois Vertus* ("The Book of Three Virtues").

52. Le Coy de la Marche, *St. Louis* (Tours, 1887), p. 194; and Susan Noakes, "The Fifteen Oes, the 'Disticha Catonis' and Dick, Jane, and Sally," *University of Chicago Library Bulletin* (Winter 1977):2–15.

53. Viriville, pp. 668–69.

54. MS Douce 231, fol. 3, Bodleian Library, Oxford.

55. John F. Benton, *Self and Society in Medieval France: The Memoirs of Abbot Guibert of Nogent* (New York, 1970), p. 45.

56. Maurice Roy, ed., *Oeuvres poetiques de Christine de Pisan*, 3 vols. (Paris, 1886–96), vol. 3, iv–ix and 27–57; and MS Harley, 4431, British Library, London.

57. Franz Unterkircher, *A Treasury of Illuminated Manuscripts* (New York, 1967), pp. 144–47. The primer ordered by Anne of Brittany for her six-year-old daughter Claude in 1505 begins with the alphabet and proceeds with the Lord's Prayer, the creed, grace to be said before meals, the story of the creation, and other short details from the New Testament. See M. R. James, *A Descriptive Catalogue of the Manuscripts in the Fitzwilliam Museum* (Cambridge, 1895), item no. 159, pp. 356–59; and John Harthan, *Books of Hours and Their Owners* (London,

1977), pp. 134–37. Gospels also may have served as reading exercises particularly for learning new languages; for example, English Gospels were especially translated for Anne of Bohemia when she arrived in London as a young bride in 1382. See Margaret Deanesly, *The Lollard Bible and Other Medieval Biblical Versions* (Cambridge, 1922), p. 20. Vincent de Beauvais's educational treatise, *De eruditione filiorum,* was commissioned by Margaret of Provence, who also suggested what he should include for the education of her children, as we have seen.

58. Isabeau ordered the book from Perrin Cauvel in 1398 and paid eleven livres and four sous for it. Jeanne married at the age of six, like many aristocratic girls, and the book served educational purposes as well as being a wedding gift. See Viriville, p. 681.

59. Exceptions to this rule have been discussed in James Westfall Thompson, *The Literacy of the Laity in the Middle Ages* (Berkeley, 1920); and W. Wattenbach, *Das Schriftwesen im Mittelalter* (Leipzig, 1871).

60. On Herrad, see Eckenstein, pp. 238–55; and A. Straub and G. Keller, *Herrade de Landsberg, Hortus Deliciarum* (Strassburg, 1901).

61. Susan Groag Bell, "Christine de Pizan (1364–1430): Humanism and the Problem of a Studious Woman," *Feminist Studies* 3:3/4 (1976):173–84, esp. n. 8.

62. Mayor, ed., p. 292.

63. William A. Pantin, "Instructions for a Devout and Literate Layman," in *Medieval Learning and Literature: Essays Presented to Richard William Hunt,* ed. J. J. G. Alexander and M. T. Gibson (Oxford, 1976), p. 400.

64. Eileen Power, *Medieval English Nunneries, 1275–1535* (Cambridge, 1922); and Deanesly, *Lollard Bible,* p. 166.

65. W. H. Woodward, *Vittorino de Feltre and Other Humanist Educators* (Cambridge, 1897), and *Studies in Education during the Age of the Renaissance, 1400–1600* (Cambridge, 1906); Foster Watson, *Vives and the Renaissance Education of Women* (London, 1912); Ruth Kelso, *Doctrine for the Lady of the Renaissance* (Urbana, 1956).

66. See Walter Ong, "Latin Language Study as a Renaissance Puberty Rite," *Studies in Philology* 56 (April 1959):103–24.

67. Alison Klairmont Lingo, "The Rise of Medical Practitioners in Sixteenth Century France" (Ph.D. diss., University of California, Berkeley, 1980); and see Joan Kelly, "Did Women Have a Renaissance?" in *Becoming Visible: Women in European History,* ed. Renate Bridenthal and Claudia Koonz (Boston, 1977), pp. 137–64.

68. Mary Dominica Legge, *Anglo-Norman Literature and Its Background* (Oxford, 1963), p. 10.

69. Thompson, *Literacy of the Laity,* p. 144. In the same century, Aliz de Condé asked Sanson de Nanteuil to translate the "Proverbs of Solomon" into French (MS Harley, 4388, British Library, London); see also Karl Holzknecht, *Literary Patronage in the Middle Ages* (Philadelphia, 1923), p. 92. The Byzantine princess Theodora Comnena (niece of the famous author Anna Comnena), who married the German Henry Jasomirgott and with him established an important literary court in Vienna, ordered a German translation of the *Song of Roland* in about 1170, perhaps with the intention of learning the German language. See William C.

McDonald, *German Medieval Literary Patronage from Charlemagne to Maximilian I* (Amsterdam, 1973), pp. 98–100. In the 1290s, Jeanne de Navarre commissioned a French translation of the *Speculum Dominarum,* which described ethics for women and was written by her confessor. See Karl Wenck, *Philip der Schöne von Frankreich: Seine Persönlichkeit und das Urteil der Zeitgenossen* (Marburg, 1905), p. 19. Mahaut, Countess of Artois, ordered the *Lives of the Saints* and a Bible translated into French in 1328 (see Richard, p. 239). Clemence of Hungary, the second wife of King Louis X, left thirty-nine books at her death in 1328; twenty-four were written in French and one of them in both English and French. See *Bulletin du bibliophile,* 2d ser., no. 18 (1836–37):561–63.

70. See L. Delisle, "Exemplaires royaux et princiers du Mirroir historial," *Gazette archéologique* 11 (1886):pl. 16.

71. Deanesly, *Lollard Bible,* p. 248.

72. Ibid., pp. 278–79, and p. 20; Anne's sister Margaret, having benefited from Anne's experience in a foreign land, left home as a child bride in 1388 to marry the king of Poland, carrying with her a Psalter in Latin, German, and Polish.

73. Margaret Deanesly stressed the increasing ownership of vernacular books in England in the late fourteenth and the fifteenth centuries. She is not explicitly concerned with women's book owning, but it is significant that twenty-nine of her examples are women book owners. See Deanesly, "Vernacular Books," pp. 349–58.

74. A third area for discussion might be women as patrons of new genres of literature—e.g., twelfth-century love poetry and romances, and books praising women that developed in the mid-fourteenth century. These important developments, however, are outside the scope of this study, which concentrates on women's role in the development of lay piety and the transmission of religious culture. See Herbert Grundmann, "Die Frauen und die Literatur im Mittelalter," *Archiv für Kulturgeschichte* 26 (1936):129–61.

75. Millard Meiss, *French Painting in the Time of Jean de Berry* (New York, 1975), p. 109.

76. Gertrud Schiller, *Iconography of Christian Art,* trans. Janet Seligman, 2 vols. (Greenwich, Conn., 1971), vol. 1, p. 42.

77. Hans H. Hofstatter, *Art of the Late Middle Ages* (New York, 1968), p. 182; and Plummer, ed., no. 10.

78. See, e.g., Caxton's translation of the *Golden Legend,* reprinted as *The Golden Legend; or, Lives of the Saints by William Caxton,* (London, 1900), vol. 3: pp. 97–101; or M. R. James, *The Apocryphal New Testament* (Oxford, 1924), p. 74.

79. *Virgin in the Garden of Paradise,* Städesches Kunstinstitut, Frankfurt (reproduced in Hofstatter, p. 163); and Plummer, ed., no. 97.

80. André Grabar, *Christian Iconography: A Study of Its Origins* (Princeton, N.J., 1968).

81. Isaiah 7:14.

82. Schiller, vol. 1, p. 42.

83. The Bodleian collection in Oxford has at least twenty such examples: MS Douce, 237, fol. 9v; MS Liturg., 401, fol. 30v; MS Rawl., D. 939; MS Astor, A.

18, fol. 82, (i) and (ii); MS Astor, A. 17, fol. 154v; MS Keble, fol. 148v; MS 311, fol. 100; MS Douce, 268, fol. 31; MS Rawl. Liturg., d. 1., fol. 100v; MS Add., A. 185, fol. 65v; MS Buchanan, E. 8, fol. 144v; MS Lat. Liturg., fol. 2, fol. 104v; MS Auct., D. Inf. 2.13, fol. 41v; MS Canon. Liturg., 178, fol. 101v; MS Auct., D. Inf. 2.11, fol. 51v. In an article on miniatures representing reading in late medieval manuscripts, Frank Olaf Büttner points out that the act of reading represents transmission of religious ideas, and that the user of the manuscript recognized "a mirror image of himself" in the reading motif. It is interesting, however, that, while every one of Büttner's many examples portrays either a reading Virgin Mary or a real medieval woman book owner, he does not develop the connection between his examples and females as actual readers and owners of books. See Frank Olaf Büttner, "Mens divina liber grandis est: Zu einigen Darstellungen des Lesens in Spätmittelalterlichen Handschriften," *Philobiblion* 16 (1972):92–126, and "Noch Einmal: Darstellungen des Lesens in Spätmittelalterlichen Handschriften," *Scriptorium* 27 (1973):60–63.

84. Meta Harrsen, "The Countess Judith of Flanders and the Library at Weingarten Abbey," *Papers of the Bibliographic Society of America* 24, pts. 1/2 (1930):1–13.

85. MS 708, Pierpont Morgan Library, New York.

86. MS BB 437, Monte Cassino Library; and see Harrsen.

87. MS Egerton, 1139, British Library, London.

88. Deanesly, *Lollard Bible*, p. 20.

89. "Inventaire des Livres Apportés en France par Valentine de Milan et Compris dans sa Dot (1388)," in Pierre Champion, *La Librairie de Charles d'Orléans* (Paris, 1910), pp. lxix–lxx.

90. A. Cim, *Le Livre*, 2 vols. (Paris, 1923), vol. 2, p. 372.

91. From the reminiscences of Giovanni Rucellai, cited in Yvonne Maguire, *The Women of the Medici* (New York, 1955), p. 69.

92. Elisabeth Pellegrin, *La Bibliothèque des Visconti et des Sforza, Ducs de Milan, au XVe Siècle* (Paris, 1955), p. 69.

93. Ibid., p. 67.

94. Ibid. Hyppolita Sforza's books are now divided among Valencia, Milan, Paris, and London. Another member of the family, Bianca Maria Sforza, became Maximilian I's second wife in 1494, and brought eight books in her trousseau from Milan to Austria. At least five of these were devotional volumes. See Pellegrin, p. 69.

95. See Margaret Rickert, *Painting in Britain: The Middle Ages* (London, 1954), p. 152; and Sabrina Mitchell, *Medieval Manuscript Painting* (New York, 1965), p. 37. Note, however, that many historians still cite Anne as importing only fashions in clothing from Bohemia to England.

96. Samuel Moore, "The Prologue of Chaucer's 'Legend of Good Women' in Relation to Anne and Richard," *Modern Language Review* 7 (June–October 1912):488–93, esp. 490.

97. John Wycliffe, "De triplici vinculo amors," cited in Deanesly, *Lollard Bible*, p. 248.

98. MS 333, fols. 26–30b, Trinity College Library, Cambridge, England; re-

printed in Deanesly, *Lollard Bible,* pp. 278–91. Deanesly also cites the 1405 text in the English. See *Lollard Bible,* p. 445.

99. Ottocar Odlozilik, "Wycliffe's Influence on Central Europe," *Slavonic and East European Review* 7:21 (March 1929):634–48.

100. Roland H. Bainton, *Women of the Reformation: In Germany and Italy* (Minneapolis, 1971), p. 14.

101. These medieval developments foreshadow the close involvement of women in the Reformation. See Nancy L. Roelker, "The Role of Noblewomen in the French Reformation," *Archive for Reformation History* 63:2 (1972):168–95; Bainton (ibid.), and Roland H. Bainton, *Women of the Reformation: In France and England* (Boston, 1973); Patrick Collinson, "The Role of Women in the English Reformation Illustrated by the Life and Friendships of Anne Locke," *Studies in Church History* 2 (1965):258–72; Charmarie Jenkins-Blaisdell, "Renée de France between Reform and Counter-Reform," *Archive for Reformation History* 63:2 (1972):196–226; Miriam V. Chrisman, "Women of the Reformation in Strasburg 1490–1530," *Archive for Reformation History* 63:2 (1972):143–67; and Natalie Zemon Davis, *Society and Culture in Early Modern France* (Stanford, Calif., 1975), esp. chap. 3, p. 76.

Lady Honor Lisle's
Networks of Influence

Barbara A. Hanawalt

W omen's access to power—their ability to be influential in spite of their exclusion from magisterial positions—has been a favorite subject among historians. Because women were barred from officeholding and from direct lines of political influence, historians have often described their role in the power structure as manipulative and have characterized their tools of influence as deceit, intrigue, fickleness, and even witchcraft. When an undeniably outstanding woman did appear on the historical stage, she was described as acting with "manly virtue."[1] Omitted from these accounts are the ordinary acts that the wife of an official or prince performed that solidified political successes or saved careers. The kind word or the right gift from an ambassador's wife, for instance, might make the difference in concluding a treaty and yet might not be recorded. Also passed over in official chronicles and political histories are the many ways in which a woman used her influence or acted as a patron to place people in office, resolve lawsuits, or form marriages.

Our way of analyzing power needs to be adapted if we are to understand women's practice of power. Anthropologists have observed the gender asymmetry that exists in all cultures of ascribing to male activities more value and importance. However vital the women's contribution to the survival of the social group, all cultures accord men some dominance over women. Women who seek to exercise power, therefore, must function within the context of male authority. The spheres in which women can act are socially limited, and the avenues that women have open to them for manipulating their environment are circumscribed. Because women are relegated to the domestic as opposed to the public arena, they try to procure a share of the power through kinship, gifts, patronage, and such weapons as gossip and humiliation.[2]

One limitation of the anthropological literature is that most of it does not consider upper-class women in more developed societies. A noblewoman in sixteenth-century England had many of the same constraints that primitive and peasant women experienced, but she was also a power broker in her own right, and this role set her apart from other women in the society. Through her networks of well-connected kin and friends, she could expect access to decision makers and she would assume a major role in patronage that could influence the lives of those below her. In this essay I will investigate the ways that a noblewoman's power could be used and its limitations by examining the correspondence of Lady Honor Lisle.

Lady Honor Lisle and the Lisle Letters

Exploring the exercise of political influence by a woman married to a highly placed royal official during the reign of Henry VIII—Honor Lisle, wife of the Deputy of Calais, Arthur Plantagenet Viscount Lisle—will lead us into the web of the woman's political world. We should not be surprised that a woman's political influence was closely tied to her other roles as wife and mother and to her station in society. The very lying-in ceremony at the birth of a child was replete with political meanings, as we shall see. The placement of children for fostering in another person's home did not merely secure an education for the child but also formed close political bonds for both the parents and the child. Management of the accounts of landed estates required knowledge of farming and the market as well as of the character of employees. The pursuit of legal matters arising from dower property and inheritances demanded elaborate political networks. In order to run a large, official household with a considerable retinue and a variety of offices in its gift, the prominent sought Lady Lisle's patronage for their clients. A range of people from princes to poor scholars had to be entertained with generosity and cordiality, for a particular individual could become politically useful in time. Gifts and tokens of affection solidified an important contact so that favors might be forthcoming when they were needed. Finally, as Henry VIII's reign of terror led to the elimination of so many of Arthur Lisle's kin and associates, Lady Lisle had to be sensitive to the possibility that only her gifts, letters, tokens, and entreaties would save her husband from the chopping block. In the sixteenth century, letter writing also helped to cement political bonds and to further political causes. Through Honor Lisle's correspondence we gain the access to a woman's political world that official records deny us.

The Lisle correspondence has some advantages over other letter collections in that it was less self-consciously preserved than most. The seven years of correspondence dating from 1533 to 1540 include a body of letters found in household chests when the suspicious ministers of Henry VIII accused Lord Lisle of treason and confiscated his Calais letters and papers. Although a few of the letters were destroyed out of prudence when they were received, and some were thrown into the "jakes" (latrine) in the hasty days after Lisle's arrest, letters of friendship, business, gossip, and diplomacy are all mixed together. Muriel St. Clare Byrne has edited the letters in a six-volume collection.[3] Her edition contains all of Honor Lisle's own letters (only forty-one have been preserved) and most of those addressed to her (between four and five hundred). It also contains her children's letters, Lord Lisle's letters, and a large proportion of those addressed to him. Byrne's purpose in compiling the letters was to tell the story of the Calais household, and thus some of the diplomatic and official correspondence is excluded. For the purposes of studying Honor Lisle's networks of influence, Byrne's edition is most complete.

A brief introduction to Honor Lisle, her family, and correspondents is necessary in order to place her access to power in perspective. Honor Grenville Basset was the second wife of John Basset, a West Country knight with landholdings and connections in Cornwall and Devonshire. The Grenville family was upcoming gentry from the same region, who rose to prominence under the Tudors. Honor, who had been left a widow with seven young children, married for the second time considerably above her country gentry background. Arthur Plantagenet, Lord Lisle, was a bastard son of Edward IV by a young gentlewoman from Hampshire. His very pleasant, nonthreatening personality stood him in good stead so that he survived the transition to Tudor rule and was even taken into the household of Elizabeth, Henry VII's wife. His valued service to his Tudor nephew, Henry VIII, was rewarded in 1533 by his appointment as deputy of Calais, the last English possession on the Continent. Arthur's first marriage to the widow of Henry VII's minister, Sir John Dudley, brought him the title of Lord Lisle and supplemented the land he possessed from his mother's family with considerable estates in Hampshire. His second marriage to Honor Grenville Basset strengthened his West Country connections, for her jointure and lands held in wardship for her son included land in Cornwall and Devonshire. Honor's new position as Lady Lisle and as the wife of the deputy of Calais moved her swiftly into powerful court circles and a new life abroad that increased the significance of her patronage. It is a measure of her intelligence and good management abilities that she adapted so well to a changed environment.[4]

In addition to accumulating land and titles, Arthur and Honor put together one of those large families characteristic of Tudor country gentry, who remarried when their spouses died. Arthur's first wife had three sons by her first marriage, and she and Arthur had three daughters. Honor's first husband was a widower with four children, and their own marriage produced seven children. The Lisles did not have a child, although Honor was still young enough and did undergo a false pregnancy during the Calais years.

An early assessment of Honor's personality will help the reader in forming some idea of her abilities and her opportunity for gaining access to power. In a century replete with notable women, Honor Lisle appears to the reader as a competent but ordinary woman of the privileged class. She was not particularly well descended, nor did she have the humanistic education of the Cooke sisters, whose husbands became Tudor statesmen,[5] or of Margaret Roper, daughter of Thomas More. She came to historical notice not because of brilliance of position or social distinction but solely because of her correspondence. Her own letters and those addressed to her give us a strong sense of her interests and accomplishments. Byrne describes them well: a "decidedly religious bent, . . . housewifely competence, . . . knowledge of physic, . . . love of pets of all descriptions, . . . social accomplishments such as dancing, card-playing, shooting with a bow, and the more practical ones such as reading and riding."[6] The letters to Lord and Lady Lisle indicate that she had the better business sense and in major matters it was she who made decisions. One correspondent wrote of Lisle that " 'with a few words and the present of a penny' a man might have his lordship's good will, 'so that my lady was not in the way.' "[7] She could be decisive and forthright, as her letters to Cromwell indicate. She was also a warm person valued for her kindness and esteemed for her good sense by her numerous correspondents.[8] As a wife and mother she provides a valuable corrective to the many cold portraits that have been painted of Tudor domestic arrangements. The letters exchanged between Arthur and Honor show marital tenderness, and the letters concerning the children indicate a vigilant and concerned mother.

We have, then, a woman who was happily married, capable of running a large official household, comfortable entering into the world of lawsuits, estate management, and the court, and valued as a hostess, friend, and correspondent. The king's treasurer, Sir Brian Tuke, wrote to Lisle, "I may say without flattery, [she] is the best that ever I saw in any noble lady of her estate: reputing you, my lord, amongst many other great graces, that God hath sent you to have of her ladyship as great a jewel as any nobleman may wish or desire." That some viewed her as overconfident and full of pride we know from Foxe's *Book of Martyrs,* for he described her as incessantly urging her gentle husband on to wickedness. With some she had a reputation as a demanding and aggressive ("very sharp and hasty") woman.[9] She was active and able, but she was also criticized and more than once asked correspondents for assurances of their continued goodwill or inquired of connections in court if she were still in good favor.[10]

Forming and Maintaining Networks

Keeping in mind Honor's character and family connections, we may now turn to her web of interactions, for this was the source of her power. Certain connections could place children in appropriate households, secure appointments in service, help to influence the correct people in lawsuits, or lend money. Both sexes expended great efforts in extending their networks and consolidating those that they already had. Everyone was potentially useful. The arrangements were reciprocal; one expected to perform the same services for those within one's power in exchange for the friendship. For both men and women, contacts were not exclusively male or female, although for some matters the connections of one sex could be more useful than those of the other.

The basis of a significant network was the family. With the frequency of intermarriage among the nobility, kin networks were large, overlapping, and crucial. A business agent wrote to Lisle of a man: "because he is my Lady's nigh cousin and thereby allied unto your lordship, I would be loath to see him have displeasure."[11] Honor's Grenville family included a number of rising men and women who married well and occupied major positions in court. Both the Bassets and Grenvilles were well connected with local gentry families and clergy in the West Country.

Two examples will illustrate the reciprocity that such kin ties brought. The set of letters from Walter Staynings and his wife, who was Honor's niece by marriage, illustrates the strength of the claims that kinship could exercise for a ruined relative. Walter's case was a hard one indeed. When the letters begin, he was in prison for a bad debt, and the merchant had so blackened his name that he could not get further credit or leave prison to arrange for payment. Honor applied first to their businessman in London, who could only say that Staynings must pay his debt. Since he could not do so while in prison, Honor used her influence with people at court to have him released. Meanwhile, Elizabeth Staynings had become pregnant. Perhaps with Honor's influence or that of other well-placed kin, the Staynings won the king to their side. Elizabeth then wrote Honor to appeal to Cromwell to do the necessary paper work.[12] The second example also involves a niece of Honor's who became the wife of the Duke of Sussex. Her influence, as we shall see, eventually procured Honor's daughter, Anne, a position as maid-of-honor to the queen.

Had Honor remained the wife of a West Country gentleman, her network would have been limited to her relatives and other similarly situated families. The first few years of correspondence indicate the comfortable exchange of such local courtesies and gossip. These kin and neighbors also proved useful in looking after her estates and taking in the children the Lisles had left behind in England. Honor's brilliant second marriage, however, made her an aunt by marriage to the king and tied her fate to that of Arthur's other royal-blooded relatives, the Pole family. It moved her into the social and political world of the court.

Beyond the network of kin, both those of the natal family and affines from marriage and godparenting, a person's networks were enhanced with friends acquired in various ways. For the Lisles the friendship of the current queen and minister of the day were most important along with that of the various people who carried out their business for them. Introductions to the court circle were a matter of course in their station, but much of the time and effort of both husband and wife and of their agents was spent in sustaining these friendships, as we shall see shortly when we turn to the fine art of network maintenance.

For the most part, Honor's life centered around the Calais household in the years covered by the letters. Her responsibilities and opportunities were great, since Calais was a major link between England and the Continent. Merchants kept headquarters there, ambassadors passed through routinely, such great personages as Anne of Cleves and Cromwell visited, friends came for extended visits, and a variety of other, lesser people stopped on their business there, among them Lutherans and Catholics and other enemies of Henry VIII's efforts to create an English church. Because Calais was continually threatened by the French, a military garrison and a naval presence were prominent. Other English officials and their families resided there, in addition to the lord deputy, and helped administer the holding. Aristocratic French neighbors visited, exchanged gifts and letters, and eventually fostered two of Lady Lisle's daughters.

The picture of Honor's interactions would not be complete without mentioning that the system also relied upon what might be called a "piggybacking" of networks. For instance, an acquaintance that Honor made in Calais, Lady Whethill, writes to her, asking Honor to use her connections with Cromwell to help Elizabeth Staynings.[13] Usually we see network upon network acting in the case of the various gentlemen servitors and estate managers who worked for the Lisles. Men such as their faithful gentleman servant John Husee maintained their own networks with various members of the court, nobility, Inns of Court, London merchants, sea captains, and clergy so that they could advance their own careers; they could use these contacts to promote the business of their masters and mistresses.

The crucial contacts had to be maintained and solidified by careful and solicitous measures. Gifts, favors, entertainment, and letter writing were all employed. Lady Lisle's first correspondence with Cromwell and her first gifts to Anne Boleyn illustrate this process. Lord and Lady Lisle had been part of the great party attending Henry VIII at a diplomatic meeting with Francis I at Calais. At the close of the meeting, Henry secretly married Anne Boleyn. As the English departed, a terrible storm came up that made the passage terrifying. Lady Lisle, upon her safe return, writes to Cromwell: "Heartily we thank you for our good supper on All Hallows day, and for many divers other kindness that you shewed unto my lord and me, which I do not forget. Signifying you that I have sent you a teg [doe], because I would know of your good return to England, and how you passed the perilous danger of the sea."[14] She wishes to know of him by the return messenger and offers their services to himself or his friends. He replies by the messenger, and she writes immediately, thanking him for "his kind and loving letter, which I have sundry times perused; and for the great kindness that you shewed my lord and me, when he was far from home and in a strange place, in lending him £20, which I have sent by this messenger."[15] In addition she sends two cheeses and wildfowl, the first in the large number of gifts needed to persuade Cromwell to move on their various suits, lend money, or secure a pension for Lord Lisle.

Honor had been one of the ladies who accompanied Anne Boleyn in dancing with the French king and his nobles at Calais. As a result she had an introduction to the new queen that she did not allow to lapse. She was quick with her gifts and requests. George Taylor, Anne Boleyn's gentleman-servant, wrote to Honor about the reception of her gifts: "I have delivered to my lady the bow you sent her by this bearer, which she did greatly esteem, and commanded a string to be set on it and assayed it, but it was somewhat to big." Honor had cleverly perceived that Anne would want to learn to hunt with Henry and sent her a bow. The gift accompanied a request for a license for Honor's ship, which the queen put off, saying that she would be glad to do another favor, but the time was not right for that one.[16] The queen's goodwill was solicited with many subsequent gifts, including dotterels (plovers) when the queen was pregnant, a linnet to sing in her chamber, and even Honor's own beloved lapdog, Purquy.[17] The queen reciprocated with gold beads and other gifts.[18]

The exchange of gifts was a time-honored way of cementing friendships and procuring goodwill. Honor must have spent a good part of her time supplying people with the dogs, hawks, songbirds, dotterels, quail, wine, and venison that they directly asked her to find or that her servant, Husee, suggested she send to sweeten some official or to thank some friend. To Arthur also she applied for horses, boars' heads, wine, and the rest of the numerous gift animals and birds. Much of the gift trade was international; the Lisles supplied spaniels for the English and greyhounds for the French. The problems in the gift exchange may be seen from the letter of one correspondent. "Your servant who had the carriage of my bird [a linnet] and the stool ye gave to me, by occasion that the ship he came in did leak, was driven to be set a land. And the said ship after being perished the said stool was lost therein. And also he brought my bird a'land and left her with his host in London, till he might inquire out my house, in which time, through the negligence of his said host, a Cat killed her."[19] The Lisles received similar gifts. The only gift the poor who begged favors could offer in return was mention in their prayers.

Although many of these reciprocal exchanges involved costly items, some merely indicated personal regard. Honor was famous for her very fine preserves and sent them as gifts. Her daughter, Anne, presented some to the king and wrote to her mother, "The King doth so well like the conserves you sent him last, that his Grace commanded me to write unto you for more of the codiniac of the clearest making, and of the conserve of damsons, and this as soon as may be." When the next batch of codiniac was sent, Honor commissioned Anne to ask the king for a token. Anne was more reticent than her mother, however, and replied: "I durst not be so bold to move his Grace for it no other wise, for fear least how his Grace would a'takyt it."[20]

A more intimate way of expressing the bonds of friendship was through the exchange of tokens, which served a variety of purposes. These were reminders of time spent together; they could authenticate a letter or message; they could be simply a mark of special friendship. No gift needed to accompany a token; the person might recall a particular incident such as a shared joke or handshake and ask that the event serve as a token. Items of small value, such as cramp rings,[21] sufficed as tokens to show esteem and friendship. Lady Lisle sent tokens to her daughters and the ladies at court and also occasionally to men as well. She gave her cousin, Thomas Leygh, a ring when he left Calais, which he returned as token of his safe arrival. Her business agent, John Husee, received a ring and wrote: "I will be your ladyship's treasurer of that and of your turquoise till my coming over, for they shall keep my credence."[22] Among ladies the exchanged token might be a piece of personal jewelry. Honor sent Lady Ryngeley, a Calais friend, her bracelet of coral beads with the gold heart on it when Lady Ryngeley was in England, and Lady Ryngeley reciprocated with a diamond ring.[23] Some of these tokens had a considerable history. Lady Sussex, Honor's niece, wrote to request that Honor return a token she sent, for it had belonged to the Queen of Hungary, who gave it to another woman, who gave it to Lady Sussex.[24]

The line between tokens and gifts on the one hand and fees and bribes on the other is sometimes difficult to draw. Some people preferred to be paid with wine rather than money, and some of the gifts were obviously given as inducements to transact a piece of business, as when a merchant's wife tells Honor that, if Lord Lisle will give her husband a needed permit, he will bring her "some pretty thing from Paris."[25] Others offered bribes and pay for positions in the Calais garrison.[26]

Letters were a new and useful device for maintaining network ties. Byrne observes that letters "gave a man a chance to express himself to his betters without interruption. What is perhaps of even greater significance is the fact that it gave this same opportunity to women."[27] Through letters Lady Lisle could state her causes to Cromwell when personal access would have been difficult. She could manage her English estates from Calais and pursue lawsuits in London. Her letters (Byrne estimates that over the seven-year period she probably wrote about eight hundred) reached the humble as well as the powerful and were in their own way a token of esteem to the receiver. One of the best illustrations of her use of letters to firm a friendship is the note sent to Archdeacon Thomas Thirlby, who had stopped at Calais on a diplomatic mission. She wrote to him that "I was not so glad for your fair passage but I was as sorry for your departure, and that you would tarry no longer at my desire; but my Lord of Winchester and you will do nothing after a woman's advice." Prettily protesting that they perhaps did not tarry because they did not receive sufficient cheer, she concludes by asking Thirlby again for his recipe for preserves and by calling herself "your poor scholar."[28]

For a king's son and deputy of Calais, the extension of grand hospitality was another way of cementing networks. Notables passing through Calais expected the hospitality of my lord and lady deputy, and they were not disappointed. One guest commented that "all strangers that came you did feast them for the King's honour," adding that the best duke in England could not do more honor to the king.[29] This entertainment was expensive. Arthur's cousin warned Honor that the post would prove to be a difficult one for a person of Arthur's "large stomach"—that is, his generous disposition.[30] So it proved, as Honor and her agent, Husee, struggled to pay the grocery bills and Arthur became more deeply indebted to Cromwell.

Beyond simply feeding a large household and its frequent visitors,

Lady Lisle had to treat everyone, of any degree, with diplomacy and warmth. Each person who passed through was a potentially valuable contact who could aid her, be her need as humble as a dozen French caps or as important as influence in a legal case. That she succeeded is evident in the most charming letters of thanks which she received. Sir Drue Williams wrote to Honor, asking that he be remembered to Lord Lisle "upon the token that your ladyship laughed heartily at dinner for the great wise answer which I gave unto my lord; with thanks many for my good cheer at my last being with you."[31] The admiral of France was so taken with her that he presented her with two Brazilian monkeys, including instructions for their care and feeding. A poor English scholar, on his way to the University of Paris, thanked her for her kind reception, saying that he had never met anyone of her degree who treated an ordinary person like himself so well.[32]

As was expected of the lady of a large household, Honor treated the sick with her own recipes. Although not as sought after as her preserves, they were apparently effective. Lisle wrote to her while she was in London on business that "your powder for the stone hath saved Highfield's life and the boy's."[33] Her cure for the stone was described with great wit by Lord Edmund Howard, one of her patients.

> Madam, so it is I have this night after midnight taken your medicine, for the which I heartily thank you, for it hath done me much good, and hath caused the stone to break so that now I void much gravel. But for all that, your said medicine hath done me little honesty, for it made me piss my bed this night, for the which my wife hath sore beaten me, and saying it is children's parts to bepiss their bed. Ye have made me such a pisser that I dare not this day go abroad, wherefore I beseech you to make mine excuse to my Lord and Master Treasurer, for that I shall not be with you this day at dinner. Madame, it is showed me that a wing or a leg of a stork, if I eat thereof, will make me that I shall never piss more in bed, and though my body be simple yet my tongue shall be ever good, and especially when it speaketh of women; and sithence such a medicine will do such a great cure God send me a piece thereof.[34]

One of the traditional ways for the great lady both to expand her contacts and to show significant consideration for people already connected to her was through patronage. As lady deputy, she found that the household and the retinue in Calais established her as a patron in a large and complicated network of requests for service and positions. It was the rule of the day for younger sons, impoverished clergy and gentlewomen, and people on the rise to seek places in noble households that would provide training and hope for advancement. Honor herself would have to place

her sons and daughters. To accept someone's protégé was a compliment
to the recommender and obligated that person to reciprocate. To be a
patron, therefore, was to have power.

Honor had been accustomed to patronage requests in the country.
Lady Weston, for instance, asked her to take a gentlewoman as a servant
because the woman had fallen in love with one of the serving men and it
seemed best to move her to another household.[35] What changed in Calais
was the volume of requests, which now came from every sort of connection. Her sister-in-law, Margaret Grenville, wrote to ask that a young
man be taken into service;[36] George Taylor, a gentleman servant to Anne
Boleyn, asked her to place a young man:[37] Thomas Warley, a member of
the Calais household, recommended priests with a variety of accomplishments, including writing, physic and astronomy, singing, gardening,
and so on.[38] Not all of the people recommended to her and to Lisle
proved to be friends of their house, but the worst of all was Clement
Philpot, who came with the recommendation of a steady old Hampshire
friend, Sir Anthony Windsor. Honor and Husee had apparently arranged
this appointment without consulting Arthur. Under the bad influence of
Gregory Botolf, one of the household chaplains, he connected the Lisles
with a popish plot that contributed to their ruin.[39]

Although Lord Lisle received most of the requests for official positions
and posts in the retinue, many people, even royal officials, chose to address Lady Lisle as well. William Popley, for instance, was one of the
prominent men assisting Cromwell, but he wrote to her when he wanted
to place a man. She replied, noting that, by a recent parliamentary act,
Lord Lisle did not have the control over appointments he had once had,
but she adds: "Nevertheless, I pray you send your friend as shortly as you
may. Let him be a tall man and a good Archer. And my lord will admit
him. . . . And where ye write he shall recompense me, good Mr. Popley,
I would not for £100 take one penny, nor never did of no man, what-
soever hath been reported; and loath I would be to begin with you."[40]
Lord Edmund Howard wrote to thank her for her efforts for one of his
sons, but as he was already placed, could the position be left open for
another son?[41]

By virtue of their position, Lord and Lady Lisle were continually called
upon to "be good Lord/Lady to" some petitioner or other. Often they
were required only to give some financial reward to a person carrying a
letter or a gift. Because of the esteem in which Honor Lisle was held for
her practical turn of mind, and because of her closeness to her husband,
people often appealed to her in matters involving the retinue or other
business of Calais. Young men requesting that their leave of absence from
their posts be extended often wrote to Honor and asked that she impor-

tune her husband on their behalf,[42] or they requested that she ask Lord Lisle to write a letter to one of his connections at court, speeding their suits.[43] Another member of the retinue wanted to set up a brewhouse and asked Honor if she would persuade Arthur to write for the king's license.[44] The popish conspirator, Gregory Botolf, knew the influence of Honor over her husband so well that he wrote to one of his contacts in the household about getting a license to study in Louvain: "And no doubt if ye make the writing ready to his [Lisle's] hand he will not fault to assign and seal it. If he suspect anything then take my lady's advice, showing her ladyship in that I most heartily besought you to procure for me of my said lord and lady the same in writing."[45] Her ready action in these cases must have generated considerable affection for her among the retinue, as indeed the chatty tone of the letters indicates. In return for her aid they carried tokens for her to friends and sent gifts of gratitude.[46]

Some petitioners were not in her networks but requested favors from her as a sympathetic and well-connected noblewoman. Her letters on these matters show that she was easily moved by pity for people she knew only slightly and that she was effective in communicating legal matters to Cromwell. Of particular interest is a letter she sent on behalf of a widow deprived of her jointure. She says that "pity moved [her] to write." She then tells Cromwell that one of his servants purchased a subpoena for the widow when she was lying in childbed so that she could not respond. He pushed it through court and impoverished her.[47] In another case she pleads for a man who killed in self-defense.[48] Her direct address in dealing with Cromwell and her good sense for law appear again, as we shall see, when she was forced to negotiate directly with him for her own jointure.

Exercising Power Through Networks

Having established and skillfully expanded networks, how did Lady Lisle use them to exercise power? It would be prudent to consider, first, what she might hope to achieve. Foremost was the welfare of her children. Her three sons had to be trained and established with their own positions and networks. The inheritance of the oldest son was in dispute. Because he was their ward, it fell to her to pursue the lawsuit. She also had four daughters to marry advantageously. Arthur's daughters also fell to her charge. Lord Lisle's own political career was a constant source of anxiety to them both. Arthur had suits pending on his property, and Honor was concerned about these as well. As was traditional for women then, she wanted to further religious causes, but her position became increasingly difficult as religion changed. Always in the background was the worry of running a household that required considerable management skills and money. In addition, Honor was anxious to maintain her station both by outward signs of display and by being included in such power as might be associated with her position in life. We must, finally, consider those areas in which she did not attempt to exercise power and methods that she did not employ in manipulating power.

Her desire to place her children in positions that would be a credit to their elevated social status as stepchildren of Lord Lisle led her to call upon a broad network of friends, kin, and servants. John, her eldest, was to inherit the family property, but she felt that he must have a fitting training to take up this position. Law would be his career because he was likely to have magisterial positions in the county and because the estate was encumbered with lawsuits. To prepare for the law he was left in England with Richard Norton, a neighbor and gentleman, and taught Latin. The establishment of the foster parent relationship meant that Norton and his wife received gifts and tokens from Honor in generous amounts.[49] Meanwhile, all efforts were bent on finding John a room at the Inns of Court. Finally, through Lord Lisle's contacts at Lincoln's Inn, his stepson got chambers and a tutor there.[50] John kept close ties with the Nortons, frequently visited them during vacations, and also visited people with whom he had made contact at Lincoln's Inn.[51] There was even some maneuvering to get John a post with Cromwell.[52]

John's marriage was made within the family, to Lord Lisle's daughter, Frances. The marriage may have been inspired by genuine affection, but it certainly met with no obstacle on the part of the parents. Their chief concern was that Frances, given her royal lineage, should not lose any privileges of rank by marrying John. Lady Lisle inquired and had Husee inquire of Lady Rutland and of the College of Heralds about the marriage.[53]

Honor's chief problem in looking after John's interests was the lawsuit over part of his inheritance. The lawsuit covered the whole of the correspondence and required most skillful manipulation of the Lisles' networks. Honor retained legal counsel and in addition relied upon John Davy, a servant on her estates, and Husee. Their advice was to buy the land outright, but since the Lisles could not raise the money, the usual methods were employed. Honor sent the Lord Chief Justice sturgeon and got Arthur to write to Lord Norwich and his fellow justices "desiring them their favours." Her advisers also suggest that she try to befriend the adversary by sending a peace offering of wine. Perhaps the more practical advice was to place a "privy friend" in their adversary's household who would loyally report any planned actions for a fee.[54] Since the matter could not be settled, the next step was to exert pressure on connections at court, including Cromwell. As Husee assured Honor, she was "too well friended" for her adversary to get the advantage of her.[55] Husee apparently used his own access to Cromwell and other officials, as well as that of Lord Lisle, and this "piggybacking" of networks did get the king's ear and led to a brief stay of the case.[56] But matters were worse than appeared, for Edward Seymour, Earl of Hertford, was trying to buy the land, and he and Lisle were already in a dispute over other land in the West Country.[57] Finally, it was Lady Lisle's personal negotiations that won the day, as we shall see, and earned her the commendation of the king: "your son should be bound to pray for you, and that few mothers would have taken the pains your ladyship hath done."[58]

Since the second son, George, and his younger brother, James, would not inherit the family estate, they were to have an education that would fit them for a career in service. Apparently Arthur rather than Honor determined the course of their education, for it corresponded with that of the new men in the service of the Tudors. Rather than going to grammar school or spending their early training being fostered in a nobleman's house, they were taught in French and then sent to France to learn the language.[59] If Arthur outlined the education, the correspondence indicates that Honor, through her contacts, carried out the plans and worried about their success. George was taken from his initial training at the Abbey of Hyde in Winchester and was put with a priest in St. Omer who already had the son of one of the Calais retinue under his care.[60] His stay was brief because of the threat of war with France and, after returning to Honor in Calais, he was sent to Sir Francis Bryan, a well-placed courtier, to continue his education. The arrangement was so successful that, when the Lisles wanted to send George to Paris, both he and his master preferred that he stay.[61]

The French education of James drew upon contacts made in Calais. A member of the French admiral's diplomatic corps, the president of the Parlement, was solicited to interview James in London. He was impressed and generously offered to look after the boy's education in Paris. He proved to be unreliable for the task, but Lady Lisle called upon ties that she or her family had among the English scholars in Paris. They used their contacts to place James in an appropriate situation and kept up a continual correspondence with Honor about his health, complaints, and progress.[62] On James's second visit to Paris for schooling Guillaume Le Gras, a merchant with business in Calais, took care of him and incidentally supplied Lady Lisle with various Parisian luxuries. Again, most of the letters concerning James are addressed to Honor, until James himself began to take an interest in the direction of his education and requested that his stepfather put him in the prestigious College de Navarre, where he could meet the cream of French aristocracy.[63] At the end of his stay in Paris he was placed in the household of Bishop John Gardiner for his political education.

The direction of the younger daughters' careers also took a more ambitious turn with Honor's marriage. Two of the daughters by her first husband's marriage were left in England to become old maids, but her four daughters accompanied her to Calais along with Arthur's daughter, Frances, who married John. Using connections that she and Arthur had made with the French aristocracy, Honor placed her two youngest daughters, Anne and Mary, in French households to be "finished." The Lisles had intended to fit the girls into the current fashion for things French in the English court. The plan was highly successful. The two beautiful girls were beloved by their French foster mothers, and the youngest one eventually received a proposal in marriage from the son of one of these illustrious families. (Unfortunately, Lord Lisle's arrest ended this engagement.)[64] Honor and the French ladies exchanged gifts and visits, as did Lisle and the men of the families, and the girls learned French and became elegant and accomplished. When Mary fell ill, her foster mother was as concerned and upset as Honor was.[65]

Anne's beauty and wit led her mother to think that a career at court might be possible. Husee had written that Lady Lisle had two nieces serving as maids-of-honor for the new queen, Jane Seymour. This news apparently led to a discussion with Arthur about forwarding her daughter.[66] The first attempt failed, but Honor pressed on, asking that both Anne and her older sister, Katherine, be preferred to the position. As in the fostering of Anne and Mary, through the networks of women Anne was eventually placed with the queen, and Katherine found a position in one of the noble households. Kinship bonds, encouraged by gifts and exchanges of tokens, brought to Honor and her daughters the goodwill of Lady Sussex, Honor's niece, and Lady Rutland, the wife of Arthur's cousin. With the help of these two women and their connections in court, Anne found a position at court: "Upon Thursday last, the Queen being at dinner, my Lady Rutland and my Lady Sussex being waiters on her Grace, her Grace changed, eating of the quails, to common of your ladyship and your daughters; so that such communication was uttered by the said ij ladies that her Grace made grant to have one of your daughters."[67] Anne was such a favorite that Henry kept her on to serve successive queens. Apparently her French training and natural beauty served her well in this ambitious post. Katherine, probably less beautiful but more docile, was to become the comfort of Lady Rutland.[68]

It is appropriate to ask at this juncture what a network of women could accomplish. We are used to women's composing informal or formal coalitions to establish manners and morals or exert political pressures. The women of Honor's female networks did none of these things. They worked within the small political world of the domestic sphere. In the placing of daughters, as opposed to sons, the female contacts were of great importance. At that very political and splendid occasion, the lying-in of an aristocratic woman, the female network came to the fore. When Honor anticipated the arrival of a Plantagenet heir, apparently a false pregnancy, she requested her lady friends to send tapestries, bedding, rugs, and other finery to decorate the lying-in chamber. The infant was thus to be immediately surrounded by proofs of a valuable network. The French ladies wrote, offering whatever madame would need. Husee was directed to pack up the items from Lady Sussex and Lady Rutland and to see whether he could not procure some carpets from the king's supply.[69] Even in these feminine and domestic areas the husband's political ties were the precondition for the wife's influence.

Feminine networks could also be called upon for solving domestic problems. Anthoinette de Saveuses, a nun and a close relation of Madame de Rieu (a member of the family who fostered Anne and Mary), carried on a warm correspondence with Honor Lisle even though she spoke no English and Honor no French. Sister Anthoinette was so distressed by Madame de Rieu's marital situation that she wrote to Honor, asking whether she could do something. Madame's second marriage to the impoverished de Rieu was a disaster. He gambled away her inheritance and took no interest in their six children. Her own family disowned her because of the unsuitability of the match. Honor generously responded that she would address the French king about Madame de Rieu's marital problems. Apparently she meant that she would speak to her friends, the English ambassadors to the French court, or her French contacts, such as the admiral, who would speak to the king. Possibly the intervention worked, for de Rieu became a reformed man shortly afterward.[70]

Female networks also allowed one to keep up with fashions, learn what gifts would be correct, and acquire items of clothing and the names of good tailors and dressmakers. When Husee was commissioned to buy the nightgown for Honor's lying in, he consulted with Honor's friends to find the style that the queen wore. When Honor was unsure whether or not a gift should be given for the churching of a woman, Lady Rutland was consulted. In all these little matters so important for establishing one's social status the female network was the final arbiter.

For business matters Lady Lisle relied on a predominantly male network of paid servants, lawyers, and some of her West Country kin and neighbors. As a diligent estate manager of both her lands and those of

Arthur, she knew the fields by their names and the number of animals
that could graze in the park. She always went over the accounts from her
estates. When she found errors, she berated her servants for mistakes.[71]
She knew her rights and kept pursuing various matters such as the right
to have a weir. Besieged with complaints of disservice and cheating that
arose from the petty quarrels among her servants, she had to determine
from afar who was honest.[72] In addition to her land, she bought a boat,
largely to provision her household and to carry on coastal trade.

The numerous family lawsuits also became Lady Lisle's concern. Finally it was she who completed the negotiations with Cromwell on their
land disputes. Cromwell was, as is well known, a manipulator and was
bent on enriching himself with land speculation. He had the final power
to settle John Basset's inheritance. Cromwell's price was to link that settlement and Arthur's pension to his acquisition of one of Lord Lisle's
estates. The estate, Painswick, was part of Honor's jointure from her
marriage to Arthur. Lisle understood from the king that his annuity was
to be four hundred pounds, but Cromwell held out for a lower payment,
hinting that if the sale of Painswick went through, he might be able to
increase the annuity. Lady Lisle was sent to England to negotiate. The
letters between Arthur and his wife reveal Honor's courage in dealing
with both the king and Cromwell as well as her sorrow at their inevitable
decline in fortune.

Lord Lisle wrote to Cromwell, explaining that his wife would come
over and negotiate the matter of her jointure and her son's lands. He
prayed Cromwell to arrange it so that she would not lose her jointure, as
he could not afford to make her an offer similar to that which he had
made in Painswick.[73] Arthur expressed to his wife his complete confidence in her as a bargainer, making such comments as "you will use such
prudent diligence therein as shall be to the contentation of both our
minds" and "I put all to your discretion and wisdom."[74] Her first reception was as warm as they could have desired. The king held a special
party for her at court and ordered both the earls who were trying to get
John Basset's lands "no further to meddle with any part of my [Lady
Lisle] son's inheritance."[75] However gracious the king might be, however, Cromwell had to make the final arrangements and persuade the
earls to sign a statement.

Lady Lisle was not backward with even so great and intimidating a
man as Cromwell. Her account of their first interview is worth quoting
at length, for it shows her perseverance.

> I was this morning with my Lord Privy Seal, to whom I declared how good
> and gracious the King's Majesty was unto me, and that his pleasure was that
> I should resort to his lordship for the expedition of mine affairs, desiring

him to be good unto you for your annuity, which he said might be no more the £200 yearly: to whom I answered, that it lay in him to obtain the £400, and that was his first motion and promise: whereunto he answered, that he thought you would not charge him with his promise. Finally he said that he would do the best therein for you and others that lay in his power.

Then resumed I with him of the taking of possession of my son's lands, how the good earls had handled me; and his lordship made me answer that they should undo that was done, and that he would be in hand with them for the same within ij hours after. And forasmuch as he moved me not for Painswick, I opened the matter unto him myself; saying that Mr. Pollard had moved me in his behalf for it, and how that notwithstanding I had refused diverse and sundry great offers for mine interests therein, yet forasmuch as I found him always good lord unto me, and specially now in my need, I could be content to depart with it to him, so that he would see me no loser.[76]

Honor was bold indeed, for as she was making her pleas for settlement, Cromwell was trying to round up all of Arthur's Pole kin in England, intending to have them executed.

In the end the negotiations did not prosper. The many gifts and tokens to Cromwell, and the numerous appeals made to him through Arthur's and Honor's networks, could not move the rapacious man. Although the two earls were prevented from trying to steal John Basset's inheritance, Honor was forced to concede her jointure in Painswick, and Arthur received only two hundred pounds for his annuity. Arthur's letters to Honor were consoling: "Touching Painswick, I am sure you will not depart from it with loss; and you and I cannot live on fair words."[77] Honor, however, was clearly despondent. She realized that she would have to give in to Cromwell or jeopardize her husband's life. Being in London during the trials of his relatives, she could not help but worry about the future, and she closed one of her letters: "I beseech you keep my letters close or burn them; for though I have sorrows, I would no creature should be partaker, nor of knowledge with me."[78]

Arthur never lost confidence in her as his agent in these depressing settlements and wrote rather sentimental love letters, saying repeatedly that he missed her more than a babe could miss its nurse, that he could not sleep at night, and that "for my part I never loved none so well, neither thought so long for none since I knew a woman."[79]

Honor's Role in Politics and Religion

For the most part, Honor's power lay in the domestic realm of family, friends, household, and lawsuits related to family lands. It is difficult to demonstrate how far her influence extended into the public sphere. The confidence that Arthur placed in Honor led some contemporaries to feel that she took too active a part in the official business of Calais. A homey glimpse of the two given by one letter suggests that the gossip was not wrong. As he and Honor sat together, opening the mail, Arthur mistakenly broke the seal on a letter directed to another official. It was Honor who discovered the mistake.[80] Cromwell was so concerned about her possible meddling that he hints in a letter of reprimand to the Council of Calais that her popish leanings had sheltered two priests: "It is thought against all reason that the prayers of women and their fond flickerings should move any of you to do that thing that should in any wise displease your prince."[81] The action that had elicited Cromwell's displeasure was Lady Lisle's attempt to save two priests who were imprisoned for upholding the papacy against the king.[82] When the religious unrest in Calais became serious enough for a commission to investigate, the gossips accused Lady Lisle of trying to influence its work.[83] That she played a significant role in Arthur's official life beyond entertaining the right people and procuring gifts and tokens for them cannot be doubted, but she did not call upon her networks to support Arthur's governmental policies.

She had, moreover, no official role. Her title of "lady deputy" was purely honorific. While Arthur may have privately asked her advice, Calais was run by a council and by directives from the central government. Even Lord Lisle continually complained to the king and his ministers regarding his own lack of discretionary powers in governing Calais.

Honor's role in politics was not unlike that advocated by Christine de Pisan for a princess. She was available to petitioners who wanted to influence her husband, and she gave counsel to him.[84] Hers was a subordinate position in the male world of politics. It was her duty to be circumspect and to accept male dominance. She knew the limit of her power, and she sometimes mentioned her inferior position as a woman. Her contemporaries were concerned that her advice was so frequently forthcoming, and they suspected that Arthur acted on it.

Cromwell's complaint about Lady Lisle's meddling in religious affairs, for instance, was not without grounds. Like other noblewomen, she was expected to be a liberal patron of the Church, and the correspondence makes plain that she was attached to traditional Catholicism rather than to Henry's reform. She was quite accustomed, as a landholder with livings to bestow, to making ecclesiastical appointments. Clergymen applied to her for various positions or for aid in lawsuits, and clergy of all ranks wrote to her as frequently as they did to her husband.[85] Her traditional piety caused Husee some anxiety. He begged her in 1538 not to be angry with him for warning her "to leave part of such ceremonies as you

do use, as long prayers and offering of candles, and at some time to refrain and not speak, though your ladyship have cause, when you hear
things spoken that liketh you not, it should sound highly to your honour
and cause less speech . . . to conform yourself partly to the thing that is
used and to the world as it goeth now."[86] Shortly afterward he begged
her "to leave the most part of your memories and have only one mass,
matins, and evensong of the day."[87] Husee spoke frequently enough with
Cromwell to know that Lady Lisle's fidelity to the old ritual annoyed
him. He wrote to Lord Lisle that Cromwell had asked about their religious persuasion because he had heard rumors about Lady Lisle.[88]

The exclusion of noblewomen from their traditional influence over religious patronage and practice was perhaps the most pronounced change
that these women experienced in the sixteenth century. Friendship with
Catholic clergy and nuns and adherence to the old rituals exposed them
and their families to enormous personal risk during this period of Tudor
despotism. A once safe and assured role for women as arbiters of small
religious disputes and dispensers of charity and patronage was transferred
to males. Moreover, involvement in this traditional area in which women
had previously demonstrated their status became potentially treasonous.
The torture and execution of the Pole family made it apparent to Honor
that Husee had been correct in calling for caution.

Gossip and Intrigue

Medieval and Tudor historians thought that women relied upon gossip
and intrigue to get their way. Modern anthropologists have confirmed
that the powerlessness of women forces them into gossip, ridicule, and
other intrigue in order to gain their ends. If we may judge from the
letters, the Lisles were very much afraid that these weapons, although
ineffectual for their own purposes, would be used against them.

The fear of acquiring a bad reputation about court, of being the butt of
malicious gossip, and of losing the king's or Cromwell's friendship continually haunted both Lord and Lady Lisle. Lady Lisle pursued every
report she heard that someone spoke ill of them. She wrote and taxed the
abbot of Burton about such rumors.[89] All friends at court were solicited
for information. Sir Edward Ryngeley wrote in 1534 that he had not heard
the rumor that Honor was unhappy in Calais and that the queen had
inquired warmly about her.[90] She was her usual direct self in pursuing
the suggestion that Cromwell was no longer her friend in 1534. His servant, William Popley, first wrote to reassure her that this was not true and
her businessman in London wrote the same. Finally, Cromwell himself

wrote and reassured her of his respect and favor. He signed himself her
"loving friend."[91] When several gentlewomen-in-waiting refused to
serve because she was "hasty," she demanded to know from Husee who
had said so, and he reassured her that these were "back-friends" who
could not hurt her. He wished her to throw off such fantasies both for her
sake and for that of Lord Lisle.[92] Lady Lisle might have felt that she was
often too plain spoken with Cromwell on matters that did not concern
her, but she may simply have expressed the anxiety of those living close
to the center of power in a period of despotism.

We must ask whether, in a political climate dominated by gossip and
intrigue, Lady Lisle herself indulged in these methods of gaining power.
The letters do not present evidence that she engaged in gossip about various people who passed through Calais, but perhaps such matters did not
appear in letters, and so few of Honor's own letters are preserved that we
cannot know from them. It is also possible that the precarious position of
the Lisles would have made gossip too dangerous a weapon to use. A
loose word could be turned into a treasonous one.

Honor enjoyed gossip, and her correspondents among her old friends
from the West Country regaled her with the petty scandals of people she
knew.[93] The Calais household was full of jokes and gossip, as Lady
Ryngeley's letters show, for she admonishes Lady Lisle not to let the
widow, Lady Banaster, come between her and her husband.[94] Other gossip was essential for knowing the political drift in England. Court news
such as the progresses of the king, his impending marriage, the pregnancy of the current queen, changes in ministers, and information on
powerful friends are all included, but the most disturbing news was
transmitted by word of mouth rather than in letters. The response to
these serious matters of gossip was gifts and letters to turn the new situation to advantage or to avoid damage from it.

The evidence that Lady Lisle indulged in major intrigues is also limited. She did try to influence and flatter people, and she perhaps wrongly
encouraged her younger daughter's engagement without the king's permission. She threw letters down the jakes when Arthur was arrested. For
the most part, however, her letters and the responses to them indicate that
she was outspoken and direct in her undertakings. Indeed, the chief criticism of her related to her ready words and action. Although more forceful than Lord Lisle in negotiation and business, she appears to have been
in accord with him in always acting honestly. Intrigue, like gossip, was
probably too risky for the Lisles.

To what extent was Lady Lisle successful, and to what did she owe her
successes? In the sphere of family affairs she certainly achieved a great
deal. Her marriages were happy, especially that with Lord Lisle. She edu-

cated her children and placed them advantageously. She was a very good estate manager, capable of reading the accounts, dealing with tenants and markets, and judging the abilities of those who served her. She had a good sense of the law and a fine, clear mind in dealing with court officials, lawyers, and even Cromwell. She succeeded in securing her son's inheritance. Although the Calais household was somewhat extravagant, she managed to maintain the social status of the establishment and keep Lord Lisle contented. Their debts were not disproportionate to those of previous Calais governors or of the nobility in general. Her informal participation in the politics of Calais might have been rather large because of her great influence with Lisle. It was not, however, her indiscretions about religion or her possible political influence that brought about Lord Lisle's arrest, nor could her power save him from being sent to the Tower.[95]

Such power as she exercised came from her reliance upon Arthur's regard for her, the station in society which her kinship and her marriage provided, and her own abilities. All of her advantages would have accounted for little had she not paid careful attention to increasing and maintaining her networks. The contacts, both male and female, furthered her ambitions. Men as well as women built their careers and their access to power on exactly the same basis: spouse, kin, and connections. While the basis of male and female power might be similar, the spheres in which men and women could exercise power were very different. Women's power was, for the most part, limited to the domestic realm. Though they might have informal access to the broader political scene, because they were denied magisterial roles they could not command, but could only attempt to manipulate, their environment beyond the home.

Notes

1. "Manly virtue" and forthrightness were attributed only rarely to women by the Tudor historian Polydore Vergil in describing Queen Margaret of Anjou. For the sixteenth-century debate over women's nature, see Katherine Usher Henderson and Barbara F. McManus, *Half Humankind: Contexts and Texts of the Controversy About Women in England, 1540–1640* (Champaign-Urbana, 1985).

2. For the anthropological discussion, see *Women, Culture, and Society,* ed. Michelle Zimbalist Rosaldo and Louise Lamphere (Stanford, 1974). In particular in that volume, see Michelle Zimbalist Rosaldo, "Women, Culture, and Society: A Theoretical Overview," pp. 17–42, and Jane Fiskburne Collier, "Women in Politics," pp. 89–96. See also Peggy Reeves Sanday, *Female Power and Male Dominance: On the Origins of Sexual Inequality* (Cambridge, 1981), pp. 113–135.

3. Muriel St. Clare Byrne, ed., *The Lisle Letters,* 6 vols. (Chicago, 1981).

4. An account of the lives of the correspondents appears in volume 1 of *The Lisle Letters*. Byrne has also provided background information and a commentary at the beginning of each chapter and a running commentary interspersed in the letters.

5. Sheridan Harvey, *The Cooke Sisters: A Study of Tudor Gentlewomen* (Ph.D. diss., Indiana University, 1981). The sisters were trained in Greek and Latin and translated pieces into English. One married Cecil (Lord Burghley) and the other two married Lord Russell and Lord Bacon, respectively.

6. *Lisle Letters*, vol. 1, pp. 29–31.

7. *Lisle Letters*, vol. 5, p. 249.

8. Letter 1316.

9. *Lisle Letters*, vol. 1, p. 31. Letters 421, 1149, and 1328.

10. *Lisle Letters*, vol. 1, pp. 31–32.

11. Letter 998.

12. Letters xxvii, xxxviia, 202, 202a. *The Lisle Letters*, vol. 2, pp. 163–171 for his story and for the very distant kinship that he could claim with Honor.

13. Letter 201.

14. Letter xv.

15. Letter xva.

16. Letter xxxii.

17. Letters 109, 182, 193, 199a.

18. Letter 307.

19. Letters xxxvii, 54, 109, 111, 216, 234, 241, 290a, 299, 450, 513, 529, 537, 830, 846, 847, 850, 855, 855a, 862 are but some of the many examples. Letter 1379 has the story of the bird and stool.

20. Letters 1620, 1653.

21. *Lisle Letters*, vol. 2, pp. 362–65, for a discussion of tokens. Cramp rings were narrow rings of gold and silver made of coins that the king had blessed. They were supposed to be good for the health.

22. Letters 308, 833.

23. Letter 390. Letter 1372a from Husee gives a good idea of the delivery of the tokens: "My Lady Sussex is in Essex, so that I have reserved your token, and my Lady of Rutland is at Enfield. I have sent thither your ladyship's letter, and also Mrs. Katherine's French hood and your ladyship's letter to her by one which I sendeth thither, but I have your ladyship's token to my Lady Rutland by me till her coming, the which shall be immediately after the holidays, and then will I deliver the same myself. Mrs. Denny doth also greatly thank your ladyship for the caps, and saith your ladyship shall have a token. Mrs. Baynham, having her humbly commended unto your ladyship, was not a little glad of her token, and Mrs. Grene of her letter, but yet I do not know how she doth speed in her suit."

24. Letter 895.

25. Letters 203, 332.

26. *Lisle Letters*, vol. 2, pp. 366–68.

27. Ibid., vol. 1, p. 64.

28. Letter 1237.

29. Letter 1011a.

30. *Lisle Letters,* vol. 1, pp. 22–23. Letter 119.

31. Letter 116.

32. Letters 290, 290a, 555. Ruth Kelso, *Doctrine for the Lady of the Renaissance* (Urbana, 1956), pp. 224–36. Books of advice recommended treating everyone with respect, according to station.

33. Letter 1280. See also *Lisle Letters,* vol. 5, pp. 215–16.

34. Letter 399.

35. Letter xxxi.

36. Letter 25.

37. Letters 35 and 175.

38. Letters 245 and 690.

39. *Lisle Letters,* vol. 5, pp. 53–57, 69–70, and vol. 6, pp. 53–54. Letters 861, 1108, 1116, and 1125.

40. Letter 721.

41. Letter 398.

42. Letters 59, 443.

43. Letters 158, 922, 922a, 936, 945, and 962 contain examples.

44. Letter 503.

45. Letter 1668.

46. Letters 332, 466, 471.

47. Letter xxv.

48. Letter 56.

49. Letters 525, 527, and 529.

50. *Lisle Letters,* vol. 4, pp. 12–13; letter 825.

51. Letter 839.

52. Letters 1219, 1222, 1231.

53. Letter 856.

54. *Lisle Letters,* vol. 5, pp. 132–35.

55. Letter 1174.

56. *Lisle Letters,* vol. 5, pp. 167–70.

57. Ibid., pp. 187–90.

58. Letter 1218.

59. *Lisle Letters,* vol. 3, pp. 75–82.

60. Letters 541–48.

61. Letters 1120 and 1654.

62. Letters 553–67.

63. Letters 1042–82.

64. *Lisle Letters,* vol. 6, pp. 140–43.

65. Letters 571–97a.

66. Letters 717 and 847.

67. Letter 887.

68. *Lisle Letters,* vol. 4, pp. 104–97. Letters 1404 and 1649 show how close the relationship became. Neither Lady Rutland nor Katherine wanted to be separated when another offer of a place was made to Katherine.

69. Letters 801, 864, 866, 868, 868a, 870a, 872, and 873.

70. *Lisle Letters,* vol. 3, pp. 176–91.

71. Letters 14, 25, 70, 71, 80, 89, 157a, 172b, 231, 289a, 341, and 344. Kelso, p. 251. Christine de Pizan advised her princess to go over the accounts herself.

72. Letters 394, 453, 514, 515, 519, and 520.

73. Letter 1261.

74. Letters 1266, 1267.

75. Letters 1269, 1270.

76. Letter 1272.

77. Letters 1279–97.

78. Letter 1298.

79. Letter 1267.

80. Letter 999.

81. Letter 980.

82. *Lisle Letters,* vol. 4, p. 350.

83. Ibid., vol. 6, pp. 69–70. Letter 260a.

84. Kelso, pp. 236–38.

85. Letters 25, 56, 118, 119, 214; *Lisle Letters,* vol. 1, p. 53.

86. Letter 1120.

87. Letters 1131, 1133.

88. Letter 1124.

89. Letters 119, 200.

90. Letter 212.

91. Letters 268, 284, 286. See also 987 for an example of Lisle's anxiety about rumor and concern with favor.

92. Letter 1154.

93. Letters 58, 63, 118.

94. Letter 377.

95. Arthur Lisle was imprisoned in the Tower for two years while the rest of his kin were led to the chopping block. He was finally released by his nephew, but when the messenger arrived, he died. By Byrne's estimate he would have been in his early eighties. Honor was kept under house arrest in Calais during the two years. She was released and returned to the West Country to live out her life. She did not remarry.

Public Postures
and Private Maneuvers:
Roles Medieval Women Play

Joan Ferrante

With limited opportunities to exercise real power over their own or
others' lives, women in medieval literature and sometimes in real life find
subtle or hidden ways to exercise such power, to manipulate people and
situations, and to spin out fictions which suit them better than their reality, fictions by which they can, or hope to, control reality. They cannot,
with rare exception, go to war or battle; only a few of them have the
opportunity to rule lands. Their sphere is more limited, their tools more
subtle. Outwardly many accept the role society expects them to play, that
of the quiet figure with no public voice, but secretly they subvert it often
to serious effect. They rely for the most part on their wits, on intrigues,
on the clever and sometimes devious use of words—fictions, lies, false
oaths, hidden promises—or the practice of magic, which involves cleverness and specialized knowledge. [1]

I shall first consider the roles women play in literature, particularly epic
and romance, showing the similar means that women in both genres
adopt to influence their worlds indirectly;[2] I shall then examine the careers of three women writers whose activity virtually spans the Middle
Ages (the tenth, twelfth, and fifteenth centuries). These women, two
religious and one secular, all adopt a posture of helplessness and ignorance when speaking of themselves and at the same time use their writings, as the women in literature do their maneuvering, to influence their
societies.

In epic, women are frequently passive victims of male feuds. In *Beowulf*, for instance, they are "peace-weavers," given in marriage to unite
warring families or tribes, destined more often than not to see their sons
fighting their brothers and to assume another traditional female role, that

of the mourner. The women in *Beowulf* seem to accept these roles—the poet gives them no choice—but in other epics, the poet reveals their frustrations and occasionally permits them to take corrective, and usually destructive, action.

When Raoul de Cambrai refuses to listen to his mother's sound political advice warning him against engaging in a feud, she turns to prophecy, often a woman's gift. She provides a detailed foretelling of his death in that feud, and still he pays no attention. Worse than that, he shows only contempt for her advice because she is a woman:

> Maldehait ait, je le taing por lanier
> Le gentil homme, qant il doit tornoier,
> A gentil dame qant se va consellier.
> Dedens vos chambres vos alez aasier:
> Beveiz puison por vo pance encraissier,
> Et si pensez de boivre et de mengier;
> Car d'autre chose ne devez mais plaidier.

Let him be cursed and called a coward, who takes a woman's advice before he goes into battle. Go back to your rooms and relax, drink potions to fatten your belly, and give your thought to food and drink; you shouldn't be meddling with other things. [1100–106][3]

Unfortunately for Raoul, his mother is not the retiring sort; she will later threaten another knight with a crowbar (11.5244–45). She reminds him of all she has done to preserve his inheritance, and then she curses him: "Et qant por moi ne le viex or laisier, / Cil Damerdiex qi tout a a jugier, / Ne t'en ramaint sain ne sauf ne entier" (1131–33: "If you won't give this up for me, may God who judges all not let you return safe and sound and whole"). Raoul's mother very quickly wishes her curse unsaid, but there is nothing to be done about it. It is the result of an understandable frustration and anger at her total impotence. An intelligent and competent woman—she has protected his lands for more than fifteen years—she is powerless to interfere with what she knows is a disastrous course of action for him and for those lands. Deprived of her public (beneficial) voice, she resorts to a private voice which is effective but also destructive.

A similar kind of frustration can be seen in the two female protagonists of the *Nibelungenlied*. Both Brunhild and Kriemhild are denied their feudal or legal rights and both find other—destructive—ways to exercise power over their society. When Brunhild marries Gunther, her land is left in the hands of a regent and she has nothing more to do with the governing of it. Her treasure is lavishly dispensed by her husband's men, who fear her strength, so that she arrives in his land without power, men, or enough money to buy them. She shifts from being a powerful queen, who not only rules her own land but defeats all male suitors in tests of strength, to being the impotent consort of a weak king. Is it any wonder that she broods and looks for ways to assert herself, pressing for the visit of her sister- and brother-in-law, which must end in the confrontation of the two women and the murder of Siegfried?

Though she is only a young girl when she marries Siegfried, Kriemhild also attempts to assert her feudal rights. She claims her share of the family lands and men, but her husband refuses the lands, though he lets her take the men. After his death, she claims her husband's treasure, but since she uses it to buy loyalty (in order eventually to avenge his murder), the treasure is taken away from her and hidden, becoming the focus of the struggle between her and her family, particularly between her and Hagen. Her one attempt to take revenge openly and legally is rebuffed: she publicly accuses Hagen of murder when Siegfried's body bleeds in his presence, but nothing is done. Had a man like Siegfried's father made the same public accusation, it is hard to imagine how he could have been so easily ignored.

When Kriemhild is ignored, she turns to devious methods. She marries a powerful king, Etzel, in order to secure a new base of operations. She tricks one of her husband's most honorable men, Rudeger, into an oath which means one thing to him and another to her, that he would avenge whatever happened to her ("swaz ir ie geschach," 1257). He assumes that the oath refers to the future; she means it to refer to the past and will force him to honor it in that sense. She waits more than thirteen years to avenge Siegfried—women must often wait a long time for the right opportunity—and takes a revenge that involves not only the deaths of her brothers and the destruction of her people but severe loss to Etzel and his men, who had no connection with Siegfried's death. While the poet clearly thinks that women should be kept out of public affairs, and the only king in the poem who allows them free use of men and money, Etzel, certainly lives to regret it, the story also suggests that if you rob women of the rights and powers they are entitled to, they will find other ways to assert those rights and powers that may be far more harmful to society.

In the *Lai of Kudrun,* a German poem composed in the epic tradition, with some reference to the *Nibelungenlied,*[4] the heroine brings about peace rather than destruction through her manipulations, but the poem emphasizes the suffering women endure in their traditional roles as a result of mens' wars. Most of the women are the objects of bride quests, the captives of victorious armies, or givers of sound military advice which is ignored. They try to persuade the men to bar the gates and stay inside until the invaders leave, but the men insist on going out to fight and are defeated, leaving the women to be captured. The heroine and all but one of the sixty-two women who are captured with her show great strength and endurance during their fourteen-year captivity. They refuse to yield to their captors, though Kudrun is forced to do heavy work and even to go barefoot in the snow to wash the linens in the sea. Only when she knows the rescuing army has arrived does she take action, and she takes it in the only way she can, deviously, albeit in a good cause. She pretends to be willing to marry her captor in order to get him to bring all the other captive women together so that she can protect them when the army enters; she also persuades him to send a hundred men out to announce the wedding, so that the castle defenses will be depleted. Once Kudrun has been set free, instead of demanding revenge on her captors she persuades her mother and the various warring factions (her brother, her fiancé, and her two rejected suitors) to marry in a way that resolves all the old enmities. Unlike the *Beowulf* poet, the *Kudrun* poet gives us no reason to think that these marriages will not accomplish the peace she seeks.

It is, of course, rare for a woman to have such a positive effect on her society, in either epic or romance, and not coincidental that she does so only after fourteen years of bitter suffering. For the most part, women in epic are passive victims of power struggles and war, ignored when they attempt to participate openly, forced to maneuver behind the scenes. The women in romance, though more central to the story than in most epics, are rarely at the center of power; they too rely on subtle and devious methods. Their most common tools are words and magic, both involving skill and cleverness, both employed to manipulate without the object's being aware of it. Manipulation by words takes various forms: the hidden promise, the false oath, the forged letter, the beneficial fiction, the malicious lie. None of these is an exclusively female tool, but in the romances all are practiced far more widely by women and all, potentially or actually, have social repercussions.

The hidden promise, in which the crucial factor is not spoken (a variation of the ambiguous oath Kriemhild imposes on Rudeger), is used by the lady of the Joie de la Cort in *Erec* to keep her lover always with her. She extracts the promise of a favor from him in the first bloom of their love when he is willing to promise anything. She only later reveals that he has promised never to leave her until he has been conquered by another knight in battle, which traps him in a very uncomfortable situation: he can escape only by the loss of his life or his honor as a knight, yet by staying, by defeating and killing all his opponents for no real purpose, he is denying, indeed subverting, one of the basic tenets of knighthood—to serve society.[5]

The false oath, which also leaves the essential truth unspoken, is a more public abuse of trust and manipulation of reality. It is a statement sworn to before the entire society, technically true but intended to convey to the audience a sense very different from the real truth. Probably the most famous example in medieval literature is the oath Iseut takes to deny her affair with Tristan. In Béroul's poem, she carefully avoids the words suggested by Arthur, that she swear Tristan had never loved her with an improper love ("amor / de putée ne de folor," 4193–94) and instead swears that no man ever came between her thighs except the leper who carried her across the ford and her husband king Mark ("entre mes cuises n'entra home, fors le ladre . . . et li rois Marc mes esposez," 4205–208).[6] By the explicit reference to the sexual act, and the sweeping "no man," she seems to be swearing a much stronger oath, which satisfies them all, but since the leper who carried her is Tristan, the oath means nothing. In both Béroul and Gottfried, the false oath is only the last step in an elaborate plan, which is devised and staged entirely by Iseut. Béroul's heroine chooses the setting (the Blanche Lande), the costumes and makeup (Tristan as a pock-marked leper), props (the goblet for begging), and the audience (Arthur and his court along with all of Mark's vassals) as well as the crucial dialogue. In Gottfried, Isot concentrates less on the external details and characters in the drama and more on the real force behind it; she puts her effort into winning over (manipulating) God. To impress Him, she prays and fasts, gives away her jewels and gold and horses, and wears a hair shirt when she swears on the relics. The heroines of both poems use the oath for self-protection; it is a conscious deception to convey a false sense of innocence to the audience within the poem, to avoid punishment, and to enable the lovers to carry on as before without suspicion.

A tool related to the false oath in its intention and effect is the forged letter, in which the woman maintains her silence publicly but attempts to get her way by putting her words into another's mouth (or hand). In the *Roman de Silence,* the queen makes several passes at the hero (the heroine in disguise), forces her indulgent husband to send Silence away from court, and exchanges the letter he is to carry from the king asking for good treatment with one she has written asking that he be killed.[7] No harm is done in this case because the other court is loath to hurt Silence, but the dangers posed by an ill-intentioned woman who can forge royal documents and use the royal seal do not need to be spelled out. A very different kind of silence is maintained by the hero/heroine of the romance, whose very name, Silence, indicates its importance in her life. Born in a land where girls are not allowed to inherit because of a foolish law, she is raised from birth as a boy and must preserve silence about her identity despite various misgivings during her youth. Like her person,

her name, Silentia, is made masculine with the addition of *us,* which is
both a masculine ending and the noun "usage"; by removing the ending,
her father says, she can return to natural usage:

> Il iert només Scilencius;
> Et s'il avient par aventure
> Al descovrir de sa nature
> Nos muerons cest -us en -a,
> S'avra non Scilencia.
> Se nos li tolons dont cest -us,
> Car cis -us est contre nature,
> Mais l'altres seroit par nature.
>
> [11.2074–82][8]

Male usage is thus imposed on female silence, enabling the woman to act
fully and successfully as a man in a man's world. Deprived of her legal
rights by male authority, compelled to silence, she can act and speak only
through a disguise, but since it is a male disguise, she is able to take
public action and indeed to put things right in her world, to inspire the
repeal of harmful laws, while the queen, who is cast in the passive female
role of the desired and indulgent wife, takes deceptive action (lies and the
forged letter), surreptitiously usurping the male role in order to harm the
hero and betray her husband.

   Implicit in the episodes of the forged letters[9] may be the fear of wom-
en's intellectual powers. Since women are given to deception and trickery
anyway, the more education they have, the more dangerous they become.
This is not to say that trickery is always a negative factor, but the attitude
toward women's use of it is usually at least ambivalent. The attribution to
them of magic powers seems at times to be a manifestation of fear of
women; as it is practiced in courtly literature of the twelfth and thirteenth
centuries, magic is both an intellectual power and a secret one. In the
earlier romances women usually employ the magic to good ends but always to shape and control situations they cannot influence in any other
way and not always successfully. When Isot's mother, who is known for
her considerable skills in medicine, has to send her daughter off to marry
a man none of them knows, a national enemy of long standing, she prepares a potion for the couple that will ensure a happy marriage. The
potion, of course, is drunk by the wrong man and so has exactly the
opposite effect, giving rise to the love affair, and necessitating all the other
female intrigues (of Brangaene and Isot) to keep it hidden.

   In Chrétien's *Cliges,* the servant, Thessala, has the knowledge of medicine and herbs; she may not be educated in other spheres, but she is
knowledgeable about medicine and capable of faking a urine analysis.
She prepares two potions to help her mistress, Fenice, by creating a false

reality for her husband: one potion makes the husband dream he has possessed his wife, the other makes the wife appear to be dead. Both the feigned copulation and the feigned death are intended to keep Fenice chaste and free to love only her lover, since she has been forced to marry a man she does not love, who also happens to be the usurper of her lover's throne. Faced with a reality she cannot accept, she creates one of her own, managing with her complicated fictions to keep her husband happy without giving herself to him and to go off with her lover without arousing suspicion. Her plotting almost backfires, however, when she becomes restless inside the self-imposed prison and insists on going outdoors, where she is seen. Fortunately, the husband is so distressed by the truth when he must finally face it that he dies, leaving the lovers free to turn their fiction into reality. A happy ending, perhaps, but too much based on hypocrisy and deception to be really satisfying to the author or the audience.

In two other romances, *Le Bel Inconnu* and *Partenopeu de Blois,* highly educated heroines use their magic powers to control the life of the hero from early on, but their magic is countered by the effective if less skilled manipulations of other women. Both heroines use their powers to draw the hero to them from far away and to win his love, but neither is able to keep him through those powers. In *Bel Inconnu,* the heroine, la Pucele, plans elaborate schemes to test her men, which ultimately backfire. To ensure herself a worthy knight, she offers herself to anyone who can for seven years fight and defeat all comers. The current contender has lasted five years and appears to be well on his way—but she does not like him. She fashions a still more elaborate scheme to entice the hero, a young, untried knight anxious for adventure. He is to rescue her, en route to the exotic adventure she uses to lure him, the freeing of another woman imprisoned by a spell in an enchanted castle. The scheme begins well— the hero rescues the heroine, falls in love with her, and does not want to leave—but the other lady's servant makes her own plans to get him away so he will complete the rescue of her lady. As might be expected, the other lady, the Blonde Esmeree, also falls in love with her rescuer and wants to marry him. He tries to put her off, saying he will need Arthur's assent, but she sets out immediately to secure the permission. Clever as she is, the Pucele has not anticipated the counterplotting of the Blonde. Without the heroine's extraordinary education or magic powers, the Blonde has the common sense to understand that the hero cannot resist the challenge of chivalry. She plots with Arthur to call a tourney, which the hero attends, against the Pucele's wishes; he wins it and the prize is marriage to the Blonde. The action of the hero, who is free to move openly in the public sphere, is limited to fighting, which has far less effect on the plot than the women's manipulations, almost as if they sent him out to play with his weapons while they worked behind the scenes to control his life. Both women manipulate the hero, though neither is entirely successful—the Blonde gets him but not his love; the Pucele has his love but cannot keep him from pursuing chivalry. Though she is the more skilled manipulator, the Pucele outwits herself by her own cleverness.

The hero of *Partenopeu de Blois* is manipulated by not two but three women—his mother, his love, and her sister. He is something of an emotional yo-yo, drawn back and forth between the demands of the mother and the love until the love finally rejects him and he goes off to the woods to die. Here the sister takes over and manipulates both hero and heroine into the marriage both want. The hero, like the Bel Inconnu, seems to be effective at nothing but fighting and attracting women (he wins a kind of beauty contest as well as a tourney to get his bride). All three women in *Partenopeu* use clever and devious ploys to control the hero: the sister uses lies and forged letters to persuade the hero of his lady's love for him; the mother uses a potion to make him forget the love, so she can fix him up with a nice French princess; and the love uses her considerable magic to draw him across the sea to her land and then to keep herself and her people invisible from him for over a year. She visits him to make love only in the dark—a reverse of Cupid and Psyche but also a female version of the possessive husband. There seems no need for all her secrecy, except to create the illusion, the fiction, of an impossible and therefore more appealing love. It is intriguing but perplexing that the heroine is an empress, a woman in a position to act openly, who should not need to rely on subterfuge, and yet she chooses to operate in the same manner, in the typical female role, as if she were totally dependent on the will of others, or as if she were trapped by her culture's expectations of woman's role.

Melior wins her hero in this romance despite her mistakes. La Pucele in the *Bel Inconnu* does not, but the poet of *Bel Inconnu*, Renaut de Beaujeu, leaves his ending open; he tells the lady who inspired him to write the story that he will return the hero to his real love if the lady will be kind to the poet. This seems to give the poet's lady a certain control over the content of the story, a way to manipulate the poet so that he will give her the ending she wants for the characters, but of course this is only a concealed way for the poet to manipulate the lady, by enticing her sympathies to the heroine so he can make his lady do what he wants. This is, apparently, the reverse of the situation in Chrétien's *Lancelot*, where the Countess of Champagne imposed the subject matter on the poet before he began to write it. He accepted the assignment but, finding no way to resolve its central problem, refused to finish it. In fact, he may well be commenting on the countess's attempt to control him by his treatment of the heroine Guenevere, who imposes such extraordinary and sometimes pointless burdens on the hero. If so, then the real woman's attempts to manipulate the reality of fiction have no more success than fictional women's attempts to manipulate their own reality.

Yet another way of manipulating reality through fiction and letters is to write them yourself. Many women writers in the Middle Ages when they speak in their own voice adopt the traditional posture of humility, the frail "little woman," modest about her talents. In their writings, however, they are aggressive, and the objects of their attack are frequently men of great power and authority. I will consider three women writers here, Hrotsvit of Gandersheim (tenth century), Hildegard of Bingen (twelfth century), and Christine de Pizan (fourteenth century to fifteenth). Though almost five centuries apart, one living in a German convent, the other in the secular world of Paris, Hrotsvit and Christine are very similar in their presentations of themselves and in the way they treat the women characters in their works. Hildegard, though not a writer of fiction, presents the same sort of contrast between what she says of herself in the first person and what she says to those she is addressing. Sometimes, of course, she claims to be speaking with the voice of God, which, if not a fictional character, is surely the equivalent of the allegorical women in Hrotsvit's plays and Christine's narratives.[10]

Hrotsvit, the tenth-century nun who wrote Latin poems and plays, speaks of herself and her work in the most deprecating and self-effacing terms, but many of her women characters put down the highest male authority in their world, the Roman emperor. While one might object that the emperor in the plays is a pagan, one should not forget that Hrotsvit was writing under his Christian heirs, Otto I and Otto II, and that her abbess was closely related to them. Furthermore, these emperors identified with their pagan predecessors, consciously modeling themselves and their courts on ancient Roman forms.[11]

In the prologues to all her works—the poems, the plays, and the epics—she presents herself as a poor little thing, without much learning or talent but diligent and anxious to do the right thing—the quintessential female posture. Though the humility topos was a standard medieval rhetorical device, a means of gaining goodwill in order to be able to move the auditor more effectively,[12] Hrotsvit exaggerates the conventions with heavy use of diminutives and deprecation of her female self. Hildegard and Christine do the same, though Marie de France, interestingly, does not. On the contrary, she asserts herself and her abilities, proclaiming her gifts and her duty to use them for the instruction of others, though she too attacks established authority, indirectly in the *Lais* (e.g., "Equitan" and "Lanval") and directly in several of the fables.

Hrotsvit's prologues are filled with such phrases as "feminea fragilitas" (I, II), "nesciola" (II, Ep., "an ignorant little thing"), and "vilis mulierculae" (II, Ep., "a vile little woman"—note the tendency to use diminutives about herself and her work), "propriae pigritia inertiae" (II, Ep., "the laziness of my inertia"), "vilitas meae inscientiae" (II, Ep., "the worthlessness of my ignorance"), "rusticitas" (I, III), "ultima ultimarum" (III, "the last of the last"), "aliis meae inscientiae opusculis" (II, "in other little works of my ignorance"), "sexus fragilior, scientiaque minor" (III, "[my] weaker sex, lesser in learning").[13] She describes her work in the same way: "hunc libellum, parvo ullius decoris cultu ornatum" (I, "this little book, adorned with little cultivation of any beauty"), "opusculi" (I, III), "male composita" (I), "ingenioli" (I, "feeble little intellect"), "carminula" (I, poem, "little songs"), "vilitatem laboris" (II, "the worthlessness of my labor"), and "rusticitatem meae dictatiunculae" ("the lack of sophistication of my little compositions"). Her work, she says, is filled with errors which others, more learned, must correct; others have praised it, finding a little knowledge of the arts in it, but their "subtlety has long evaded my womanly wit" (II, Ep.: "quarum subtilitas longe praeterit mei muliebre ingenium"). She has perhaps plucked out a few threads from the rags torn from Philosophy's robes (II, Ep.: "si qua forte fila vel etiam floccos de panniculis, a veste Philosophiae abruptis") and has inserted them in her work, mixing nobler matter with the baseness of her ignorance.

Of course she does not hesitate to correct Terence, substituting proper Christian material for the bawdy stories of the popular Roman writer, nor does she give up the stories she had taken from the Apocrypha, when she learns that biblical scholars question their authenticity—what seems false might prove to be true after all. In contrast to the overwhelming expression of her own inadequacy, she gives unstinting praise to her teachers' wisdom and learning, and the two she mentions are women, the "sapientissimae atque benignissimae Rikkardis magistrae" (I, "the most wise and kind teacher Rikkarda") and Gerberga, "scientia provectior" (I, "advanced in learning") and later "illustris moribus et studiis" (I, poem, "illustrious in her ways and her studies"). Most significant, however, is the forcefulness of her female characters, whose "feminine fragility" (the same phrase she had used of herself) "conquers while virile strength is subjected to confusion" (II, "cum feminea fragilitas vinceret et virilis robor confusioni subiaceret").

The best examples of this triumph of weakness are in the plays *Dul-*

citius and *Sapientia*. In both, Christian women or girls are brought before the pagan emperor, who tries to befriend them and persuade them gently to give up their madness, but they respond with contempt and make fools of him and of his major officers. In *Sapientia*, the emperor Hadrian is warned of the threat to the state from a few Christian women. He asks, "What possible harm could the arrival of little women [*muliercularum*] do to the state?" He is told that they are persuading Roman women to abandon religious rites and to refuse to eat or sleep with their husbands. He summons them and treats them with condescending graciousness: "are these the little women . . . ?" He praises their beauty and the dignity of their dress (as if to ask why a nice, pretty girl like you wants to get mixed up with this sort of thing), and he attempts to win them over with flattery. His adviser comments that the "fragility of the female sex" is easily softened by flattery. When the mother, Sapientia, refuses to worship his gods or to accept his friendship, he tells her he is moved by paternal love for the good of her daughters. She immediately tells the girls, apparently in an aside, not to trust the "snake-like panderings of this satan" ("serpentinis huius satanae lenociniis") but to despise him, as she does.

As the emperor continues to be gracious, inquiring the ages of the three girls, Sapientia asks them if they would like her to wear out this fool ("hunc stultum") with an arithmetical disputation. They say they would love it, and she begins: "Charity completed a diminished evenly even number; Hope, a number also diminished, but unevenly even; and Faith, an augmented number, unevenly even." The poor emperor, beginning to lose his grasp, says, "With that answer I know less than I knew before." Sapientia continues to taunt him, seeming to explain but in fact becoming more and more complicated. He tries to keep up, showing off what little knowledge he has—he knows that Charity's two olympiads are eight years, Hope's two lustres ten, Faith's three olympiads twelve, if not why ten is diminished or twelve augmented—but he falls further and further behind as her talk becomes more technical. He eventually says, "I don't know the term or the denomination or the quantity you're talking about," and then, plaintively, "what a precise and twisted question came out of the age of these children." At the end he explains that he has put up with this long argument in order to persuade them to worship his gods. When Sapientia still refuses, he gives up and condemns her. It is, of course, not unusual for martyrs to mock their tormentors and assert the truth of their faith, but these do so in a way which shows the intellectual rather than the religious superiority of the women at the expense of the men who hold the highest positions in their world. In the dialogue she writes, Hrotsvit identifies herself with her characters by putting the condescending terms she has used of herself, "muliercula," "fragilitas sexus feminei," in the mouth of those men, to describe the women in the plays who oppose them. The implication is that, either consciously or subconsciously, she does not consider herself a poor little thing any more than she does the women she writes about, but this is the role men expect her to play, and if she plays it, she can get away with a good deal more than she otherwise might have.

Hildegard of Bingen, a twelfth-century abbess and figure of international reputation, adopts a similar posture in her letters and some of her other works: "ego paupercula forma" (Ep. 127, "I, a poor little thing"), "debilem et indoctam femineam formam" (Ep. 58, "a weak and untutored female form"), "Ego misera et plus quam misera in nomine femineo . . . indignam famulam tuam" (Ep. 19 to Bernard of Clairvaux, "I, miserable and more than miserable in the name woman . . . your unworthy servant"), "ego paupercula et imbecillis forma" (*Liber divinorum operum*, "I, a poor little powerless thing"), and "Ego paupercula et fictile vas" (45, "I am a poor little earthen vessel, and I say, not from me but from the serene light, Man is a vessel which God made for himself and imbued with his inspiration . . . like a trumpet [*tuba*] which only gives sounds, when another blows in it. . . . I who lie in the pusillanimity of fear, sound a little, like the small sound of the trumpet from the living light").[14] The trumpet may only sound when someone blows in it, but it makes a sound no one could ignore, not unlike the "loud voice" of Gandersheim, as Hrotsvit interpreted her own name. Since it is God who blows Hildegard's trumpet—her visions were authenticated by a papal commission in 1147—she can say anything with impunity, and she does. She takes on popes and emperors, telling them how they neglect their duties, how they allow evil to triumph, how they will feel the wrath of God, but her posture of ignorance is belied, like Hrotsvit's, by her medical writings, her musical compositions, and her visions, in which she reveals a knowledge of scientific and philosophic thought, of current developments in Neo-Platonism and perhaps Arab science.

Christine de Pizan adopts the same postures and also belies them in her writings. She was a woman who knew well what it was like to be defenseless in the world of male bureaucracy. After the deaths of her father and her husband, she found herself a young mother, the sole support of her children, her own mother, and her niece, and she spent years trying to collect the money that was owed her husband before he died. She returned to her studies, perhaps the first secular example of a phenomenon that is common in our time, of a woman forced by economic or emotional circumstances to return to school after marriage and children, who carves out a successful career for herself in midlife (in Christine's case at twenty-five). She wrote a great deal, not only poetry, but also works on politics, the nature of government, the ideal of a world empire, the exploitation of the poor, corruption in government, factional struggles and civil war in France, and she was highly regarded. Though she claims that her books were successful because of the novelty of a woman writing, in fact learned men discussed and circulated them. The poet, Eustache Deschamps, called her a

> Muse eloquent entre les ix, Christine,
> Nompareille que je saiche aujour d'ui,
> En sense acquis et en toute dotrine,
> Tu as de Dieu science et non d'autruy;
> Tes epistres et livres, que je luy
> En pluseurs lieux, de grant philosophie,
> Et ce que tu m'as escript une fie,
> Me font certain de la grant habondance
> De ton sçavoir qui tousjours monteplie,
> Seule en tes faiz ou royaume de France.[15]

Muse eloquent among the nine, Christine, without equal today in acquired wisdom and all doctrine, you have learning from God and from no other; your letters and books, which I read in many places, of great philosophy, and what you once wrote me, make me certain of the great abundance of your knowledge which continues to multiply—you are alone in your deeds in the kingdom of France.

Nonetheless she adopts the posture of the frail, ignorant creature and not only for herself but in the name of all women.

At the beginning of the *City of Ladies,* influenced by her reading of misogynist authorities, she begins to detest herself and the entire female sex as monstrosities of nature and feels sorry for herself because God made her inhabit a female body (1.1.2: "Je determinoye que ville chose fist Dieux quant il forma femme . . . , desprisant moy meismes et tout le sexe feminin, si comme ce ce fust monstre de nature").[16] When the three allegorical ladies approach her in a vision to correct the errors about women, she calls herself a "simple and ignorant student" and protests that her "weak, feminine body" cannot support such a task (1.7.1: "simple et ignorent estudiente," "mon foible corps feminin"). She insists that women have weak bodies, are tender and feeble in deeds of strength, and are cowards by nature (1.14.1: "c'est chose prouvee que femmes ont le corps foible, tendre et non puissant en fait de force, et par nature sont couardes"). When the figure of Reason notes that strong-bodied men can be cowards and that weakness keeps women from committing the worst cruelties, and then cites examples of women's victories in battle, Christine concedes but raises a new question about learning. Reason tells her that, if girls were sent to school like boys and were taught the sciences, they would learn as thoroughly and would understand the subtleties of the arts and sciences as well as boys. They may have weaker bodies, but they also have sharper minds if they apply themselves (1.27.1: "de tant comme femmes ont le corps plus delie que les hommes, plus foible et moins habille a plusieurs choses faire, de tant ont elles l'entendement plus a delivre et plus agu ou elles s'applicquent"). After another impressive series of examples, Christine asks whether they have ever discovered any new arts or sciences (1.33.1). This question leads Reason to her most extreme defense: women have invented alphabets, grammar, music, armor, cloth, and agriculture. Anyone who doubts her, she says, can find it all in Boccaccio (1.37.1). If it's in a male authority, it must be true. Christine probably does not expect her audience to accept all of this as fact, but she is making a point about the contributions of women to civilization, and she makes it not in her own voice but through the allegorical figures of Reason, Right, and Justice (Rayson, Droitture, and Justice), sent from heaven to correct her own (and her audience's) erroneous notions about women. They can take a much more extreme position than she could.

Yet Christine was not unwilling to defend herself in her own words. She tells us in *L'Avision-Christine* that, when a man told her learning was not suitable to women, however little they might have of it, she responded that ignorance was even less suitable to men, however much they might have of it (59v: "disant que il napertient a femme avoir science comme il en soit pou et lui dis que moins apartent a homme ignorance comme il en soit beaucop"). In the debate in which she became involved when she attacked Jean de Meun and the *Roman de la Rose,* she took on major figures of the intellectual establishment. Of course, here too she adopted the useful posture of the poor little woman. She asked the Prevost of Paris for "compassion de ma femmenine ignorance," to join his wisdom to hers against the noteworthy and select masters whose subtle arguments would have defeated "my just cause" for lack of learning (7–8). She speaks of the "legiereté de mon petit engin . . . , moy Christine de Pizan, femme ignorant d'entendement," to the Prevost of Lille and of her slight understanding of subtle matters (12).

Christine's opponents are not entirely taken in by her pose; they address her as "prudent, honnouree et sçavant . . . , femme de hault et eslevé entendement" (9). At the same time they are condescending. Gautier Col is astonished that she should attack the work of maistre Jean de Meun, "vray catholique, solempnel maistre et docteur en saincte theologie, philosophe tres parfont et excellent sachant" (9); he begs her to correct her manifest error, the folly that came to her out of presumption or audacity as a "femme passionee" (23). Jean de Montreuil speaks of the arrogance with which some attack, particularly a certain woman named Christine, who has even written publicly, and not without understanding, inasmuch as a woman can have it (42), but Christine is not inhibited by their objections. If she, a woman, dares to attack so subtle an author, she comments, it should not be considered folly, or arrogance, or presumption, when he, a single man, dared to defame and blame an entire sex. She tells Pierre Col, canon of Notre Dame, secretary of the royal chancellery, that if he wants to hear about Hell and Paradise in more subtle terms than Jean's, with more exalted theology, more profitably, more poetically, and effectively expressed, he should read the book by Dante, or have it explained to him, since it was written in the Florentine tongue (141–42), rubbing in the fact that she can read Italian and he cannot. She reminds Gautier Col, also of the royal chancellery, that the small point of a little knife can pierce a great sack stuffed with goods (25: "une petite pointe de ganivet ou cotelet puet percier un grant sac plein et enflé de materielles choses"). Clearly she adopts the posture of the poor ignorant woman in order to attack as the little knife all the more effectively.

Christine and Hildegard and Hrotsvit, the "little knife," the "small trumpet," and the "last of the last" (who is also the "loud voice of Gandersheim"), were able to put their intelligence and their learning to good use. Instead of rejecting the role of the frail, ignorant woman imposed on them by their culture, they embraced it and made it work for them. Like the women in the romances and epics who worked behind the scenes, secretly, sometimes deceptively, because they were not given the opportunity to act openly, these writers exercised powerful influence from positions of apparent weakness. Like the characters in literature who had to rely on magic and intrigue to assert their will, these three writers felt the need to disguise their learning and their strong views under a modest unthreatening exterior, but because they found a public mode of action, they could make a contribution that was beneficial to society and not destructive of it, whereas the surreptitious actions of the women in literature were threatening and often harmful to it.

The point seems to be that not all women will accept the passive role imposed on them; if they are denied a direct and open role, they will find a way to assert their will, and the secret, hidden way can be dangerous. It is likely that these three women writers knew exactly what they were doing in using the posture of humility to make stunning criticisms of male authority, but it is also possible that the male authors of the epics and romances I cited recognized, perhaps not always consciously, that women would assert themselves despite or because of the constraints imposed upon them and that it might be safer for society to allow them to operate more openly.

Notes

1. Women in medieval literature respond in at least two other ways to the male concept of woman. The woman as image, the reflection of the male ideal, in literature has little life of her own, existing mainly to inspire the man's mood (if he is a lyric lover) or action (if he is a romance hero); see my *Woman as Image in Medieval Literature* (1975; repr., Durham, N.C., 1985). Woman as realist cuts through the rhetoric of courtly love, the fictions and postures of the noble lover, and shows up the hypocrisy, the emptiness of the pretense; see my "Male Fantasy and Female Reality in Courtly Literature," *Women's Studies* 11 (1984):67–97.

2. Despite the differences in spheres of activity of which Penny Schine Gold speaks in *The Lady and the Virgin* (Chicago, 1985), women in both genres must resort to similar means in order to exercise power in the male world.

3. *Raoul de Cambrai, Chanson de geste,* ed. P. Meyer and A. Longnon (Paris; repr., New York, 1965).

4. The names of many characters and the heroine's long wait before she can take action are suggestive. For a recent study of the poem, see Stephen L. Wailes, "The Romance of Kudrun," *Speculum* 58 (1983):347–67.

5. He is disturbed about the deaths of other knights, as he makes clear to Erec after their battle when he says that the guilt is not his—he had no choice unless he wanted to be false and cowardly (6058–64), ed. Mario Roques (Paris, 1955).

6. Béroul, *Le Roman de Tristan,* ed. Ernest Muret (Paris, 1957). In Gottfried's version, the oath is put somewhat more delicately, but the essence and effect are the same.

7. The queen also uses the malicious lie against Silence, accusing him of rape when he rejects her advances. The Potiphar's wife motif also occurs in Marie de France's *Lanval*.

8. *Le Roman de Silence,* ed. Lewis Thorpe (Cambridge, 1972).

9. There are other instances in thirteenth-century romance (e.g., in the Prose Lancelot) where a false Guenevere announces herself to Arthur's court by letters purporting to come from the real queen, denouncing the other as an impostor (Lancelot, 4.13).

10. Barbara Newman, *Sister of Wisdom: St. Hildegard's Theology of the Feminine* (Berkeley, 1987), p. 255, notes that Hildegard has no female role models. If she identifies with women, it is with allegorical figures, e.g., Ecclesia, Caritas, Scientia Dei.

11. See Peter Dronke, *Women Writers of the Middle Ages* (Cambridge, 1984), p. 59, citing E. R. Labande, "Mirabilia mundi: Essai sur la personnalité d'Otton III," *CCM* 6 (1963):297–313, 455–76. Dronke also notes the close connections

between the imperial court and Gandersheim, Hrotsvit's convent, and suggests that her plays may well have been read at court (58).

12. See Alain de Lille, *De arte praedicatoria, Patrologia Latina,* vol. 120, c. 113: "Praedicator debet captare benevolentiam auditorum a propria persona per humilitatem, et a rei quam proponit utilitate dicendo, se iis proponere verbum Dei, ut fructum fáciat in mentibus eorum . . . ad provectum et profectum eorum." As E. R. Curtius shows in Excursus II, *European Literature and the Latin Middle Ages,* trans. Willard R. Trask (New York, 1953), the humility topos was taken over from the classical rhetorical tradition.

13. *Hrotsvithae Opera,* ed. Karl Strecker (Leipzig, 1930); the numbers refer to the three books of her works. The intensity of her self-deprecation and the frequency of diminutives far exceed the normal "captatio benevolentiae" of a poet. For a recent study of the writer, see Katharina M. Wilson, "The Saxon Canoness: Hrotsvit of Gandersheim," *Medieval Women Writers,* ed. Katharina M. Wilson (Athens, Ga., 1984); for a new and accessible translation, see Wilson's *The Dramas of Hrotsvit of Gandersheim* (Saskatoon, 1985).

14. The text is taken from the *Patrologia Latina,* vol. 197, which must serve until we have a better edition. Peter Dronke has an interesting study of Hildegard in his recent *Women Writers of the Middle Ages* (Cambridge, 1984).

15. *Oeuvres complètes de Eustache Deschamps,* ed. Le Marquis de Queux de Saint-Hilaire, vol. 6 (Paris, 1889), pp. 251–52, Ballade 1242.

16. The *Livre de la Cité des Dames* was edited by Maureen Curnow (Ph.D. diss., Vanderbilt University, 1975) and translated by Earl Jeffrey Richards (New York, 1982). *Lavision Christine,* cited below, was edited by Mary Louis Towner (Washington, D.C., 1932), and *Le Débat sur le Roman de la Rose* by Eric Hicks (Paris, 1977).

The Powers of Silence:
The Case of the Clerk's Griselda

Elaine Tuttle Hansen

To take a stand would be to upset the beautiful balance of the game.

Richard A. Lanham, "Chaucer's *Clerk's Tale*"

To most Chaucerians, it is by now either commonplace or irrelevant to note that the *Clerk's Tale,* like so many of Chaucer's poems, situates a strong female character in what one modern editor describes as "a context of masculine authoritarianism."[1] Recognition of this situation does not seem to resolve the interpreter's fundamental confusion about the Tale's meaning. This confusion, in fact, is one of the few things on which a number of critics can agree: whatever its specific significance, this poem appears to be bound up with its ambiguities and ambivalence, the "insolubility" of its many problems. The force of gender conflict in the Tale is thus at once recognized and neutralized; if Chaucer takes no definitive position on the victimization of women that he so clearly depicts, then we do not need to raise charged and difficult questions about misogyny and great Western art. We can instead see "beautiful balance" and aesthetic resolution to the problems of sexual politics and sexual poetics.

In this essay, I want to reconsider the question of the ambivalence of the *Clerk's Tale* in light of the "masculine authoritarianism" in the poem. The text offers readers a fundamentally equivocal—and hence rich and compelling—confrontation with patriarchal power, a confrontation negotiated by a not uncommon situation in Chaucer's works: the representation of a male author telling the story of a female character. In the first part of my discussion, focusing on the female character and her multiple, slippery significations, I argue that the tale of patient Griselda addresses questions about women and power and articulates a clear paradox: woman's insubordination is, as our lexicon suggests, no more and no less than an inflection of her subordination. In the second half of the essay, focusing on the representation of the male author, I ask what kind of *men*, according to Chaucer, choose to tell such stories about women and why such men might well refuse to take a stand.

"This is ynogh, Grisilde myn"

Viewed in a certain way, the plot of Griselda's story demonstrates how a woman may rise to the highest position of hegemonic power, becoming the honored wife of a wealthy lord and a coruler of his kingdom through her archetypally acceptable behavior: by being utterly submissive and fundamentally silent. As the story begins, the people of Saluces (Saluzzo) approach their bachelor lord, Walter, to urge him to marry. He complies with their reasonable wishes, on the condition that he choose the bride. He then selects Griselda, a beautiful peasant girl whom he has often noticed while out pursuing his favorite pastime—hunting. The terms of his marriage proposal underscore his determination to brook no insubordination from the wife whose origins are clearly intended to remind Walter's subjects of their subjugation, and to constrain Walter himself as little as possible within an institution that he explicitly views as "servage" (147).[2] Walter tells Griselda's father, the poorest man in the kingdom, that he will marry the girl "if it hire wille be / To be my wyf, and reule hire after me" (326–27), and then he expands on the conditions or "demandes" (348) of his offer to Griselda herself:

> "I seye this, be ye redy with good herte
> To al my lust, and that I frely may,
> As me best thynketh, do yow laughe or smerte,
> And nevere ye to grucche it, nyght ne day?
> And eek when I say 'ye,' ne sey nat 'nay,'
> Neither by word ne frownyng contenance?
> Swere this, and heere I swere our alliance."
>
> [351–57]

Griselda's antiphonal response puts her willing submission to Walter's authority above life itself:

> "But as ye wole youreself, right so wol I.
> And heere I swere that nevere willyngly,
> In werk ne thoght, I nyl yow disobeye,
> For to be deed, though me were looth to deye."
>
> [361–64]

The subsequent plot is designed to prove, in both senses of the term, Griselda's promise—to test and testify to her perfect submission, through a series of three trials. First, shortly after the birth of their first child, a girl, Walter takes the baby away; some time later, after their son is born, he again pretends to have the child murdered, although in both cases he in fact sends his offspring into his sister's care. Third and finally, Walter announces that he is going to marry a younger, well-born wife (who turns out to be his twelve-year-old daughter) and that Griselda must therefore return to her father's hovel. Griselda passes each test and on each occasion speaks only to assert that her children, like herself, are Walter's to "save or spille" (503), that his command is her will, that she left her freedom at home when she moved into the palace, and again that she would gladly die if it would please him to have her do so.

After the third trial, Walter announces that Griselda has finally proven her worth, and amid tears, kisses, and swoons she is reinstated as his wife and reunited with her children. Griselda thus succeeds in rising from peasant to aristocrat—and at another level even serves, the Clerk tells us, as an allegorical figure for the patient Christian soul—by living up to her culture's image of perfect femininity, by willfully accepting, even reveling in, the powerlessness of her position. To the modern reader, of course, Griselda may in this way represent not a positive model of female power but rather the kind of prescriptive antifeminist propaganda for which the medieval period is well known.[3] Indeed the Clerk's peculiar handling of the Griselda story supports and complicates this seemingly "modern" response by exploring the implications of Griselda's paradoxical position as a woman: the fact that she attains certain kinds of power by embracing powerlessness; the fact that she is strong, in other words, because she is so perfectly weak. The Tale suggests on the one hand that Griselda is not really empowered by her acceptable behavior, because the feminine virtue she embodies in welcoming her subordination is by definition both punitive and self-destructive. On the other hand, the Tale reveals that the perfectly good woman *is* powerful, or at least potentially so, insofar as her perfect silence and submission are fundamentally insubordinate and deeply threatening to men and to the concepts of "human" identity upon which patriarchal culture is premised.

The *Clerk's Tale* implies in more ways than one how the prescriptive idealization of women in which it ostensibly engages is punitive. The nature of Griselda's reward for feminine perfection, in the first place, is problematic from the "realistic" point of view that the Clerk sometimes at least prompts us to take; the "happy" ending, after all, brings her permanent union with a man whom the Clerk has carefully characterized as a sadistic tyrant, worst of men and cruelest of husbands (although not unrealistic or even atypical in this regard, the storyteller suggests). At another level, the series of unmotivated trials leading to this "reward" suggests that the better Griselda is, the more she must suffer, or that the more she suffers, the better she must be. We shall see that one logical conclusion of this fatal prescription for female virtue proves troubling at the close of the Tale: the end of the heroine's suffering must in a sense spell the end of her virtue, and any voice Griselda has is silenced, her story finished, when Walter finally stops torturing her.

Power, in this case the ability to impose one's will on someone else, is also shown to be both out of the question and potentially dangerous to a woman's well-being in another interesting way. Immediately after his description of Walter and Griselda's marriage, before the story of the trials begins, the Clerk, following his sources, notes how swiftly and remarkably the good peasant girl is transformed into the perfect no-blewoman. In the space of a few stanzas (393–441), we learn that after her marriage Griselda is beloved by Walter's people and famed in many regions; people in fact travel to Saluzzo, we are told, just to see her. Not merely a paragon of "wifly hoomlinesse," she can also serve the public interest (the "commune profit"), acting in her husband's absence as a peerless adjudicator who settles all disputes with her "wise and rype wordes" (438). The passage seems in its own right to document Griselda's innate "virtue"—but the root of the word "virtue" itself, from the Latin for "male person," may suggest what the *Clerk's Tale* affirms: a virtuous *woman* is by definition a contradiction, an aberrancy, and a threat to nature itself and the stability of the gender system. Walter apparently recognizes this threat. Griselda's public virtue, her ability to exert a power masculine in kind and superhuman in degree, would seem to vindicate Walter's choice of a bride beyond what we might imagine to be his wildest dreams; people say, according to the Clerk, that Griselda is literally a godsend. The situation of this passage describing her perfection within the plot as a whole, however, implies on the contrary that Walter is less than delighted with his perfect spouse, since his decision to torture and humiliate her as a mother and a wife comes, according to the narrative, *after* she has been acclaimed as a saintly ruler. The Tale thus implies that virtue in a woman in fact provokes male aggression and that a woman's public powers, even if they are divinely sanctioned, matter little to her identity or fate as a female, both of which are shown to be ultimately and utterly under the control of her husband. Griselda's supposedly unusual ability to rule wisely and well, to pass good judgments and speak in ways that men admire and respect, to assume, that is, the power and position normally assigned to the best of men, does not and cannot empower her or enable her to escape her subordinate status. Her situation may in this way remind us of a point made by modern feminist analyses of history: the occasional existence of a strong, wise, and successful female in a position of exceptional power is if anything the exception that we need to prove the rule, and the token queen or abbess or bourgeois female entrepreneur does not alter the position or definition of the feminine in the dominant gender system. To prove her "wommanhede," again, Griselda must suffer and submit; her virtue—her allegedly inherent but nevertheless unnatural manliness and power—must be punished and contained.

At the same time, however, the Clerk's version of the Griselda story also invites us to see the other side of Griselda's supremely feminine powerlessness, the subversive potential of her "acceptable" behavior. Walter, as the narrative structure of the tale implies, is goaded into unexpected and irrational cruelty by the very virtue of this woman that he himself discovered, the unacceptable power of the female that he unwittingly unleashed in an attempt to demonstrate and protect his own power. His reaction is in various ways highly plausible; any reader's experience will confirm, for one thing, that it takes a saint to live with one, and Griselda strikes many irreverent readers as far too much of a Pollyanna, or a little Goody Two Shoes. It is equally obvious at another level that, if a peasant woman can in fact be as good a ruler as a noble man—or an even better one—then Walter's birthright and the whole feudal system on which it depends are seriously threatened. This, I suggest, is part of what the Clerk means when he remarks, near the end of the Tale, that it would be "inportable," or intolerable, unbearable, if real wives behaved like Griselda. His comment seems intended to heighten the pathos and abstraction of his portrait of Griselda and to express his alleged sympathy with her situation; it also suggests, however, his at least equal sympathy with Walter, his understanding that it is precisely Griselda's saintliness, her superhuman—or inhuman—goodness, her ability to be just what he asks her to be, that enrages her husband. Walter perceives at some level that he is shown up, defeated, and made powerless first by the position and authority he hands his wife, which she so easily and successfully wields, and then by the self-abasement that he demands and that she, ever obedient and adaptable to her situation, so easily and successfully provides. Galled by the unbearable way in which this woman eludes his tyranny by refusing to resist and define it, he can only torture her again and again, seeking to determine her elusive identity as well as his own, to find the "other" in Griselda, someone he can master in order to find himself.

What makes Walter stop, after the third trial, may be his understanding at last of the paradoxical sense in which this woman continues to win by

losing so fully and graciously to a tyrannical man. Here the last scene of
the Tale becomes crucial to our understanding of the complex interaction
of the subordination and insubordination of a woman, as Griselda almost
beats Walter to the draw. She has been called back to the palace to clean it
up for Walter's second wedding. As the nobles sit down to dinner, Walter
calls the old wife over to ask how she likes his beautiful new bride. In the
preceding stanza, however, we have learned that Griselda is already busy
praising the girl and her brother "so wel that no man koude hir prise
amende" (1026). When Walter, who apparently has not noticed what
she's up to, foolishly invites her to come center stage for a moment—in
her rags—Griselda seizes the opportunity to protest and celebrate, at the
same time, her own treatment at Walter's hands. First she wishes him
well of the lovely young thing; at the same time that she is accepting and
cooperating as usual in her own abasement here, she is unwittingly praising herself, born again into better circumstances, as well as directly engaging in the competition between women, even between mother and
daughter, that her culture enforces. Then she warns Walter not to tor-
ment the maiden as he has tormented "mo" ("others"), as she tactfully
puts it. The well-born creature could not endure, Griselda predicts, what
the poor one could. Her strategy here recalls her earlier move, when she
responded to banishment with the longest, most pathetic speech in the
poem (814–89), but this time Walter knows better than to let his patient
wife have the floor for more than one stanza. He is at this point said to
"rewen upon hire wyfly stedfastnesse" (1050), and while the chief sense
of "rewen upon" is "to feel pity or compassion for," we may also think of
the more familiar sense of the verb, one which was current in Middle
English—"to regard or think of . . . with sorrow or regret, to wish that
(something) had never taken place or existed."[4] Walter must indeed regret
Griselda's surpassing wifely steadfastness because it has all but defeated
his lordly urge to dominate. When in the next stanza he tells Griselda,
"This is ynogh, Grisilde myn," we are reminded that he said this once
before, when she gave her initial promise (365), apparently without
meaning it. And this time we cannot be sure whether he intends to call a
halt to her suffering or to her emergent powers of subversive speech—
powers paradoxically dependent on his continued oppression. When he
goes on to seal Griselda's lips with kisses, her reaction is telling. She is so
stunned, the Clerk says, that for a moment she cannot hear Walter's astonishing concession that she has finally proved herself in his eyes—"She
herde nat what thyng he to hire seyde; / She ferde as she had stert out of a
sleep" (1059–60). Griselda's temporary deafness represents, I suggest, her
unwillingness to hear that the nightmare is over, because she presumably
knows at some level that any power she has lies only in suffering, that she

can speak only to assent to being silenced, and that with the promise of a happy ending her potential for martyred subversion is fatally precluded and she must awake into the reality of her powerlessness.

In the second half of this essay I will explore what happens after this climactic moment, in the multiple endings of the *Clerk's Tale,* but let me conclude this section of my discussion by underscoring one implication of the reading I have just offered. Griselda has threatened to escape Walter's tyranny by refusing to resist it, I have suggested, and it is possible to argue that he keeps testing her because, given his view of selfhood and power, her behavior can only seem to him unmotivated, implausible, irritating, and even inhuman. As the Clerk says after the second trial, Walter "wondered" at his wife's patience; if he had not known better, he would have thought that she took some perverse or treacherous delight in seeing her children murdered (687–95). Modern readers have also frequently complained that Griselda was not a good mother. There is certainly a way in which Griselda's behavior is, I believe, both perverse and treacherous, not because she fails to protect her children against paternal infanticide and thus to live up to ideals of motherhood but because she lives up all too well to ideals of womanhood. Walter cannot and does not solve the mystery or negate the threat that her womanly behavior poses—he merely stops trying to do so and stops giving his wife the chance to act in ways he cannot understand or control. Just as she remains a mystery and a threat to Walter, so too Griselda remains an unresolved problem for the Clerk and for his audiences. The *Clerk's Tale* suggests, and generations of modern interpreters confirm, that Griselda is a "humanly unintelligible" entity,[5] as one critic puts it, comprehensible and coherent only at the allegorical level that the Clerk at once entertains and undermines, as we shall see. The problem she presents—the unintelligibility of the perfectly good woman, or of any woman—is the most threatening thing about her; Griselda's archetypally feminine position thus marks not only the absence and silence and powerlessness of "real" women in history but also the limits of power for masculine authority (Walter), for the male author (the Clerk), and for the audience attempting to fix the "meaning" of the character and the Tale.

"Grisilde is deed, and eek hire pacience"

Viewed as a poem about either a woman's subversive silence or her silenced subversion, the *Clerk's Tale* thus affirms two central conclusions about masculine and feminine power in Western culture. It suggests that "maleness," as Catharine MacKinnon has put it, is "a form of power that is both omnipotent and non-existent, an unreal thing with very real consequences."[6] It also explains why "woman" is of necessity defined as an equivocal, troublesome figure, at once utterly powerless and fundamentally threatening. Such conclusions, however, do not resolve a further question that many modern readers, even though we ought perhaps to know better, insist on asking in one way or another: so what was "Chaucer's" attitude toward women? Does he sanction or criticize the gender system that is so oppressive to women, and whose workings he so clearly seems to understand? For reasons that will I hope become clearer, I do not think we can answer this question. More accurately, I think that the *Clerk's Tale,* like all of Chaucer's work, offers a thoroughly and deliberately ambiguous answer. Still, I do think that asking the question is nevertheless a necessary and useful first step in understanding something more about the strategy of male authors who speak through or in sympathy with female characters.

Turning the focus of my reading of the *Clerk's Tale* 180 degrees now, I want to suggest that the ambiguity of the Tale is most fruitfully read as a reflex of the narrator's position as a male poet and hence of his necessarily equivocal attitude toward women and power. In an important sense, this is not a poem about women at all, and it certainly offers no solution to the problems faced by human beings bound to debilitating definitions of femaleness. It is, rather, a poem about men and, like so many of Chaucer's poems, about the men who tell and listen to stories about women. In the second half of this paper, I support and flesh out this claim by comparing the subtle Clerk of the *Canterbury Tales* with another male narrator more obviously related in a problematic way to his female characters, the poet of Chaucer's earlier *Legend of Good Women.* In conclusion I suggest that the carefully constructed ambiguity of both poems with regard to the question of women and power is in fact a strategic equivocation that empowers the male poet while (and through) affirming the powerlessness of the female with whose position he sympathizes and which he usurps.

Comparison of the *Clerk's Tale* and the *Legend of Good Women* is authorized by the text of the *Canterbury Tales.* The Legends are directly invoked in the preface to the *Man of Law's Tale,* a poem which in the most common ordering of the Tales comes right before the *Wife of Bath's Tale,* to which the Clerk in turn is responding. The link between the Man of Law's and the Clerk's tales is reinforced by the fact that both are female saints' lives, bracketing and containing the Wife's monstrous tale of feminine misrule, and the Clerk emphasizes this point by directly alluding to the Man of Law's heroine, Constance, twice—once when Walter says

Griselda is "constant as a wal" (1047) and once when the Clerk says that
we should all be, like Griselda, "constant in adversitee" (1146). The anal-
ogies between the virtuous Constance and Griselda in the *Canterbury
Tales* and the female saints of the *Legend of Good Women* are obvious. All
these women are archetypally passive. They put the love of a man above
all other responsibilities, even life itself. As a direct consequence of this
"love" they endure great suffering. (The heroines of the earlier poem, of
course, almost all die; Griselda's survival may thus indicate either a
"flaw" in her goodness or the story's need to punish and contain her
perfection.) The unremarked similarities between the narrator of the
Legends and the Clerk, I would argue, are equally obvious and perhaps
even more telling. Three prominent features of their performances war-
rant comparison: the ostensible circumstances under which they tell their
stories, the changes they make in their sources, and their closural strategies.

In both the *Legend of Good Women* and the *Canterbury Tales,* the audience
is made privy to specific circumstances or preconditions, outside and
prior to the narratives of good women, that occasion each act of storytelling and hence oblige us to speculate about the motives and attitudes of
the poet/dreamer of the earlier poem and the Clerk of Oxenford and to
see each narrator's voiced "personality" as part of the "meaning" of his
fiction. Chaucer, as others have noted, seems to be dramatizing again and
again what we might call the inherent bias in all verbal utterances, in all
literary texts.[7] The Legends are framed by a dream vision in which the
speaker, identified as the translator of the *Romance of the Rose* and the
author of a poem about Criseyde (G. 255–66), meets Cupid in a field of
daisies. The God of Love compares the dreamer unfavorably with a
worm (G. 2433–44); then Cupid harshly rebukes the dreamer for his en-
mity to the religion of Love and for betraying women by telling the story
of one who was unfaithful (Criseyde) instead of the many more, available
in literary accounts, who were good and true to Love. Cupid's wrath
is assuaged by Alcestis, the queen who accompanies him, and who,
like queens in the *Knight's Tale* and the *Wife of Bath's Tale,* intercedes on
behalf of the accused male. She decrees that the poet's penance for his
"trespas" will be to spend most of the rest of his life writing "a gloryous
legende / Of goode women, maydenes and wyves, / That were trewe in
lovynge al here lyves" (G. 473–75) and of the false men who betrayed
them. Cupid agrees to the punishment and departs; the dreamer, either
awake or still asleep, begins to serve his sentence by composing the *Legend of Cleopatra.*

In the *Canterbury Tales,* not in a dream but in the framing matter of his tale, the Clerk is also commanded to tell a story—"Telle us som murie thyng of aventures" (15)—by the Host, a figure who like Cupid assumes godlike powers of judgment and behaves like a tyrant. The Host first makes fun of the Clerk's unaggressive, even effeminate behavior—"Ye ryde as coy and stille as dooth a mayde / Were newe spoused, sittynge at the bord" (2–3)—and reminds the Clerk that he agreed to submit to the Host's authority when he entered into the "pley." The Clerk's professional status is also underscored by the Host's prohibitions against an overly didactic or boring tale in the "heigh style" associated with learned clerks. In the Wife of Bath's prologue (separated from the *Clerk's Tale* only by the *Friar's* and *Summoner's Tales*), of course, clerks in general, again like the poet/dreamer of the *Legend of Good Women,* have already been associated with literary antifeminism and castigated for it. The Clerk appears to accede more meekly to the tyrant's commands than the dreamer does—just as we would expect from the quiet, virtuous, willing learner we met in the General Prologue. Even before the tale proper begins, however, the coy Clerk subtly defies the Host's orders by translating, within an ostensibly disparaging framework ("Me thynketh it a thyng impertinent," 54) almost all of Petrarch's "prohemye" to the story. This is presumably just the kind of elevated, clerkly speech that the Host hoped to forestall, and its inclusion clearly suggests that this Clerk has his own share of the impertinence he displaces onto Petrarch, that crafty impudence associated with others of his profession throughout the *Canterbury Tales.*

If we are obliged to recognize even before we begin to listen to their stories that both the Clerk and the poet/dreamer of the *Legend of Good Women* have on these particular occasions of storytelling similar axes to grind, their subsequent representations of good women confirm the wary reader's suspicions that, as in all literature, bias and resentment and special pleading color the stories. The Clerk, as we shall see, covers himself and his motives more cleverly than the poet/dreamer of the *Legends* (or other storytellers, like the Wife of Bath and the Pardoner); he is so discreet, in fact, that at least one modern critic sees his performance as "a rarefied act of literary-critical wit," executed not in the "voiced style" of the other Canterbury pilgrims but in the manner of Petrarch himself, as "man *of letters,* a posited ideal character, created, displayed, and caught only in the act of writing."[8] This argument represents the Clerk's *intentions* quite accurately, but his alleged neutrality does not stand up to close inspection of the apparently "minor" additions and revisions the Clerk makes to his two apparent sources, Petrarch's Latin version of Boccaccio's Griselda story and an anonymous French translation of Petrarch. In one early addition, for instance, the Clerk aims a direct blow at the Wife of Bath by supplementing the original description of Griselda with these lines:

> No likerous lust was thurgh hire herte yronne.
> Wel ofter of the welle than of the tonne
> She drank. . . .
>
> [214–16]

No such comment is found in either the Latin or the French version of the story, and it must recall to attentive listeners the Wife's self-proclaimed drinking and sexual habits and particularly her observation that "a likerous mouth moste han a likerous tayl" (III.466). In light of the insults that the Wife hurled at clerks as a profession and at Janekyn in particular, the Clerk's allusion cannot seem accidental or innocent, and so too the subject matter of his tale—the story of a patient, submissive married woman who is faithful to one husband despite his insufferable exercise of *maistrie*—must be interpreted by the audiences of the *Tales* as a central part of the interpersonal, "voiced" drama of the poem as a whole.

In another set of additions and revisions, the Clerk's strategy may again be profitably compared to the narrator's in the *Legend of Good Women*. The latter's rich and subtle play with the earlier stories and traditional reputations of his heroine is too complex to detail adequately here. I have argued elsewhere that alterations in all of the Legends consistently reshape the heroines into figures like the narrator's Cleopatra, less active, aggressive, and passionate, or like his Thisbe, less noble, more flawed and feminine.[9] So too, as J. Burke Severs notes, Walter in the Chaucerian version is "more obstinately wilful, more heartlessly cruel," while Griselda's "gentleness, her meekness, her submissiveness" are more pronounced.[10] Together, these changes call attention, as do alterations in the Legends, to the heroine's powerlessness with respect to a ruthless, self-centered, all but omnipotent man with whom she is in love and hence to her victimization. Griselda's suffering, no matter how we view its "meaning," arises specifically from the actions of a "cruel," deliberate, and decidedly male oppressor. At the same time, the Clerk's version of the Griselda story, like the poet/dreamer's treatments of his good women, stresses the heroine's archetypal femaleness, as Petrarch certainly does not. Note, for instance, this minor change in Walter's motivation: according to the Clerk, what he is seeking and testing in his wife is not her patience or obedience or ability to live up to her vows, but her "wommanhede." Whereas in Petrarch (as in the anonymous French version) Walter is said to admire her "virtutem eximiam supra sexum supraque etatem" ("a virtue beyond her sex and age"),[11] the Clerk gives us Walter

> Commendynge in his herte hir wommanhede,
> And eek hir vertu, passynge any wight
> Of so yong age.
>
> [239–41]

The "translation" effectively alters the entire thrust of the passage; Griselda still transcends her youth, but notably she does not transcend the expected limitations of gender. Instead she exemplifies, first and foremost, what has become an almost holy ideal, in the *Clerk's Tale* as in the *Legend of Good Women:* the abstraction of certain gender-specific characteristics into the ideal state of "wommanhede." After Griselda passes her last test, Walter reiterates his motivation:

> "I have doon this deede
> For no malice, ne for no crueltee,
> But for t'assaye in thee thy wommanheede."
>
> [1073–75]

Again his self-justifying claim, original to the Clerk's version, brings Griselda into line with the heroines of the Legends as type and embodiment of the idealized good woman.

In another set of even more obvious additions to his source materials, his own intrusive comments on the characters' behavior, the Clerk also underscores the issues of gender and marital conflict so central to the *Legend of Good Women.* Just as Walter celebrates Griselda for her "wommanhede," the Clerk repeatedly notes that Walter's behavior is typical of a certain kind of "housbonde" or "wedded" man (698, 622) who needlessly tries his "wyf" (452, 461) and her "wyfhod" (699—note that in this line "wyfhod" is mentioned before "stedefastnesse," just as in 239–40 "wommanhede" precedes "vertu"). In another original comment, after drawing a direct analogy between Griselda and Job in line 932, the Clerk observes:

> but as in soothfastnesse,
> Though clerkes preise wommen but a lite,
> Ther kan no man in humblesse hym acquite
> As womman kan, ne kan been half so trewe
> As wommen been, but it be falle of newe.
>
> [934–38]

This particular "moral" to the story—just one of many that we will be offered—is found nowhere in Chaucer's sources; the superiority of women to men, especially in their humility and fidelity, is, however, the main point that the narrator of the *Legend of Good Women* has been commanded to make. The qualifying, tonally odd turn at the end of the Clerk's comment—no man can be as humble or half as true as woman can, "unless it's just happened recently," is also reminiscent of the odd jokes that the poet/dreamer often throws off at the end of his legends.

Moreover, the Clerk's implicit separation of himself from those other clerks who "preise wommen but a lite" is, I suggest, part of his attempt to show himself sympathetic to the cause of women, even at the expense of professional solidarity. So too in an earlier intrusion he poses a rhetorical question to the female members of his audience:

> But now of wommen wolde I axen fayn
> If thise assayes myghte nat suffise?
> [696–97]

The Clerk's strategy is remarkably similar to the poet/dreamer's attempts in the *Legend of Good Women* to ingratiate himself with women and demonstrate his unique sympathy with their gender. Despite his apparent eagerness to side with women, however, and to show himself, like the Clerk, innocent of the antifeminist charges that have been lodged against him, the narrator of the martyrology identifies with "us men," as he puts it at the end of *Thisbe*. Like all members of his gender (which he appears to regard, like the opposite sex, as a unitary class), he is naturally inclined to fool "ye wemen" whenever possible. His increasing boredom with his good women, culminating in his inability to complete the poem, is just one more piece of evidence of the narrator's allegiances, his inability to transcend, in the war between the sexes, the bias of his gender.

This inability is shared, I suggest, by the poet/dreamer's figurative son and heir, the Clerk of Oxenford. As we have seen, the heroine he constructs, unlike her prototype in Petrarch, is the epitome of *wommanhede,* and the Clerk, despite his efforts to deny that he is the epitome of *clerkhede,* to condemn needless male cruelty and to sympathize with the archvictim of patriarchal tyranny, is finally not able to distance himself from a specifically masculine attitude toward feminine virtue. The fact that the Clerk's perspective is not morally universal, as many modern critics have assumed,[12] not actually sympathetic to women,[13] and not, as Middleton and others claim, artistically neutral, is dramatically confirmed at the conclusion of the tale, where what we might call the excess of endings has the same effect as the apparent incompletion of the *Legend of Good Women*. Although they appear to close in such radically different ways, both endings are definitely and strategically equivocal, designed to compound the reader's uncertainty about the "meaning" of the narratives, about the narrators' respective attitudes toward the purposes of stories and storytelling, and especially about "Chaucer's" attitudes toward the problematic issues of gender and marital conflict.

There are several endings to the *Clerk's Tale,* and it may be useful to describe them here in some detail. The narrative itself first concludes with a completely closed and "happy" ending worthy of the most conventional nineteenth-century novel: Walter and Griselda live "ful many a yeer in heigh prosperitee"; their daughter is married to one of the worthiest lords in Italy; Walter brings Griselda's old father to court and takes care of him for the rest of his days; and Walter's son succeeds to the lordship of the land and makes a fortunate marriage (1128–37). At this point the Clerk departs briefly from Petrarch to add that Walter's son, however, did not test his noble wife, and that "this world is nat so strong . . . As it hath been in olde times yoore" (1139–40). This implicit comparison between the hardiness of wives then and now—also a comparison, of course, between the fabular or literary and the "real"—is echoed three stanzas later, where it leads directly to the Clerk's reference to the Wife of Bath and then to the Envoy. First, however, another possible ending to the story, a religious moral, is offered, prefaced by a closing call to attention, "And herkneth what this auctour seith therfoore" (1141). This moral is found in both Petrarch and the French versions: the point is not that wives should adopt Griselda's humility, but that all human beings should be as "constant in adversitee" as she is. As St. James says, God does not tempt us but causes us to suffer "as for oure excercise." The Clerk explicitly attributes this religious application of the story to Petrarch (1147) and with perhaps another subtle dig at the Host recalls, erroneously, that it was originally written in the "heigh stile" (1148).

Following this, a third conclusion to the tale is initiated with a second closing formula, "But o word, lordynges, herkneth er I go" (1163). In the next two stanzas the Clerk does precisely what he has just told his audience not to do. Returning to the notion that it would be hard "now-a-dayes" to find two or three live Griseldas in a town, he de-allegorizes the notion of "assay" from the religious interpretation of Griselda's trials to offer this comment on material women, who fall so short of the ideal female malleability his tale prescribes:

> For if that they were put to swiche assayes,
> The gold of hem hat now so badde alayes
> With bras, that thogh the coyne be fair at ye,
> It wolde rather breste a-two than plye.
> [1166–69]

He then goes on to dedicate a blessing (in contradistinction to the Wife's parting curse) and a song—the Envoy—to the Wife of Bath and "al hire secte," who are implicitly presented as living examples of that superficially fair coin that will not bend. With a third parting call to attention—"Herkneth my song that seith in this manere" (1176)—as if he realized that our minds may well be wandering or at least confused by this plethora of contradictory conclusions and applications of his tale, the Clerk (or Chaucer?)[14] offers what now stands as the last ending to the text, the Envoy. Here of course, as in the preceding two stanzas, he directly engages in the ongoing dramatic interaction at the level of the pilgrimage and links the story he has told to the question of marital sovereignty. Now treating his heroine not as a paradigm for all humanity but as a historically real character, dissociable from her ideal virtue, he reminds husbands that "Grisilde is deed, and eek hire pacience, / And bothe atones buryed in Ytaille" (1177–78) and warns them that they will fail if they test their wives. Turning to "noble wyves," he advises them not to let any clerks tell a story about them like the story of Griselda. In the remaining stanzas he presents, clearly with tongue in cheek, advice couched as the most extreme version possible of the Wife's already extreme philosophy of female dominance. The Clerk's explicit disclaimer two lines before the beginning of the Envoy—"lat us stynte of ernestful matere" (1175)—explicitly encourages us with Middleton and others to see this as "play," but together with the tale he has told, the cruel exaggeration of the Wife's enormities in the Envoy must be also seen as perhaps the most serious revelation of the Clerk's not finally so hidden agenda in his performance as a whole. The Clerk's turnabout wants to look either playful or deranged, but it is serious and strategic. The Clerk (or Chaucer) preempts the voice of the opposition by exaggerating and satirizing the only response that a subversive female speaker like the Wife of Bath could offer to his story. The Wife is silenced and disarmed by this masculine impersonation of her voice—just as Griselda is made deaf and dumb when Walter suddenly undergoes a dramatic reversal and agrees that Griselda has proved her worth and can stop suffering.

The conflict, moreover, between a "religious" interpretation, in which Griselda is seen as emblematic of the human soul, and a more "realistic" reading, in which she is viewed as the ideal woman and wife and hence as a victim, has been intensified in the alterations the Clerk makes throughout the tale; this conflict, which has been the central problem for many modern readers, is not resolved but heightened in the conclusion, as inconclusive as the *Legend of Good Women* by virtue not of its incompletion but of its abrupt shifts in tone, its anticlimactic repetition and self-contradiction. As other readers have suggested, although to different ends, we are therefore obliged to consider that such conflict and inconclusiveness are in fact the "point" of the performance as a whole.[15] The heightened religious symbolism of the Clerk's version of the Griselda story coexists with the heightened pathos of her sufferings as a "real" human being, and more specifically with her plight as a female victim of male marital tyranny, because this is the *Clerk's* tale, and the Clerk's motives in telling it, which we are forced by the framing "facts," by his own internal commentary, and by the Envoy to consider as an integral part of its meaning, are complex, contradictory, and deliberately obscured. It may be suggested that the Clerk needs to release what we might term his repressed sexual aggression and to defend himself and his profession from the subversive attacks of the Wife of Bath. If this is the case, he does so, as I have suggested, in a much more subtle and clever way than the Host might or the Merchant does: by disassociating himself from the kind of anti-feminist clerical narrator that the Wife has so tellingly portrayed in Janekyn and his book; by showing his idealization of and sympathy with a paradigm of female virtue; by exposing and decrying her victimization at the hands of a tyrannical husband; by rewarding Griselda's brand of female virtue with the allegedly happy, fruitful marriage to a forceful but loving man that the Wife of Bath so wanted and so clearly failed to find; and finally by cleverly suggesting that after all he is above a merely literal or personal response to the tale's pathos and distanced by his superior learning from the whole field of sexual warfare. The happy ending for Griselda, together with the dignity she retains throughout her trials, is the masterstroke of the Clerk's strategy, making his bias and aggression more difficult to spot than the narrator's in the *Legend of Good Women,* where the dangers of the clerical and literary idealization of women are much more readily seen. Tellingly, however, and like many of his fellow pilgrims, the Clerk does not stop talking quite soon enough. Contradiction at the end of the tale is a clear signal that this teller is not in perfect control and not any more aesthetically or philosophically or morally removed from the "real" uses of literary texts than other men whose anti-feminism often takes the subtle form of celebrating and hence prescribing ideal female behavior.

A comparison of the *Clerk's Tale* and the *Legend of Good Women* with respect to their narrators thus confirms, I submit, that these are both poems about the masculine imagination and that when we ask whether they are anti- or profeminist—a question that both texts, of course, invite us to raise—we fall into a neatly laid trap from which there is no escape. The poems are neither for nor against the cause of women's equality because, as I have argued, they are poems about men, and more specifically, about male poets. Here, as another feminist reader has recently observed, we watch the figure of the poet and his heroes as they "enter ideology and inherit its privilege."[16] As he is conscribed into ideology, the male poet, according to Chaucer, is *both* pro- and antifeminist in certain critical respects. The Clerk's empathy with women, for instance, may be suspect, but his identification with the feminine position and hence his insight into the nature of oppression is probably "genuine." As a figure for the poet, as a man whose manhood is openly questioned, as a young unbeneficed cleric, the Clerk occupies a marginal and insecure position in the dominant culture, the hearty heterosexual world organized and ruled by the Host of the *Canterbury Tales*. Like his heroine, as others have noted, the Clerk is patient and idealized, although like Griselda too his apparently submissive behavior can be subversive of the Host's demands. At the same time, I have suggested, the Clerk's antifeminism is hard to argue away and is more disturbing and effectual than less subtle varieties.

Speaking now of that elusive and finally nonexistent position or voice that we must crudely call "Chaucer," I want to affirm the distance between "Chaucer" and the Clerk, although I am not sure we can or should even begin to estimate how great that distance is. To the extent that Chaucer both is and is not the Clerk, he manages at once to write about his limitations and his bias with a self-scrutiny, an ironic self-reflexivity, that we cannot help admiring and hence at the same time to imply that he has in some sense escaped them. (Like Griselda, again, he transcends apparent limits because he admits to perceiving and accepting them.) Equivocation about the "woman" question is the most salient feature of his persona, the one that most clearly seems to validate our sense of "Chaucer's" ability to see both sides of an issue, to sympathize with victims and victimizers, and simultaneously to understand and critique the misogyny of his world. This equivocation fosters, then, the well-known myth of the great artist's androgyny or transcendence. Furthermore, this myth about the artist's escape from the prison house of gender in turn offers a strategic place, at once decentered and all encompassing, in which the male poet in patriarchal culture, in retreat from tyrannical forces that would subjugate and silence his own subversive voice, can situate himself. Disguised, but not completely successfully, as a pro-feminist (and in other tales as a female impersonator), the male poet thus disarms the threat that misogyny entails for men, like Walter, who fail to understand and control the dangerous power of the feminine behavior they have defined as "acceptable." The incompletion of the disguise, however, readily affirms the poet's proper maleness, as the reaction of the audience characterized in the text itself suggests. In the link between the *Clerk's Tale* and the *Merchant's Tale,* for instance, Chaucer supplies us with the Host's enthusiastic response to the story of Griselda, which he wishes his wife could hear. The Merchant, another manly man, begins the next Tale in the series by comparing his own shrewish wife to Griselda. The Host and the Merchant have been accused of distorting the *Clerk's Tale,* [17] and indeed they do simply ignore the Clerk's halfhearted and clearly ambivalent warning that we should view Griselda not as a woman but as a figure for the human soul. Their response, however, biased as it may be, is in fact invited by the Clerk's presentation. The audience outside the poem may be more alert to the Tale's subtleties, but we are not able to fix its significance in a completely persuasive way either. The Clerk offers manly men a comforting (if unreal) example of how both virtuous and vicious women alike may be silenced, and at the same time dooms more skillful and high-minded interpreters to failure in their efforts to pin down the politics and the meaning of his Tale, and the identity and intention of its equivocal author. The male poet thus realizes the powers of silence and unintelligibility that he usurps from and must finally deny to his female heroines.

Notes

1. John H. Fisher, ed., *The Complete Poetry and Prose of Geoffrey Chaucer* (New York, 1977), p. 145.

2. All quotations from the *Canterbury Tales* and the *Legend of Good Women* are from *The Works of Geoffrey Chaucer*, ed. F. N. Robinson, 2d ed. (Boston, 1957). I will give line numbers for passages from the *Clerk's Tale* parenthetically, without citing fragment (IV) or group (E).

3. For a discussion of Chaucer's relation to the antifeminist tradition as it emerges in "images . . . which celebrate, with a precision often subtle rather than apparent, the forms a woman's goodness is to take," see Hope Phyllis Weissman, "Antifeminism and Chaucer's Characterizations of Women," in *Geoffrey Chaucer: A Collection of Original Articles*, ed. George D. Economou (New York, 1975), pp. 93–110.

4. See the *Oxford English Dictionary*, s.v. "rue," v. 1, sense 7.

5. Marsha Siegel, "Placing Griselda's Exemplary Value by Way of the *Franklin's Tale*" (Paper presented at International Congress on Medieval Studies, Kalamazoo, May 1982).

6. Catharine A. MacKinnon, "Feminism, Marxism, Method, and the State: An Agenda for Theory," *Signs* 7 (1982):543.

7. As Myra Jehlen puts it in "Archimedes and the Paradox of Feminist Criticism," *Signs* 6 (1981):575–601, "as a way of judging the literary work per se, exposing its bias is essentially beside the point. Not that literature, as the New Critics once persuaded us, transcends subjectivity or politics. Paradoxically, it is just because the fictional universe is wholly subjective and therefore ideological that the value of its ideology is almost irrelevant to its literary value" (p. 578). Robert B. Burlin, in *Chaucerian Fiction* (Princeton, 1977), nicely summarizes Chaucer's specific and pervasive understanding of the subjectivity of all literature: "Whatever the narrative method, these works all testify to a strong sense on Chaucer's part of the unavoidable implication of the teller in the thematic import

of his fiction. The idea that a story could have a meaning independent of and unaffected by the formulations of its narrator is a naive assumption that Chaucer thought better left to the fictional storytellers themselves and perhaps a few in his own audience" (p. 82).

8. Anne Middleton, "The Clerk and His Tale: Some Literary Contexts," *Studies in the Age of Chaucer* 2 (1980):149.

9. For a more complete discussion of this point and others in the Legends, see my "Irony and the Antifeminist Narrator in Chaucer's *Legend of Good Women,*" *JEGP* 82 (1983):11–31.

10. *The Literary Relationships of Chaucer's Clerk's Tale* (New Haven, 1942), pp. 231, 233.

11. I take the Latin quotation from the convenient edition of Petrarch's *Epistolae Seniles,* Book XVII, Letter 3 (with a facing edition of *Le livre Griseldis*) in *Sources and Analogues of Chaucer's Canterbury Tales,* ed. W. F. Bryan and Germaine Dempster (Chicago, 1941), pp. 296–331. The text of Petrarch's version is translated in Robert Dudley French, *A Chaucer Handbook* (New York, 1927), pp. 291–311.

12. The assumption that the Clerk's answer to the Wife of Bath presents the obviously sensible, beautiful, and "universal" refutation of the Wife's obviously irrational, monstrous, and one-sided argument, her blatantly ridiculous perversion of "what is commonly thought true and proper in an ideal wife" [Jerome Taylor, "*Frounceys Petrak* and the *Logyk* of Chaucer's Clerk," in *Francis Petrarch Six Centuries Later: A Symposium,* ed. Aldo Scaglione, North Carolina Studies in the Romance Languages and Literatures: Symposia 3 (Chapel Hill, 1975), p. 381], need not be fully documented here, since in a variety of forms it is the standard, purportedly "historical" reading. For a sampling of different approaches and conclusions, all based on this fundamental premise, see S. K. Heninger, Jr., "The Concept of Order in Chaucer's *Clerk's Tale,*" *JEGP* 56 (1957):382–95; Thomas H. Jameson, "One Up for Clerks," *Arts and Sciences* (Winter 1964–65):10–13; Lynn Staley Johnson, "The Prince and His People: A Study of the Two Covenants in the *Clerk's Tale,*" *Chaucer Review* 10 (1975–76):17–29; Alfred Kellogg, "The Evolution of the *Clerk's Tale,*" in *Chaucer, Langland, Arthur: Essays in Middle English Literature* (New Brunswick, N.J., 1972), pp. 276–329; Patrick Morrow, "The Ambivalence of Truth: Chaucer's 'Clerkes Tale,'" *Bucknell Review* 16 (1968):74–90; Irving N. Rothman, "Humility and Obedience in the *Clerk's Tale,* with the Envoy Considered as an Ironic Affirmation," *Papers in Language and Literature* 9 (1973):115–27; Jerome Taylor, *Frounceys Petrak.*

13. For this reading of the tale, see, e.g., Harriet Hawkin, "The Victim's Side: Chaucer's *Clerk's Tale* and Webster's *Duchess of Malfi,*" *Signs* 1(1975):339–61; Velma Richmond, "Pacience in Adversitee: Chaucer's Presentation of Marriage," *Viator* 10 (1979):323–54; and J. Mitchell Morse, "The Philosophy of the Clerk of Oxenford," *Modern Language Quarterly* 19 (1958):3–20, who believes that the Clerk "at heart . . . was on the side of the Wife of Bath" (p. 4), although "a man of such a conventional attitude toward women could not altogether disapprove of Griselda's invincible 'wyfhod' and 'stedfastnesse'" (p. 19).

14. The scribal heading of these final stanzas (1177–1212), "Lenvoy de Chau-

cer," suggests that this passage is spoken by the author rather than the Clerk, and John Koch argues for such a reading (*Anglia* 50 [1926], 65). Robinson disagrees and states in his note on this passage: "It belongs dramatically to the clerk, and is entirely appropriate" (p. 712).

15. For other readings like Richard Lanham's (see "Chaucer's *Clerk's Tale:* The Poem, Not the Myth," *Literature and Psychology* 16 [1966]:157–65) that locate "meaning" in the contradictions and tensions the Clerk brings to his story, see Dolores Warwick Frese, "Chaucer's *Clerk's Tale:* The Monsters and the Critics Reconsidered," *Chaucer Review* 8 (1973):133–46; Warren Ginsberg, "'And Speketh so Pleyn': The Clerk's Tale and Its Teller," *Criticism* 20 (1978):307–23; Lloyd N. Jeffrey, "Chaucer's Walter: A Study in Emotional Immaturity," *Journal of Humanistic Psychology* 3 (1963):112–19; Patrick Morrow, "The Ambivalence of Truth"; J. Mitchell Morse, "The Philosophy of the Clerk"; and Robert Stepsis, "*Potentia Absoluta* and the *Clerk's Tale,*" *Chaucer Review* 10 (1975–76):129–42.

16. Janet Halley, comment on "The Literary Traffic in Women," panel presented at "Collaborations and Connections in Women's Studies Research," University of Pennsylvania, March 1985.

17. Middleton, "The Clerk and His Tale." The Host's words, in lines 1212a–g, appear in only one family of manuscripts, including the Ellesmere manuscript and Hengwrt 154. Robinson identifies them as "without doubt genuine," perhaps part of a canceled job. See also Eleanor Hammond, *Chaucer: A Bibliographical Manual* (New York, 1908), pp. 302–303, and Aage Brusendorff, *The Chaucer Tradition* (London, 1925), p. 76.

The Power of Sisterhood: Marie de France's "Le Fresne"

Michelle Freeman

The poem begins on a note of harmony, a harmony constructed of symmetries linking two knights. Two noblemen, wealthy and worthy knights, live near one another in Brittany. Each man takes a wife. Here the symmetry ends—temporarily. One wife gives birth to twin boys. The new father, wishing to share his joy with his neighbor, sends a messenger to him in order to break the news. The father has decided to send one of his sons to his friend; his purposes in so doing are phrased somewhat ambiguously, however:

> L'un li tramettra a lever:
> De sun nun le face nomer.
> [Ll. 17–18][1]

Do these lines mean that the child will be sent to the neighbor in order for the knight to give him a name at baptism, *lever* having the meaning, according to Rychner's *Glossary,* of "to hold over the baptismal font, in the role of godfather"; or "to give the child his [i.e., the neighbor's and godfather's] name" at that time? The antecedent of *sun* is not clear. Or does the text mean that the child will be sent to the knight to be raised as well as named by him? In any case the knight is pleased for his friend and thanks God for his neighbor's good fortune.

His wife, meanwhile, smiles and wonders aloud—hers are the first words of direct discourse in the text—what the neighbor has intended in communicating the news of his shame and dishonor: she purposefully decides to interpret the birth of twins as always signifying that the mother is adulterous. As she avers, different men must have fathered the two children (ll. 31–42).[2]

The gloss placed by the second wife on the twin birth may have been motivated by her feeling that her own barrenness was rendered all the more obvious by the neighbor's producing not one but two male children. She may also have feared that the arrival at her household of one of the boys—and his taking her husband's name?—would make definitive her failure to provide her husband with a proper heir, with a child to bear and continue his name. Indeed, could not these fearsome possibilities lead to her dismissal and to annulment of the marriage, to her being—as her daughter will later be—traded in for a fruitful second wife? In speaking out against the innocent wife whose good fortune menaces her, she is indirectly arguing, I believe, that a faithful wife, though barren, is superior to a fruitful but adulterous one. The barren wife's words against the woman who has given birth disrupt everything. Her speech has thwarted the original storyline and the fruit it could have borne. The jealous wife falsified another's story, rewriting it through her misapplication of gloss, so as better to exploit matters in her own self-defense.

The symmetry of events, despite the wife's words, does continue, but with a twist, since the lady soon gives birth to twin girls. Because of her speech, however, the birth is viewed in a context different from that in which it would otherwise have been seen. The mother regards the birth as a direct consequence of her own words, as a just punishment for her calumny, which puts her in the unfair position in which she had placed her neighbor. An ironic dimension has thus been added to the process of symmetrical structuring. In the lady's second quoted speech, a lament uttered in private but within the hearing of her women servants, we listen to the ending of a minifable: the poetic justice meted out to the villainess, with the appropriate lesson drawn. The lesson, however, is articulated by the transgressor herself rather than by an all-knowing and somewhat removed narrator:

> "Sur mei en est turnez li pis!
> Ki sur autrui mesdit e ment
> Ne seit mie qu'a l'oil li pent;
> De tel hume peot l'um parler
> Ki meuz de lui fet a loër."

> "The worst has befallen me!
> He who calumniates and lies about another
> Is completely unaware of what lies before him;
> One may gossip about someone
> Who is better fit for praise than oneself."
> [Ll. 86–90]

This lady refuses, however, to submit to any higher authority. She once again insists on taking matters into her own hands, rewriting her role at least as far as the public is allowed to perceive it. She doctors appearances so as to mask reality and thus avoid judgment. Once more she violates a text, one that would now be falsely glossed by all, or so she fears, because of her prior misinterpretation. This time she strikes deeper, tampering with the text itself, in order to influence the application of gloss. The lady wishes to protect herself, that is, her reputation and status, by murdering one of the two children. She has recognized her previous sin, but instead of making retribution for it, she decides to compound her fault with the crime of infanticide.[3]

By glossing the text publicly in this manner, the lady seems to have misapplied a certain womanly *escïence* (or knowledge) concerning birth and sexuality in order to devalue another woman. Her speaking the hidden but false meaning of the text publicly has the consequence that many hear it and that the pronouncement is many times repeated. This multiple recounting, however, results ironically in its author's—and not its protagonist's—condemnation. The female community of Brittany, who consider that the lady's knowledgeable judgment against one specific woman potentially threatens all womankind, collectively come to hate her for her infringement of womanly solidarity (ll. 49–56).

The servant women refuse to permit the gruesome solution to be carried out. One in particular suggests an alternative. She is the first in a series of women who act as surrogate or adoptive mothers to the jeopardized child—individual women who carry and/or care for the girl, hide her, and preserve her from harm. They participate in the mother's plan to conceal the child, to keep her true identity a secret (although most do not refrain from relating their roles in the infant's history to some other person). The servant girl persuades the mother that, by following the scheme she proposes, the lady will not be dishonored because she will never have to confront the child again. The servant promises to leave the baby in a church where some good man (*produm*, l. 115) will be bound to find her and take her in as his own. This, however, is not exactly what eventually does take place.

Together, the women wrap the little girl in fine linen, placing over her a "paile roé," the finest they had ever seen, which the child's father had brought back from Constantinople. This cloth, made either of gold or of silk, is woven (or possibly embroidered) with circular designs. Among its related meanings, *roé* counts as a synonym for *rodné,* a term used to designate a pregnant woman (or "round belly").[4] Since this cloth will be so closely associated with Le Fresne and the uncovering of her true identity, I cannot help but conclude that the superlatives used in its description also apply metonymically to the child it protects. A gold ring set with a *jagunce* (a precious gem known as jacinth)—a love token exchanged between husband and wife before their marriage—is laced to the child's arm as well.[5] The two objects, gifts from the father to the mother, are the two signs the daughter will bear in order to indicate to those who find her that she is of noble birth. The mother had received and saved these two presents as she had received the father's two children. Now one daughter will carry away with her these signs of class that are tokens of the father, relics of his love story and possibly of his prowess as a crusader. Unlike her mother, she chooses never to abandon these gifts, never to forget them or what they mean. She keeps them with her always, never separating the two items except on her lover's wedding day in order to do him and his new bride honor. In sacrificing one of the objects that preserves her veiled history, Le Fresne will make it possible for that history to emerge clearly and for the sisters finally to be reunited.

The servant girl does carry the day-old child all night long through a forest out to a town where she comes upon a convent, complete with nuns and their abbess, the narrator informs us, a kind of "cité des dames." Because of the fiction of her foundling status, the best life an aristocratic female in Le Fresne's position could hope for was, of course, a place in a nunnery.[6]

The servant prays to God to keep the child from harm; it is significant that the prayer is quoted verbatim and that, as if in answer to the servant's request, she notices the ash tree, the *fresne*, which is

> lé e branchu,
> E mut espés e bien ramu;
> En quatre furs esteit quarrez
> Pur umbre fere i fu plantez.

> broad and spreading,
> Thick with leaves and branches;
> It was split into four forks
> And was planted to give shade.
> [Ll. 167–70]

She places the baby wrapped in the cloth within the forks of the tree, commends her to God, and returns to her mistress to relate what she must now consider to be the end of the story.

The *portier*, or gatekeeper, of the convent, upon noticing the rich cloth, at first believes it to be stolen goods that a thief has hidden. And stolen goods they indeed are, stolen from the father, placed in the tree to be hidden from him but also to be found by another father. The gatekeeper discovers the baby, rejoices over the child, and brings her to his own daughter, a widow with an infant of her own. She bathes, warms, and suckles the child—performing those actions that would normally follow the birth of the child that we did not see described when the baby was born. Thus this woman ensures the child's natural life and makes of her a kind of twin by adoption to her own baby, a "soeur de lait," or foster sister. The father and the daughter marvel at the cloth and ring, drawing the conclusions intended. Presumably the child is of too high a station to be raised by the likes of them, so the porter bears the message of the discovery to the abbess. She orders him to carry the baby to the convent, takes a long look at her, and resolves to raise the girl in the convent. She goes so far as to admonish the gatekeeper not to speak of the circumstances of the child's being found, thereby doubling or confirming the natural mother's desire to silence the story of the child's identity. Just as the mother in her act of hiding the child endows it with objects that signify its origins, however, so the abbess, in wishing to silence the porter about the child's having been abandoned in the tree, retains that feature of her history by having the baby baptized Le Fresne, or Ash Tree.[7]

The abbess also invents the fiction that the child is her niece, the daughter of her sister or sister-in-law—we are not told which. The aunt/niece relationship might well suggest an opposition between two sisters, one of whom produces offspring whereas the other does not. Later, when the tale reveals that Le Fresne's twin has been named La Codre, or Hazel Tree, we see this dichotomy in its most emphatic form.[8]

When we think of the theme of sisterhood in this context, we cannot forget that Le Fresne will be raised in what is, after all, a community of sisters! The abbess's act of charity, her adoption, baptism, and raising of another's daughter, reminds us of the original plan of the neighbor who wished to have one of his sons sent to his childless friend to be named and educated. We recall that at that time the plan was announced by a messenger, just as here the parallel plan is concocted in the presence of the gatekeeper, who bears the joyful message of the child's surprising arrival. The patterns of symmetry persist, despite the mother's previous efforts to alter the history.

The softening of the mother's endeavors to thwart God's plans originates with the servant girl. The narrator elaborates on the background of this character, who attracts our attention during a considerable portion of the poem (some eighty lines). This young woman is "de franche orine" (l. 100), that is, of noble origin. She has been kept and raised ("gardee e nurie," l. 101) and greatly loved and cherished ("mut amee e mut cherie," l. 102) for a long time by her mistress. Consequently, we must recognize that the mother in this piece is hardly an unregenerate stock villainess; she is devoid neither of charitable impulses nor even of feelings akin to maternal love. In return for this love, the young girl wishes to comfort her mistress; she also has the wit to invent a more acceptable solution than the mother's. She devises an alternative plot for the daughter, which, however, will not be respected in every detail. She takes the "materials"—literally and figuratively—which are provided by the mother/benefactress and supplies them with new avenues of existence, all the while respecting the intentions of the mother, namely, her desire to conceal her part in the baby's life, to hide her signature because that signature will be perceived as illegitimate.

The components of this revised narrative are the gifts of the father—cloth, ring, and baby—which now find themselves transferred to what is for the most part a purely woman's world. (The chain of exchange, however, does include such males as the gatekeeper/father and later the lover. Each of these men serves as a point of transition; each introduces the girl into a new situation that brings her to a new mother in the series.) The serving maid and Le Fresne, who will herself become a serving girl, stand, opposed, at the penultimate points in the series, the one bearing the infant and gifts away from the mother, the other returning them all to her. The gatekeeper/father ferries the baby back and forth between a surrogate—and husbandless—mother, the one who sees to the child's physical needs, and the abbess, who takes charge of her spiritual and cultural education. Might not this dual mothering in fact make of these two female characters, abbess and porter's daughter, another sisterly pair, one playing the part of "la codre" and the other of "le fresne"? The tale's individual segments which feature characters who carry the child in a variety of ways are represented, I believe, by (and in) the designs of the baby's blanket, each of which is *roé,* round like the series of metaphorically pregnant mothers who carry the child. The detail of round patterns is further mirrored in the circular pattern of the narrative as a whole, which permits the mother to complete her delivery of the child into the world.

When Le Fresne matures, a lord named Gurun falls in love with her and, in order to be near her, becomes a principal benefactor of the abbey, visiting it frequently. Finally he persuades Le Fresne to run away with him; they live happily for many years in his castle until his knights intervene, pressing Gurun, because of Le Fresne's childlessness and low social status, to take an appropriate wife—a woman whom the reader recognizes as Le Fresne's twin La Codre (i.e., the fruitful Hazel Tree).

Le Fresne's acquiescence is complete, even extending so far as placing on the marriage bed the rich cloth which had wrapped her as an infant. When La Codre's mother sees and recognizes this cloth, she asks Le Fresne to explain how it came into her possession, acknowledges her child, and reveals all to her husband. The results are happy: the archbishop severs La Codre and Gurun and marries Le Fresne and her lover.

When Le Fresne returns the text and the objects to her mother, she allows her story to be removed from the private context of women, rendering it possible for her true identity to be made public, complete, and legitimate. Her unique and brief speech, a response to the mother's urgent command to explain the origins of the cloth, allows the mother to confess and make retribution for her sin. She finally assumes responsibility for her role in her daughter's life, providing Le Fresne's narrative with a suitable prologue and the possibility of one last happy detour when she cries out, "Tu es ma fille, bele amie!" (l. 450), "You are my daughter, beautiful beloved!"

At this point we may recall the scene at the narrative's opening in which the mother slanders her neighbor's wife. Both scenes take place during meals of celebration. The prevailing mood is altered in each case once the mother speaks. Both the mother, earlier, and Le Fresne, at the tale's end, are dishonored by the good fortune of another woman, a counterpart: the neighbor's wife in the first instance, and Le Fresne's sister, in the second. The unexpected occurs, however, in both cases. The mother's desire during the opening scene to maintain her status—in the eyes of male society—paradoxically brought on her debasement in the consideration of other women, whereas her later confession of guilt brings joy to all concerned.

Le Fresne's behavior occasions everyone's admiration and elicits sympathy for her plight. Her apparent infractions of the legal and moral codes are consequently pitted against the reality of her obvious natural virtue. Le Fresne's topsy-turvy presentation of virtue in lieu of law enables the mother to recount her two stories of dishonor: the widely diffused prevarication concerning the male twins' birth and the true circumstances, albeit known to only a few, attending her own maternity.

In the first scene the mother's words manufacture a triangle composed of a woman and two men—a husband and a supposed lover. In the conclusion, another triangle is created as the heroine's lover has recently become the husband of a different woman. Nature's—or God's—story will restore balance by disrupting the real triangle which had temporarily provided a parallel for the fictive one. In this the principle of symmetry, or twinness, is preserved despite the various attempts made to do away with it.

The father receives the pieced-together narrative. I use this quilting metaphor, since each woman has contributed a segment of the *vita* and has, at some time, narrated a portion of the story (with the exception of the gatekeeper's daughter; her father presumably speaks for her as well as for himself, as he duplicates the role of the messenger from the opening segment of the story). Le Fresne's father merely repeats the mother's account to his son-in-law.

Both members of the new masculine audience rejoice in the narrative and its truth. Once all the roles of the complex of female characters and narratrixes have been linked together in the one fabric of Le Fresne's life, the tale reverts to the peripheral world of the male characters. They are the ones who see to stamping the story and the heroine with the seal of approval, as it were. The father accepts his daughter; the lover, his new wife; the archbishop arranges the particulars of the annulment and remarriage.

The role of the serving maid, enacted twice, seems to enclose this female circle of narrative continuation begun by the pair composed of mistress and daughterlike servant. The outer framework for the enclosure of the feminine world of narrative transactions involves the male personages: the two knights who are neighbors at the outset of the tale and the two noblemen—father and son-in-law—who complete the reception of the history whereby all the characters occupy once again their rightful places in society. Are we not asked to infer that the role of servant at court, so privileged by this poem, is analogous to the position Marie de France adopts for herself with respect to the tales which, in the *Lais*, she preserves and to which she adds?

Despite the appearances, however necessary, of this power to make legitimate, to accept, to approve, and to name, the male characters seem to be less powerful than the parts they play might at first intimate. The husband of the wronged wife is manipulated into destroying his own and his family's happiness. The jealous wife's husband, although of a generous and charitable nature, is unable to save his daughter and is duped for a long time into believing that he has only the one child. Gurun, the lover, is unable to marry the woman he really loves because he concedes the necessity of listening to his vassals and of adopting their choice of spouse. Even the archbishop agrees to disregard the rules of the Church concerning annulments in order to obey the dictates of true love.

Comparing Marie's fiction with the motifs of the Patient Griselda story—and it certainly does have affinities with this narrative[9]—we notice immediately the weak roles played by the men in Marie's text in contradistinction to the strong network of maternal roles responsible for the fiction. These roles are reversed in the Griselda tradition, where the lord takes an apparently unsuitable wife, a peasant girl, in defiance of his subjects' wishes but in positive answer to their injunction to marry. He feigns to kill her two children in order to test her obedience to him but actually sends the children to be raised elsewhere. He also pretends to obtain an annulment from the Pope so that he might make a more suitable match. He asks his former wife to act as servant in his house while preparations are undertaken to receive his new bride. All of these trials

Griselda accepts without a murmur until her husband reveals that his behavior has been a ruse designed solely to try her. He publicly restores her children and station to her.

Power in this example rests exclusively with the man, with his right to defy those whom he rules and to justify that right by virtue of his indisputable authority and competence to judge correctly. His right and his ability to rule are mirrored in his wife's capacity for taking abuse—disguised as obedience—and in the control she exercises over her feelings and over her natural instincts as a mother."[10] As Chaucer himself concluded in the *Clerk's Tale,* this heroic example is in part meant to teach Christian acceptance of God's will. Although a female protagonist is ostensibly at the heart of his story, her conflicts serve above all to ensure the legitimacy of the lord and his ordering of society.

The contrary seems to prevail, however, in Marie's "Le Fresne." For one thing, despite a wife's rebellion, God's plans appear to be fulfilled, thanks to a daughter's exercise of freedom and initiative. In the Old French poem the testing of the heroine's loyalty and love is not based on law at all. Le Fresne's love, obedience, and silence in the face of adversity are freely given; they do not constitute mere examples of obedience to a vow. Her unexplained acts of self-effacement mystify the reader. Nevertheless, precisely this loving nature of hers, acting outside the confines of legal code, provides the lynchpin holding together this uniquely feminine version of the Griselda story, and Marie's stroke of genius invented it.[11]

In her poem there is no test per se; the lover is not at all in control of his own situation. Unlike the lord in Petrarch's, Boccaccio's, or Chaucer's tales, Gurun is manipulated by his men; he does not possess the courage to choose a socially unacceptable wife—though, as we know, Le Fresne is worthy in every way. He cannot call a halt to the plot's twists and turns, to his own and his beloved's suffering, by revealing, as do his fourteenth-century analogues, that his new wife-to-be is in actuality his own daughter. The lover is not on the verge of remarrying; he is already married to Le Fresne's rival. The situation is not, as in the Patient Griselda story, a trick but a stubborn reality that all seem powerless to change. The heroine is no wife with certain rights but a concubine without legal claims. Law and order are everywhere against her. In "Le Fresne"—but not in the Patient Griselda story—the power to deprive a spouse of his or her children devolves upon the wife, and this deprivation comes close to being implemented. Likewise the identification of a daughter as the wife-to-be occurs in both tales. Since in "Le Fresne" the daughter is not the child of the patient heroine but rather her sister, however, it becomes her mother's right and duty, instead of the husband's prerogative as played out in the Griselda tale, to disclose that identification.

Marie reverses the procedures we have come to associate with the Griselda model so that power rests in the hands of women, especially in those of one woman who, as paradoxical as this may seem, refuses to exercise power over others, preferring to allow them their freedom. Even Le Fresne's own display of virtue appears not to be the result of a struggle to cause one side of her nature to dominate the other. She is, as one critic has put it, all generosity,[12] all love, with neither sadness nor regret. This ideal woman's actions which restore harmony are portrayed in a fashion diametrically opposed to the lesson of the proper use of male power in a feudal society. The fact that we may have some difficulty in comprehending Le Fresne's motivation while we have an easier time understanding her mother's abuse of power (the type of power wielded by masculine figures in the Patient Griselda stories) might well be Marie's way of commenting upon, and eliciting her reader's response to, this kind of power and its ordering of society. The systematic reversal of the devices and lessons of the Griselda model makes of "Le Fresne" a woman's narrative in every way, but one which seeks to enlighten the whole of society, beginning with the one individual who has been given responsibility for it, namely, the "noble king" to whom she presents this collection of stories ("General Prologue").

"Le Fresne"'s exemplarity as woman's narrative is further confirmed when we note that what has been withheld from the heroine, when it is finally restored to her at the close of the history, is never spoken and so is never revealed to the audience. Presumably, when the mother breaks her silence and, as it were, signs her text by admitting the link between herself and Le Fresne, her daughter then recovers her father's name. Since in less than a day her marriage is celebrated, she trades this name for her husband's. We do not know the father's name, however, nor do we ever learn more than the lover's Christian name. In short, we never discover what the heroine's official public titles are; she is not identified by Marie's text in terms of the men to whom she ostensibly belongs. In fact the public and masculine signs of acceptance into society are lost to us—erased from the history. What remains in their place is the *narration* of that history and *its* being named—what, in other words, the paile roé and the ash tree have come to represent.

Although the narrator assures us that the father, in his happiness at finding a daughter, has divided his inheritance with the new couple, the legacy fêted and transmitted by Marie's poem is not the husband's or the father's lineage but Le Fresne and her history ("herstory") formed and

forged (respectively) by a company of women. In the concluding lines
we learn that an anonymous group of people composed a *lai* about this
aventure and gave it the name "Le Fresne" after the lady:

> Quant l'aventure fu seüe,
> Coment ele esteit avenue,
> Le lai del *Freisne* en unt trové:
> Pur la dame l'unt si numé.

> Once the adventure was known,
> And how it had come about,
> They composed the *lai* of the *Ash Tree* from it:
> They named it so for [because of] the lady.
> [Ll. 515–18]

Marie makes no mention (as she is usually so wont to do) in this composition of "li Bretun" as the originators of this tale. Might we infer from
this silence that the anonymous composers of "Le Fresne" were a group
of Breton *women* comparable to those who had previously repeated the
tale of the slanderous wife? Such an inference would add yet another
dimension of symmetry to the work's poetic structure. In the end the *lai*
bears a woman's name, paradoxically also the name of the tree that supposedly could not bear fruit, the name given by the abbess and planted in
her mind by the servant girl's invention. This is the poetic fruit which a
number of women have fostered; it is the heroine's legacy, the result of a
matrilinear transmission. It is what we receive when we learn that Le
Fresne will lie in another bed under the same cover that once warmed her
as she lay (*cuchiee*, l. 298) in the four-forked tree, when we see that she
receives in the last line of the poem the well-deserved title of *dame* (l. 518),
and when we hear of this heir, or bequest, that is the "lai del Freisne."

We recall, moreover, that it was the intention at the outset of the poem
to have the neighbor's son named after/by Le Fresne's father: a plan that
was never carried out. At the close of the poem, a name has been con-
ferred but through the mother's side of the family line and through the
workings of a voluntary sisterhood. When the narrative is pictured in this
light, I think we understand that Marie de France also clearly participates
in this sisterhood, in this matrilineage. She also shares in the preservation
and transference of "Le Fresne," while hiding, as did her sisters before
her, the lady's "true" identity, her name as it derives from a man, be it
husband's or father's. These names which the *lai* and Marie's account
have suppressed have been replaced by the name, and the *aventure* it symbolizes, fabricated by a sisterhood, a name ironically of masculine gender, le fresne.

Marie has thus preserved and furthered a celebration of an alternative birth-giving, the sort in which maiden aunts, servant women, and concubines might well participate, that is, those women who are marginal in the public arena of a male-dominated society. She has created this alternative possibility by appropriating the terms of masculine-styled discourse, which she has exploited for the sake of reordering the scale of values applied to men and women (both independently and in their relationship to one another). By the close of "Le Fresne," the public domain and the male scheme of legitimacy has become a silenced, forgotten, and peripheral history, whereas the domain of women, formerly private, hidden, and inconsequential, has been publicly commemorated so that it might endure. By means of her revolutionary, and feminine, clerkly efforts, Marie has substituted a lineage born of sisterhood for the more familiar patriarchy. She has questioned the power upheld by the male, lineage-oriented feudal social structure, and she has affirmed the truly potent marvel of love given freely—even when this gift most unquestionably appears to violate patriarchy's central code.

Notes

1. In citing the *Lais* I refer to Jean Rychner, ed., *Les Lais de Marie de France,* Classiques français du Moyen Age 93 (Paris, 1966).

2. Numerous examples (from a variety of literatures) of multiple births considered (correctly or incorrectly) as a sign of adultery are assembled by Karl Warnke in his introductory remarks on "Le Fresne"; see his *Die Lais der Marie de France,* 3d ed. (Halle [Saale], 1925), pp. cxi–xxi. A negative interpretation of multiple births, although judged in many texts to be erroneous, seems to have been widespread in medieval Europe.

3. Infanticide as the solution to the stigma associated with multiple births figures prominently in the traditional handling of this theme. In her remarks about infanticide (a practice apparently historically more common among peasant women than among the gentry), Shulamith Shahar informs us that desperate women resorted to it in order to escape judgment as well. The motive for this sort of murder did not stem from economic considerations, at least not centrally: "The expression 'because of fear and disgrace' occurs again and again in the arguments cited by girls, widows, and married women. The married women justifiably feared the violent reaction of their husbands if they were unable to conceal the true paternity of the child" (*The Fourth Estate: A History of Women in the Middle Ages,* trans. Chaya Galai [London and New York, 1983], p. 19).

4. Godefroy (s.v. *roé*) and Tobler-Lommatzsch (s.v. *röé*) furnish many examples of rich cloths with circular patterns indicated by terms such as "paile roe," "pourpre röee," and the like. Only Godefroy mentions that *roé* is a synonym for *rodné* (other forms of the latter term are given as *rosné, roné, ronné,* and *rogné*). When *rodné* is applied to physical appearance, it usually means "round" or "fat,"

with the particular significance of "pregnant." See Godefroy (s.v. *rodné*) for two
examples derived from *fabliaux* (F. Godefroy, *Dictionnaire de l'ancienne langue française* [Paris, 1892; Kraus reprint, 1969], vol. 7, p. 217; Tobler-Lommatzsch, *Alt-
französisches Wörterbuch* [Wiesbaden, 1971], vol. 8, cols. 1370–71). Given, in addition, the obvious connection between *roé* and *röe* ("wheel"), perhaps an indirect
reference to the Wheel of Fortune is intended here as well by the cloth's specific
pattern. The Wheel of Fortune makes a quick downward turn at the beginning of
Le Fresne's life but finally comes full circle at the end of the story.

   5. According to Marbode of Rennes's *De Lapidibus*, the *jagunce* (or *hyacinthus*)
has the power to make sadness and vain suspicions vanish, a property that will
apparently have direct bearing upon the final outcome of Le Fresne's situation.
See Marbode of Rennes (1035–123), *De Lapidibus*, trans. J. M. Riddle (Wiesbaden, 1977), pp. 51–52. At the close of the twelfth-century *Roman d'Enéas*, a text
well known to Marie de France, Enéas defeats Turnus in combat. In courtly fashion he is about to spare his adversary's life when he catches sight of a ring on
Turnus's hand. Enéas had originally given the ring as a gift to Pallas. It was removed from his dead body by Turnus, who had killed him. The ring prompts
Enéas to recall the circumstances of his friend's death and suddenly renews for
him the pain he suffered upon losing his young comrade. He decides to wreak
vengeance upon Turnus and to show him no mercy. In this way he also definitively rids himself of a dangerous rival in his pursuit of Lavine's hand in marriage.
The poem describes Pallas's ring as follows:

> Molt i ot bon ancestané
> un lioncel fet d'un jagonce;
> bien i avoit d'or plus d'une once.

> It was splendidly set with
> a lion cub made of a jacinth;
> it contained well over an ounce of gold.

> (*Enéas: Roman du XIIe siècle*, edited by J.-J. Salverda de Grave, vol. 1,
> Classiques français du Moyen Age 44 [Paris, 1964], 5766–68).

   When Le Fresne's mother recognizes the jagunce-set ring that she has given to
her baby daughter in the possession of Gurun's mistress, the recognition also
leads to an unexpected act of remembrance and to the definitive elimination of a
rival. The story's intended lineage is thereby ensured. We note, however, that, in
Marie's story, all the comparable roles are played by women.

   6. "Only in the laboring classes were there unmarried laywomen; in the upper
classes almost without exception unmarried women entered the nunnery";
"those [girls] destined to take the veil were often placed in nunneries as small
children, while others who were not earmarked for the monastic life were sent to
nunneries to be educated" (Shahar, *The Fourth Estate*, pp. 96 and 140).

   7. I have departed from Rychner's practice of entitling this poem "Fresne" and
instead have followed Warnke's edition (*Die Lais der Marie de France*) and Ewert's
(*Marie de France, Lais*, ed. Alfred Ewert [Oxford, 1944]; both give the title accompanied by the definite article. The heroine's name in l. 230 is clearly "Le Freisne";

therefore her entire birthname should be consistently capitalized. I am indebted to Alfred Foulet for pointing out these discrepancies and for suggesting editorial emendations to me.

8. The relationship between aunt and niece that Marie's account invents underscores her consistent appropriation for a woman's narrative of the typical male pairing of uncle and nephew which we encounter so often in chanson de geste and romance traditions (Charlemagne/Roland, Arthur/Gauvain, Mark/Tristan, and many more). The fact that the relationship in "Le Fresne" is a fabricated and freely chosen one also contributes to the poem's deliberate feminization of (largely male) clerkly concerns and procedures.

9. "Some commentators have seen a connection between Marie's two *lais* ["Le Fresne" and "Eliduc"] and what is sometimes called the Griseldis theme, but more correctly, the Calumniated Wife. This theme, though ancient and widely-distributed, is particularly common in Celtic stories. . . . Clearly, this popular theme has influenced the presentation of the man with two wives" (W. Ann Trindade, "The Man with Two Wives: Marie de France and an Important Irish Analogue," *Romance Philology* 27 [1973–74]:466–78 [p. 475]). For earlier discussions of Marie's "Le Fresne" within the context of "The Man with Two Wives," see also Gaston Paris, *La poésie du Moyen Age,* vol. 2 (Paris, 1906), pp. 109–30; J. Matzke, "The Lay of *Eliduc* and the Legend of the Husband with Two Wives," *Modern Philology* 5 (1907–1908):211–39; and W. Küchler, "Schöne Annie: Fraisne und Griselda," *Die neueren Sprachen* 35 (1927):489–97. François Suard reminds us that the documented versions of these two types of stories do not precede Marie's text: "Sans doute n'avons-nous pas pour cette histoire, ni pour celle que conte la ballade populaire, de témoignage écrit antérieur à Marie de France. Les occurrences les plus anciennes de la calomniatrice punie ne remontent pas au-delà du XIIIe s., avec *Octavian* ou la chanson du *Chevalier au Cygne;* il s'en faut même de beaucoup pour la ballade qui semble attestée en Allemagne à la fin du XVe s. mais pourrait remonter, selon les éditeurs de la version germanique, à un modèle commun avec Marie de France" ("L'utilisation des éléments folkloriques dans le lai du 'Frêne,'" *Cahiers de Civilisation Médiévale* 21 [1978]:46). His suggestion that "Le Fresne" is located at the intersection of the ballad and the legend (p. 46) prompts one to wonder whether Marie has not situated a version of the former within the context of the latter, so that, by underlining the pair of mother and daughter, she might erect a framework of matrilineage for her own version. If this is the case, we observe that the coupling of a *pair* of stories—a double narrative—lies at the heart of her enterprise, which emphasizes twinness at every turn.

10. "At the end of the Middle Ages and in early modern Europe, the relation of the wife—of the potentially disorderly woman—to her husband was especially useful for expressing the relation of all subordinates to their superiors, and this for two reasons. First, economic relations were still often perceived in the medieval way as a matter of service. Second, the nature of political rule and the newer problem of sovereignty were very much at issue. In the little world of the family, with its conspicuous tension between intimacy and power, the larger matters of political and social order could find ready symbolization." Furthermore: "One set of reversals portrays women going beyond what can ordinarily be expected of a

mere female; that is, it shows women ruling the lower in themselves and thus deserving to be like men" (Natalie Zemon Davis, "Women on Top," in her *Society and Culture in Early Modern France* [Stanford, 1965], pp. 127 and 132).

11. "Fresne présente cette unicité, cette transparence d'âme qui caractérise les personnages merveilleux. Son geste n'exprime pas plus de vie intérieure que ne font les complaintes des malmariées dans d'autres lais" (Edgard Sienaert, *Les Lais de Marie de France,* Collection Essais sur le Moyen Age [Paris, 1978], p. 84). Although I strongly concur with Sienaert's view of Le Fresne as a "personnage merveilleux," I believe that this characteristic is more than merely a mechanical narrative device. Meanwhile Glyn S. Burgess notes that the ash is "symbolic of adaptability, flexibility, modesty, and nobility" and that thus "Le Fresne has been aptly named" ("Symbolism in Marie de France's 'Laüstic' and 'Le Fresne,'" *Bulletin bibliographique de la Société Internationale Arthurienne* 33 [1981]:265). Furthermore, the ash, in reality, "not only bears a flower but also a fruit" (p. 265). Therefore, the vassals, in interpreting the heroine's name as a sign of barrenness, have falsified her text, her signature. Following upon this interpretation, we might see Marie's role as once again appropriating male techniques in her celebration of woman's text as she causes this "lie" ironically to be subverted in the begetting of the text's lineage. A switch of this sort would impart an additional symmetry to the poem, since yet another calumny is put right and proven to be unsound.

12. Sienaert, *Les Lais de Marie de France,* p. 84.

Contributors

Susan Groag Bell is an affiliated scholar at the Stanford Institute for Research on Women and Gender. Her publications include *Women from the Greeks to the French Revolution* (Stanford: Stanford University Press, 1973) and, with Karen Offen, *Women, the Family, and Freedom: The Debate in Documents, 1750–1950,* 2 vols. (Stanford: Stanford University Press, 1983). At present she is working on a book tentatively titled "Women and the Garden."

Judith M. Bennett received her doctorate from the University of Toronto in 1981. An associate professor of history at the University of North Carolina at Chapel Hill, she is the author of *Women in the Medieval English Countryside: Gender and Household in Brigstock Before the Plague* (Oxford: Oxford University Press, 1987).

Stanley Chojnacki, who earned his Ph.D. at the University of California at Berkeley, is professor of history at Michigan State University. His studies of patrician politics, society, and culture have appeared in the *American Historical Review, Journal of Interdisciplinary History, Renaissance Quarterly, Studies in the Renaissance,* and several multiauthored collections.

Mary Erler, associate professor of English at Fordham University, took a Ph.D. at the University of Chicago in 1981. Her work on early English printing and drama has appeared in *Modern Philology, Library,* and *Huntington Library Quarterly.* She is currently editing a volume in the *Records of Early English Drama* series published by the University of Toronto Press.

Joan Ferrante is professor of comparative literature at Columbia University. The first woman to be elected president of the Dante Society of America (1985–1988), she is also a fellow of the Medieval Academy. She is the author of *Women as Image in Medieval Literature* (New York: Columbia University Press, 1975) and, with Robert Hanning, has translated *The Lais of Marie de France* (New York: Dutton, 1978). Her most recent book is *The Political Vision of the Divine Comedy* (Princeton: Princeton University Press, 1984).

Michelle A. Freeman, who earned her doctorate at Princeton University, was assistant professor of French at Columbia University from 1977 to 1985 and received a fellowship from the National Endowment for the Humanities for 1982–1983. Her publications include *The Poetics of "Translatio Studii" and "Conjointure"*

(Lexington, Ky.: French Forum, 1979). Two of her other studies of Marie's *Lais* appeared in *PMLA* (1984) and *Romance Notes* (1985), respectively.

Barbara A. Hanawalt, professor of medieval history at the University of Minnesota, received her Ph.D. from the University of Michigan. Her publications include *Crime and Conflict in Medieval England, 1300–1348* (Cambridge: Harvard University Press, 1979) and *The Ties That Bound: Peasant Families in Medieval England* (New York: Oxford, 1986). She is the editor of *Women and Work in Preindustrial Europe* (Bloomington: Indiana University Press, 1986).

Elaine Tuttle Hansen, associate professor of English at Haverford College, completed her graduate studies at the Universities of Minnesota and Washington. She has published articles on Chaucer and on several contemporary women writers and has a book on Old English poetry currently in press.

Martha C. Howell received her doctorate from Columbia University and is currently associate professor in the Department of History at Rutgers University. She is the author of *Women, Production, and Patriarchy in Late Medieval Cities,* Women in Culture and Society (Chicago: University of Chicago Press, 1986).

Maryanne Kowaleski received a Ph.D. from the University of Toronto and is assistant professor in the history department at Fordham University. She has published articles on women and work and the history of the urban family in medieval England. She is also the author of *Local Markets and Regional Trade in Late Medieval Exeter,* forthcoming from Cambridge University Press.

Jo Ann McNamara is professor of history at Hunter College. In 1984 she published *A New Song: Celibate Women in the First Three Christian Centuries* (New York: Harrington Park Press). She is currently working on a history of Catholic nuns, to be published by Macmillan.

Brigitte Bedos Rezak, *archiviste-paléographe,* a graduate of the Sorbonne and of the Ecole Nationale des Chartes, was formerly the curator in charge of the section of seals at the French National Archives (Paris). She is currently adjunct associate professor of history at the State University of New York, Stony Brook. Her scholarly interest in the social, cultural, and political history of France is evident in *La châtellenie de Montmorency des origines à 1380: Aspects féodaux, sociaux, et économiques* (Pontoise: Société historique et archéologique, 1980) and in *Corpus des sceaux français du Moyen Age,* vol. 1: *Les sceaux des villes* (Paris: Imprimerie nationale, 1980) as well as in some thirty published articles.

Jane Tibbetts Schulenburg is professor of history, Department of Outreach and Women's Studies, University of Wisconsin—Madison. She is the author of a number of articles on women in the medieval church and society. Her *"Forgetful of Their Sex": Female Sanctity and 'Deviancy,' ca. 500–1100* is forthcoming.

Suzanne Wemple is professor of history at Barnard College. In 1981 she published *Women in Frankish Society* (Philadelphia: University of Pennsylvania Press). The project that she is currently directing, which is sponsored by the National Endowment for the Humanities, examines women in Italian and English monastic life between the years 500 and 1500.

Index